Jerome H Long

Fagen

David Fagen (private collection of Anthony L. Powell)

FAGEN

An African American Renegade
in the Philippine-American War

Michael Morey

The University of Wisconsin Press

The University of Wisconsin Press
1930 Monroe Street, 3rd Floor
Madison, Wisconsin 53711-2059
uwpress.wisc.edu

3 Henrietta Street, Covent Garden
London WC2E 8LU, United Kingdom
eurospanbookstore.com

Printed in the United States of America

This book may be available in a digital edition.

Library of Congress Cataloging-in-Publication Data
Names: Morey, Michael, author.
Title: Fagen: an African American renegade in the Philippine-American War / Michael Morey.
Description: Madison, Wisconsin: The University of Wisconsin Press, [2019] | Includes bibliographical references and index.
Identifiers: LCCN 2018013081 | ISBN 9780299319403 (cloth: alk. paper)
Subjects: LCSH: Fagen, David, 1878-1901? | African American soldiers—Biography. | Guerrillas—Philippines—Biography. | United States. Army. Infantry Regiment, 24th (1869-1951)—Biography. | Philippines—History—Philippine American War, 1899-1902.
Classification: LCC DS676.8.F34 M67 2019 | DDC 959.9/031092 [B]—dc23
LC record available at https://lccn.loc.gov/2018013081

publication grant by

Figure Foundation

---

deserted to justice

To Barbara and Michael Anthony

Contents

Part Three: Ladrone

Illustrations

Preface

In 1903 the African American novelist Charles Chestnutt wrote that "the rights of the Negroes are at a lower ebb than at any time of the thirty-five years of their freedom, and the race prejudice is more intense and uncompromising." Many observers of the time, black and white, had reached the same dire conclusion.[1]

The mounting hostility between the races had escalated sharply on April 23, 1899, with the savage lynching of Sam Hose, a man whom many believed had killed his employer in self-defense. A white mob of thousands in Newnan, Georgia, turned Hose's lynching into a drawn-out ritual of torture and frenzied celebration. After that, observers described the worsening race relations in the South as verging upon a "state of war." John S. Bassett, a professor at Trinity College in North Carolina, wrote that "today there is more hatred of whites for blacks and blacks for whites than ever before" with both races caught "in a torrent of passion which, I fear, is leading to an end which I dare not name."[2]

In July 1900, that "torrent of passion" flared into open revolt in New Orleans when a man named Robert Charles, roughed up for no reason by two policemen, had the temerity to fight back even though he knew it meant his doom. Charles had lived in a state of rage at the injustices heaped upon southern African Americans, and nothing had so infuriated him as the lynching of Sam Hose. Being assaulted by white officers with their nightsticks was the last straw for Robert Charles. When the shooting stopped three days later, Charles had killed four police officers and three civilians, seriously wounded eight, including three additional police officers, and delivered lesser wounds to twelve more—twenty-seven in all. And he had only fifty cartridges for his Winchester to begin with. Smoked out, Charles had gone down to meet his death in a blaze of gunfire. Mobs rampaged for four days as the young white males of the city took out their frustrations on the black citizens of New Orleans, murdering more than a dozen blacks and injuring many more before the police and militia could bring them under control.[3]

Ida B. Wells-Barnett wrote of Charles: "It is now, even as it was in the days of slavery, an unpardonable sin for a Negro to resist a white man, no matter how unjust or unprovoked the white man's attack may be."[4]

Also in July 1900, an African American deserter from the U.S. Twenty-Fourth Infantry committed the unpardonable sin of resisting the white man in the mountains of the faraway Philippine Islands. His name was David Fagen. Had Robert Charles known of him, he would have found the young black man's position an enviable one: a fighting chance to make war upon his white oppressors without incurring a certain and swift death.

I had never heard of David Fagen—his name more often spelled Fagan or Fagin—until I came across this passage from Leon Wolff's *Little Brown Brother*, a history of what was then called the Philippine Insurrection, 1899–1902: "An enormous Negro named Fagan deserted the U.S. Army, taking with him all the revolvers he could carry, and was commissioned a captain in the insurgent forces. . . . Fagan drank heavily, played a guitar, fought like a wildcat, and lived in camp with a native woman."[5]

From the moment I came upon these few lines about Fagen, I was struck by the image of an American black man leading Filipino guerrillas in jungle and rice paddy. Where did Fagen come from? What was he like? What happened to him? My interest was more than just curiosity about this one man but also about the period. It seemed to me that to understand something about the American character, particularly when it relates to matters of race, a meaningful starting point would be that time when conditions for blacks in America had sunk to the lowest point since the end of the Civil War. Lynching had reached its peak, Jim Crow laws were being enacted all over the South, and the doctrines of the extreme racists were increasingly taking hold in the North. As Malcolm X later phrased it, from the African American's perspective, the American dream had become an American nightmare.[6]

In 1900 white people had the starring roles in the great pageant of American life. Blacks, Latinos, Native Americans, and Asian Americans were bit players, extras cast in nonspeaking parts or perhaps allowed a line or two for comic effect. Being a "real" American was all about being white. And for many white Americans here in the twenty-first century, this view still pertains. Despite great progress, African Americans find themselves fighting a seemingly permanent racist headwind, a condition that Derrick Bell, a Harvard professor, saw as a bitter fact of life: "Black people will never gain full equality in this country. Even those Herculean efforts we hail as successful will produce no more than temporary 'peaks of progress,' short-lived victories that slide into irrelevance as racial patterns adapt in ways that maintain white dominance."[7]

One would like to believe that Professor Bell was overstating his case, but a review of the tortuous course of race relations in the United States since 1900 makes Bell's argument sadly persuasive. As Bell saw it, there is nothing to do but fight on.

Southern blacks in 1900 lived in a state of terror. Most of them also lived in a permanent state of rage, a rage kept hidden from their white oppressors until, as with Robert Charles, their fury might erupt in an explosive outburst of violence. Blacks fought back in race riots north and south, in numerous confrontations with the law. But to answer white violence in kind was almost always fatal, which is why a black man's story of armed resistance in that age of terror is so unusual. David Fagen traveled to the other side of the world, and the racist abuse he had known as a young man in the South traveled with him. But in the Philippines, he found himself in the middle of a revolution of brown-skinned people fighting against white domination. That revolution gave him the chance Robert Charles and so many others never had, the means to fight against white oppression as part of a larger struggle. He could give full vent to his rage and, if his luck held, live to fight another day.

This is his story.

Fagen

Introduction

DURING THE FIRST DECADE of the twentieth century, the name Fagen, the "notorious renegade," was virtually a household word in America, particularly among African Americans. And then, like most popular figures of any era, his name faded from the public memory. I had never heard of Fagen—his name more often spelled Fagan or Fagin—when I became interested in the conflict first known as the Philippine Insurrection, 1899–1902. But as I read both about the war and of what little was known of David Fagen, his story seemed the ideal way to address multiple issues: the racist hypocrisy of a supposed "land of the free," and the projection of that hypocrisy abroad as America asserted itself upon the global stage. What does it really mean to be an "American"? Does the answer to that question depend upon whose America we are talking about? Perhaps it is like some ancient riddle for which there can never be a clear answer.

The Philippine-American War, as it is now more often called, has been described as a "forgotten" war, as if it were of such little consequence that it just faded naturally from historical memory. Historians like Paul A. Kramer and Stuart Creighton Miller argue persuasively that the war has been purposely "hidden"—in Kramer's words, "smothered beneath the protective mantle of the much shorter war that immediately preceded it, the Spanish-American War." That sense of a hidden war only drew me to read more about it, to try to understand why it had been "swept under the rug," as Richard O'Connor phrased it.[1]

The war in the Philippines, which some would argue lasted until 1913, was America's first great counterinsurgency conflict, Vietnam being the second, and the wars in Iraq and Afghanistan can now be added to the list. Though all share the characteristics common to irregular warfare, they can be understood as much by their contrasts as their similarities. What can be said is that none has worked out well for the United States, and the suffering inflicted on the people in these war zones has been catastrophic.

If left-leaning American historians have viewed the war in the Philippines through a lens of "moral outrage," more conservative historians have been inclined to focus on the lessons to be gained from the military's success—at horrific cost to the Filipinos—in quelling a determined guerrilla resistance. But even the conservative Brian McAllister Linn, America's foremost military historian of the war, has concluded, "In fact, perhaps more than most wars, the 'lessons' of the Philippines are confused, ambiguous, and controversial."[2]

That said, both conservative and liberal American historians, as well as Filipino historians, are in agreement upon the centrality of the war in the Philippines to understanding America's evolution from newcomer on the world's stage in 1898 to global empire in the twenty-first century. And more recently, in *Policing America's Empire: The United States, the Philippines, and the Rise of the Surveillance State*, Alfred W. McCoy has tracked the parallels between the wars in Iraq and in the Philippines, finding the consequences of both misadventures anything but positive. The techniques of surveillance and suppression of dissent developed by the army in the Philippines were imported back to America during World War I and the Red Scare that followed; that two-way process—the projection of power abroad and increasing governmental intrusion upon the private lives of citizens at home—has continued to the present. "In both the Philippines and Iraq," McCoy writes, "the U.S. military, thrust into the crucible of counterinsurgency, developed innovative methods of social control that had a decidedly negative impact on civil liberties back home."[3]

In 1899 the McKinley administration cited the racial inferiority of the Filipinos—among other rationales—as justification for denying them sovereignty and engaging in a bloody war of conquest. The irony of sending black American soldiers to "take up the white man's burden" in the Philippines was not lost on the commentators of the day and became the subject of debate among the circles of power: Would they remain loyal or would they side en masse with their brown-skinned "cousins of color"? The army needed the manpower and, in the end, six thousand African American soldiers, beginning with 2,100 of the famed Buffalo Soldiers, were sent to the Philippines at a time when the fortunes of blacks in America had hit rock bottom. This was the dawn of the Jim Crow era. That many of the black soldiers sent to the Philippines felt conflicted in their loyalties should hardly be surprising—or that a small number of them, perhaps no more than fifteen, would decide that their place, rather than helping suppress the Filipinos' struggle for independence, was in joining them in revolution. The most famous of those black deserters was David Fagen.[4]

Fagen's story is a hard one to tell, taking place in the context of a bewilderingly complex Philippine-American War and in a time when it seemed the plight of African Americans could get no worse. Fortunately, witnesses left a number of vivid anecdotes of their encounters with Fagen: all indicate a charismatic personality, a gifted leader of men, a master of the art of guerrilla warfare. But Fagen himself left nothing in writing and was never interviewed at any length; the precise nature of his views, his grievances, the subtleties of his thinking, will remain more to be inferred by his actions than fully known.

General Frederick Funston described the conflict in his district of central Luzon as "a nasty little war." The fighting there was not on the same scale as the resistance in Batangas or the Ilocos region, but neither was the guerrilla war in central Luzon a small affair. Filipino revolutionaries were peasants with inferior weaponry and limited military training, particularly in marksmanship, and they were no match for the Americans in stand-up fights. Their hit-and-run tactics were meant to wear the Americans down, in effect, harassing them until they might just give up and go away. For the most part the engagements in Funston's district were small, the notable exceptions being a number of ambushes and assaults led by David Fagen. As word of his exploits spread, he became a mythic figure among both Filipinos and the Americans in the islands. Eventually Fagen's fame would spread to the United States, particularly among an increasingly militant African American community inspired by the heroism of the Buffalo Soldiers at San Juan Hill.[5]

David Fagen's revolt harks back to the tradition of black revolutionaries from Toussaint L'Ouverture through Gabriel Prosser, Denmark Vesey, and Nat Turner. By his actions he was a revolutionary, whether he thought of himself precisely as such. His challenge to U.S. military authority, with its potential to inspire a full-scale revolt among his former African American comrades-in-arms, was an ongoing source of consternation, if not alarm. He represented not only a political threat but also an affront to their supremacist sensibilities. Black men were supposed to know "their place," a premise he emphatically rejected.

Almost from the day of his desertion, the "notorious renegade Fagan" became the subject of rumor and speculation, some accurate, some wildly fanciful. The result was a lively blend of man and myth, of fact and fiction. Tracking the real David Fagen in the files of the National Archives, old newspapers, autobiographical accounts, and elsewhere has proven almost as difficult as tracking him through the jungles and rice paddies had been for his host of pursuers. But a trail begins to emerge as first we catch sight of him and follow him on his way—until he turns, fleetingly now and then, to meet us face to face. In trying to render a portrait of such an elusive figure, a degree of speculation is unavoidable.

In a departure from the usual conventions of historical writing, I give the reader fair warning when I am venturing into the realm of the speculative. Perhaps the reader, taking in what I have presented here and given the fragmentary nature of the evidence, will see a different Fagen.

Like the war itself, memory of David Fagen had been "swept under the rug" until the 1960s. Since then, historians of the Philippine-American war have been laboring with notable success at correcting that case of purposely induced national amnesia. In telling David Fagen's story, my intention has been to add one more piece to that vital work of historical reclamation.

The Young Man from Tampa

Part One

I remember one big red-eyed black whom we met by the roadside. Forty-five years he had labored on this farm, beginning with nothing, and still having nothing. . . . As it is, he is hopelessly in debt, disappointed, and embittered. He stopped us to inquire after the black boy in Albany, whom it was said a policeman had shot and killed for loud talking on the sidewalk. And then he said slowly: "Let a white man touch me, and he dies. . . . I've seen them whip my father and my old mother in them cotton-rows till the blood ran; by—" and we passed on.

W. E. B. Du Bois,
The Souls of Black Folk

The Twenty-Fourth Infantry
Comes to Tampa

1

D AVID FAGEN STARTED OUT HIS LIFE in Tampa, Florida, the sixth and last child of former slaves Samuel and Sylvia Fagen. The year was 1878, probably in October. According to the 1880 census, Samuel Fagen was born in Mississippi in 1840, but Florida's census of 1885 records his birth year as 1844 in North Carolina; the Florida entry is probably the correct one though the reasons for the discrepancy remain unclear. Samuel ("Sam" according to D. B. McKay, the *Pioneer Florida* chronicler and *Tampa Bay Tribune* editor) came down to Florida in the great migration following the Civil War. South Carolina and Mississippi were the first states to enact what were known as the Black Codes, provisions that criminalized every aspect of black life; the severity of these attempts to re-constitute the conditions of slavery may have influenced Sam Fagen's decision to move elsewhere. According to the historian Eric Foner, "Florida's code, drawn up by a three-member commission whose report praised slavery as a 'benign' institution whose only shortcoming was its inadequate regulation of black sexual behavior, made disobedience, impudence, or even 'disrespect' to the employer a crime."[1]

Despite the Black Codes (they were soon struck down by the military authorities and congressional legislation), conditions in Florida were still considered better for blacks than they were elsewhere in the South. The *New York Times* estimated that fifty thousand former slaves had left South Carolina and that most of them had gone to Florida. "Nearly every day brings trains and wagons to Tallahassee from South Carolina." Presumably a good many came from the other states of the South as well.[2]

There is also confusion about Sylvia Fagen's birth year. In the 1870 census she is recorded as born in 1842 in Georgia; in the 1880 census, the birth year is 1853. Whether Sam met Sylvia on his way south or in Tampa is not clear, but in 1870 they had their first child and in the coming years would live at the corner of Nebraska and Constant Streets in what is now the core area of Tampa. Sylvia

9

already had two sons, John and George Douglas, and over the next decade six more children would follow—four boys, Charles, Joseph, William, and David; and two girls, Louisa and Alice.[3]

A visiting journalist described Tampa as "a city composed of derelict wooden houses and drifting in an ocean of sand." Plagued by periodic outbreaks of yellow fever and isolated from any decent road or rail line, the failing little town had actually lost population over the preceding decade. Tampa went from a population of 796 in 1870 to 720 in 1880, when David Fagen was just one year old. In those early days Tampa's sandy streets were so wide that the larger mossy oaks were left for a wagon to skirt around. There were picket fences where Spanish moss was hung out to dry and used to stuff mattresses and in making blankets, packing materials, and even voodoo dolls. Much of the land was covered in palmetto and oak scrub, but there were also cypress trees, sweet gum and black tupelo, magnolia and chinaberry, as well as bougainvillea, flame vines, and Carolina yellow jasmine.[4]

In 1880 Sam Fagen was a laborer, primarily housepainter, and a colorful—one might say "resourceful"—character in that he was not above stealing a chicken now and then or some oats for his horse, activities that occasionally landed him in jail. A local paper, the *Sunland Tribune*, made much of his "catching an alligator" and the impression is that Sam Fagen was as given to hard play as to hard work, arrested on one occasion for being "drunk and disorderly." The Fagens probably raised vegetables and poultry while Sam engaged in wage labor of various sorts. Sylvia Fagen "kept house," an important distinction for African Americans at the time when black women wanted to be known for taking care of their own families, not those of white people who had ordered them about as menials for so long. Women worked outside the home when they had no choice, often listing themselves as "laundresses."[5]

Sadly, for the Fagen children, Sylvia died in 1883; she was either forty-one or only thirty years of age, depending on which census birth date was the accurate one. That same year, her town, after languishing as a backwater for so long, began to undergo a transformation. Phosphate was discovered in the Bone Valley southeast of Tampa and also in the Hillsborough River that ran through town. Phosphate had many uses, primarily as fertilizer but also in baking powder, matches, and other products. The following year, the railroad tycoon Henry Plant ran a line down from Jacksonville, connecting Tampa and the phosphate trade to the outer world. In 1886 Vicente Ibor moved his cigar-making factory from Key West to the east side of Tampa. The Cuban enclave, called Ibor City, was quickly annexed to Tampa proper with the so-called Scrub, the town's growing black ghetto, encompassed by white and Latin neighborhoods. Cuban and Spanish cigar workers poured into the city along with Sicilian and eastern

European Jewish immigrants, turning sleepy Tampa into a bustling town of 5,552 diverse citizens in 1890. About a fourth of that number was African American.[6]

The Scrub was a private world for the blacks, a warren of dirt alleyways and unpainted shacks without running water or sewers. But impoverished as it was, the closed community offered a retreat from the overbearing vigilance of white Tampa. Without a mother, the Fagen children probably did not have an easy time of it. By the 1885 Florida census the three oldest children, still in their early teens, were out of the house. Sam Fagen had become a merchant with three employees; the four youngest children, including seven-year-old David, were enrolled in school.[7]

Young David was not the silent, brooding type. Later, his fellow soldiers would describe him as "lighthearted, careless and full of jokes" while to the white officers he was a "loud-mouthed" troublemaker who didn't take well to military discipline. Cocky and irrepressible, David was likely influenced in his high-spirited disposition by Sam Fagen, and perhaps in the art of the trickster as well.[8]

While D. B. McKay, the editor of the *Tampa Tribune*, could dismiss Sam Fagen as "a shiftless old Negro who was never known to work, but had about twenty children," the reality of who Sam Fagen was, apart from the whites' racist assumptions, was undoubtedly more complex. The fragments of information we have about Sam Fagen suggest the strategy of the trickster about him, the wily subversive in the guise of the indolent and simpleminded black man. With the whites he could play humble and dumb; after all, he had spent his first twenty-one years as a slave where, in the absence of a valid social contract, the master-slave relationship justified any and all strategies by the powerless: pilfering, deceit, feigned ignorance, arson, sabotage, and even assassination, if one could get away with it. Slaves, in some instances maintained on the edge of starvation, learned to steal in order to survive. By the stark days of the 1890s conditions seemed only to have gotten worse in the years since the end of Reconstruction. "In 1877 we lost all hopes," a former slave recounted to a congressional committee, "the whole south had got into the hands of the very men that had held us as slaves. We felt we had almost as well be slaves under these men." A merchant, an artful thief by necessity, a horse trader, a storyteller, a man adept at finessing his way through a world of capricious and domineering whites—and a man who could catch alligators!—was probably a man to be respected in the Scrub. Later evidence suggests that Sam Fagen was a more upstanding member of his community than the ne'er-do-well a white chronicler would have him.[9]

David Fagen grew up in an environment rich in myth and mystery, with a tradition of song and folk tales that stretched back far into the slavery era, featuring marvelous trickster stories of the weak outwitting the strong and of hoodoo doctors and their otherworldly powers. In the tales of tricksters and conjurers, animals were invested with human traits. The conjure man could turn himself into a fox or a black cat; the trickster in the form of a small animal could outwit the bear or the fox—a metaphor for the unequal contest between whites and blacks in the Jim Crow South. In describing African Americans in turn-of-the-century Florida, the folklorist Stetson Kennedy writes, "Beneath the outward cloak of Christianity, there is an underlying mass of inherited superstitious belief, much of it pagan (non-Christian) in character." The Tampa police rarely arrested a black man who didn't have a silver-encased rabbit's foot or "weirdly assorted bags, bones, and other voodoo charms" in his pocket. According to Kennedy, "Transplanted African cults and practices thrive in the Palmetto Country as in no other part of the United States; besides the Southern Negro stuff variously known as hoodoo, voodoo, and cunjervation, there is the *brujeria* and ñañiguismo brought by the Afro-Cubans, and the *obeah* of the Bahaman blacks."[10]

What influence growing up in this environment, with its potent mix of West Indian and southern black folklore, had on young Fagen is impossible to know. There is no evidence that he claimed the attributes of the trickster or the conjurer for himself, even if others thought of him in those terms.

All indications are that Fagen was never at a loss for words, and he would have spoken in the African American English vernacular—the Florida variation—so vividly rendered by Zora Neale Hurston. Later, he would be noted for his volubility, a verbal cockiness and aggressiveness that matched his boldness in the field. His gift for the mot juste, in the style of the most audacious southern blacks, is suggestive of the black "badman" phenomenon of the 1890s. In fact, the officer with whom he would most come into conflict would label him "a rowdy soldier and a 'bad man'"—"loud mouthed and given to slang and profanity."[11]

In *From Trickster to Badman*, John W. Roberts describes the evolution of the badman from the slavery-era trickster and the conjurer. The trickster was a master of guile and deception, noted for his wit and craftiness. If a man was going to make you work for free at the point of a gun, there were other forms of resistance besides direct confrontation. The conjurer was the master of supernatural trickery. Both roles have clear antecedents in West African folklore. The badman of the 1890s—the outlaw folk hero—combined the characteristics of both folk types, the trickster's craftiness and mischievous sense of humor and the conjure man's supernatural powers, usually gained by some kind of pact with the devil. If the trickster was the perpetual child, the badman was the teen-age rebel.[12]

There is nothing to suggest Fagen ever thought of himself as a badman, but certainly others, both black and white, saw him as one. During his youth, there were rugged black men, sometimes called the "Winchester Negro," who lived at a wary distance from the law in the piney woods and swamps. And there were badmen like Harmon Murray, leader of the North Florida Gang, eventually killed in 1891 by another young black man after several years as a dangerous bandit and gunfighter. Murray killed more than ten men, eluded capture repeatedly, and became a legendary figure in the Florida of 1890.[13]

Perhaps the most famous of the badmen was Railroad Bill, born Morris Slater. Slater worked in a turpentine camp in Escambia County, Alabama. In 1893 he shot a sheriff who tried to relieve him of his rifle, then escaped into a swamp. For three years Railroad Bill plundered railcars as they rolled along the tracks in southwestern Alabama and the Florida Panhandle. By some accounts he killed as many as twelve men, including two sheriffs in desperate gun battles. The Pinkertons sent a black undercover agent to locate Bill; the agent was never heard from again. On March 7, 1896, Railroad Bill was lured into a trap at a station on the Louisville & Nashville line and gunned down by bounty hunters.[14]

David Fagen would defy white authority with complete contempt, and the stories of badmen and tricksters may have been an important influence on him, perhaps even a source of inspiration. It is even tempting to see him as a sort of Railroad Bill but in the context of the Philippine Revolution, a man who, rather than rob trains in solitary defiance of the white man, joined Filipino freedom fighters in their struggle for independence. It is tempting—but there is no evidence to show that Fagen identified with badmen such as Harmon Murray or Railroad Bill or in any way thought of himself in that tradition. More significant is the insistence of whites upon labeling him as a "badman"—a "criminal"—even as he led Filipino revolutionaries against them in what were clearly military operations.

In 1891, when David Fagen was thirteen, Henry Plant built the Tampa Bay Hotel, a quarter-mile long and topped by silver minarets that looked as if they belonged more in Istanbul or Samarkand. Black men worked in the railyards and loaded and offloaded cargo ships at Port Tampa, nine miles away. They moved cedar and mahogany logs, barrels of turpentine and rosin, bales of tobacco, and phosphate by the ton. Sometime in the late 1890s, David Fagen went to work at Hull's Phosphate: ten hours a day for a dollar a day. White foremen supervised from dry land while black men worked waist-deep in the river breaking off chunks of phosphate with picks, shovels, and crowbars. They heaved the chunks into small boats or wheelbarrows on shore to be carted away for the process of drying and crushing. Young Fagen may have worked close to home in the Scrub, or he may have worked at times at a phosphate camp away from town.[15]

These camps were rough places, like the turpentine, lumber, and phosphate camps that Zora Neale Hurston described in *Mules and Men*. After a day of laboring in the hot sun amid swarms of mosquitoes, men gambled and drank in a camp barrelhouse with prostitutes and rowdy music making for a heady mix. The workers brought that same boisterous spirit to their relations with the foremen and the mining bosses, and there were violent clashes over wages and work conditions.

Sometime during his youth, David Fagen acquired several scars on his face. His enlistment papers note a "curved scar ¼ inch on chin" and an "oval scar ½ x ¼ in on left cheek," the result perhaps of fighting or roughhousing. He was noted for his astounding luck at stud poker (and obviously not a little skill), regularly relieving his fellow soldiers of hundreds of dollars at payday. And General Jose Alejandrino would later write of his "looking for a guitar to serenade the ladies." His time at Hull's Phosphate probably served as an apprenticeship in those diversions, even as it conditioned him for the toughest kind of physical labor. The seeds of his contempt for white authority may have found fertile soil at the work camps as well.[16]

When there was a shortage of workers, the mine owners brought in prison contract labor. When the Black Codes were struck down, plantation and mine owners looked for other ways to ensure an adequate labor supply. According to C. Vann Woodward, "the conviction prevailed that Negroes could not be induced to work without compulsion." The sharecropping system, whereby indebted black farmers were granted advances in return for a lien on their crop, was a way to exploit the black farmer, stringing him along in a marginal existence with no hope of advancement. And if a farmer should run, he risked, in the words of George Frederickson, being "consigned to a fate that was often worse than slavery."[17]

With the exception of Arkansas and Tennessee, every state in the South made vagrancy a crime, and any black man not vouched for by a white could be classed as a vagrant. The state incarcerated these men, as well as men charged with petty crimes and minor debts, then leased them to mine and plantation owners for a fixed annual sum. When their supposed release time arrived, white authorities discovered provisions in the fine print of contracts, such as money owed for debts incurred while imprisoned, that required many to serve more time, and still more time. By variations on this system, thousands of

African Americans were kept in a permanent state of imprisonment. According to Douglas A. Blackmon, author of *Slavery by Another Name: The Re-Enslavement of Black Americans from the Civil War to World War II*, "hundreds of men charged with petty crimes were simply worked to death."[18]

Young Fagen worked alongside men being paid forty cents a day and then locked up at night in stockades that were "but little more than cow sheds, horse stables, or hog pens." David Fagen's rage was almost certainly built upon a lifetime of grievances; the humiliations visited upon his father, his friends, and his neighbors; and surely the many offenses he himself suffered. In describing the mental state of southern blacks in the 1890s, Arnold H. Taylor could have been charting the very course young Fagen's life was soon to take: "Under the façade of accommodation virtually every black person harbored feelings of bitter resentment. These feelings were carefully kept under control but were liable to flare into open revolt under the provocation of a specific event or a long train of abuse."[19]

While laboring for Mr. Hull in Port Tampa, the eighteen-year-old David Fagen found time to woo a young woman by the name of Maggie Washington. In October 1897, they were married. The union would last at the most eight months, maybe less. About their courtship and marriage nothing is known.[20]

While the city bustled with enterprise during the late 1890s, the Cuban side of town seethed with a revolutionary fervor. Cuban exiles in Ybor City rolled fine cigars in the factories and cheered the fiery speeches of Cuban rebel leaders. At night, the Cuban expatriates loaded small sailing vessels with weaponry to be smuggled to the rebels at home, a violation of the McKinley administration's strict neutrality laws. For thirty years, Cubans had risen up repeatedly in revolt against Spanish rule. An independence movement in 1868 had dragged on for ten years before Spain could quell the resistance, bringing ruin to the economy and misery to the people. Over the next two decades, short-lived rebellions followed with regularity, most of them put down within a matter of weeks, if not days. But in February 1895, after so many false starts, the Cuban rebels mounted an independence movement that took hold.[21]

The uprising started in Cuba's eastern Oriente Province, and within eighteen months it had swept across the entire 780-mile length of the island. Under the leadership of generals Maximo Gomez and Antonio Maceo, the revolutionaries adopted a scorched-earth strategy, dynamiting railroads and burning Spanish-owned plantations, cane fields, and sugar mills, all with the purpose of cutting off food supplies to the cities and limiting Spain's ability to wage war.[22]

By the first months of 1898, the McKinley administration had concluded that the Cuban rebels were almost certain to prevail. The government in Spain had reached the same conclusion. Spanish forces had lost the will to fight; ravaged by yellow fever and malaria and profoundly demoralized, they could claim control of only the seaports and a scattering of inland towns. The insurgents controlled the countryside, and by early spring General Gomez's rebel army was preparing for the final assault on the Spanish-occupied cities. All parties understood that the struggle would be resolved over the coming summer with the revolutionaries almost certain to win their independence. Louis A. Perez Jr. stresses that while we cannot know for sure that the Cuban rebels would have won on their own, "What can be determined and documented, however, is that all parties involved had arrived at the conclusion that the days of Spanish rule were numbered. This was the perception that, in the end, served as the basis on which the vital policy decisions were made and actions were taken."[23]

The Spanish, under General Valeriano Weyler, had been brutal in their reaction to the rebels' scorched-earth tactics. Particularly infamous were the *reconcentrado* camps where Cuban civilians starved and suffered under the most wretched and disease-ridden conditions. The American press reported on Spanish atrocities in graphic detail, reports embellished and supplied mainly by the Cuban Junta in New York; they dubbed the Spanish general "Butcher" Weyler. Joseph Pulitzer's *New York World* and William Randolph Hearst's *New York Journal* engaged in a duel of one-upmanship, each topping the other with sensational and often fabricated accounts of Spanish outrages. Newspapers across the country picked up the drumbeat, echoing the cry of *Cuba Libre*, which worked the American public into an increasingly bellicose mood. Backed by popular support for the insurgent cause, politicians in Washington began to call for American intervention in support of Cuban independence.[24]

But Cuban independence was the last thing the McKinley administration wanted, and eventually McKinley would lead the United States to war, not to secure Cuban independence but to prevent it. Throughout the nineteenth century, American politicians, starting with Thomas Jefferson, had dreamed of incorporating Cuba into the United States. James Polk offered Spain $100 million for the island, Franklin Pierce $130 million. The Grant administration also contemplated making an offer. The consistent view, expressed repeatedly by political thinkers throughout the century, was that Cuba was essential to America's security, and that as Spain's empire continued to crumble, acquisition of the island by the United States was all but inevitable. What could not be tolerated, and would amount to a *casus belli*, was if Spain attempted to sell the island to another power. An independent Cuba was equally unacceptable. There were only two outcomes that America would tolerate: either Cuba remained a Spanish colony, or dominion over the island would pass to the United States.[25]

Should armed intervention be deemed necessary, conditions were ripe for war. The economy had been in collapse for five years, with deep political disaffection everywhere; a foreign adventure to distract a restive public had become increasingly attractive to politicians of both parties. Assistant Secretary of the Navy Theodore Roosevelt, Admiral Alfred Thayer Mahan, and Senator Henry Cabot Lodge, among others, saw in a war with Spain a great opportunity for American expansion. Already they had envisioned an American empire that included Cuba, an isthmian canal in Central America, and acquisition of the Hawaiian Islands as linchpin of an island chain that stretched all the way across the Pacific to Spain's other remaining major colony—the Philippines.[26]

What part President William McKinley played in Roosevelt and Lodge's grand scheme has long been the subject of debate. In the words of the historian Warren Zimmerman, "McKinley remains a tantalizing enigma. The view of historians differs on whether he masterminded America's war with Spain or was dragged into it." I would argue for the former, that this most inscrutable of presidents knew precisely what he wanted and achieved his ends like a poker player who wins without ever showing his cards. Walter Karp makes this argument best, quoting John Hay in a letter to Henry Adams: "I was more struck than ever by his mask. It is a genuine Italian ecclesiastical face of the fifteenth century. And there are idiots who think Mark Hanna will run him." (Hanna ran the Republican party at that time and helped put McKinley in office.) In Karp's opinion, "The White House has rarely known a president more devious, crafty, or subtle than the amiable, mild-mannered McKinley." Walter LaFeber was of a somewhat different view: "Although [McKinley] did not want war, he did want what only a war could provide: the disappearance of the terrible uncertainty in American political and economic life, and a solid basis from which to resume the building of the new American commercial empire." William McKinley may not have wanted war, as LaFeber and others have maintained, but he wanted control of Cuba.[27]

On a February night in 1898, the battleship USS *Maine* blew up in Havana harbor, killing 268 American sailors. As it turned out, the explosion was an accident, the fault of a poorly designed coal bunker. The American people kept their patience while a court of inquiry convened to determine whether the explosion had been caused by an accident or by an act of sabotage. Though Roosevelt and others suspected the accident was the result of an internal explosion (and suppressed a report to that effect), they were delighted when the court concluded that the sinking of the *Maine* had been caused by the external explosion of an underwater mine. The court did not name a culprit, but American newspaper readers had already made up their minds. With the yellow press fanning the flames of a growing outrage, cries of "Remember the *Maine*" and

"*Cuba Libre*" reverberated across the country and in the halls of Congress. Spanish men were depicted as swarthy lechers leering over pale Cuban beauties, and young American men could hardly wait to charge to the rescue. Hundreds of thousands of young men rushed to enlist. According to Chaplain Theophilus Steward of the African American Twenty-Fifth Infantry, the men in the regular army did not share the young enlistees' enthusiasm: "Officers and men were ready to fight if the stern necessity came, but they were not so eager for the death-game as were the numerous editors whose papers were getting out the extras every half-hour."[28]

The sinking of the *Maine*, however tragic in the loss of life, could not have been more fortuitous for the purposes of the McKinley administration. Rather than have to invent a pretext for insinuating the United States into the Cuban conflict, McKinley had merely to sit back, feigning reluctance, and thus be swept along by the tide of public opinion. On April 21, 1898, "caving in" to public and political pressure, the president signed a Joint Resolution of Congress authorizing the use of force to intercede on behalf of the Cuban revolutionaries against Spain.

Yet, in all of the public announcements leading up to the resolution, McKinley had avoided any mention of Cuban independence. This telling omission sent a wave of alarm through the Cuban rebel leadership. General Gomez made it clear that without some assurance that America was intervening as guarantors of Cuban independence rather than using it as a pretext for annexation, the Cubans would have no choice but to see the Americans as invaders and fight them as such. This impasse was resolved by a late addition to the Joint Resolution—the Teller Amendment. Put forth by Senator Henry Teller of Colorado, the fourth provision of the amendment read:

> That the United States hereby disclaims any disposition or intention
> to exercise sovereignty, jurisdiction, or control over said island except
> for the pacification thereof, and asserts its determination when that is
> accomplished, to leave the government and control of the island to its
> people.[29]

Spain, a fifth-rate power that had desperately tried to avoid war with the United States, was left no honorable way out but to declare war. America answered in kind. As it would turn out, Teller's promise was not worth the paper it was written on, but it sufficed to allay the Cuban revolutionaries' fears and the McKinley administration had what it wanted: America was going to war.

With the declaration of war, the army that had all but dried up and blown away in isolated posts in the West had to be reconstituted overnight. The job fell to General William Rufus Shafter, and Tampa was chosen as the assembly point. Shafter—in the words of Walter Millis, "an extremely corpulent warrior"—made his headquarters at Henry Plant's Tampa Bay Hotel, holding forth on the veranda in a wicker rocking chair. Old soldiers from the plains and the Rockies, even Civil War veterans, gathered here and enjoyed warm reunions at Henry Plant's hotel.[30]

Supplies from the industrial north streamed down the rail lines and overwhelmed Tampa's railyard, clogging the siding for miles out of town. Thousands of raw recruits and their rugged noncoms were bivouacked in Tampa Heights and Ybor City. Soon the logistics pile-up became more than Shafter could handle, but still the matériel and the troops—eventually twenty-five thousand of them—continued to arrive. Almost overnight orderly Tampa became a place of chaos.

And then, into the midst of this tumultuous scene, came the Buffalo Soldiers. Composed of black regulars under white officers and formed just after the Civil War, the four regiments—Twenty-Fourth and Twenty-Fifth Infantry, Ninth and Tenth Cavalry—had spent thirty years on the plains and in the Rockies from the Rio Grande to the Canadian border. They had fought Indians, chased rustlers, kept the whites out of Indian Territory and the Indians in, put down mining strikes and railroad strikes, and all the while looked out for one another with a loyalty that transcended all else. They had shot a few sheriffs and liberated more than one comrade from a local jail. They served under white officers, some good men and some deeply racist. "There is one great desire among the colored soldiers now-a-days that did not exist probably a decade ago," Sergeant M. W. Saddler of the Twenty-Fifth Infantry wrote to the *Indianapolis Freeman.* "That is to be represented in the file as well as in the ranks." Nonetheless, the day when deserving black enlisted men would be admitted to the officer corps still appeared far distant when they boarded trains in Montana and the Dakotas, in New Mexico and Utah, and set off for Tampa.[31] The Buffalo Soldiers arrived in Tampa in early May 1898. Even in the isolation of their scattered western posts these men had suffered their share of racist abuse and hostility, but conditions in Tampa went beyond anything they had ever encountered: to a man they were appalled when confronted by the "humiliating treatment" accorded the local blacks. Chaplain George Prioleau wrote: "The prejudice against the Negro soldier and the Negro was great, but it was of heavenly origin to what it is in this part of Florida." And another put it more bluntly: "With all its beauty, it is a hell for the colored people who live here, and they live in dread at all times." For always, just beneath the surface, was the specter of lynching. Between

The Twenty-Fourth Infantry comes to Tampa (private collection of Anthony L. Powell)

1882 and 1930, Florida would have the highest per capita rate of lynching in the South, with one of every 1,250 African Americans there falling victim to mob violence.[32]

In *The Strange Career of Jim Crow*, C. Vann Woodward corrects the popular misconception that the Jim Crow system of segregation fell into place quickly in the years following the Civil War. That was not at all the case. Throughout the period of Reconstruction and the establishment of "home rule" after 1877, and despite the climate of violent repression, relations between blacks and whites had yet to be codified, with blacks and whites frequently working side by side and living in mixed neighborhoods. "Subordination there was but it was not yet an accepted corollary that the subordinates had to be totally segregated and needlessly humiliated by a thousand daily reminders of their subordination."[33]

There are many reasons why over the decade of the 1890s, the South and the country as a whole gave in to the doctrines of the extreme racists, but a primary catalyst was the depression of 1893, the most severe in American history to that point. Five hundred banks failed and sixteen thousand businesses went bankrupt; factories, mills, and mines everywhere shut down, throwing two and a half million men out of work. The economy ground to a halt.[34]

In addition to the economic pressures following the collapse of 1893, there was the challenge of the Populist Movement to the southern Democratic Party and its powerful planter-class interests that had kept rural people in a state of penury for decades. Most threatening was the potential for an alliance of black and white farmers as the Populist leader Tom Watson and other white radicals across the South welcomed black farmers into the movement. In reaction, the southern Democratic Party abandoned its long-held position of racial moderation and took a virulently racist turn; maintaining white supremacy became the party's central theme and remained so through the first half of the twentieth century. Working crowds into near-paroxysms of "negrophobia," politicians warned of unrestrained bestiality and the dreaded prospect of amalgamation if the black population were not "kept in its place."

In hard economic times, black people made for convenient scapegoats, and the growing number of African Americans who were achieving economic success presented not only an economic threat to poorer whites but, even more intolerably in their minds, a threat to their social standing. Lynchings and the terror they created among southern African Americans served, in the words of Stewart E. Tolnay and E. M. Beck, "as crucial mechanisms for assuring the perpetuation of the southern status quo, especially the continuation of the exploitative plantation economy." According to Leon Litwack, the black southerner was "trapped in a web of controls that encouraged neither initiative nor hope," as white southerners took an increasingly fanatical turn in their determination to maintain a strict racial caste system. The message was clear: the only acceptable role for a black person was one of complete subservience to whites. But the more brutal the white southerners' attempts to affirm the old order, the less submissive the younger blacks and the deeper their contempt. "The impression conveyed was not so much the racial superiority of whites," Litwack wrote, "as their enormous capacity for savagery and cowardice, the way they inflicted their terror as crowds and mobs, rarely as individuals."[35]

Tolnay and Beck cite more than eighty reasons that were given for lynching a southern African American. The charge in approximately half the lynchings was murder or assault; another 30 percent was attributed to rape and sexual assaults. That left 20 percent to cover the other eighty stated reasons, and there one encounters such charges as "miscegenation," "voodooism," "inflammatory language," "race hatred," "being obnoxious," "improper with white woman," "indolence," "trying to vote," "offended white man," "insulted white woman," and "impudence to white man."[36] An African American never really knew when some slight misstep—a hard look, a muttered word—might set off a chain reaction that would career out of control. In such an atmosphere of terror, it is understandable why the black citizens of Tampa "lived in dread at all times."

W. Fitzhugh Brundage describes the fine line blacks in the South were required to walk in their dealings with whites: "The elaborate codes of racial etiquette dictated even the most minute details of everyday conduct and determined how blacks addressed whites, how they comported themselves in the presence of whites, and even how they expressed humor, anger or any other emotion. Blacks had to observe scrupulously the exacting standards of behavior lest they offend whites."[37] At the heart of this was the suppression of black men. Again, "the circle of black transgression and white extralegal punishment was intended to lead back to the brutal confirmation of white, male power."[38]

The Buffalo Soldiers were of no mind to answer to the customary "boy" and "uncle" in exchange for "sir" and "mister" to the whites. From the first, they clashed with the white citizens of Tampa. The black regulars refused to step off the sidewalk and tip their hats when white people passed; they insisted on purchasing goods across the same counter as a white person and even on sitting down in a white café to eat. A journalist for the *Tampa Morning Tribune* summed up the problem: "The colored infantrymen stationed in Tampa and vicinity have made themselves very offensive to the people of the city. The men insist upon being treated as white men are treated and the citizens will not make any distinction between the colored troops and the colored civilians."[39]

The sight of a black man in a military uniform, while thrilling to the black citizens of the region, represented the ultimate affront to the white people of Tampa. When a saloonkeeper refused to serve a black soldier a drink, the soldier returned with forty of his comrades. Left little choice, the saloonkeeper served them, but then proceeded to smash all the glasses in a barrel. The blacks closed his establishment down and did the same with a number of other saloons. Throughout the month of May the white citizens lived in a state of outrage, the papers itemizing and inflating any perceived transgression by a black soldier in an evermore hysterical indictment. According to Willard B. Gatewood Jr., "Sensational accounts of 'rackets' and 'riots' by 'these black ruffians in uniform' appeared regularly in dailies throughout the South." The behavior of the Buffalo Soldiers in Florida only increased the tension between the whites' resolve to keep blacks on the bottom and the black soldiers' determination to gain their full rights.[40]

Willard Gatewood concluded that the Buffalo Soldiers' "presence in Florida contributed to the final capitulation of the white South to extreme racism. The presence of so large a contingent of Negro soldiers in the South hastened the collapse of whatever remained of internal resistance to racism. The tendency of the black troops to resist discrimination and to defy regional customs regarding race conjured up frightful prospects in the minds of white Southerners. . . . In such an atmosphere racist demagogues throughout the South came into their own."[41]

To the black people of Tampa, the sight of a black soldier on horseback, all spit and polish and unfazed by white hostility, was like nothing they had ever seen. The cavalrymen put on displays of trick riding and galloping charges for awed crowds of ragtag youth. And when the call came for new recruits—750 for each of the four regiments—young black men lined up at recruiting stations by the hundreds. Among them was nineteen-year-old David Fagen.

As a married man, Fagen was ineligible to enlist, and his age, only nineteen, told against him. On both counts he lied, declaring, "I have neither wife nor child," and stating his age as twenty-two years and seven months. Charles Tayman, the white recruiting officer, also fudged on the enlistment papers, recording that Fagen read and wrote English "satisfactorily." But Fagen signed the document by making his mark, an X, bracketed on each side by his name entered and undersigned by Corporal Anthony A. Morrow.[42]

On June 4, 1898, David Fagen became a private in the Twenty-Fourth Infantry, Company H.[43]

———————

Fagen's height was recorded as 5 feet 10¼ inches, his weight only 140 pounds. At the time of his desertion sixteen months later, he was again listed as the same height, but his weight was estimated at 163 pounds. One of his noncommissioned officers later described him as "a man of medium height." Clearly, Fagen was not "gigantic," as several breathless journalists had described him, but it seems that he gave the impression of being larger than life. General Jose Alejandrino, whom Fagen would carry on his shoulders in the late days of the war, referred to him as "a Negro giant of more than six feet in height," and in 1960 Wolff passed that description on in *Little Brown Brother*. Five feet ten and 163 pounds put him two inches taller than the average black recruit of the day and thirteen pounds heavier. He was a little bigger than average, and certainly all muscle, but no giant. In that he was only nineteen when he enlisted, there is an outside chance that he grew during his time as a guerrilla leader, but more likely he had grown in General Alejandrino's imagination over the years. That the average Filipino fighter stood around five feet tall would also have made a man just under six feet seem quite large.[44]

———————

Four days after Fagen's enlistment, rumor spread that the troops would be boarding ships at Port Tampa but that late-arriving companies might not get to board at all. Each company of the Buffalo Soldiers was limited to seventy-five men. David Fagen is listed on the rolls of Company H along with other new recruits, but it is not likely that he sailed with the company only four days after enlisting. But the record is inconclusive. After the Battle of San Juan Hill, Chaplain Theophilus Steward quoted Captain Leavel of Company A of the Twenty-Fourth: "It would be hard to particularize in reporting upon the men of the company. All—non-commissioned officers, privates, even newly joined recruits—showed a desire to do their duty, yea, more than their duty, which would have done credit to seasoned veterans." Given the way the nineteen-year-old laborer had bluffed his way into the army, it is not out of the question that the enterprising young man might have talked his way on board a transport as well. There is simply no way to know, but the fact that 950 new recruits remained in Tampa for further training would make it more likely that the young private of four days stayed behind while the old hands joined the stampede across the nine miles of palmetto scrub to the port. In twenty-four chaotic hours, 16,887 men crowded onto thirty-two transports.[45]

And there they sat. At the last minute a rumor of three Spanish cruisers on the prowl off the coast put the entire enterprise on hold. Until the navy declared the seas off Tampa safe they could only wait, in sweltering heat, day after day. The white soldiers were allowed to come and go while the blacks remained confined to a segregated portion of the deck and quartered in the darkest stifling holds of the ship.

At last, after idling for an interminable six days, the navy gave the all clear. On June 14, 1898, the rotund General Shafter and his makeshift army sailed off to war.

Santiago

2

IN THOSE FEW WEEKS IN JUNE, while his fellows in Company H sailed off to war, young Fagen took the first steps to becoming a soldier. From reveille at 5:30 a.m. the bugle calls regulated the recruits' routine throughout the day. They trained under the baking sun, early morning hours spent on the firing line learning to handle their five-shot Krag-Jorgensens, a smooth-firing rifle of such long range the Crow Indians called it "shoot today, kill tomorrow." "It was exceedingly hot at this place," a soldier of the Twenty-Fourth recounted, "and many were prostrated while drilling four and five hours each day, generally in heavy marching order."[1]

Three weeks was not much time to prepare for war, but on June 30, the 950 new recruits and other reinforcements, teamsters, mule packers, and artillery drivers crowded onto six transports and set off on the eleven-day voyage. Their comrades in Cuba—twenty-six regiments in all—were poised on the eve of battle before San Juan Hill and the heights of El Caney.

A month earlier, the Spanish fleet under Admiral Cervera had taken refuge in the harbor at Santiago on the southeast coast. The American fleet under Admiral Sampson soon had Cervera's fleet bottled in. General Shafter chose Daiquiri, seventeen miles east of the heavily fortified Santiago, for the disembarkation of his Fifth Corps. Matériel, men, mules, and horses had to be landed through the heavy surf, and in keeping with the chaos that characterized every part of this mercifully brief war, disorder reigned. The flamboyant journalist Richard Harding Davis, who went about in sack suit, tramping boots, and Legionnaire's puggaree, later referred to the Santiago campaign as an expedition "prepared in ignorance and conducted in a series of blunders."[2]

Both Shafter and the War Department knew the coming rainy season would bring the dreaded yellow fever. They had a month, at best, before the first cases would appear. There was a belief that black people were immune from the fever and were better suited constitutionally for fighting in the tropics, hence the inclusion of the four black regiments and the urgent recruitment of additional regiments of African American volunteers. The blacks turned out to be just as susceptible to malaria and yellow fever as whites. The medical experts thought the fever spread by poor hygiene and human contact and did not yet understand that it was a mosquito-borne illness. From the first, the specter of an army decimated by yellow fever was in the back of Shafter's mind. In 1741 a British invasion force had landed at Guantanamo to the east and within days had been incapacitated by yellow fever and forced to withdraw. The leaders at the War Department feared a similar fate.

From the black regulars' perspective, the war gave them a chance to prove their mettle at last. If they could fight with courage and skill and, if it came to it, lay down their lives for their country, they could gain the respect of whites and improve the lot of blacks back home. For three years, the African American community had been roiled by conflicting opinion on the Cuban question. Why, some asked, should black Americans fight and die for Cuban independence when they were denied the rights of full citizenship at home? Until the federal government acted to stop the wave of lynchings and the disfranchisement and oppression of blacks throughout the South, many in the black community believed that African Americans should refuse to participate in what they saw as a travesty—America clamoring for war to bring freedom to Cubans (about half of whom were black) while denying freedom to its own black citizens back home.[3]

Others were just as adamant that if African Americans ever hoped to be accorded their full rights, they had to demonstrate their patriotism and loyalty on the battlefield, as they had in all of America's wars going back to the Revolution. When the explosion of the USS *Maine* made war all but inevitable, the debate among the African American community became less heated and support for the Buffalo Soldiers took precedence. It is doubtful that David Fagen had given these controversies much thought. Facing the prospect of years in a phosphate camp, he had grabbed the same opportunity the army had offered countless young men—an escape from the drudgery of life on the farm or the assembly line.

On the other hand, white males in America had been undergoing something of an identity crisis throughout the 1890s. There was the worry that with the closing of the West the American male was going soft. Additionally, the depression of 1893 had put two and a half million men out of work, generating anxiety and self-doubt among men of all social classes. For men like Theodore Roosevelt, the need to prove one's manhood became something of an obsession. And for the white male of the late nineteenth century, any notion of manhood was predicated upon the belief in the superiority of the "Anglo-Saxon" race. From that lofty ideal, other "races" descended in a hierarchy of worthiness that generally corresponded to darkening skin color and social class. Relegated to the bottom rung of the ladder below the Irish, the Slavs, and Italians, the rest of the Mediterranean world, the Jews, the Arabs, the Asians, the Native Americans, the mestizos of Latin America, and all other shades of brown-skinned peoples, were the blacks. True manhood was reserved for the white male; the black male was of a "child-race."[4]

From boyhood, Theodore Roosevelt had been a believer in Aryan theories of racial superiority and, as Gregg Jones wrote in *Honor in the Dust*, "had dreamed of battlefield valor as the ultimate test of manhood and honor." Roosevelt was more than ready for the war; he had been clamoring for it—for any war—for years. This bellicosity was hardly unique; political figures outdid themselves in extolling the virtues of battle and heroic conquest as proof of both individual manhood and a nation's manly character. With the declaration of war, the rush to enlist was more like a national stampede. This explosion of "popular fury," as Chaplain Theophilus Steward described the country's reaction, "represented a spirit quite like that of a mob . . . which could not be directly opposed." Dissenters were labeled as cowardly and unpatriotic, a charge that effectively silenced the opposition. Young men were going to liberate Cuba and prove their manhood before the eyes of the nation.[5]

While David Fagen and the 950 men known as "Shafter's recruits" were just beginning their eleven-day sea voyage, the Buffalo Soldiers were covering themselves in glory, charging up Kettle Hill with Roosevelt and his Rough Riders, and in taking both the fortress at El Caney and the blockhouses on San Juan Heights. Richard Harding Davis, reporting for the *New York Herald*, along with a phalanx of other journalists, made sure that Theodore Roosevelt received the bulk of the attention as if it had been a one-man show. But in fact eight thousand men—nine infantry regiments and six cavalry troops—were all in the thick of it, including 1,750 men from four regiments of the Buffalo Soldiers. In the opinion of the journalist and witness Stephen Bonsal, "The services of no four white regiments can be compared with those rendered by the four colored regiments."[6]

The long day's combat on July 1, 1898, the brutal heat and exhausting charge, had left the men victorious on the Heights but entirely spent. For the next two days they had remained under constant fire, without sleep or food, with little water, and exposed to a fierce July sun. They could look down upon the harbor town of Santiago, but between them and complete victory awaited tangles of barbed wire, more lines of trenches, and ten thousand Spanish regulars.

On July 4, Admiral Cervera received orders to break out of the harbor of Santiago where his squadron of nine ships had been blockaded by the American fleet under Admiral Sampson. One by one the Spanish warships steamed through the narrow passage and were pulverized by the American battleships. With the destruction of the Spanish squadron, the war was effectively won for the Americans. But General Toral declared his intentions to fight it out. When Shafter issued an ultimatum—surrender or Santiago would be bombarded and attacked—Toral ordered a flag of truce raised and entered into negotiations.

On July 10, 1898, David Fagen, aboard the transport *Hudson*, arrived off the beach at Daiquiri. In the ten days since taking the heights, the black soldiers had dug trench after trench for the white regiments. As soon as they finished one, they were ordered on to dig another. A black soldier wrote home: "Now we are almost naked, no medicine, not much to eat, hot water to drink, sleeping on the bare ground and no papers of any kind." The Twenty-Fourth Infantry had lost 104 men killed or wounded.[7]

While the Spanish General Toral and General William Rufus Shafter went back and forth in seemingly interminable negotiations, the cases of malaria and dysentery began to mount up, and the first cases of yellow fever were correctly diagnosed. In the belief that yellow fever was contagious, Shafter had designated the coastal village of Siboney, seven miles west of Daiquiri, as the place of a hospital quarantine camp. The first order was to burn the town under the theory that the yellow fever germs had to be exterminated. The next step was to determine which regiment was to take on the dreaded task of serving as nurses and cooks for the camp. Eight white regiments refused the assignment. On the night of July 15, the Twenty-Fourth Infantry was ordered to proceed immediately to Siboney, the enlisted men as yet unaware of the nature of their assignment.

Several months later, a reporter from a small-town Ohio newspaper, the *Piqua Daily Call*, interviewed Major Markley and men of the Twenty-Fourth Infantry as they passed though the train station traveling west. One of the soldiers recounted that the men of the Twenty-Fourth marched a distance of fifteen miles that night, "passing through places so dense and dark that they were compelled to clasp hands in order to find their way. This was the worst night experienced while in Cuba." At three o'clock in the morning they arrived at a hilltop overlooking Siboney and collapsed on the wet ground for a few hours sleep. The reporter went on: "Early that morning Major Markley went down the hill alone, poked around and found out what his command was expected to do. The climb back to the top of the hill . . . must have been made with sinking heart, for he had learned that his men, having fought the Spaniards so bravely, were now to be used as nurses and laborers."[8]

When Major Markley called for volunteer nurses, Captain A. A. Auger, Company H, stepped forward; fifteen men of the company followed his example. Others volunteered for burial detail, as cooks, for policing and all manner of work in the camp of thirteen hundred patients. Soon the first contingent of

The Buffalo Soldiers at Montauk Point (private collection of Anthony L. Powell)

sixty-five volunteer nurses set off down the hill. Stephen Bonsal recounted that at Siboney they found the hospital "in a deplorable condition," the town reduced to charred lines of blackened houses "still smoky and sooty with the fires which had been lighted too late to destroy the germs of the dreaded yellow jack." Rows of white tents had been erected in the midst of the ashes and there, for the most part unattended, American soldiers were dying hourly.[9]

The physician in charge, Major La Garde (who himself was stricken with the fever several weeks later), had warned of "the terrible contagion," but in fact Bonsal had touched upon the source of the illness when he described the camp's location in "pestilential, fever-breeding swamps that stagnated behind the beach." Although the fever is not spread by human contact, a mosquito that bites a yellow fever victim then transmits the fever to everyone else that it bites. The volunteers worked in a camp swarming with infected mosquitoes.[10]

While Fagen and the men of the Twenty-Fourth went to work at Siboney and new cases of yellow fever began to pour in, Shafter determined that he could wait no longer for General Toral to concede defeat. He ordered the Fifth Corps to prepare for attack at one o'clock on July 16, 1898. He knew that his army was on the point of collapse and that each succeeding day would only weaken it further. "The nervous tension of the line was terrific," Lieutenant Parker wrote. "The troops . . . were only waiting the word to dash forward upon the intrenchments [sic] of the enemy." But Shafter's gambit worked. An hour before the promised assault, General Toral accepted an unconditional surrender.[11]

According to Walter Millis, within two days of the surrender, "malarial and yellow fever swept the Fifth Army Corps like a scythe." Shafter had received orders to remain "until the fever has had its run." But Roosevelt went behind Shafter's back, organizing a round-robin letter, signed by a number of officers and dispatched straight to the press. "The army . . . is in a condition to be practically entirely destroyed by the epidemic of yellow fever to come in the near future." An infuriated William McKinley relented, despite fears of a yellow fever epidemic in the homeland.[12]

Various regiments, starting with the Rough Riders, boarded transports as they became available and sailed for Montauk Point, Long Island, the site designated as the quarantine camp for the returning soldiers. Yellow fever cases were left behind, abandoned with a shameful haste in what amounted to "a mad scramble," "an unqualified panic" to escape the island. Three hundred and fifty of General Kent's Division were left with fifty cots, the rest consigned to the wet ground, too weak to dig latrines and many delirious. They cursed their fleeing "comrades" for deserting them in their hour of peril. Eventually they were moved to Siboney, in Bonsal's words, "the charnel-house of the army, where many of our best and bravest had been brought back to die, and worse — to rot."[13]

As if consigned to a lower rung of Dante's hell, the remaining 456 men of the Twenty-Fourth Infantry rose each day for forty days to face their daunting task. Eventually all but a few would become ill, some felled for several days at a time before regaining the strength to return to their labors. The first stage of yellow fever lasted three or four days, accompanied by severe muscle aches and pains, headaches, fever, and nausea. In most cases there was no second phase, but for the unlucky minority a toxic phase returned after a remission of several days, marked by jaundice and the "black vomit," by liver, kidney, and lung failure. Many even survived the toxic phase, though with permanent organ damage.

Private "David Fagin" served as a nurse with Company I rather than with Company H. Company I's contingent consisted only of five sergeants, six corporals, a wagoner, and two privates—Fagen and one other. This unexplained attachment to Company I will be of significance the following year.[14]

On August 21, David Fagen contracted yellow fever. Four days later the death camp at Siboney was closed down. On August 26, the last remaining patients were carried on board the *Nueces*. Fewer than half the men of the Twenty-Fourth were able to walk unaided. White soldiers cheered them as they passed. Thirty-six remained behind in graves dug by their comrades.[15]

Stephen Bonsal paid them eloquent tribute.

In and out among the tents where the yellow pest was raging, I saw the groups of the black soldiers of the Twenty-fourth Infantry carrying into their places the sick as they came and carrying out the dead as they died, and burning the infected clothing, and scrubbing the place with chloride and other disinfectants. Superb as was the behavior of the Twenty-fourth Infantry in the San Juan charge, the battle they fought for forty days in the yellow fever hospital here was a still more gallant fight, and one which cost more dearly in precious lives; and there is no name that more deserves to be inscribed in letters of gold upon the regimental flag than that of Siboney, to commemorate those who faced in that slough of despair, that charnel-house of the wrecked army, a danger and a death more terrible than they had to fear from the Spanish fire.[16]

An article in the *Salt Lake (UT) Tribune*, September 30, 1898, concluded: "The country does not know the debt it owes to the Twenty-fourth Infantry, colored."[17]

The Far Side of the World

3

WHILE EVENTS IN CUBA were unfolding before young Fagen's eyes, another of Spain's last possessions, the Philippines, a tropical archipelago of more than seven thousand islands, was similarly roiled by an insurgency. The Spanish Empire that had once included the greater part of South and Central America was enduring its final unraveling. And William McKinley, under the influence of Assistant Secretary of the Navy Roosevelt and Senator Henry Cabot Lodge, saw in one empire's decline the opportunity for another's ascendancy.

With the declaration of war on April 25, 1898, Commodore George Dewey sailed from Hong Kong with his squadron of cruisers and, on May 1, in what amounted to an exercise in target practice, destroyed Admiral Montojo's decrepit fleet in Manila Bay. Several weeks later, Dewey brought the Filipino revolutionary leader Emilio Aguinaldo back from exile. With American ground forces still being organized in San Francisco, Dewey encouraged Aguinaldo to raise an army and attack the Spanish garrisons throughout Luzon. What assurances, if any, that were given remains a matter of controversy. Dewey saw Aguinaldo as useful to his purposes, and Aguinaldo, however suspicious of American intentions, was finally persuaded by the imposing commodore's exhortations.

In a matter of weeks, Emilio Aguinaldo mounted an army of fifteen thousand—a force that, according to James Blount, "kept growing like a snowball"—captured Spanish garrisons everywhere and drove thirteen thousand Spanish soldiers into Intramuros, Manila's old walled city. Hailing America as "the harbinger of their liberty," Aguinaldo declared himself dictator until a constitution could be written. Over the summer the revolutionaries established control and a provisional government throughout the towns and provinces of Luzon. "Compatriots!" the revolutionary leadership announced in a

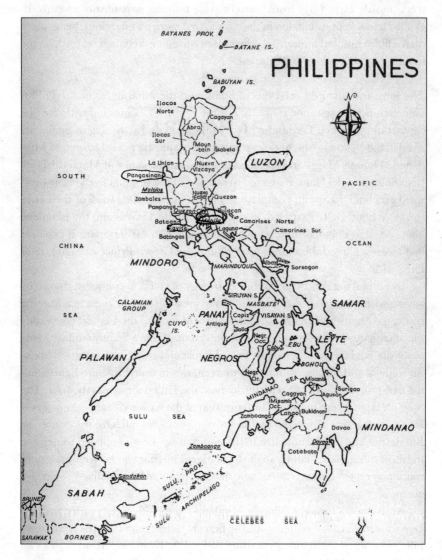

Philippines (George Farwell, *Mask of Asia* [1966])

proclamation, "Divine providence is about to place independence within our reach . . . where you see the American flag flying, assemble in numbers, they are our redeemers!" The United States had guaranteed Cuba's independence; it could only follow that it would do the same for the Philippines.[1]

But no promises were made—or at least none that were admitted to later— and an American force of four thousand regulars and eleven thousand volunteers, mostly farm boys from western state militias, was hastily assembled. While Dewey kept Aguinaldo in the dark as to America's intentions (being more than a little confused himself), the first twenty-five hundred men set forth on the month-long voyage to the Philippines.

The long and tortured relations of Spain and the inhabitants of the Philippine archipelago spanned more than three centuries, beginning with the first contact in 1521 when Ferdinand Magellan, sailing under the flag of Spain, arrived in the Visayas—the middle grouping of islands between Luzon and Mindanao. Though Magellan was killed in battle on the shore of Mactan Island, Juan Sebastian del Cano managed to sail one of the original five vessels westward and back to Spain, completing the first circumnavigation of the earth. In 1565 Miguel de Legazpi led an expedition to the Visayas and the islanders' long ordeal as colonial subjects of Spain began. (An earlier Spanish explorer had already named the islands after Philip, the Crown Prince of Spain, later Philip II.)

By employing the divide-and-rule strategy of colonial conquest, that is, by allying with the *datus* (town leaders) of one area to conquer their neighboring rivals, the Spanish were able to take control of most of the islands, converting the inhabitants to the Catholic faith as they went. While a Spanish military governor directed the colony's affairs from Manila and small contingents of Spanish soldiers and locally conscripted mercenaries manned scattered garrisons, the true representative of Spain throughout the settled areas was the friar. The Spanish largely kept the social organization of the native villages—*barangays*— intact, with a *datu* supported by the town's prominent citizens, the *principalia*. But despite the *datu*'s eminence in the community, he was obliged to defer in the most subservient manner to the local friar. The friar was both civil administrator and religious authority, usually the only Spaniard the "natives"—*indios*— ever saw.

Arab traders brought Islam to Mindanao in the fifteenth century and, except for some coastal settlements, the fiercely independent Moros were never fully conquered by Spain. According to Paul A. Kramer, "Mindanao's vast interior was sparsely populated and difficult to reach, and powerful, militarized polities under Muslim datus actively resisted the imposition of Spanish control."[2]

In time the friars acquired vast estates, particularly in the Tagalog regions of central Luzon, eventually controlling great tracts of arable land, estimated at 185,000 hectares (ca. 458,000 acres) or one-fifteenth of the island's cultivated land. Many of the ancestral *datus* were displaced by mestizos, both Spanish and Chinese, who also became large landholders (*hacenderos*) or prominent merchants. The largest hacenderos were called *caciques*, the most powerful figures in their respective regions, something like the largest plantation owners of the antebellum South, or a count in medieval Europe. Lessees on both the friar and *cacique/hacendero* lands were called *inquilinos*; some inquilinos rented properties large enough to be considered hacenderos in their own right; others might lease only several hectares of land. At the bottom of the social ladder was the *kasama*—the sharecropper, or subtenant. With few exceptions, the kasama remained on the bottom, barely subsisting as tenant farmers, beholden in every way to the inquilino, the hacendero, and the friar. The Filipino historian Renato Constantino catalogs the various abuses perpetrated by the friars, among them "corporal punishment such as whipping and lashing of both men and women for the slightest offense, onerous fees for confessions and other religious rites, sexual offenses against native women, and the native's virtual reduction to a slave and servant of the friar."[3]

Resentment festered continually among the indios, and an agrarian uprising occurred somewhere in the islands about every twenty years. The indios in one area, largely isolated from contact with other regions, were unaware that they shared the same grievances with indios throughout the islands. And all the while, the principalia—in Constantino's words, "the intermediaries between the Spanish colonizer and the masses of the people"—prospered, assuring their deepening loyalty to their colonial benefactors over the generations.[4]

With the Mexican Revolution of 1815, the galleon trade that had lasted for two centuries came to an end. In 1834 Spain opened Manila to the world economy, intent on extracting the maximum profit from the islands' resources, in particular tobacco, sugar, copra, hemp, and coffee. With the proliferation of commercial trading houses, shipping companies, banks, and other enterprises, an educated class of Filipinos to handle the required clerical work became a necessity. These were the first indios to receive a more extensive education, and by late in the nineteenth century they would form a "middle level" of urban workers who, in turn, would form the heart of the resistance to Spanish rule.[5]

As Spain tried to squeeze every ounce of wealth it could from the islands, conditions for the indio, burdened by the *polo*—an annual tribute—and weeks of forced labor on public works, only worsened. In 1841 a major agrarian revolt in Tayabas signaled a more widespread disaffection among the people. In 1872 the colonial authorities used the occasion of a mutiny by workers in an arsenal, protesting a renewed imposition of forced labor, to conduct a purge of those believed to be plotting against Spanish sovereignty. They not only exiled business leaders and members of the educated class but executed three prominent native clerics, accusing them of inciting the Cavite mutiny. This brutal crackdown by the colonial authorities fomented a resentment and frustration that increased in intensity over the last three decades of the nineteenth century.[6]

Many of the children of the mestizo elite—the principalia—studied abroad in Europe, particularly in Madrid: these young intellectuals became known as the *ilustrados*—the enlightened. When these urban intellectuals returned home, the stifling environment they encountered seemed all the more repressive. Initially, the ilustrados were not seeking independence but an end to racist discrimination and full inclusion as citizens of Spain. In 1889 Marcelo H. Del Pilar founded *La Solidaridad* in Barcelona, and for six years the periodical featured the writings of the most prominent of the ilustrados, most notably those of Jose Rizal, an artist, physician, and novelist. Rizal's subversive masterpiece, *Noli Me Tangere* (Touch Me Not), gave voice to the native population's grievances, particularly the abuses of the friars. In the face of these challenges, the friars became even more resistant to change, the Spanish authorities more repressive.

In 1892 Rizal returned to Manila and founded La Liga Filipina. The league's constitution advocated mild reforms achieved through legal means, even if some of its members were more revolutionary-minded. One of those more radical thinkers, and a founding member of La Liga, was Andrés Bonifacio. Raised in poverty and largely self-educated, Bonifacio worked his way up to become an agent for a commercial firm, all the while reading widely and developing his ideas. In July 1892, by order of the Spanish governor-general, José Rizal was exiled to Dapitan in Zamboanga, Mindanao, and La Liga Filipina disbanded. On the night of Rizal's deportation, the charismatic Bonifacio founded the Katipunan, a secret revolutionary society that advocated not reform but separation from Spain. The core members of the movement came from the middle level of what we would today call white-collar workers. The resulting uprising was not initiated by the laboring masses while most of the principalia elite, fearing the loss of their wealth and status, clung to the hope of reform.[7]

In 1896, when Spanish authorities discovered the Katipunan's plans for an uprising in Manila, fighting broke out. But Bonifacio proved to be a poor military leader. Another member of the Katipunan, Emilio Aguinaldo, was more successful militarily in defeating Spanish forces in his home province of Cavite. A rivalry grew between the self-educated Bonifacio and Aguinaldo, a Chinese mestizo raised in a family of some prominence. When Aguinaldo was elected

Emilio Aguinaldo (Marrion Wilcox, *Harper's History of the War in the Philippines* [1900])

leader of the Katipunan over Bonifacio, Bonifacio led a separatist movement of
his supporters; Aguinaldo had him arrested, tried, and executed in 1897.

But under Aguinaldo the revolutionaries proved no more successful than
under Bonifacio in the face of the Spanish regulars' superior weaponry. In a
Treaty of Biak-na-Bato, Aguinaldo and his leadership reached a strange accommodation with the colonial administrators: for a promised payment of eight

hundred thousand pesos they agreed to go into exile. On the last day of 1897, Aguinaldo and twenty-seven leaders of the Katipunan arrived in Hong Kong, where they lived frugally, scheming and plotting an eventual return and continuation of the revolution. Their prospects looked bleak and the day of their return a distant possibility until the Americans' entry into a war with Spain changed all their political calculations.

———•·•———

Dewey and Aguinaldo had already been well along in their various exchanges and interactions when President McKinley finally got around to cabling instructions to the commodore: he was under no circumstances to recognize the legitimacy of Aguinaldo's revolutionary government or offer any assurances of Philippine independence. But before these policy directives could be transmitted from the other side of the world, it seems that Dewey may have already compromised himself; American consular officials appear to have done the same. Dewey insisted that he had made no promises but was effusive in his praise of the Filipinos, pronouncing them "far superior in their intelligence and more capable of self-government than the natives of Cuba." Aguinaldo remained adamant that promises had been made but had nothing in writing to back his claim. Two years later, before a Senate committee, Dewey, feigning bafflement, testified that he had no idea the Filipino leadership had sought independence but instead thought their aim had been "revenge, plunder and pillage."[8]

With the American volunteers still making their way across the Pacific, Dewey was content to let Aguinaldo's "plunderers and pillagers" do the fighting and dying against their common enemy. Later, Dewey would explain that "he had used the Filipinos as the Federal troops used the negroes in the Civil War."[9] Suspicious as the Filipinos were of American intentions, they could only hope that this encouragement, including the distribution of rifles and ammunition, meant that the Americans were allies in the pursuit of Philippine independence. But should the Americans prove to have other ambitions, the weaponry would be useful in trying to evict the new would-be colonizers as well.[10]

Emilio Aguinaldo was a young man, not yet thirty years old, and George Dewey was a gruff and glowering presence with a volatile temper. Swept up in a whirlwind, Aguinaldo seemed confused about which direction he should take; he had been in Singapore when called back by Dewey to Hong Kong and brought to Manila aboard the *McCullough*. When Dewey first encouraged Aguinaldo to raise an army against the Spanish garrisons, Aguinaldo returned a short time later and asked to be taken to Japan; Dewey prevailed upon him to stay. This tendency to vacillation, to indecisiveness, would critically impair the revolutionaries' conduct of the coming war with the American invaders. Aguinaldo wanted to put his faith in the United States and in Dewey, but he was puzzled by the commodore's refusal to make clear America's intentions. Instead, Dewey put him off day after day while the transports carrying the first contingent of volunteers drew closer.

"I speak not of forcible annexation, for that cannot be thought of," President McKinley had said only months earlier in reference to Cuba. "That by our code of morality would be criminal aggression." But, in fact, long before the first hint of war with Spain, McKinley had planned at least one small act of criminal aggression should the possibility present itself—acquisition of the port city of Manila, if not all of the islands, as part of his design for an American commercial empire. Some contend that the mercurial McKinley's idea was to retain Manila and give the rest of the islands back to Spain. But it quickly became apparent that Aguinaldo and his revolution, which was now spreading like wildfire, precluded any return to Spanish control and presented McKinley with a dilemma.[11]

For if Spain was not returning, there were other nascent imperial powers ready to move in. Already, German warships were anchoring in Manila Bay, waiting for the Americans to leave. The Japanese had "kindly" offered their assistance should America need help in administering the islands. The British and the French looked on with more than passing interest. Cuba nestled securely ninety miles off the tip of Florida, but the Philippines hung like a ripe fruit in the open vastness of the southwest Pacific. McKinley faced a quandary: he was hardly inclined to share the remainder of the Philippines with rival powers such as Germany or Japan. Nor would an independent Philippine nation be conducive to his projected plans for an "open door" to China. As a convenient rationale, the president's military advisors assured him that were the Filipinos left to manage their own affairs, islandwide chaos would follow.

As McKinley deliberated, Aguinaldo and the revolutionary leadership grew more anxious, and dissension set in. The revolutionaries did not want to alienate their benefactors; they needed America as guarantors of their fledgling independence. But American intentions had become increasingly obvious: the longer they waited to take action the harder it would be to dislodge the interlopers. Yet Aguinaldo counseled patience: "I have studied attentively the Constitution of the United States and I find in it no authority for colonies," he told General Anderson. "I have no fear." And then the first transports steamed through the Boca Chica. The raw and undisciplined volunteers disembarked at Cavite, a short distance across the bay from Manila. The United States now had its toe in the door. In many ways, it has never left.[12]

Westward

4

ON SEPTEMBER 2, 1898, the *Nueces* docked at Montauk Point. No doubt David Fagen was relieved to be free and clear of Siboney after what must have seemed like a bad dream that would never end. He was just recovering from the miserable first stage of yellow fever when he boarded the transport. The period of remission must have been profoundly unsettling, if not terrifying, as he waited for the return of the dreaded toxic phase. Mercifully, he was spared where others were not so fortunate. More than forty men of the Twenty-Fourth Infantry survived the toxic phase but were left permanently disabled.[1]

Another soldier of the Twenty-Fourth Infantry, Company H, who "suffered near to death with the disease" was Corporal John W. Calloway, who had signed as second witness at Fagen's enlistment. Calloway would rise to the rank of battalion sergeant major, and Corporal Anthony Morrow, who also signed for Fagen, would rise to the rank of regimental sergeant major. These two men, so impressive in their bearing, must have made a strong impression on the young laborer. During the Santiago campaign, Calloway was promoted from regimental quartermaster sergeant to acting sergeant major of his regiment, according to First Lieutenant J. D. Leitch, "performing the duties of his office entirely unassisted." At Siboney, "he remained zealously at his post" until he contracted yellow fever on August 21, the same day as Fagen.[2]

Just how the two men got on is unknown, but from the day of Fagen's enlistment until the morning of his desertion, the two men's careers were intertwined. Calloway may have been an important influence on the younger man, or they may have been at odds, but their stories have been the two most often cited as contrasting examples of the Buffalo Soldier experience in the Philippines. John W. Calloway was born in Bristol, Tennessee, in 1872, making him seven years older than Fagen. He enlisted in the Twenty-Fifth Infantry in 1891 at the age of nineteen and was soon on his way to Montana, where he spent his first three-year tour of duty. Just 5 feet 7½ inches tall and a slight 125 pounds,

Calloway was light-skinned, according to scholar Gil Boehringer, "the grand-son of a union between a white planter of an old Virginia dynasty and a 'mulatto slave.' His father was an emancipated 'mulatto' slave, while his mother's Mary-land family had been 'free born coloreds' since well before the Civil War." Calloway had received a good literary education and while still a teenager moved to Boston, where he learned the printer's trade. What inspired him to enlist and set off for the wilds of Montana is unknown, perhaps a young man's desire for adventure.[3]

John Calloway loved the army and was a model soldier, taking part in putting down the Coeur d'Alene miners' strike in 1892, and railroad strikes in Colorado and New Mexico in 1894. But he was most useful for his secretarial skills. White officers lamented the illiteracy of so many of the black noncommis-sioned officers (although literacy rates improved throughout the 1890s), and a man who could make the company rolls and returns, keep the accounts and books, was highly prized.

After recuperating for three weeks, the regiment boarded a train for the army post at Fort Douglas, Utah. Newspapers covered their passage across the country with such headlines as OUR BLACK HEROES and COLORED HEROES FROM SANTIAGO. The men clearly relished the praise and the ce-lebrity; at great sacrifice they appeared to have accomplished what they had set out to do.[4]

In barely two months, David Fagen had traveled a long way from the Scrub—to Cuba, to Long Island, and now he was taking in the great sweep of the farmlands of the Midwest, the Great Plains, and the Rocky Mountains. Along the way, the young private was docked twelve cents for ordnance lost—a knife and a fork. Twelve cents out of a soldier's monthly pay of thirteen dollars would hardly be noticed; eventually the fines could consume the better part of his wages.[5]

Upon the regiment's return to Salt Lake City, they were welcomed home by a parade, the regimental band proudly leading the way. Julius F. Taylor, the firebrand publisher of the *Broad Ax*, one of the city's two African American newspapers, noted that the regiment's return from Cuba was greeted with con-siderably more enthusiasm than when it had first arrived at Fort Douglas in 1896 and faced widespread protests. A reporter from the *Salt Lake (UT) Tribune* interviewed a number of the veterans: "Some of the men showed scars where bullets had ripped through their bodies. Others were visibly emaciated from attacks of the fever, but not one talked boastfully of his achievements or the achievements of the command."[6]

With their ranks swollen from the 511 who had gone off to war to the 958 returning, the regiment settled into its old post near the city with its spectacular view to the west. Life at Fort Douglas was exceedingly tame, a monotonous round of drill, practice marches, the maintenance of post grounds, gardens, and stables. One other activity, attendance at the post school for those regulars of limited education, was strongly encouraged. John Calloway was a teacher at the Post Military School, highly praised by Chaplain Allensworth, who supervised the school. The evidence suggests that Fagen was a pupil.[7]

Calloway was what was then called a "race man." He was a strong advocate of Booker T. Washington's gradualist approach to race relations with its emphasis on the long view, on self-improvement, on forbearance rather than confrontation. Like Washington, Calloway believed that education was the key to improving the status of the black man in America. But beneath the young man's polished, carefully modulated exterior—he was repeatedly praised for his honesty, efficiency, accuracy, faithfulness, promptness, and sobriety— burned a deep rage at the unending oppression of African Americans. As Calloway's career advanced, he would find it increasingly difficult to reconcile John Calloway, the loyal soldier, with John Calloway, the advocate for racial justice.[8]

Fortunately, an article in the *Salt Lake City (UT) Herald*, October 30, 1900, provides a vivid description of the irrepressible young Fagen and also one of the two known likenesses of him, this one (reproduced here) either a letterpress or halftone reproduction taken from a photograph. The article, published two years after Fagen's time in Salt Lake City, was prompted by a report in the *New York Times* of a guerrilla attack led by Fagen in the Philippines, October 25, 1900. As it happened, "Captain" Fagen was so revered by his Filipino fighters that they referred to him as "General" Fagen. In picking up the rumor, the *New York Times* promoted the young guerrilla captain to "General" in "the Filipino army." A reporter for the *Salt Lake City (UT) Herald* interviewed a number of people, both soldier and citizen, who had known Fagen in Utah in that fall of 1898 to get their reaction to this astounding news.

The article states, incorrectly, that Fagen had enlisted in the regiment at Fort Douglas, then goes on to say that while at Salt Lake City he

> was a frequent visitor of the gambling resorts on Commercial Street, where he was known as a jovial, reckless player with a penchant for stud poker and an exhaustless fund of luck.
>
> Among his former comrades, many of whom are now residing in Salt Lake, he passed for a very poor excuse for a soldier. Sergeant Williams of No. 49 Franklin Avenue, a veteran of the Twenty-fourth Regiment of more than twenty years' service and recently returned from Manila, wore a very disgusted look yesterday while discussing his

DAVID FAGIN.

"David Fagin" (*Salt Lake City [UT] Herald*, October 30, 1900)

former companion in arms who had cajoled the Filipinos into making him a general.

"That man Fagin was no soldier," exclaimed the gray-haired veteran. "He never would make a soldier. He was just naturally too lazy and had too much book learning in his head. He had been through the university of Nashville and when he joined the regiment here he wanted to be giving orders and didn't like to take them. That's what made him join the Filipinos. He wanted a chance to be a high boss."

According to Williams's description, Fagin is a man of medium height, and in complexion, "half-way between mulatto and gingerbread."

He added that the man looked enough like a Filipino to pass for one if he donned the native costume . . .

Before quitting his regiment to don the epaulettes of a native general Fagin took advantage of a lay-off last March, and his usual run of luck at stud poker to take about $200 from his comrades. This was only one of his regular winnings every time there was a payday. He was similarly successful while in Salt Lake on Commercial Street, but the money slipped through his fingers as fast as he won it, and he seldom had any in his pocket.

W. D. Robertson, a colored milkman who used to cater to the men of the Twenty-fourth when they were stationed at Fort Douglas, remembers Fagin well as one of his best-paying customers. Robertson says it was like coining money to lend Fagin a few dollars to stake him in a game of stud poker.

"In five minutes he'd give me back twice as much as I let him have," said the milk vendor. "He was always good pay when he had the money, and he could borrow from almost anybody because he was so lucky."

When off duty Fagin seemed to have been always light hearted, careless and full of jokes, gambling or drinking when he could get the money. In the restraint of camp life, though, he was sullen and had the reputation for shirking drill for a bed in the hospital every time he could impose on the surgeon. . . .

"Fagin would make a wild general," said one ex-member of the regiment. "Why, that boy didn't know a column of fo's from a box of hardtack. That's right; he didn't know nuthin' at all about soldiering, an' he was too blame lazy to learn. But I reckon his soldiering days are about over now, for when the co't marshall gets after him he'll sho' take the elevator.[9]

I was pleased to come across this long-buried article, both for the likeness of Fagen that I had given up hope of finding and, more importantly, for its vivid description of young Fagen as a devil-may-care charmer—"jovial" and "reckless," "light hearted" and "careless." The image, a halftone print from a photograph, would indicate a young gambler with a taste for sartorial elegance, probably outfitted by some of his winnings. If his enlistment papers confirm that he was not a giant, this article confirms that Fagen was not the brooding black man, smoldering in barely controlled rage, as he was sometimes portrayed. Here again, the image of the trickster comes to mind. He charms the milkman into loaning him money (and how many others?), persuades the surgeon he's too sick for drill, and convinces Sergeant Williams he's a graduate of Fisk University when he's just learning to sign his name. It seems dissimulation, if not a natural trait, was one he had cultivated as a means of navigating in a difficult world.

His routine success at stud poker was obviously due to more than an "exhaustless fund of luck." He could "read" people, he could bluff, he could remember the deck several hands back. And, obviously, he took real delight in the game.

Was he conning the surgeon or was he genuinely ill? The following May, he would be assigned to a mountain detail, its men chosen because they had continued to suffer from the effects of the malarial fever contracted in Cuba. Then again, maybe he used his close call with the yellow jack as an excuse to put his feet up and loaf in bed while the others trudged through their monotonous routines.

Did Sergeant Williams, the gray-haired veteran, just assume that Fagen was a graduate of Fisk because of his brash, fast-talking manner? Educated blacks were sometimes perceived as "uppity." Maybe there was a touch of haughtiness in the young man's air of confidence that made him sound educated. Or maybe the smooth-talking private was just putting the gullible old-timer on, bragging of his university days and laughing at the older man's naïveté.

As for Fagen's demonstrated lack of enthusiasm for the rigors of military life, his later renown as a guerrilla strategist would indicate that he was learning a good deal more about soldiering than his instructors imagined. Perhaps he found it an advantage to employ that old survival tactic of feigned ignorance, of appearing useless, another way of playing his cards close to his vest. Or, perhaps, he was simply bored, uninterested, or genuinely incapable of grasping the difference between a column of fours and a box of hardtack. Maybe those lessons sunk in later.

This is speculation on my part. This extraordinary article presents the reader wide latitude for interpretation.

Fagen would mark his twentieth birthday that October. During his time in Utah, he was fined two dollars in summary court, with accompanying fatigue duty and possibly a short stay in the guardhouse. The files do not describe the nature of infractions that led to company punishment, just the amount of the fine. We wonder just how Fagen was getting into trouble, and not knowing the particulars is frustrating. As best I can tell, he remained a private during his time in the army, a private on a downhill trajectory rather than on the rise.[10]

The Waiting Game

5

WHILE DAVID FAGEN AND THE MEN of the Twenty-Fourth Infantry trained at Fort Douglas, the situation in the Philippines developed into something of a waiting game: the Americans waiting for more troops to arrive and some clear direction from Washington, and the revolutionary leadership waiting for an unequivocal sign from the Americans that they had come as liberators and not conquerors. The revolutionaries had been suspicious of American intentions from the first but remained hopeful that deliberations in Washington would evolve in favor of Philippine independence.

The Filipino army ringed Manila, where they had corralled thirteen thousand Spanish soldiers; Aguinaldo believed his Army of Liberation could take the city but only with the support of American naval artillery, an offer of help that was not forthcoming. Rather than chancing it without that help in a full-out assault, Aguinaldo stayed his hand. It was a grave miscalculation, one of many to follow.

On June 12, 1898, Aguinaldo and the leaders of the Katipunan signed a declaration of independence. Over the summer months, elections were held in towns throughout Luzon, but the franchise was limited to members of the provincial elite whose support Aguinaldo feared losing should he signal any lessening of their social preeminence. By a decree on June 18, Aguinaldo granted equal authority to both military and civil officials, which led to all manner of confusion and dissension. But if there had been no change in the social order and the administration of the provincial towns remained something of a shambles, the revolutionary government could still claim sole authority over the island of Luzon.[1]

Frustrated and anxious, the president continued to seek reassurances of America's good intentions, but he only got the runaround—and a large dose of condescension—day after day. Little by little the Filipinos were eased,

47

grudgingly, farther to the suburbs of Manila, while General Wesley Merritt's eighty-five hundred men took over the Army of Liberation's trenches. These curious requests, the insults and evasions, continued to add to the Filipinos' growing resentment and distrust. In the meantime the troops kept coming, proof enough for many of those around Aguinaldo of American intentions.

The Spanish commander in chief, General Fermin Jaudènes, fearing a blood-bath at the hands of the Filipinos, arranged through secret negotiations to surrender to the Americans. General Merritt and Admiral Dewey agreed to accommodate Jaudènes by staging a mock battle that would allow the Spanish general to save his honor (as well as his neck, should he return to Spain in disgrace).

Accordingly, on the morning of August 13, 1898, Dewey's warships lobbed some shells at Fort San Antonio Abad while General Merritt's volunteers sloshed up the coastal marshes in a drenching rain. They entered the fort to find it vacated and a white flag flying above the old walled city. Aguinaldo had been warned to stay out of the city, but his men, furious at having been excluded from the action, rushed forward; for a time the mock battle threatened to turn into a real one. But in the end only six Americans and forty-nine Spaniards died to save a Spanish general's honor.[2]

In another costly moment of hesitation that day, Aguinaldo had refrained from ordering an assault on the Spanish defenses at the first onset of hostilities. The Americans now had all of Manila, and the revolutionary leadership was thrown into further disarray.

Emilio Aguinaldo was a Chinese mestizo of "very slight education." He was by all accounts a remarkable orator, with a gift for inspiring the masses in soaring speeches. According to Aguinaldo's early biographer, Edwin Wildman, the people "looked upon him as a demigod." But the American journalists who met Aguinaldo were almost universally of the opinion that he was a figurehead. Wildman counted four men as the true power behind Aguinaldo, none more influential than Apolinario Mabini.[3]

Apolinario Mabini was the son of peasants and small landholders. A brilliant student and early member of La Liga Filipina, he had worked diligently through the years to become a skilled lawyer noted for his political acumen. But in 1896, at the age of thirty-two, he was stricken with polio, his legs paralyzed.[4]

When Aguinaldo returned to Cavite, across the bay from Manila, in May 1898, he ordered twelve municipalities to "prepare a hammock" and provide teams of men to convey "the paralytic" to his headquarters. In this dramatic fashion, the two most important figures of the revolution—Aguinaldo, "the

Apolinario Mabini (Marrion Wilcox, *Harper's History of the War in the Philippines* [1900])

undisputed leader of the masses," and Mabini, "their intellectual spokesman"—
were brought together for the first time.[5]

Apolonario Mabini was a true radical. He would settle for nothing less than
complete independence; with his icy detachment and razor-sharp intellect he
inspired a deepening hatred on the part of many in the elite who referred to
him as "the president's dark chamber." If Mabini was not exactly the fierce

champion of the indios that Teodoro A. Agoncillo made him out to be in *Malolos: The Crisis of the Republic*, his views still set him apart from those of the other ilustrados, and certainly from the principales. Mabini believed in a "simultaneous external and internal revolution." In his opinion, independence had to go hand in hand with a social leveling; if a successful revolution led only to a continuation of rule by a privileged elite, then the masses would have every right to revolt. Without the promise of internal reform, he predicted the support of the masses for the revolution would wither away. "In Mabini's view," Guerrero wrote, "this 'social regeneration' would be implemented 'from above' with the initiative coming from the revolutionary leadership." This was not the sort of radical talk most of the principales wanted to hear.[6]

Mabini needed no further convincing of American perfidy. "The conflict is coming sooner or later and we shall gain nothing by asking favors of them which in reality are our rights." But Aguinaldo continued to see what he wanted to see. The United States and Spain had signed a peace protocol on August 12 whereupon it was agreed that American forces would remain in control of Manila "pending the conclusion of a Treaty of Peace which shall determine the control, disposition, and government of the Philippines." And upon that slender thread Aguinaldo appended his hope. The Americans had guaranteed Cuba its independence; surely in time they would come around to a similar disposition of the Philippines.[7]

In Manila, the Americans and their involuntary Filipino hosts settled into a tense waiting period. From the day of the mock battle in August—a clear act of betrayal—the Filipinos ceased to see the Americans as their benefactors. They were now interlopers, unwelcome visitors who exhibited all the unsettling signs of a long, if not permanent, stay. Troops and matériel continued to arrive, piling up on the docks. "Passenger steamers disgorged a civilian army of American speculators, swindlers, prostitutes, gamblers and adventurers converging on Manila. Scores of new saloons, whorehouses, gambling halls and opium dens sprouted along the narrow streets," writes Gregg Jones. The volunteers got their first taste of the rainy season in the tropics; the streets and drainage streams ran with sewage, and in the sweltering heat and humidity the stench was overwhelming. Hospitals filled to overflowing with cases of typhus, malaria, dengue fever, and a score of other tropical diseases.[8]

In the arcaded streets and dank alleyways, many an encounter between American and Filipino turned violent. Shoving matches, knife fights, and even gunplay were daily occurrences. "We have to kill one or two every night," a private wrote home. According to Leon Wolff, "Many a Filipino civilian was punched, or slugged with a beer bottle, many a fruit vendor jostled and robbed of his wares." This practice became known as "bulldozing the natives," and William Thaddeus Sexton itemized the various offenses committed by these young men so far away from home for the first time—assault, extortion, larceny, rape.[9]

Into September the waiting game dragged on, while in Paris Spanish and American delegations negotiated the archipelago's fate. Puerto Rico was in America's possession, and the McKinley administration showed no inclination of letting it go. But the disposition of the Philippines remained unresolved. Most historians maintain that it was not until September that McKinley privately elected to keep the islands, having gauged public opinion favorable. Walter Karp argues that this most inscrutable of American presidents had determined to acquire the islands from the first: "To conquer and rule the Philippines as an American colony was William McKinley's principal war aim." Getting the public on board required some delicate sophistry. The press obliged. By then the American people had become persuaded of the administration's narrative, that the Philippines had come to America as "a gift from the Gods," a responsibility foisted upon the nation by "happenstance." "Destiny is duty," William McKinley solemnly explained.[10]

In Manila, the rains continued without letup, and the American camps became mosquito-ridden quagmires; in the stifling heat and humidity, some companies trained in their underwear. There was a general agreement among observers that the U.S. Army was "a mob without discipline." Along with the small horde of fortune-seekers—whom journalist Frederick Palmer called "the curse of the city"—the volunteers found diversion in dives such as the Ah Gong Saloon and Montana Chop House where they puffed on Maria Cristina cigars and consumed great quantities of Schlitz and Pabst Blue Ribbon and hard liquors whimsically dubbed "Chinese tanglefoot." Chaplain Bateman confided to a reporter, "The people have reason to believe that the United States is a nation of drunkards." These were young men away from home for the first time, free from the restraining eye of their parents, the local minister, or the town fathers. Admiral Bradley Fiske took note: "The army . . . began to call them [the Filipinos] 'niggers' and treat them as 'niggers,' so that friction between them and the Filipinos increased as the size of the American camp increased."[11]

Aguinaldo had removed his government to Malolos, twenty-five miles north of Manila, and on September 15, a congress of ninety-five influential Filipinos set about writing a constitution. Apolinario Mabini was firmly against writing a constitution, believing that nothing good could come of a document conceived by men whose primary aim was to protect their interests. He quoted a character, Padre Florentino, from Rizal's *Noli Me Tangere*: "Why independence, if the slaves of today will become the tyrants of tomorrow?"[12]

Mabini proposed a military dictatorship until the revolution might succeed; the Filipinos, he believed, needed to present a unified front to the world. He was also justifiably concerned about the excesses of the military; without a tight control the soldiers in the field had demonstrated a marked tendency to lawlessness and brutality, behaviors that threatened to alienate many who might otherwise support the revolution. "No revolutionary people," he wrote, "should adopt a definitive constitution but should confine themselves to the declaration of principles with which they intend to complete their work."[13]

If most of the younger and less affluent ilustrados wanted independence, it would be a carefully managed independence, one with themselves at the helm of what they termed "an oligarchy of intelligence." They were particularly keen on excluding the military leaders of the revolution from power. These were the men of the Katipunan who had initiated the struggle against Spain and had done the fighting while the privileged classes remained on the sideline. Most of the fighters came from the lower middle class and from the peasantry and imagined that an expulsion of the Spanish would mean land reform, tax relief, and an end to centuries of injustice and oppression. To the ilustrados, they represented a dangerous rabble, undisciplined and led by men whose volatile nature was only matched by their ignorance.[14]

Aguinaldo, perhaps not fully aware of the composition of the delegates or their intentions, may have still been under the illusion that he could persuade the elite to support the revolution. The conservatives were out to consolidate power in the legislative branch, which they would control, and severely limit that of the executive, in effect, to hamstring Aguinaldo in his effort to carry on the revolution. Mabini, who saw what Aguinaldo came to see too late, was overruled.[15]

———————

The volunteers had a new general, Elwell S. Otis. The mutton-chopped Otis was described as looking like a beagle; the men referred to him as "Grandma Otis." Major General Arthur MacArthur privately ridiculed him as "a locomotive bottom-side up, its wheels revolving at full speed." Otis had been wounded in the head in the Civil War and suffered from insomnia, so rather than delegate much of his paperwork, he sat at his desk until late in the night attending to administrative trivia. James H. Blount, a lieutenant in the volunteers, later U.S. District Judge in the Philippines, and in 1912 the author of a blistering critique of America's colonial appropriation of the islands, wrote of Otis's "unswerving devotion to a desk in time of war."[16]

Otis was a capable administrator but strangely incurious, rarely venturing forth from Malacañang Palace and uninterested in learning about developments beyond the perimeter surrounding Manila. Control of Manila seemed sufficient to Otis to claim authority over the entire archipelago, conveniently ignoring the reality that Aguinaldo and the revolutionary leadership had established local and provincial administrative control throughout Luzon and into the Visayas.

Many historians agree with Blount that Otis's uninformed rosy assumptions about the disposition of the Filipinos toward American authority led to an equally misinformed administration in Washington. If Otis had given McKinley an accurate account of conditions in the islands, the president might have understood that denying sovereignty to the Filipinos was going to be a bloody proposition. Blount cites Otis's "total misapprehension of conditions in the islands . . . a misapprehension due to General Otis's curious blindness to the great vital fact of the situation, viz., that the Filipinos were bent on independence from the first, and preparing to fight for it to the last."[17]

With no hope of recovering its lost colonies, Spain signed the Treaty of Paris on December 10, 1898. The Philippines, Guam, and Puerto Rico were now colonies of the United States. In return, the country recompensed Spain twenty million dollars for "Spanish improvements" to the islands. Earlier, in July, at the height of the Santiago campaign in Cuba, Congress voted to annex Hawai'i as a territory of the United States. The uninhabited Wake Island in the western Pacific was quickly added to the collection, and with the addition of Guam even farther west Roosevelt and Lodge had their string of coaling stations, key to the contemplated American commercial empire. It only remained to bring the obstreperous Filipinos into the fold.

In Manila, the revolutionaries resigned themselves to the coming war, a war that threatened to break out at any moment. Edwin Wildman, a witness to these events, described the scene in his biography of Aguinaldo: "A storm was brewing. Nightly knifing affairs kept the inhabitants at a fever pitch. Every white man carried a loaded revolver, and most of the natives secreted bolos or knives in their clothes . . . the least spark would start a conflagration."[18]

Though some of the officers in the revolutionary army had fought in the first phase of the revolution against the Spanish, the majority of them — "the relatives and favorites" of the generals — were young men who knew nothing of military science. Brigades were organized by provinces under command of "native sons" who treated their forces as private armies and were inclined to disregard orders they found objectionable.[19]

Aguinaldo had demonstrated little aptitude for military leadership, but he insisted on retaining command of the forces surrounding Manila. Mabini believed the revolution would be better served if General Antonio Luna were placed in command. Luna was an ilustrado, a core member of the Propaganda Movement who had returned from Madrid, where he had been imprisoned by the Spanish authorities for his provocative writings in *La Solidaridad*. He brought with him a suitcase full of military textbooks, having received some instruction in military tactics from a Belgian general, and he fashioned himself a military strategist.[20]

Antonio Luna was the most passionate and courageous of patriots, a man of fiery temperament, prone to such volcanic rages that his mental stability would come into question. His rage was compounded by the constant infighting among his brash young officers and their undisciplined commands. Time was of the essence, the shadow of the American army looming over them; he had somehow to make a coherent fighting force out of rural peasants and the violent and intemperate offspring of the provincial elite. None of this augured well for the revolutionary forces in the conflict to come.

Permissions to Hate

6

DAVID FAGEN HAD BEEN AT FORT DOUGLAS for only five weeks when the congressional bi-elections took place. In Wilmington, North Carolina, the Fusionists—a coalition of Populists and Republicans—had successfully controlled the state government for the previous four years. In the November election, the Democrats took over the state and most local governments, largely by suppressing the black vote through intimidation and violence. Blacks were threatened with death if they ran for office or even voted; some had shotguns held to their heads and were forced to sign oaths promising not to vote. All over the South, white paramilitary organizations called the Red Shirts, violent vigilante groups, had succeeded in denying blacks the right to vote. In *Williams v. Mississippi*, the Supreme Court had upheld Mississippi's plan for depriving blacks of the franchise, and the other states of the South were following its example.

In Wilmington, the editor of a black-owned newspaper, Alex Manly, responded to an incendiary letter written by a white woman in support of lynching, calling on white men to do a better job of protecting white women. Manly answered fire with fire, suggesting that rural white women used the charge of rape when they were discovered having clandestine affairs with black men. He also attacked the whites' double standard in the matter of sexual relations between the races. "Tell your men that it is no worse for a black man to be intimate with a white woman than for a white man to be intimate with a colored woman," and he reminded white men of their long history of taking sexual advantage of black women. "You set yourself down as a lot of carping hypocrites; in fact you cry aloud for the virtue of your women, when you seek to destroy the morality of ours."[1]

Manly's strong words enraged the white men of North Carolina, and in the months leading up to the election the tension between blacks and whites reached a fever pitch. According to Edward L. Ayers, "Every facet of life seemed touched by racial anger and anxiety, every kind of racial interaction had become tainted by diseased politics." When the black-majority city of Wilmington elected a Fusionist mayor and biracial city council, it was too much for the whites in the eastern part of the state. Two thousand white voters invaded Wilmington and burned the offices of the offending black newspaper, then proceeded to gun down blacks in the streets, killing an unknown number of people. More than two thousand blacks, among them the most prominent citizens, fled the city, abandoning their homes and businesses. Nearby federal troops did not intervene; President McKinley remained silent. Democrats took office in what is now acknowledged as a coup d'état, the only one in American history. African Americans throughout the country were enraged, especially at the indifference coming from Washington.[2]

In Salt Lake City, the fiery publisher of the *Broad Ax*, Julius F. Taylor, expressed his outrage at the forced resignations of the Wilmington mayor and chief of police. From the safety of the far side of the Rockies, Taylor chided the *Wilmington Record*'s editor, Alex Manly, for allowing himself to be run out of town, his offices burned: "For our part we would not leave. The man or men who would extend such an invitation to us in this city would find that repeating rifles can be purchased by colored as well as white. . . . Colored men, when the state and national governments do not protect us, we must defend ourselves, and not be afraid of the shotgun, the gibbet and the stake in doing so."[3]

For all of Julius Taylor's refreshingly bold talk, his provocative editorials would so offend the elders of the Church of Jesus Christ of Latter Day Saints in Salt Lake City that he would feel compelled to close up shop and take the *Broad Ax* to Chicago in June 1899. If Taylor was not exactly run out of town, there was the added incentive of reaching a larger readership in the big city and the possibility of furthering his support for William Jennings Bryan in the Great Boy Orator's second run for the presidency.[4]

There were scarcely one thousand African Americans in Utah, not counting the men of the Twenty-Fourth, who must have constituted a significant part of the *Broad Ax*'s readership. Julius F. Taylor despised Booker T. Washington's acquiescent approach to race relations, and the editor's talk of guns and "a long and bloody race war" in the South probably created some discomfort for an advocate of moderation like John Calloway. It is doubtful that Fagen was able to read Taylor's broadsides, but given that many of the regulars could not read, it is likely that articles of interest were read aloud. If Taylor's threatening words might have sounded a jarring note to John Calloway's ears, they may well have been music to young Fagen's. In the not distant future, he would more than match Julius Taylor's bold talk with bold action.

At first it seemed as if the Buffalo Soldiers had accomplished their purpose by performing so heroically in the Santiago campaign. While at Montauk Point, stories of the black regulars' heroism at San Juan and El Caney began to spread, and "for a few brief weeks they enjoyed the status of national heroes."[5]

But this acclaim was to be short-lived. While some African Americans were convinced that the performance of the Buffalo Soldiers in Cuba would improve the lot of African Americans and lead to a lessening in racial tensions, the great majority of blacks remained skeptical. That skepticism was soon borne out as "assiduous efforts were made to poison the public mind toward the black soldier, and history can but record that these efforts were too successful."[6]

As reports of lynchings, race riots, and slanderous attacks on the Buffalo Soldiers continued, many in the black press began to dismay, one voicing the opinion that the "Negro soldiers had died for nothing." "El Caney and Santiago may as well not have been," wrote another. The poet Paul Lawrence Dunbar captured the irony of the moment: "You may be heroes in war but you must be craven in peace."[7]

Perhaps the biggest blow to the black regulars' morale was the War Department's continued refusal to allow blacks to serve as officers. Deepening the insult, young graduates fresh out of West Point were placed over black noncoms, experienced veterans who had led the fighting at San Juan and endured the hell of Siboney.[8]

Harry Smith, the editor of the *Cleveland Gazette*, summed up the bitterness that had supplanted the black soldiers' initial euphoria: "What has been his reward? Has honor, promotion, assured citizenship, or protection crowned his career at El Caney or San Juan Heights? Ingratitude, discrimination, humiliation are the only trophies which, so far, he can thank his country's star for."[9]

No one sounded a more despairing note than Julius F. Taylor: "We fear that within a very short time the relations will become so estranged between the whites and the blacks of the south that nothing can prevent them from plunging into a long and bloody race war. And we still believe that the negro would have been ten million times better off if the slave ships which brought him to these shores had sank to the bottom of the sea."[10]

African Americans looked on with horror and with full knowledge of what was happening: North and South, estranged since the Civil War, were reconciling—but at the black man's expense. The McKinley administration "had used the war [in Cuba] to make its final peace with the white racists of the South." "It was getting toward the yuletide season," James Blount wrote, "President McKinley was engaged, quite seasonably, in putting the finishing touches to the great work of his life, which was welding the North and the South together forever by wise and kindly manipulation of the countless opportunities to do so presented by the latest war." Blacks would pay a terrible price for this reconciliation, as the North acquiesced to the "doctrines of the extreme racists," an arrangement that would obtain until the 1960s.[11]

As the year 1898 drew to a close, the violence against African Americans continued, in South Carolina, in Illinois, and elsewhere. President McKinley toured the South and said not a word about Wilmington, not a word about lynching; crowds of whites greeted him with great fanfare. Most blacks supported the party of Lincoln, believing that even if it did little for African Americans, at least it might hold the white South somewhat in check. But Julius F. Taylor had long since become terminally disgusted with the Republicans; from the end of the Civil War, they had done nothing but sell out the black man over and over. In an inspiration that was prescient but counterintuitive at the time, Taylor maintained that the only hope for African Americans lay in the Democratic Party. After moving to Chicago he continued to publish the *Broad Ax* for more than three decades and died in 1934.[12]

In *The Strange Career of Jim Crow*, C. Vann Woodward best describes this cascade of events that led, seemingly overnight, to a drastic worsening of the plight of blacks in the South and throughout the country.

> Economic, political, and social frustrations had pyramided to a climax of social tensions. No real relief was in sight from the long cyclical depression of the nineties. . . . There had to be a scapegoat. And all along the line signals were going up to indicate that the Negro was an approved object of aggression. These "permissions-to-hate" came from sources that had formerly denied such permission. They came from the federal courts in numerous opinions, from Northern liberals eager to conciliate the South, from Southern conservatives who had abandoned their race policy of moderation in their struggle against the Populists, from the Populists in their mood of disillusionment with their former Negro allies, and from a national temper suddenly expressed by imperialistic adventures and aggressions against colored peoples in distant lands.[13]

Christmas and the New Year came and went. Undoubtedly, David Fagen got his first experience of snow and bitter cold. In mid-January, by order of the War Department, more than five hundred men who had enlisted for the war in Cuba were discharged, each soldier receiving seventy-five dollars in travel pay: "The gain is a pecuniary one and every man who is qualified has the privilege of re-enlisting." Rumors were rife that the regiment would soon be on its way to the Philippines and an urgent call for new recruits went out.[14]

On January 28, 1899, Fagen was discharged, his conduct recorded as "good," and he set off on the long train ride to Tampa. Fagen's father, Samuel, had died in his absence. On the slow journey home, riding through the South in a cold and spare Jim Crow car, he would have pondered his future.[15]

Fagen hadn't even reached Tampa when he got his answer. In Manila, a clash of American and Filipino patrols had gone from taunts to gunfire. The American Eighth Corps and the Filipino Army of Liberation were at war.

Benevolent Assimilation

7

O N JANUARY 4, 1899, the Benevolent Assimilation Proclamation was "let loose on the Philippines." The wording of this document was so strident in proclaiming American authority over the islands that even the tactless General Elwell Otis tried toning it down for Filipino consumption. But the revolutionaries managed to obtain an original copy and, finally, Emilio Aguinaldo had in writing his long-sought-for answer to the question of American intentions. If he had done everything in his power to avoid war, endured insult after insult, granted concession after concession, the end result would nevertheless be war, but at far greater disadvantage to the revolutionaries than if he had accepted the fight early on. The proclamation in small part read:

> . . . the mission of the United States is one of
> ### BENEVOLENT ASSIMILATION
> substituting the mild sway of justice and right for arbitrary rule. In the fulfillment of this high mission . . . there must be sedulously maintained the strong arm of authority, to repress disturbances and to overcome all obstacles to the bestowal of the blessings of good and stable government upon the people of the Philippine Islands under the free flag of the United States.[1]

Apolinario Mabini responded with his usual eloquence to McKinley's high-sounding words: "Thus we take as legitimate norm, not absolute but relative justice, established with the tacit consent of the great powers, for their glory and aggrandizement, to the prejudice and ruin of the weak, in the pompous name of international law. It is this relative justice that usually sanctifies the most iniquitous spoils and the most marvelous usurpations, whose controlling sanction is the reason of force and not the force of reason."[2]

With war imminent, more than forty thousand citizens fled from Manila, clogging the roads for miles out of the city. Many were going to join the Army of Liberation. But Aguinaldo refused to unleash his troops. A great debate in the U.S. Senate was underway and there was still a slender thread of hope that America might avoid what James Blount would term "the one great blunder of our history, the taking of the Philippine Islands."[3]

On the night of February 4, 1899, the tension that had been building for months culminated in an altercation between Filipino and American patrols, scouting between the lines. In an impulsive exchange, Private Willie Grayson fired the first shots, killing a Filipino soldier who had challenged Grayson's command to halt, or so Grayson's story went. Grayson and Private Miller killed two more Filipinos in a flurry of gunfire, then beat a rapid retreat to their lines, warning that an attack was imminent. What actually occurred that night on a darkened bridge remains in dispute. Soon there was general firing all along the sixteen-mile perimeter surrounding Manila. An estimated two million rounds were expended during the night to little effect.[4]

Some American historians argue that the outbreak of fighting was a matter of spontaneous combustion. Others are just as certain that the Americans deliberately provoked the fighting, taking advantage of the absence of Aguinaldo's generals, who were away with their families or meeting with him in Malolos. The U.S. Senate vote on the Treaty of Paris was to take place in two days, and there was still a chance the Democrats might block McKinley's imperial gambit. In *Republic or Empire*, Daniel B. Schirmer makes the most convincing case for a deliberate provocation ordered from Washington. The *San Francisco Chronicle* reported on February 5, "the general opinion in Washington is that the news from Manila insures ratification of the treaty tomorrow afternoon." Dozens of other newspapers reached the same conclusion, yet Otis's claim that the Filipinos had initiated the hostilities went unchallenged.[5]

At first light that day, American naval vessels opened up with long-range artillery followed by land-based artillery. At last the raw American youths were let loose. Their old Springfields "kicked like a mule" but the western farm boys could shoot. The slow-moving .45 caliber slugs were devastating in effect compared with the Filipinos' high-velocity, small-bore Mausers. And, far more lethal, artillery fire left the Filipino trenches piled with dead.

No one ever questioned the bravery of the young Filipinos, but their command system broke down from the first. They had limited supplies of ammunition, much of it of inferior quality, and their marksmanship without any training was abysmal. For every man with a rifle, another waited to take his

weapon should he fall, others to carry away the wounded. Despite these de-
ficiencies, Brian Linn maintains that with a coordinated response under
proper leadership they could have taken advantage of the American volunteers' mistakes. In their exuberance, the young volunteers rushed far beyond
their designated objectives and "became scattered, disorganized, and danger-
ously exposed." "Had their enemies' skill matched their courage," Linn wrote,
"the results would have been catastrophic." As it was, the Filipinos managed to
inflict significant damage in ambushes behind the lines and in vicious house-to-
house fighting in the Tondo district.[6]

Aguinaldo's officers had not anticipated being thrown back so forcefully,
and large quantities of ammunition, weaponry, and supplies, stockpiled a short
distance behind the lines, were lost. The Americans bulled their way through
canebrakes, bamboo, and scrub thickets and charged headlong across rice
paddies and mudflats. They set fire to numerous villages surrounding Manila
and in many instances took no prisoners. "The orders were to let no Filipino
live," Arthur Johnson of the Colorado Volunteers wrote home. Another member of the Colorado Volunteers reported twelve villages burned that first day.
Whether Private Johnson's commanding officers actually issued such orders is
questionable, but in the heat of battle and after months of pent-up frustrations
it seems that many of the young volunteers were under the impression that
those were their orders, implied if not directly stated.[7]

On February 6, two days after the outbreak of the war, the Senate voted to
ratify the Treaty of Paris. William Jennings Bryan confounded many of his fellow Democrats by encouraging them to vote for ratification. Leon Wolff wrote
that "Senator Pettigrew accused him to his face of rank hypocrisy. Mr. Bryan
did not understand. He explained blandly that his intention was to saddle the
Republicans with a *fait accompli* which would ruin them at the polls in 1900."
The Treaty passed by one vote, 57 out of 84 senators voting for passage. Bryan
is credited with persuading "several democrats to vote for ratification," and
Walter Karp added that "a heavy dose of virtual bribery" brought some others
around. Bryan was not only instrumental in giving the McKinley administration
a green light to carry on its imperial adventure; he also succeeded in shooting
himself in the foot at the same time; that is, McKinley would be anything but
ruined at the polls. "Everything he [Bryan] did was wrong," it was said in a
joke that went the rounds. "He would rather be wrong than be president."[8]

The Americans consolidated their position in a wider ring around Manila,
and soon General Lloyd Wheaton was pushing up the Pasig River toward the
Laguna de Bay, a large lake only miles inland from Manila and the source of the
river. The Filipinos ambushed two companies, inflicting numerous casualties.
In response, Wheaton ordered the first reprisals against civilians, the burning

of houses and crops along a five-mile stretch of road. The journalist John F. Bass described riding through "mile after mile of this desolation."[9]

On the night of February 22, 1899, after two weeks of fighting in the region around Manila, the Sandatahan, Aguinaldo's underground militia, made a concerted attempt to burn the city while regular forces attacked the perimeter. Militiamen and infiltrators set fires, cut fire hoses, and took potshots at the military firemen. Amid the smoke and chaos, the provost guard routed them, executing some on the spot while carabaos, the native water buffalo, ran amok; various entities, particularly unaffiliated Chinese residents but also Filipinos and Americans, took the opportunity to loot and burn.[10]

The uprising was a tumultuous failure, in part due not only to a lack of adequate preparation but also shortages of ammunition and, in the opinion of Filipino historians, by the failure of Aguinaldo's Kavit (from Cavite province) battalion to come to the aid of the depleted Pampanga militia at Caloocan. Antonio Luna had given the order, and the Caviteños, in a stunning display of insubordination, informed General Luna that they took orders only from Aguinaldo. Several weeks later, Luna ordered a company of the Kavit battalion disarmed. Aguinaldo quickly rescinded the order, undercutting his own general, and the Caviteños became the mortal enemies of Antonio Luna.[11]

With the American firefighting brigades stretched to their full capacity, the Sandatahan had come close to burning the city. It was a near miss for the Americans and a golden opportunity lost by the revolutionaries. The period from the opening of hostilities on February 4, 1899, to the failed uprising on February 22 marked the best chance the Army of Liberation had to evict the invaders in a decisive defeat. If the Americans were to be forced out, it would now be through only a protracted and costly struggle.[12]

Snowbound

8

THE MAN RETURNING ON THE LONG TRAIN RIDE across the South was not the same young man who had left Tampa seven months earlier on June 29, 1898. As with anyone who has left home for the first time, the place one returns to is never quite the same. For a few brief hours, though, one sees the old familiar places with new eyes. The now twenty-year-old David Fagen was seeing Tampa and the Scrub from the perspective of the larger black experience. In his short time in the army, he was likely to have become politicized, caught up in the controversies over the regulars' performance at San Juan and El Caney, and angered by the outrages at Wilmington and elsewhere. If Calloway had not influenced him on racial issues while at Fort Douglas, there were others in the Twenty-Fourth more militant in their views. The "Race Question" was in the air, and passions were stirred as they had not been in decades.

Perhaps he was able to read the newspapers—or heard the stories read aloud—as the train rolled down from Nashville and through Atlanta. The Philippines? What kind of strange place was this? And *where* was it? And why were American troops there and now engaged in battle with these unheard-of people? This distant, unimaginable war had been underway for two days when the train pulled into the station in Tampa. Had he already made up his mind to reenlist? He had barely missed the action at San Juan; perhaps now he saw his chance to grab a piece of the glory that had so narrowly eluded him. The black soldiers who had braved the hell of Siboney had been praised by all, but it was not the kind of glory a soldier dreamed of.

Perhaps he wanted to meet again with Maggie Washington and see whether there might be a future for them. According to Frank Schubert, there is no record of a divorce; Maggie Washington still lived at her old address and under her maiden name. Without any clues as to the nature of their marriage, there are several possibilities: either Fagen had ended it and had no interest in remaining attached, or Maggie Washington had ended it. In the latter case, he would either have accepted that it was over and moved on, or he may still have hoped for a change of heart from her. No doubt his brief few days back home passed in a kind of whirlwind, with friends and siblings eager to hear of his adventures, with a father's grave to visit. And perhaps a final meeting with Maggie Washington. Factually, we only know that on February 9, some three days after returning to Tampa, he presented himself at Fort McPherson, Georgia, just outside of Atlanta. And there he reenlisted in the U.S. Army.[1]

This time, rather than simply making his mark, David Fagen signed his name. The hand is shaky, the ten letters of his name running in a quavering odd angle to the line. But it was a clear sign that he had received some education in his four months at Fort Douglas. His height was again listed at 5 feet 10, no weight given. His character was recorded as "good" (comparable to a grade "C," that is, adequate but without distinction). Although he passed the physical, subsequent information makes clear that Fagen was feeling the recurring effects of the yellow fever or of Cuban fever, a variety of malaria. Rather than return to Company H, he was enlisted in Company I, the outfit he had served with at Siboney. Presumably, he requested the assignment with Company I and perhaps the words received from the outfit both endorsed his request and vouched for his good character.[2]

The following day, on a frigid morning, David Fagen began the five-day journey back west, this time to Fort D. A. Russell outside of Cheyenne, Wyoming. Three days later, Florida experienced the coldest day in its history, minus two degrees at Tallahassee. February on the high plains of Wyoming would be even colder.[3]

As Fagen's train moved west across Nebraska, the third blizzard of the winter blew in to greet him. Eventually the train inched into Cheyenne, a windswept city of fourteen thousand. Fort D. A. Russell was three miles to the west, past a row of saloons and bawdy houses on the edge of town and at the end of a small rail line.

The post sprawled around a diamond-shaped parade ground with officers' quarters on two sides, the enlisted men's two-story brick barracks on the other two sides. Upon arriving, an appraisal of the young man's new home cannot have been a welcoming sight, with the row of imposing barracks and thin line of bare trees fronting the parade ground and a frozen landscape white for miles in every direction.

Company I's commanding officer was Captain James E. Brett. A sharpshooter, Brett commanded Company F during the Santiago Campaign and was wounded on July 4; for that action he was decorated for gallantry. He was given an extended period of sick leave and never fully recovered, delegating most of his responsibilities to his lieutenants. It appears that Brett was either a spend-thrift or had a gambling problem. He owed $176 to the post exchange at Fort D. A. Russell; he owed Bloomingdale's; he owed $60 to Pvt. Erstle in Company C; he owed more to several other men; and he owed I Company's First Sergeant George D. Powell. All of Brett's creditors were after him and one gets the sense of a beleaguered and unwell man, reliable in battle but undependable in his private dealings.[4]

On arrival, Fagen may have had a brief exchange with Captain Brett but most likely he was taken in hand by the topkick, First Sergeant George D. Powell. Powell and Fagen had served together at Siboney and were probably well acquainted. Powell, at forty-two, was a good deal older than his charges, a veteran of the Indian wars, and consistently one of the five best shots in the regiment of more than a thousand men. All the other sergeants of Company I—Sergeants Patrick Mason, Alexander Hyde, Rath Myers, and Walter Barnes—had also served at Siboney and would have known Fagen well.[5]

I Company's new first lieutenant, James Alfred Moss, had led two companies of the Twenty-Fifth Infantry in the charge at El Caney. In September 1898, Moss was promoted and transferred to the Twenty-Fourth Infantry. Born in Lafayette, Louisiana, in 1872, Moss was seventeen when he left home to attend the military academy at West Point. He graduated in 1893, one of the youngest cadets to complete his studies at that time, and also dead last in his class—"the goat." Traditionally, the goat got last choice of assignment and Moss soon found himself on a train to Fort Missoula, Montana, the greenest of young shavetails in the Twenty-Fifth Infantry.[6]

Some newly minted officers bitterly resented having to serve with black soldiers, and some even left the service rather than accept the assignment. But James Alfred Moss seems to have embraced the role without reservation. Though only 5 feet 6 inches tall, Moss was said to cut a dashing figure and thrived in the army despite his unpromising beginning. While at Fort Missoula, he received permission to organize a "Bicycle Corps," an idea that General Nelson Miles had been promoting for several years. In 1897 Moss, joined by a surgeon and a nineteen-year-old journalist, set off with twenty enlisted men—laden with blanket rolls, shelter-halves, and carbines—on a nineteen-hundred-mile bicycle ride to St. Louis. The experiment, an almost comically grueling ordeal, proved that bicycles were not the cheaper replacement for horses on the battlefield as some had hoped. (The army did find good use for bicycles in both world wars for transportation on some bases in order to save fuel.) Peddling on through mud and rain, through cactus fields and scorching heat, Moss and his men averaged fifty-six miles a day and arrived amid great fanfare in St. Louis on July 24, 1897. Moss's famous experiment with the bicycles is quite telling about the young man's character; despite his less than stellar academic performance, he remained a resourceful and inventive officer throughout a long and distinguished career, a singular enthusiast for the military life.[7]

Among the enlistees were Bible-quoting teetotalers and men of a more intellectual bent who belonged to the Frederick Douglass Memorial Literary Society; checkers and whist were more their games. But most of the enlistees were illiterate, some classed as "ruffians." On payday there were "whiskey ranches" outside the post where the men could gamble, drink, and consort with prostitutes. According to an article in the *Salt Lake City Herald*, on his first payday at Fort D. A. Russell, Fagen won two hundred dollars from his fellow soldiers.[8]

The Halfway House was a popular whiskey ranch on the small trainline to Cheyenne. It may have been there that Fagen raked in his winnings. One night, when he had been at Fort D. A. Russell for less than a month, some men from I Company went from carousing to brawling in what the *San Francisco Chronicle* called "a free for all fight with knives and razors." The main combatants, Sergeant Walter Barnes and Corporal George Greenhow, had charged up San Juan Hill together and worked side-by-side in the death camp. Now, according to the article, Corporal Greenhow lay dead on the barroom floor and Sergeant Barnes, badly wounded, had fled into the night, a posse on his heels. A number of newspapers around the country reported this incident.

Whether Fagen had been present the night of the fight is unknown, but he was known to have frequented such dives and also worked alongside both men at Siboney.[9]

On March 3, a train bound for Cheyenne ran into yet another blizzard and became snowbound at Iron Mountain, fifty miles short of its destination. The passengers cut firewood to keep the engine fires burning, and a foraging party shot a steer that provided minimal subsistence for two weeks. Several rescue parties tried to reach the train but could not get past the mountainous snowdrifts. One hundred volunteers from the Twenty-Fourth Infantry came to the rescue; the men shoveled the ten- and twenty-foot snowdrifts off the tracks for miles and the stranded passengers were rescued.[10]

During this operation Fagen received his first company punishment at Fort D. A. Russell, a one-dollar fine. Perhaps the fine had something to do with the fight at the Halfway House, or maybe the young man from subtropical Tampa was too loud in voicing his distaste for shoveling snow. At some time or another almost every enlisted man drew the ire of his superiors and received a fine and company punishment; Fagen, the "rowdy soldier," was not alone in that. A scholarly article from 1975 claimed that he was promoted to corporal while at Fort D. A. Russell, but I found no evidence of any promotion in the company rolls or elsewhere. If he were promoted to *acting* corporal, which in itself seems unlikely, that temporary promotion may have gone unrecorded in the rolls and been mentioned elsewhere . . . but I doubt it. As best as I can tell, whatever trouble occurred on March 25 marked the beginning of a downhill slide in his relations with the white officers of his company—particularly with Lieutenant James A. Moss—and that enmity would continue over the next eight months.[11]

"Fighting Fred" Funston

9

IN THE FIRST WEEKS OF THE WAR in the Philippines, no one among the Americans distinguished himself so conspicuously as Colonel Frederick Funston, commander of the Twentieth Kansas Volunteers. Funston would become the most controversial and best-known figure of the war. He would also become the mortal enemy—and foil—of David Fagen. The capture and execution of the elusive Fagen would become an obsession for Frederick Funston, but the beginning of their long duel of wits was still a year off when, on February 5, 1899, Funston first led his Kansas troop charging through thickets and across rice fields under cover of naval artillery. Pinned down by fire from the Filipino trenches on the northern perimeter of Manila, Funston ordered his men to fix bayonets and charge. Scores of General Antonio Luna's fighters, refusing to retreat even when their ammunition was expended, died in the trenches in the face of this mad rush. The young volunteers raced on far beyond their objective, and this would become the pattern of Funston's Kansans, reckless and unstoppable.[1]

A week later Funston's volunteers overwhelmed the railhead town of Caloocan and, in an early controversy of the war, were accused of summarily executing captives and injuring civilians while burning the thatched houses of the town to flush out snipers. In a letter home, a Private Brenner wrote, "Company I had four prisoners. . . . They asked Captain Bishop what to do. He said: 'You know orders,' and four natives fell dead."[2]

Dean Worcester, a member of the Philippine Commission sent to the islands to assess the situation, cabled a denial of Brenner's account to the *Chicago Times-Herald* and other newspapers, including the *San Francisco Call*, which dutifully headlined its article: PRISONERS NOT MURDERED BY AMERICAN TROOPS. After dismissing Brenner's charge, Worcester added: "The natives rejoice at the arrival of the American troops, who neither burn their homes nor loot their property, and who feed the hungry. The inhabitants are resuming their ordinary occupations, and are ready to co-operate with us."[3]

If Funston ordered prisoners shot, houses burned, and personally took part in the looting of churches, he was not alone in such inglorious behavior. Brian Linn does not mince words, citing "clear evidence of troop misconduct, brutality, criminal activity, and atrocities."[4]

What to make of Frederick Funston, one of the more improbable characters ever to parade across the American stage? Only thirty-four and with no formal military training, Funston had come by a most circuitous route to the command of an entire regiment. Born in 1865 and raised on a farm near Iola, Kansas, he had grown up reading about knights in armor, explorers and adventurers, cowboys and privateers, and especially military heroes. As with Roosevelt, adulthood had done nothing to dim the luster of youthful dreams of martial glory. Physically, Funston was a Teddy Roosevelt in miniature—five foot four and scarcely more than one hundred pounds. In just about every other respect—as adventurer in the American West, as battlefield daredevil, as ardent spokesman for Anglo-Saxon superiority, and as imprudent, garrulous talker—Frederick Funston was TR writ large (as if the future president's most salient features could bear any further enhancement).[5]

Funston had roamed the Badlands and Montana and spent nine months exploring Death Valley as part of a governmental botanical survey, barely surviving a long trek across the broiling desert floor. He had twice ventured into the Alaskan wilds on government-sponsored expeditions, rafted through a whitewater gorge on the Yukon, passed an arduous winter sledding about the Alaskan interior, then paddled a skiff fourteen hundred miles down the Yukon to its source on the Bering Sea. As a volunteer with the Cuban revolutionaries, he had been hit by shrapnel, shot in the hand, arms, thigh, and lungs; he had had horses shot out from under him—if he could be believed—more than a dozen times.[6]

From the first days of the war, Frederick Funston became a favorite of the war correspondents, counted on for his off-the-cuff references to "treacherous savages" and "bullet-headed Asians." They should know better, he growled, than to stand in the way of "Anglo-Saxon progress and decency." Funston's biographer, David Haward Bain, noted, "If some of his speeches resembled those of Theodore Roosevelt, the telling difference was that Roosevelt knew when to shut up."[7]

In 1982 Bain retraced Funston's secret mission to capture Emilio Aguinaldo and tried to achieve a balanced appraisal of his controversial subject. When pressed by a Filipino for his opinion of Funston, Bain settled on "a cad and a

Frederick Funston (Marrion Wilcox, *Harper's History of the War in the Philippines* [1900])

hero." "Cad," in the opinion of many—then and now—is too mild a word. And a qualifying asterisk should accompany the word "hero." Funston was brave, recklessly so, but he was also a self-promoter of the first order, accused of embellishing and even fabricating "feats of glory." Frederick Funston longed to be a hero on a grand scale, as if through a single epic triumph he might once and for all lay some private demons to rest. It was as if his boyhood fantasies had carried over full-blown to his command of a regiment on a real-life battlefield. While with the Cuban revolutionaries, he proposed to General Garcia that he and his artillerymen sneak up to the base of the enemy's fortress, detonate explosives, and call on the fort's defenders to surrender. As David Bain tells it, "Garcia thought the idea was insane." Funston then suggested he should "assault the fortress alone" and set off a "homemade bomb" that would signal the start of an artillery barrage. Garcia passed on that one as well. When the fighting between Americans and Filipinos broke out on the night of February 4, 1899, Funston raced to General Arthur MacArthur's headquarters. He had a plan, a way to end the war in one fell swoop! He thought he could "slip though the lines with a single platoon and capture Aguinaldo." MacArthur declined the offer. But two years later, with MacArthur's blessing, Funston concocted yet another wild scheme to capture the president in his hideout on the northeastern coast of Luzon, and this time he succeeded. If nothing else, Frederick Funston's unrelenting quest for glory is a testament to the power of visualization.[8]

In the first months after the Battle of Manila, Funston and his Kansas roughnecks spearheaded MacArthur's drive to overrun Aguinaldo's capital at Malolos. "Fighting Fred" led the way, at the front of bayonet charges through palm groves, scampering over the skeletal remains of half-destroyed bridges, swimming rivers under fire, recklessly dislodging the enemy from their trenches. The newspapers were filled with breathless accounts of Funston's exploits. But the war correspondents had picked up on something else: Frederick Funston was altogether too avid for the laurel wreath.[9]

Almost as soon as the newspapers began to sing the praises of Funston, others began to lampoon what were seen as embellished, theatricalized feats of derring-do. (It was later discovered that the hero who was decorated for swimming the Bagbag in the face of enemy fire had, in fact, never learned to swim; other vaunted achievements became similarly suspect.) As ardently as Funston longed to claim the mantle of hero, he was playing against type. First, his size, juxtaposed with his penchant for self-promotion and what Stuart Miller called his "monumental ego," lent itself to parody. To Bain, he was "a masterpiece of overcompensation." Second, the name did not have a heroic ring to it. The name Funston seemed to belong more in a Gilbert and Sullivan light opera than on the battlefield. "Fighting Fred" Funston did not work nearly as well as his father's catchy moniker—"Foghorn Funston, the Farmer's Friend." Edward Hoag Funston, a U.S. congressman for ten years, was apparently as overbearing as he was big—six foot two and more than two hundred pounds. If Funston suffered from the proverbial "small-man's-complex," having an immense and successful father probably contributed in no small part to a need to prove himself. And prove himself he did, at least to his superiors' satisfaction; for his actions during MacArthur's advance beyond Malolos, Frederick Funston was awarded the Medal of Honor and promoted to general in the volunteers.[10]

Slander

10

O<small>N MARCH 26, YET ANOTHER BLIZZARD</small> hit Wyoming, killing more cattle and stopping trains throughout the region. Finally, on April 4, on what must have been a day of jubilation, two companies of the Twenty-Fourth Infantry, including David Fagen's I Company, boarded a train in Cheyenne and set off for sunny California. Captain Brett, who still had not squared accounts with the post exchange or his other creditors, was probably as happy as anyone to be departing for San Francisco and points west. The troops encamped at the Presidio overlooking the Golden Gate and the green Marin Headlands, and there, amid the dunes and morning fog, they continued training for duty in the Philippines.[1]

Teddy Roosevelt, now the governor of New York, published his account of the Santiago campaign in *Scribner's Magazine*. A short time later the same article came out in book form as *The Rough Riders*. Not long after the battle, he had been quoted saying, "I wish no better men beside me in battle than these colored troops showed themselves to be. Later on, when I come to write of the campaign, I shall have much to say about them."[2]

As it turns out, Roosevelt had much to say about the black regulars, but the praise was backhanded at best. "No troops could have behaved better than the colored soldiers had behaved so far," he began on a promising note. But then he continued, "But they are, of course, peculiarly dependent upon their white officers. Occasionally they produce non-commissioned officers who can take the initiative and accept responsibility precisely like the best class of whites; but this cannot be expected normally, nor is it fair to expect it."[3] *cf Patton*

Roosevelt's description of the blacks' "faithfulness" and "devotion" to their white officers, words that, in the opinion of an incensed Theophilus Steward, "might well fit an affectionate dog," came as a slap in the face. But then he penned the ultimate slander: "None of the white regulars or Rough Riders showed the slightest sign of weakening; but under the strain the colored infantry-men (who had none of their officers) began to get a little uneasy and to drift to the rear. . . . This I could not allow . . . so I drew my revolver . . . and called out to them . . . that I should shoot the first man who, on any pretense whatever, went to the rear . . . and this was the end of the trouble."[4]

The trouble was in Roosevelt's imagination; within minutes of this incident Sergeant Presley Holliday explained to him that these men had been sent to the rear for entrenching tools and rations, as had several of the Rough Riders. "Everyone who saw the incident," Sergeant Holliday wrote to the *New York Age*, "knew the colonel was mistaken . . . the colonel came to the line of the Tenth the next day and told the men of his threat to shoot some of their members and, as he expressed it, he had seen his mistake. . . . I thought he was sufficiently conscious of his error not to make a so ungrateful statement about us at a time when the nation is about to forget our past service. . . . His statement was un-called for and uncharitable."[5]

To Harry Smith of the *Cleveland Gazette*, the *Scribner's* article "confirmed blacks' suspicions that Roosevelt was intent upon magnifying his own deeds and the performance of the Rough Riders at the expense of the Negro regulars who 'actually carried the day in Cuba.'"[6]

After enduring a barrage of criticism, Roosevelt changed his story in a Chicago newspaper interview on October 1900: "I had an order to hold a cer-tain position. . . . Two or three of the colored soldiers started to the rear in search of water as ordered by their captain. I rebuked the captain for lessening our force, and commanded the men to remain. . . . This is the whole story in a nutshell."[7]

That was too little, too late for prominent members of the black commu-nity. At a gathering of "the leading colored men of New England" in Boston, "the Rev. W. H. Scott of Woburn bitterly denounced Theodore Roosevelt for writing that the negroes were cowards at San Juan Hill. When he asked, 'Does he tell the truth?' the response came back. 'No; he is a liar!' causing a great commotion."[8]

Roosevelt's piece in *Scribner's* capped months of disparaging attacks on the black regulars. Through the omissions and the calumnies of the white press, their heroic service in Cuba had been rendered an exercise in futility. The tide was running against them. If that was not depressingly obvious to African Americans everywhere, it became so on April 22, 1899, when perhaps the most infamous lynching in American history occurred in Georgia. Sam Hose was accused of murdering his employer with an ax, dashing the couple's infant child onto the floor, and raping the man's wife. Most accepted accounts dispute that story, maintaining that Hose killed his employer in self-defense and fled.[9]

During the eleven days that Sam Hose avoided capture, the newspapers worked the public into a frenzy of rage, depicting Sam Hose as an evermore diabolical fiend; the now "syphilitic" Hose had raped Alfred Cranford's wife repeatedly before her husband's dying eyes. Hose, five foot eight and 140 pounds, became a "burly black brute"—a "monster in human form." When Hose was finally caught, the hysterical mob action that followed was all but fore-ordained. Special trains brought more than one thousand people from Atlanta to join the mob assembled in Newnan, Georgia. The former governor William Yates Atkinson, who happened to be in Newnan, pleaded with the "delirious, tumultuous mass" to let justice take its course. "Do not stain the honor of the state with a crime such as you are about to perform!" The crowd jeered and shouted him down; yet even with a gun pointed at him, Atkinson continued to try to reason with "the avenging mob." Judge Alvin Freeman also pleaded with the mob to release Hose to the authorities, but he, too, was pushed aside.[10]

Sam Hose was chained to a pine tree, kerosene poured on the wood fagots at his feet. A man stepped forth and with a razor-sharp knife sliced off an ear. "During all the time of torture he never uttered one cry. They cut off both ears, skinned his face, cut off his fingers, gashed his legs, cut open his stomach and pulled out his entrails, then when his contortions broke the iron chain, they pushed his burning body back into the fire."[11]

The *Newnan Herald and Advertiser* confirmed the *Richmond Planet*'s account and added, "Other mutilations followed that cannot be described here."[12] A reporter for the *New York Times* was in Atlanta when the revelers arrived home on the train: "The excursionists returning tonight were loaded down with ghastly reminders of the affair in the shape of bones, pieces of flesh, and parts of the wood which was placed at the negro's feet. One of the trains as it passed through Fort McPherson, four miles out of Atlanta, was stoned, presumably by the negroes. A number of windows were broken and two passengers painfully injured."[13]

The *Richmond Planet* laid the primary blame for this madness on the editorials of the *Atlanta Constitution*, claiming that the business manager, W. A. Hemphill, and Clark Howell, the editor, had "contributed more to the burning than any other men and all other forces in Georgia. Through the columns of their newspaper, they exaggerated every detail of the killing [of Cranford], invented and published inflammatory descriptions of a crime that was never committed, and by glaring headlines continually suggested the burning of the man when caught."[14]

Another witness of the lynching was Professor Andrew Sledd of Emory University. Sledd just happened to be on a train that had stopped in Newnan that fateful day. Three years later, he published an essay in the *Atlantic Monthly* in which he set himself the formidable task of sorting out the era's most nettle-some problem—the "race question." "The Negro belongs to an inferior race," Sledd began. "There can hardly be any need to defend this proposition in these days of the boasted universal supremacy of the Anglo-Saxon." But if northerners were mistaken in advocating social equality for blacks, Sledd maintained, white southerners were in even more serious error when they insisted that blacks would remain forever inferior to whites, their status immutable. Sledd sought a compromise between what he saw as two extremes; though he accepted the premise that blacks were indisputably inferior, he believed their status to be subject to amelioration through education and self-improvement, and that they were deserving of the same constitutional rights as white citizens. In the strongest terms, Professor Sledd condemned the brutality of the southern lynch mob: "Wholly ignorant, absolutely without culture . . . they make up, when aroused, as wild and brutal a mob as ever disgraced the earth. For them, lynching is not 'justice,' however rude; it is a wild and diabolic carnival of blood."[15]

Sledd's article so incensed white southerners that he was forced to flee for his life; he soon moved to New Haven to pursue his PhD in Latin at Yale.

Andrew Sledd's condemnation of lynching and his affirmation of the supe-riority of the "Anglo-Saxon race" was an example of the "paternalistic racism" espoused by many northerners, including Roosevelt, who would later condemn lynching while citing black criminality as the primary cause. Newspaper edito-rials throughout the North and West railed against the mob action in Georgia while southern newspapers laid the blame on the failure of the better class of southern blacks to restrain and condemn the criminal element among them. The *Newnan Herald and Advertiser* described the lynching in detail, refusing to gloss over its most ghastly particulars, and concluded: "It is bad enough, we will not deny;—yet we have no apologies to make to our northern critics. We owe nothing to that section. Our civilization is distinctly Southern, and we thank God for it."[16]

———•—•———

David Fagen had grown up in the brutally oppressive environment of Tampa, with a daily ration of fear and humiliation a constant, an outward show of sub-servience enforced by the threat of the noose and the chain gang. In Cuba, he had seen the Buffalo Soldiers' courageous service depicted as cowardice by Roosevelt; when the white mob overturned the government in Wilmington, the president had said nothing. And now came the lynching of Sam Hose, a barbaric crime perpetrated in broad daylight and for which no one would be punished. What influence the lynching of Sam Hose may have had on Fagen is impossible to know, but it seems unlikely that he would have been left un-affected by it.

Stalemate

11

A VAST WEB OF RICE PADDIES spread across the flatlands north of Manila. Bamboo thickets, high grasses, and brush grew along the earthen dikes; the occasional cart track skirted the paddies and nipa-hut villages dotted the plain. A half-dozen rivers and numerous tree-lined streams added to the Americans' difficulty in advancing on the enemy. With the Filipinos entrenched on the far side of a field or across a river, the volunteers would deploy and charge. After a brief exchange, Aguinaldo's barefoot fighters would clear out, leaving the exhausted Americans to regroup, rest, and press on, only to be sniped at from the thickets along the dikes and find the enemy entrenched beyond yet another field or river. Burdened by haversack, rifle, and cartridge belt, slogging forward across the rice fields, and wilting under the merciless tropical sun, the ranks of the volunteers began to be ravaged by fever, heat exhaustion, and lack of water. John Morgan Gates wrote that in one battalion "half the men had no shoes."[1]

Harold W. Wilson, a private in the Forty-Fifth U.S. Volunteers, wrote home: "In the past week we have had ten fights, that is a pretty fair record. In every fight, the niggers fought like the fiends of hell, showing all kinds of bravery but poor marksmanship."[2]

As the journalists understood but were prevented from reporting by General Otis's military censors, the military governor did not have enough men to sustain his supply lines and hold the positions his men had taken. Consequently, the Americans captured ground only to abandon it, retake it a few days later, and then cede it again in a seemingly endless and debilitating cycle. After several days of chasing the elusive enemy, some companies were depleted by as much as 60 percent. Added to that, Leon Wolff wrote that "25 per cent of all cases on sick report" were the result of venereal diseases the volunteers had contracted while carousing in Manila; according to Wolff, "hundreds of European, Japanese, and American prostitutes had converged upon the city."[3]

While on the losing end of virtually every engagement, the Army of Libera-tion continued to exact a price before ceding the field to the Americans. At the end of March, after a week of hard fighting, MacArthur's forces drove the Filipinos from their capital at Malolos. MacArthur proposed pushing on five miles north, but Otis ordered a halt in the advance. Brian Linn suggests that "MacArthur was speaking for the record," that he was well aware that "his di-vision was incapable of further offensive action: the one-week campaign had cost it 56 killed and 478 wounded, and roughly one man in six was incapacitated by heat and disease."[4]

By the end of April, Otis claimed control of an area only forty miles north of Manila, half of that to the east and only a few miles to the south. The elements and the Filipinos' shifting tactics had done for Aguinaldo's fighters what they could not do with their Mausers and Remingtons. The military historian A. D. Marple put it succinctly: "Had the Filipino revolutionary units been well-armed and trained marksmen . . . American losses in the exposed rice plains would have been absolutely incredible." One might even argue that the ulti-mate failure of the revolution hinged on the inability of Aguinaldo's fighters to make effective use of their rifles. "If the Insurgents had known how to shoot," General MacArthur later observed, "the losses to the American Army would have terrified the nation."[5]

By May the fighting had bogged down to a stalemate, and the demoralized young volunteers struggled to make sense of what seemed a pointless round of death and suffering in a land so far away from home. "They had a vague notion that someone had blundered," Blount, a lieutenant in the volunteers, wrote. "But it was not theirs to ask the reason why." He noted the dissatisfaction of "a lot of fellows . . . who had volunteered for the war with Spain, with intent to kill Spaniards in order to free Cubans, and not with intent to kill Filipinos for also wanting to be free." Arthur H. Vickers, sergeant in the First Nebraska, con-fided in a letter: "I am not afraid, and I am always ready to do my duty, but I would like some one to tell me what we are fighting for." Private Tom Crandall of the Nebraska Regiment spoke for many of the volunteers: "The boys are sick of fighting these heathens, and all say we volunteered to fight Spain, not heathens. Their patriotism is wearing off. We all want to come home very bad. . . . The people of the United States ought to raise a howl and have us sent home."[6]

With the ratification of the Treaty of Paris made effective on April 11, 1899, the volunteers' tour of duty could be extended no more than six months and, in the opinion of the homesick and fed-up young men, an extension of even six days was too much.

The enlisted men were not alone in seeing the war as senseless and misguided. Captain Jacob Kreps, of the Twenty-Second Infantry, kept a diary during the early part of the campaign. When his company engaged in a day-long fight with the guerrillas, they found themselves matched against Filipinos who could shoot, suffering numerous casualties and several deaths in a very hot action. That night, Captain Kreps sat over the body of Private Johnson and recorded in his diary: "However, what good is honor now? His body lies on the island of Luzon—sacrificed to a policy not to be criticized by the soldier, but which has as its objective the subjugation of a people fighting for their liberty."[7]

An editorial in the *San Francisco Call* conveyed the sense of a war threatening to turn into a much uglier and more protracted fight than anyone had envisioned: "Our troops have pushed the unavailing butchery of war with uncomplaining endurance and dash. Yet the barefooted enemy remembering his hut burned and his paddy field destroyed, lurks in the jungle and fights."[8]

If conditions were bad for Otis's volunteers, they were worse for Aguinaldo's Army of Liberation. Never a cohesive fighting force to begin with, the resistance had become a shambles early on. With the eruption of hostilities on the night of February 4, Aguinaldo had belatedly appointed Antonio Luna as commanding general. Luna set about trying to instill discipline among his fractious command. He flew into rages, slapped officers, threatened to kill others, and meted out even more severe punishments to soldiers charged with the smallest of offenses. Luna was contemptuous of Aguinaldo's fumbling leadership, and rumors abounded that he might attempt to usurp Aguinaldo's role as revolutionary president.[9]

Mabini was dismayed by Luna's tirades and realized that his violent temperament negated his usefulness as a military tactician. But Antonio Luna and Mabini shared one important thing in common, and that was their unyielding determination to fight for complete independence. They would settle for nothing less.[10]

By this time, the conservatives in Congress, led by Felipe Buencamino and Pedro Paterno, had lost all appetite for fighting. From the beginning they had been in favor of autonomy under American sovereignty. The demoralizing losses on the battlefield over the first three months of the conflict only reinforced their desire to settle with their new colonial masters and protect their interests. With their conservative majority in Congress and a constitution that gave them control over the president's cabinet appointees, they pushed for a change of government and a negotiated settlement with the Americans. On May 7, Aguinaldo acceded to their demands; the prime minister and his cabinet resigned.[11]

Mabini had become disenchanted with Aguinaldo; later referring to him as "a waxen idol" and of the Buencamino-Paterno clique, he said, "Such men are not intended for great things, they are barely useful to themselves." At last the men of wealth had succeeded in triumphing over their nemesis, and Apolinario Mabini, now a private citizen, moved north to the town of Rosales in Pangasinan.[12]

While General Otis elected to maintain little more than holding actions to the south and east of Manila, General Arthur MacArthur (father of Douglas) led the primary operation to the north in an attempt to encircle Aguinaldo's Army of Liberation and thus effectively end the war. But as Aguinaldo's men retreated and reformed, leaving spear-pits and other traps in their wake and waiting in ambush, MacArthur's supply lines fell apart. Now, with some companies reduced to as few as twenty men fit for active duty, the northern offensive came to a grinding halt. In single company and battalion garrisons, the American volunteers settled into defensive positions; the Filipinos attacked regularly and, in some cases, lay siege to the outposts. They cut the connecting telegraph lines, infiltrated between posts, sniping at supply wagons and outpost guards all the way to Manila.[13]

In June, the monsoon season arrived, and the swamplike conditions precluded any major attempt by the Americans to bring the conflict to a decisive end. The offensive had stalled, MacArthur reported, due to "the sun, field rations, physical exertion, and abnormal excitement from almost constant exposure to fire action." Shiploads of regulars and new and better-trained volunteer regiments had begun to arrive, each ship soon homeward bound with a load of mustered-out volunteers. Any grand assault would have to wait for the thousands of fresh troops to be cycled in and for the summer rains to abate.[14]

Sequoia

12

IN 1890 THE FEDERAL GOVERNMENT established Sequoia National Park in California, and from May to October every year the army was set the task of preventing illegal logging, sheep and cattle grazing, hunting, and other depredations. The war in Cuba the previous year had disrupted this usual pattern; then, before troops arrived in September 1898, "more than 200,000 sheep [had] ravaged the Park" and a fire had burned through the giant forest. On May 2, 1899, Lieutenant James Alfred Moss led twenty-five men, sixteen from Company I, to Sequoia National Park. David Fagen was among this group. Another detachment from Company H traveled to Yosemite. The *Salt Lake (UT) Tribune* reported that "the details are regarded as having been made for the benefit of the health of the colored men, many of whom are nearly broken down from the effects of Cuban fever." Sergeant Rath Myers went along as the only noncommissioned officer. Fagen was said to have clashed with First Sergeant George Powell, but there is no way of knowing how he got along with Myers. A surgeon also accompanied each detachment to monitor the men's health.[1]

Moss and his detachment traveled by train to Visalia in Tulare County, and from there on a small rail line into the Sierra foothills to Red Hill, a camp near the edge of the park. The groves of giant sequoias remained hidden several thousand feet higher above the rugged face of the mountains.

Moss's immediate concern was obtaining accurate maps of the park boundaries; local residents were complaining of illegal sheep grazing and logging and wanted the trespassers prosecuted. He received no help in the matter and set out with his men to assess conditions in the park. A year earlier, in 1898, David Fagen had been laboring waist-deep in Tampa's Hillsborough River, breaking off chunks of phosphate for Mr. Hull. Here he was now, twenty-five hundred miles away, riding patrol in some of the most spectacular wilds of America.[2]

There were few visitors to the park in those early days. There was only one road, and it was so poorly graded and maintained as to be impassable to wagons.

The Twenty-Fourth Infantry at Yosemite, 1899; Fagen's detail went to Sequoia (Yosemite Research Library)

The giant sequoias could be reached only by a nine-mile climb over a neglected trail. The men were left to get around on unmarked and little-used trails, "some made by hunters, some by cattle men, and others by the troops attempting to eject these trespassers." Through three weeks in May, Moss and his men rode on a 140-mile circuit through both Sequoia and General Grant (later part of Kings Canyon) parks.[3]

On June 9, Moss reported that they had returned on June 7 from Halstead Meadows and voiced his frustration—trespassed sheep were everywhere, the trails in "deplorable condition"—and again complained about "the present indefinite and unsatisfactory condition of park-line affairs." He called for a surveyor to resurvey the boundaries.[4]

On June 7, as the detachment was riding down from Halstead Meadows, it appeared that Moss and Fagen got into some kind of dispute. Or perhaps the trouble had occurred earlier and Moss levied the fine only when they returned to the camp at Red Hill that night. Whatever Fagen did to incur the lieutenant's displeasure, it was no small matter. Moss levied a fine of five dollars, more than a third of a private's monthly pay of thirteen dollars. Insubordination? Impudence? Dereliction of duty? The list of possible infractions runs for many pages. If the seriousness of the charge was commensurate with the size of the fine, then this was by far Fagen's most serious offense to date, one year almost to the day of his first enlistment. Fagen and Moss had known each other for about three months, and we cannot know precisely when or how the enmity between them sprang up—incrementally or in a sudden clash. But we know that David Fagen would come to despise James Alfred Moss; and in Moss's frustration at trying to bring the young private to heel, the feeling seems to have been mutual.[5]

All we really know is that Moss fined Fagen five dollars for some unknown infraction, and they became enemies. Just how all this came about is left to the imagination.

On June 20, Moss received word to rush with his detail to San Francisco for transport to the Philippines. They arrived at the Presidio on the twenty-second, too late to join the four hundred men of the third battalion aboard the *Zealandia*. On the following day, Lieutenant Moss and his twenty-five men boarded the transport *Sheridan* along with fifteen hundred white soldiers.[6]

The next afternoon the convoy of four transports set forth; soldiers lined the rails and climbed into the rigging to watch as they sailed through the majestic Golden Gate and into the sunset. An escort of pleasure craft crowded with well-wishers saw them on their way, bands and horns blaring. Soon the ships began to surge and plunge on the great swells of the open Pacific, and the afternoon's exuberance succumbed to a universal wave of nausea.

David Fagen was again sailing off to war—unaware that, before long, he would be fighting on the side of the enemy.

The White Man's Burden

13

Take up the White Man's Burden—
Send forth the best ye breed—
Go send your sons to exile
To serve your captives' need
To wait in heavy harness
On fluttered folk and wild—
Your new-caught, sullen peoples,
Half devil and half child . . .

Rudyard Kipling,

February 1899

F AGEN'S FIRST DAYS OF THE MONTH-LONG PASSAGE to Manila were the worst. In the dark freight holds, men groaned in misery on tiers of bunks knocked together from rough planking. As the ship tossed and rolled, they lurched down narrow passages to overflowing latrines, the floors slick with vomit, the air foul and stifling. After what seemed an interminable four or five days, most of them found their sea legs and ventured on deck. They brought out guitars and mandolins, cards and dice. They attended religious services and band performances, staged amateur talent shows, engaged in drills and inspections, did calisthenics and put on the gloves in friendly boxing matches. The historian Noel Jacob Kent cited a newspaper report of unsanctioned fights on the transport ships, the bare-fisted kind, between blacks and whites.[1]

Moss's twenty-five men were probably seen as something of a novelty among the more than fifteen hundred white soldiers. Three weeks into the passage, on July 14, the "rowdy" Fagen and his diminutive lieutenant got into it again. This time Moss docked him two dollars of his pay. Soon Fagen would put in his first request for transfer to another company.[2]

On July 25, flying fish and porpoises escorted the *Sheridan* through the Boca Chica and twenty-seven miles across the bay to Manila. Earlier in the decade, a spate of typhoons and earthquakes had resulted in a ban of the traditional tile roofs in favor of galvanized iron. "The buildings all have an appearance of feebleness and senility and look as if a good blow or a heavy shake would lay them flat," a young Joseph Earle Stevens wrote in *Yesterday in the Philippines*, a travelogue published that year. Flame trees and arching bamboos, coconut palms and banana fronds crowded up among the sea of palm thatch and rusting metal rooftops. The tropical air in the rainy season, a warmth sensual and oppressive by turns, brought to mind the south coast of Cuba where most of them had been the previous July.[3]

Moss's men were deposited on the quay and, legs unsteady after a month at sea, set off on a grueling six-mile trek to join their regiment at Caloocan on the northern outskirts of Manila. Like Joseph Earle Stevens, they were "much impressed with the oddity and strangeness of everything" they encountered along their way. If Moss's men marveled at these strange sights and examined the Manileños with keen interest, the locals were no less fascinated at the sight of these burly newcomers, a fascination tinged with a good deal of apprehension. A Filipino later confided to a member of the Twenty-Fourth, "White troops . . . began to tell us of the inferiority of the American blacks — of your brutal natures, your cannibal tendencies." The gregarious and affable young men of the Twenty-fourth Infantry would soon put the lie to that slander while the whites would remain tolerated, at best, when not despised. In the words of the observant Filipino: "Between you [blacks] and him [whites], we look upon you as the angel and him as the devil."[4]

During their first weeks in Manila, several typhoons blew for days and rain came down in torrents, making their days a sodden round of marches, guard duty, and work details. Fagen's I Company set up on Balic-Balic Road a mile and a half northeast of Manila. Guard and outpost duty was more than a formality: "No one can go anywhere outside of our intrenchments without great danger," Albert Gardner Robinson reported that month. "Twice within the last ten days have the guards been doubled, while soldiers slept on their arms in anticipation of a threatened uprising."[5]

In his first weeks in Manila, Fagen was not in so much trouble that he couldn't escape for a little diversion in the city. On the walk into the Sampolac district the men shared the road with bull carts pulled by carabaos, the great lumbering work animals with their massive recurving horns, and with two-wheeled carromatas drawn by the small native ponies. Far more interesting were the native fruit girls, "very shapely in their tapis" — blouses with billowy sleeves — and colorful skirts with a long train wrapped several times around and tucked in the belt in the front. Most eye-catching was the brown band of mid-riff left "shockingly exposed." With wide baskets of fruits balanced effortlessly on their heads, they carried their slippers—*chinelas*—in hand to wear once in the city. "They generally chew betelnuts," Stevens reported, "which color their mouths red, smoke cigars, and douse their hair with coconut oil." "Wild-looking women with loose hair," was the way one young soldier described the fruit girls. The men of the Twenty-Fourth would fare much better with the native women than their white counterparts, a source of resentment among the white regulars and eventually of growing concern for the military leadership.[6]

In the cluttered streets of the city, diminutive ponies pulled tramcars with ten or twelve passengers, all of whom were smoking so that the car appeared about to burst into flames. Chinese barbers carried around chair, scissors, and razor and would "stop and give you a shave and a haircut at any part of the block." Albert Gardiner Robinson described the Escolta, the main street of "chow shops and bars," as a "tangle of local carriages and wagons" with American soldiers, Filipinos, and Chinese jostling and crowding each other. Chinese porters with their shoulder-poles supporting baskets at either end darted "in and out with an astonishing dexterity and freedom from collision." On the arcaded sidewalks, shopkeepers sold "charmingly imperfect" handmade articles, woodcarvings, snakeskin canes, stuffed bats, fine cigars wrapped in silver foil and packed in rosewood boxes. The humid air was redolent with the smells of sandalwood, coriander, and fish sauce, of leather goods and musty bales of hemp. Street vendors hawked cigarettes, beno swipes (a local homebrew), and stewed grasshoppers for a penny.[7]

"The natives soon learned to dislike us," John F. Bass wrote in *Harper's Weekly*. "We plastered the town from end to end with beer and whiskey advertisements. Americans who have followed the Army have put their time and money into saloons. No other business attracts them." From this glut of bars and beer gardens, Fagen had chosen his preferred establishment. A year and a half later, an article in the *Manila Times* identified "one of his old haunts" as "a house of ill-fame at 141 Calle Sevilla."[8]

The *Manila Times* was quick to praise the exemplary behavior of the men of the Twenty-Fourth Infantry: "Our colored fighting men have conducted themselves splendidly since they came to Manila . . . drunkenness and disorder among their members has been conspicuous by its absence." By all accounts, they also got along very well with the local citizenry, Chaplain Steward writing, "The [Filipinos] are hospitable to a fault . . . and appear to entertain a decided fondness for colored Americans."[9]

But not everyone shared the *Times*'s high regard for the "Smoked Yankees," a term coined by the Spanish for the Buffalo Soldiers. According to the historian

Jack D. Foner, "White soldiers also delighted in taunting black soldiers by addressing them as 'coons' and 'niggers' and by singing 'All coons look alike to me' and 'I don't like a nigger nohow.'" Soon "white only" signs began appearing in the windows of cafes, barbershops, and drinking establishments.[10]

A photograph of Fagen that turned up years later was almost certainly taken during his brief two months in Manila in 1899 as the men of the Twenty-Fourth were not issued their summer khaki uniforms until arriving in the islands. The twenty-year-old sits in a Renaissance Revival armchair, one leg casually draped over the other. He wears a U.S. Army enlisted man's uniform—khaki war blouse, khaki pants with leggings, and campaign hat. His expression is serious, perhaps a little threatening, hinting both of insolence and the badman's subtle air of menace. One can easily see in the photo the young man who could not be brought to heel by James Alfred Moss in the peremptory manner of the white southern officer.[11]

James Alfred Moss was the youngest of six children. His father, Judge Anderson Joseph Moss, had served in Lee's army in the Civil War. Moss used terms such as "darkeys" and "pickaninnies" in his writings, and classed black soldiers who complained of racist treatment as "ruffians" and "scoundrels." It is hard not to assume that his outlook on race would have been distinctly that of the southern white male of the time. Corporal W. T. Goode, in his fine account of his service in Cuba in the Illinois Volunteers, closed a chapter thusly: "I will add, not from a prejudicial standpoint, but from actual daily observations, that, in the southern white officer's eye the man who did the most grinning . . . and could dance the best or make the best monkeyshines, was the best negro soldier."[12]

Corporal Goode quoted the Reverend H. C. C. Astwood of Philadelphia: "Colored soldiers with white southern officers are a failure, and the men who endure it are fools, slaves or cowards."[13]

Fagen wouldn't endure it. Taking Moss's background and Fagen's background and temperament together, it is not hard to see the potential for conflict.

On August 10, the first battalion of the Twenty-Fourth Infantry arrived in Manila Bay, some two weeks after Fagen's third battalion. On this occasion, instead of being drawn up the river in rowboats or cascoes, the men were dumped into the surf. One of them who struggled to make it to shore without being knocked down by the waves was the newly promoted Sergeant Major John W. Calloway. Four months earlier, Calloway, then regimental clerk, was discharged with honors at the end of a five-year enlistment. While still at Fort Douglas, Calloway applied for a position in the Civil Service as an inspector in the Customs Service. First Lieutenant Joseph Leitch, the regimental adjutant, wrote a glowing letter of recommendation, ending, "He is an excellent clerk, accurate, painstaking, honest and sober." Colonel Liscum added another letter of high praise. But at the last moment before taking a civilian position, and with some reservation, Calloway acceded to a "special request made by [the] regimental adjutant" and re-upped, now as battalion sergeant major.[14]

When Calloway reenlisted on March 7, 1899, he was recorded as "married." In the census of June 1, 1900, he is listed as single and never-before married. Whether the "married" designation had been a clerical error or John Calloway was dissimulating in some way, these seeming contradictions in his marital status will lead to trouble the following year. But for the moment, the new sergeant major's prospects looked brighter than ever while David Fagen's fortunes continued to deteriorate, literally by the day. Calloway's battalion arrived in Manila on the *City of Para* on August 10, 1899.

Sailing on board with John Calloway was a young engineer by the name of John Clifford Brown. He was a handsome blue-eyed man, blond hair parted in the middle, a sweeping waxed mustache, and clearly a charming fellow. Brown kept a journal that offers the most vivid description of the campaign soon to be undertaken in an attempt to capture Aguinaldo. In his journal entries he exhibited the racial prejudices toward both African Americans and Filipinos common to the whites of that era.[15]

On August 13, the *City of Para* had lain in anchor for three days in the bay, and Brown's initial journal entry began: "Have been kept on the ship. The niggers left on the 11th and very glad we were to have them go." More than a month passed before Brown met up with the men of the Twenty-Fourth again. On September 20, he wrote: "The Cavalry and Infantry who came over on the *Para* with us got here today. In spite of the fact we hated the colored men on the ship, it seemed good to see the familiar faces."[16]

 These casual expressions of hatred for blacks give one a sense of the routine disparagement the Buffalo Soldiers were required to endure. Brown's journal will provide a disturbing picture of the strain the men of the Twenty-Fourth Infantry were under in their first weeks in the islands.

After only a week in Manila, John Calloway wrote a hurried letter to the *Richmond (VA) Planet*: "If I had time I would drop you a few lines bearing on the subject . . . but we black men are so much between the 'Devil and the deep sea' on the Philippine question. I fear I would not know what to say should I attempt to describe it."[17]

By the end of August, twenty-one hundred Buffalo Soldiers had arrived, and two regiments of black volunteers were being organized in the states. The black press generally accepted that the regulars were obligated to serve, onerous

as the duty may have been. But they were less understanding of those who enlisted in the volunteers. "Any Negro soldier that will cross the ocean to help
subjugate the Filipinos is either a fool or a villain," wrote the editor of the
Reporter. "May every one of them get ball-stung is our sincere prayer."[18]

And, of course, Julius F. Taylor weighed in on the matter weekly in the
Broad Ax: "It is the consensus of opinion with the majority of Negroes who are
opposed to the present treatment of the Negro in the United States that any
black man who enlists to fight the Filipinos is perfectly satisfied with the abuse
heaped upon him in this country."[19]

The rain made a swamp of the camp that was all bustle with preparations for a
move to the front. On August 28, Lieutenant Moss took command of I Company. Captain Brett was not well and remained in Manila, awaiting return to
the States. Trouble between Moss and Fagen was not long in coming. On September 11, Moss ordered the unruly private to forfeit ten dollars of his pay, almost a full month's salary. And with the fine would have gone an endless round
of fatigue duty—kitchen work, digging slit-trench latrines, cleaning out culverts,
night-soil removal, as well as time in the guardhouse. On September 22, Moss
fined Fagen five more dollars and piled on more work. Fagen put in his second
request for transfer, request denied.[20]

While Fagen remained at Balic-Balic Road and bent himself to one task after
another, seething quietly—and maybe not so quietly—the first battalion of the
Twenty-Fourth traveled by rail the forty-three miles north to San Fernando.
The much-maligned General Elwell "Grandma" Otis had devised a plan to
entrap Aguinaldo and the revolutionary leadership and bring a decisive end to
the war. The previous April, Aguinaldo had been forced out of Malolos, moving his "portable capital" first to San Isidro and Cabanatuan in Nueva Ecija,
then on to Tarlac some thirty miles north of San Fernando. And there things
stood as the rainy season made the cart tracks all but impassable. By September, though the rainy season was far from over and much of the countryside
around San Fernando in flood, Otis determined his grand assault could wait no
longer.[21]

The three-pronged plan was elegant in its conception but woefully inele-
gant in its execution. General MacArthur would lead a division straight north
from Angeles, driving Aguinaldo's fighters up the central plain. General Lloyd
Wheaton would sail with two thousand men around the west coast of Luzon
and deploy at San Fabian in the Lingayen Gulf; the objective was to close off
the Army of Liberation's retreat to the north and trap it between the two
forces.

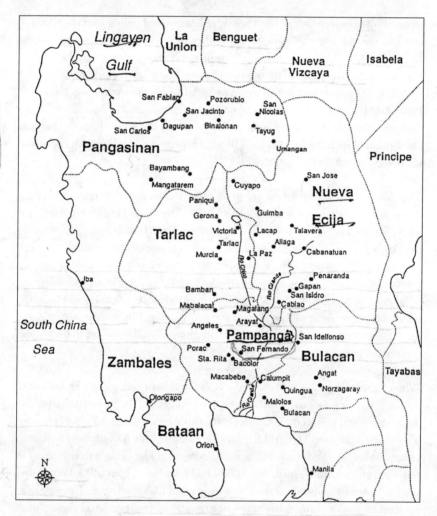

Central Luzon (Brian McAllister Linn, *The Philippine War, 1899–1902*. Used by permission of University Press of Kansas, www.kansaspress.ku.edu.)

General Lawton's assignment was the most difficult by far. He would lead his division up the Rio Grande de la Pampanga and garrison the towns along the way in an attempt to close off any escape into the Sierra Madre to the east. The Twenty-Fourth Infantry was assigned to Lawton's division. If Otis's plan worked, Aguinaldo and his ragtag army would be caught in a three-way pincer with no choice but to surrender. Then the work of benevolent assimilation could begin in earnest.

By the end of that summer, Aguinaldo's force of four thousand regulars had become a dispirited "collection of free companies each loyal to its commander but seldom able to work with others." And yet, although poorly provisioned and out-gunned, these peasant-fighters continued their daily attacks on the invaders. On September 23, a large Filipino force blew up a train near Angeles, destroyed a section of track, and fought a "heated engagement" with the Americans, killing two and wounding three. On September 26, a thirty-man detachment of the Twenty-Fourth Infantry engaged one hundred Filipinos near the town of Mexico. The brief report concluded: "Capt. Black requests authority to send out in morning to drive them off." An entry in John Clifford Brown's diary suggests the skirmish was not as routine as the various reports would indicate: "One of our reconnaissances, escorted by a detachment of the 24th, was driven back on Mexico yesterday. The niggers behaved very badly."[22]

Over the next few days, multiple engagements took place throughout the region, reports listing "Big fight near Porac," "55 minute fight, three wounded," "Big fight near Silay–1st Lt. Killed, 3 wounded." Over several weeks, Aguinaldo's fighters also attacked Guagua, Santa Rita, Santa Ana, and Baliaug. On September 27, four men of the Twenty-Fourth went fishing without permission and were set upon by "insurgents armed with bolos." Privates Edwards and Scott were captured while the other two fled. None of this reflected well on the regiment; the officers, sensitive to any disparagement from the white regiments, were not pleased.[23]

On September 28, Fagen's third battalion entrained across the flooded plain to San Fernando. The entire region out of Manila had been "gutted by fire, leaving only a landscape of dreary weed-grown rice-fields and softly waving canebrakes." The towns along the railroad to Malolos had all been burned, half by the Americans and the other half by the Filipinos under orders of General Luna, a tactic meant to inconvenience the Americans but resulting only in further hardship for the peasants. Fagen's I Company went into camp at San Fernando, a once-thriving agricultural hub of thirteen thousand, looted and burned by the Americans, now reduced to just fifteen hundred occupants. According to Albert Gardner Robinson, "A large section of the city is a wreck." Roving bands of Filipino regulars prowled in the bamboo thickets and canebrakes; the flooded rice fields reflected the low, gray sky; an air of tense expectation lingered over the Twenty-Fourth's camp. For the third time, Fagen requested transfer to another company and it was denied.[24]

Soon they would be fighting the Filipinos, the same Filipinos they had gotten along with agreeably in Manila. "We are now arrayed to meet . . . men of our own hue and color," a black soldier wrote home. "Whether it is right to reduce these people to submission is not a question for the soldier to decide.

Our oath of allegiance knows neither race, color nor nation."[25] But as scouting parties of the Twenty-Fourth Infantry patrolled the countryside, they encountered a curious message, in broken English, posted on trees.

To the Colored American Soldiers

It is without honor nor profit that you are spilling your costly blood.

Your masters have thrown you to the most iniquitous fight with double purpose. In order to be you the instrument of their ambition. Soon make the extinction of you race.

Your friends the Filipinos give you this good warning.

You must consider your situation and your history. And take charge that the blood of your brothers Samuel Hose and Gray proclaim vengeance.[26]

These posters were addressed to "The Twenty-Fourth Infantry (colored) our brother regiment." Copies of this appeal also appeared mysteriously in their camps, and bundles of them were found awaiting distribution. A Filipino boy shocked a black soldier named Richard Sims when he asked, "Why does the American Negro come from America to fight us when we are much a friend to him? . . . Why don't you fight those people in America who burn Negroes, that make a beast of you."[27]

On October 3, 1899, John Clifford Brown wrote in his diary: "While I was sitting here writing the colored infantry was drilling in extended order across the river. After the drill one of the men came down and jumped in the river drowning himself. They have just gotten his body. One did the same thing Sunday. I guess they have been driven hard since they misbehaved."[28]

Two men driven to suicide, two dishonorably discharged, many more fined and in the guardhouse, notably Eugene Young ($7), William Watson ($10) and fifteen days at hard labor.[29]

Fagen was coming to the end of the line. Did the poster rekindle the outrage at the sufferings inflicted on Sam Hose? Did the officers "driving them hard" finally push him to the edge of open rebellion? On October 1, a typhoon raged across the flat lands, destroying Nipa huts and killing more than three hundred mules, essential for the movement of supplies in the coming campaign. On October 2, Fagen stood before Lieutenant Moss and was ordered "to forfeit $15 of his pay and to be confined at hard labor 30 days per SC sentence San Fernando."[30]

Two days later, Captain James E. Brett sailed for the United States, leaving Lieutenant Moss and twenty-four-year-old Charles E. Hay Jr. as his second lieutenant in command of 114 black soldiers. As it happens, Hay Jr. was the nephew of McKinley's secretary of state John Hay, recently ambassador to Great Britain and formerly Abraham Lincoln's private secretary. Hay Jr. had joined the company on May 10, while Fagen was at Sequoia, and was immediately placed on detached service until the end of August, so Fagen would not have met the new second lieutenant until September.[31]

After three moves around the country, Captain James Brett took a position as director of the State Military Institute of Oklahoma. Perhaps his frequent moves were an attempt to keep one step ahead of the debt collectors. For when he died in Oklahoma City on March 3, 1904, he was still being pursued by his many creditors. James Brett was buried at the Presidio.[32]

That same year, *Collier's Weekly* ran a short story contest. When Rowland Thomas's winning story was later included in a collection, *The Little Gods: A Masque of the Far East*, the magazine reminded the reader that "the author of this stirring and powerful book of life in the Philippines was awarded the $5,000 prize, from 30,000 competitors, by *Collier's Weekly* for his remarkable story of *Fagan* which forms the first chapter of *The Little Gods*." For years, whenever *Collier's Weekly* ran one of Thomas's stories—and they ran many—the phrase "By the Author of 'Fagan'" went under his name. With dark hair parted in the middle and striking good looks, Rowland Thomas seemed made for the role of literary vagabond, a drifter through exotic, distant lands who then turned his experiences into page-turning tales of adventure, highly remunerative tales such as *Felicidad—A Picturesque Romance of the Tropics* and *Fatima—Or Always Pick a Fool for a Husband*. A critic described *The Little Gods* as "Philippine realism by an American Kipling."[33]

Rowland Thomas's oddly readable story is written as a fable. The outline of Fagen's story is there, in the most general way, and then embellished until it becomes a grotesque distortion of what actually happened. Thomas was at his best evoking the tropical milieu, the sultry, languid life of a remote village, at his worst in his attempt at full-phonetic black dialogue, a failing he shared with almost every other white writer of the era who took a stab at setting African American English vernacular to the page. And, as always, Fagen was depicted as a giant, in this case a "gentle" giant. "Then Fagan came to the Army, and the Army received him with joy. The surgeon's eye glistened with an artist's fervor as he thumped and kneaded the great, perfect animal and a wise old recruiting sergeant guided the pen for him to sign his name."[34]

Here, Fagan, the powerful but sweet-natured "animal" is portrayed—not surprisingly—as being simpleminded to the point of not knowing which end of a rifle is which. In the heat of combat, he instinctively takes his rifle by the barrel "as a boy might a stick" and wades through the charging Filipinos, clubbing them right and left. "From that day he was called Wild Fagan and Fagan the Nigger-Killer, and as the campaign progressed, his renown passed beyond his regiment."[35]

Ultimately, Fagan is prodded into revolt by a white lieutenant from the North—an "official bully"—who didn't possess the southern officers' gift for dealing "firmly yet kindly with the big black children committed to their charge." He is repeatedly thrown in the guardhouse for petty offenses, "for the officer had grown into the belief that Fagan was the probable cause of every misdemeanor in the company." Finally, sentenced to a month in the guard-house, Fagan emerges "still a child, but a sullen child now, moping over a bitter sense of injustice." He swears he won't be locked up again, but is soon thrown back into the guardhouse. Fagan waits until dark; then, with two hands on the bars of his window and a knee braced against the wall, he dislodges the entire window from the wall. With rifle and ammunition belt, he takes his leave of the army and the story continues from there, evermore fancifully.[36]

Rowland Thomas's depiction of Fagen as physically powerful, mentally weak, and docile was in keeping with the racist stereotypes of the day, in par-ticular, the figure of Sambo. "Finest build of a man you ever laid eyes on . . . like a cat and a grizzly rolled into one" and "a stupid, brooding, grown-up child." The Sambo caricature, popularized during the slavery era, cast the black man as an overgrown child, happy in the loyal service of his white master. In the postwar decades, Sambo evolved into the shuffling, mumbling buffoon, source of ridicule in cartoons and vaudeville acts.[37]

Throughout Thomas's story, Fagen is treated as a dullard driven to rebellion by an overbearing northern lieutenant. In reality the officer was from Louisiana, and his charge—anything but docile—knew not only which end of a rifle was which but how to fire it with a deadly accuracy.

In an article published in the *New York Age* in April 1905, the author (pos-sibly T. Thomas Fortune), first noting Fagen's reputation as "the most brilliant and dangerous of the Filipino chieftains," then addressed the recent publication of Rowland Thomas's "Fagan."

> We have read with much interest, therefore, the *Collier's Weekly* prize story by Mr. Rowland Thomas, who takes the life of Fagan as his subject. Mr. Thomas scouts the genius and vindictiveness popularly imputed to Fagan, and deprives him of heroism to make him pathetic. The legendary Fagan is metamorphosed into the simple-minded, sunny, inoffensive, forgiving child-man whom Southerners, who are to be distrusted most when they bring gifts, love to praise as the highest character of our race; the one who, whatever injuries are loaded on

him, always turns the other cheek to the smiter. Without venturing an opinion as to the ethics of apostasy, we wish, for the sake of the story, that Mr. Thomas had made Fagan a "magnificent criminal" instead of a soft-hearted simpleton; one who would revenge unmerited wrongs with violence instead of suffering himself to be broken by them.[38]

The real Fagen did not break out of the San Fernando guardhouse, as in Rowland Thomas's story, but undoubtedly the harsh sentence pushed him that much closer to his fateful decision to clear out. During the days of hard labor and long nights in confinement, there was time to consider what must have once been the unthinkable—not only to desert but also to take up arms against his countrymen. It was a conclusion he probably did not arrive at without a good deal of anguish and foreboding.

Aguinaldo Adrift

14

HISTORIANS HAVE PUZZLED OVER Emilio Aguinaldo's ineffectual leadership, his reluctance to engage the Americans early on before they had become entrenched, and, once the fighting had begun, his insistence upon continuing a strategy of conventional warfare against a militarily superior foe. In the first months of the war, Aguinaldo had presided over the loss of thousands of his best men in a futile attempt to stand up to the enemy in set-piece battles. Despite these costly defeats, he did not call for a shift to guerrilla warfare.[1]

In April, General Antonio Luna conferred with Apolinario Mabini and pressed him to urge Aguinaldo to adopt a guerrilla strategy. But Luna's rationale for the change was due to a dwindling supply of ammunition, not because he thought it a superior approach. Mabini did not see Aguinaldo until May 8, 1899, the day he was forced out of the government by Pedro Paterno and Felipe Buencamino. Paterno, the richest man in the Philippines, became the new president of the cabinet. An advocate for annexation, he had already made peace overtures to the Americans. (The possibility of a negotiated end to hostilities is sometimes given as another reason for Aguinaldo's delay in calling for a guerrilla war.)[2]

The volatile General Antonio Luna was so incensed by Paterno and Buencamino's overture to the Americans that he ordered the entire "peace cabinet" arrested and sent his own group of negotiators. In another sign of his explosive temper, he slapped Buencamino, called him a traitor, and accused his son of cowardice. When Luna turned over the cabinet officers to Aguinaldo, the president had them released. Luna, they informed him, was planning a coup d'état. Paterno and Buencamino despised Antonio Luna and wanted to bring him down, as they had Mabini. An impressionable Aguinaldo accepted that Luna was, in fact, scheming against him (Mabini did not believe so). In a cold-blooded preemptive move, Aguinaldo sent a message to Luna in Pangasinan to meet with him at his headquarters in Cabanatuan, Nueva Ecija. When Luna arrived for the meeting, Aguinaldo was not there, but soldiers of the president's Kavit battalion were. In a savage attack, they set upon the unsuspecting general with bolos and revolvers, killing him and his aide.[3]

As with the elimination of Bonifacio, Aguinaldo may have been relieved of a chief rival, but at a significant cost. "With his [Luna's] death," Teodoro A. Agoncillo wrote, "demoralization set in and the reprisals against those who were intimately or even remotely connected with him led to indifference among his sympathizers."[4]

Though born in Manila, Antonio Luna was an Ilocano, his parents from the Ilocos region on the northwest coast of Luzon. There was no great love between the Tagalogs and Ilocanos, an example of the "tribalistic and region-alistic tendencies" referred to by Agoncillo and Guerrero in their *History of the Filipino People*. With the assassination of Luna, relations between Aguinaldo and the Ilocanos became even more strained. Similarly, support for the Malolos government in the provinces of Pangasinan, Tarlac, and Pampanga—all histori-cally cool to the Tagalogs—was muted. Support in the Visayas for the Tagalog-dominated revolutionary government was even less enthusiastic. The revolu-tion was splintered not only by class differences but also by regional differences.[5]

And yet, for all the Filipinos' internal differences, there was only one invader. Despite being hampered in every way by factional disputes, class divides, and elements high and low all too eager to accommodate the new colonial masters, the Filipinos would make a fight of it, one that would take the Americans years to suppress and, in some instances, by means of only the most brutal and wanton measures. Mabini asked: "Must the Filipino people, when grown tired of the Spanish yoke, necessarily have had no other aim in view but that of submitting themselves to a new yoke?" To him, the Americans were "the same breed of dog with different collars."[6]

According to the historian John N. Schumacher, "The great majority of the masses continued to fight under the banner of the Malolos government." That allegiance, inspired by the egalitarian principles of the Katipunan move-ment, seemed apparent to John Bass the following June: "The whole popula-tion of the islands sympathizes with the insurgents." Albert Gardner Robinson and other journalists were of the same opinion, and even the new military gover-nor, General Arthur MacArthur, acknowledged as much: "Wherever through-out the Archipelago there is a group of the insurgent army, it is a fact beyond dispute that all of the contiguous towns contribute to the maintenance thereof."[7]

But, as Milagros Guerrero wrote in *Luzon at War*, with that allegiance went expectations of significant changes in return: "It is unmistakable that the peasantry throughout Luzon expected a restructuring of the economic and social relations after the Revolution, a sentiment that the ilustrado leadership in Malolos was certainly aware of but refused to acknowledge."[8]

There was one radical shift in policy by which Aguinaldo might have overcome the disparate antagonisms among the islanders and thus prevent the alienation of the laboring masses. It was a radical shift that he probably could not have implemented even had he tried—the ilustrado leadership would not have countenanced such a move. And that was to offer the indio a true stake in the revolution: land reform, tax reform, the franchise, and an end to forced labor. Aguinaldo and his government offered none of that, and yet they expected the peasant masses to continue fighting and dying for a revolution that promised them little in return. Mabini had warned, "Our strength lies within the people and without them we cannot achieve anything." But Aguinaldo and the others in the ilustrado leadership could see the struggle only in terms of their traditional privilege. Vicente Rafael wrote, "There was nothing at all proletarian about the leadership of the Revolution." Glenn Anthony May put it even more bluntly: "One important reason for the American victory was Aguinaldo's inept leadership . . . his lack of scruples, his hunger for wealth and power; but perhaps his greatest failings were as a military commander. Aguinaldo's choice of tactics virtually guaranteed defeat."[9]

The hacenderos and town leaders—the provincial elite—were the principal drivers of the war with the Americans. Despite their limited martial experience, they became the officers in charge of their respective regions. They provided the matériel support, and most of the foot soldiers were drawn from the ranks of their tenants in what has been called a "patron-client relationship." These indios were farmers, not professional soldiers, and to keep them in the field as a standing army was impractical and counterproductive. In Pampanga and Tarlac, Aguinaldo's men scoured the countryside for food and supplies, more like marauding invaders than freedom fighters. Their depredations and bullying created deep resentment among the populace and further eroded support for the revolution.[10]

And in the towns the new civil administrators, invariably drawn from the local principalia, had only their former Spanish colonial masters to serve as models. The journalist Frederick Palmer described them as "leaders who bear themselves with the air of potentates." Milagros Guerrero commented: "Rampant graft and corruption characterized the administration of many municipalities, exacerbating the grievances of the peasant masses and contributing to their radicalization." This unrest resulted in "tax riots" and "demonstrations" and led thousands of indios to join peasant messianic movements, which were antagonistic to both Aguinaldo's regime and the Americans, a development that further clouded a conflict already bewildering in its complexity. Cesar Adib Majul, Mabini's biographer, wrote that "what was claimed to be a movement supported by all classes started to show . . . signs of disintegration."[11]

Because of the inability to feed his troops, Aguinaldo's forces dwindled to four thousand men over the rainy summer months of 1899. Historians find it "baffling" that, with his rival Luna removed, Aguinaldo still did not shift to a guerrilla war. With the Americans dug into defensive positions, waiting for more troops to arrive and for the rains to abate, Aguinaldo had time to set up a guerrilla infrastructure in the towns and barrios, to create shadow governments and establish supply networks. Perhaps he feared that in adopting a guerrilla strategy he might lose control of the revolution, that other leaders might challenge his command. And however committed he was to achieving independence, he was not willing to sacrifice his own interest to attain that end. A more generous explanation is that Aguinaldo believed the Filipinos could be deemed worthy of independence only if they acted according to international norms, that is, fighting their imperial opponent in set-piece battles rather than resorting to the irregular tactics associated with "uncivilized" peoples.[12]

Along with the racial arguments, the Americans would make much of Filipino disunity, particularly the Tagalog dominance in the revolutionary leadership, and cite this as further justification for the establishment of American colonial rule. By characterizing the Filipinos as a jumble of semicivilized and uncivilized tribes tyrannized by the warlike *Tagals*, they could be dismissed as unworthy of self-government. Paul Kramer writes. "The 'tribalization' of the Republic would rhetorically eradicate the Philippine Republic as a legitimate state whose rights the United States might have to recognize under international law."[13]

In the coming years, McKinley, Roosevelt, and American politicians of every stripe would repeat what James Blount termed "the old insufferable drivel about 'tribes.'" And in tandem with this reduction of the islanders to "savages" incapable of self-government went the exaltation of that great civilizing agent, the Anglo-Saxon American, inheritor of the British imperial tradition.[14]

The peace negotiations in May 1899 had come to nothing. When Aguinaldo proposed an armistice, Otis believed the revolutionaries were only stalling for time and rejected the request. Faced with the choice of unconditional surrender or continued war, Aguinaldo and his new cabinet issued a proclamation announcing that the struggle would go on. But then they did nothing. With his revolution in tatters, Aguinaldo waited. And now, with the rainy season lessening in intensity, he found himself facing an American army intent on crushing his beleaguered and fragmented forces.

Over the Hill

15

I feel sorry for these people and all that have come under the control of the United States. I don't believe they will be justly dealt by. The first thing in the morning is the "Nigger" and the last thing at night is the "Nigger."

Sergeant Patrick Mason, Twenty-Fourth Infantry, Company I,
to the *Cleveland Gazette*,
November 17, 1899

Six weeks after penning this letter, and after twenty-nine years of service in the Twenty-Fourth Infantry, Sergeant Patrick Mason died of typhoid fever at Cabanatuan.[1]

David Fagen had six weeks remaining in the army. It was a period of turmoil, for Lawton's three-thousand-man division, and certainly for the young private whose conflict with Lieutenant Moss had culminated in a whopping fine and thirty days of hard labor. Tracking Fagen's movements during this period is problematical, and even harder to trace over those weeks is his state of mind. Though he had been sentenced to thirty days of hard labor beginning October 2, 1899, the Record of Events does not place him "in confinement" at any period. Either the officer making the rolls accidentally overlooked that Fagen was "in confinement," or the sentence might have been commuted or deferred in some way. This lack of clear evidence forces us to imagine several scenarios.

If he was, in fact, serving his sentence, he undoubtedly was not finding his stay in San Fernando all that charming. Beyond confinement and hours of hard labor, it was not uncommon for prisoners to be subjected to brutal treatment from the guards and officers in charge. Several punishments were particularly harsh: being "spread-eagled"—laid sprawled on the ground, hands and feet tied to tent stakes, and left in the sun; or the "hanging act"—strung up by the thumbs or wrists until one's toes just touched the ground. An uncooperative prisoner might also be made to stand on a barrel in the hot sun for long periods of time. Corporal punishment in the military was common in those days, as it was in civilian life; cuffs and hard knocks and even severe beatings were not unusual.[2]

There were other men from the Twenty-Fourth in the guardhouse, most notably William Watson, serving fifteen days of hard labor. It seems likely that Fagen and Watson toiled alongside one another and were well acquainted. Exactly one year later, on October 10, 1900, William Watson would become Fagen's prisoner and remain a captive for two months. And in November 1901, a Corporal William Watson would lead nineteen privates from Fagen's I Company in a joint expedition to track Fagen down in the mountains of Bongabong. Though they would press Fagen closely, as with numerous other expeditions, they would fail to catch up with the notorious renegade. Undoubtedly, William Watson would have had some lively stories to tell of his old acquaintance from I Company.[3]

If Fagen had a friend on the outside, it would have been Sergeant Major John W. Calloway. Calloway had been assigned to the Provost Marshall's office in San Fernando. Just what his duties were is not clear, probably clerical, but as sergeant major, it also seems a possibility that he served in some sort of capacity as counsel to the black prisoners from his battalion, of whom Fagen was one, and a young man Calloway knew with some familiarity.

Whether in the San Fernando guardhouse or advancing upriver with his company, sometime in October David Fagen marked his twenty-first birthday.

A young ilustrado named Tomas Consunji, son of a wealthy planter, also worked in the Provost Marshall's office. Consunji spoke English and served as translator and interpreter. He and John Calloway struck up a friendship. Out of hearing range of the white Americans, the two men could speak frankly of their shared misgivings about the war and about the oppression their ancestors had suffered for generations under the heel of white racists.

Like the other black regulars, Calloway had been dismayed to find that the white Americans' "home style" treatment of blacks had been transported intact to the islands. And now it was being applied to the Filipinos as well as to the black Americans. "The whites have begun to establish their diabolical race hatred in all its home rancor," he wrote in a letter to the *Richmond Planet*, "even endeavoring to propagate the phobia among Spaniards and Filipinos." For all of the McKinley administration's flowery talk of democracy and freedom, the only thing the occupation seemed to promise the Filipino was subjugation and humiliation at the hands of white overseers.[4]

"The future of the Filipino, I fear, is that of the Negro in the South," a Dr. Santos told Calloway. "Matters are almost to that condition in Manila now. No one (white) has any scruples as regards respecting the rights of a Filipino. He is kicked and cuffed at will and he dare not remonstrate."[5]

Calloway and the other black soldiers had to be circumspect in voicing their reservations about their country's mission in the islands, but their letters home, especially those written anonymously, attest to a deep ambivalence toward the task they had been assigned.

Always on the lookout for an opportunity for advancement, John Calloway applied for "a commission in one of the regiments of Volunteer Infantry, (colored) now being organized in the United States." Over the course of four days, his request for a commission moved through channels with almost lightning speed, with letters of glowing praise through each endorsement. On October 13, Otis signed the Fifth Endorsement and forwarded it to the Adjutant General, U.S. Army.[6]

But there Calloway's path to a lieutenancy stalled, for no reason that was explained. The only response that came from the War Department in Washington was a resounding and inexplicable silence. Why this happened is one of the mysteries that would bedevil the career of John Calloway. By any reasonable assessment of his record to mid-October 1899, he was destined to soon pin a first lieutenant's silver bar on his lapel and embark on a new career as an officer with either the Forty-Eighth or Forty-Ninth Volunteer Infantry. But it was not to be. Fifteen noncommissioned officers from the ranks of the Buffalo Soldiers would be granted commissions in the new volunteer regiments, but Calloway wasn't among them.[7]

———————

The delta region of Pampanga was the home of the Macabebes, traditional enemies of the Tagalogs. Most historians believe the trouble started before the Spanish arrived, in what has been called "the time of the rajahs." By the early seventeenth century, the Macabebes had become, along with Kapampangans in general, a main source of colonial troops for the Spanish, key to their "divide and rule" strategy for maintaining control in the islands. Vastly outnumbered by the Tagalogs, the Macabebes in turn received favorable treatment and protection from their colonial sponsors. A Macabebe regiment had fought for Spain throughout the revolution of 1896 and 1898 and now, after three centuries of this "marriage of convenience," they were left without a protector.[8]

Lieutenant Matthew Batson, whose manservant was a Macabebe, and who had traveled to the Macabebe region, was convinced that the Macabebes could be an invaluable resource as scouts, guides, spies, and translators. But Otis was wary of arming any Filipinos, afraid they would "turn traitors." Batson took the idea to General Henry Lawton, who endorsed the plan and proposed it to the secretary of war Elihu Root. Root did not bother consulting Otis and gave Lawton the go-ahead. In October, when General Young received orders from Lawton to advance on Arayat, Batson was ready with two companies of his fearsome Macabebes to take part in the campaign.[9]

On October 10, 1899, General Samuel B. M. Young led the first contingent of Lawton's three-thousand-man division out of San Fernando. Looming directly behind the charming little town of Arayat was the extinct volcano of the same name. The steep, symmetrical sides of Mount Arayat rose 3,366 feet above the floodplain that averaged no more than 40 to 120 feet above sea level. At the top, a crater more than a kilometer wide opened like a gaping maw to the skies. On the eastern edge of Pampanga, Arayat was the mythical adversary of another volcano far to the west of the province, Pinatubo. Arayat was home to the god Sinukuan, rival to Namalayan of Pinatubo; between them spread the fertile plain of Pampanga, long a region for growing sugarcane and food crops for the

Mount Arayat (photo by author)

city of Manila. Fagen would have looked to the fabled mountain daily while bending to his labors, whether in confinement or with his company.

With the town of Arayat as their first goal, Young's brigade began its grueling advance up the muddy cart track. The next day the scattered remnants of Aguinaldo's army did little to impede the column's progress as the first battalion of the Twenty-Fourth Infantry plodded toward them in a line that stretched across flooded rice paddies. General Young remained in Arayat as he assembled his force and waited for the supply wagons and artillery to catch up. The division commander, General Henry Lawton, arrived on October 16. The tall "Indian fighter," with his granite jaw, drooping mustache, and a weakness for hard liquor, wore a pith helmet—"aping the British" some said, "America's Lord Kitchener." Some have speculated that Lawton, only recently diagnosed with tuberculosis, was all the more inclined to tempt death on the battlefield.[10]

The Rio Grande de la Pampanga was key to Lawton's advance. The great challenge was supplying Young's lead troops. Given the near impassability of the cart trails, the plan was to bring supplies up the river to San Isidro in Nueva Ecija; from there bull trains and mule wagons would continue north overland and upriver.

Though fully one-third of Lawton's three-thousand-man division, the black regulars' participation received little mention in the communications between Lawton and other officers. They were relegated to the role of backups for the white units and Batson's Macabebes that spearheaded the advance. Their job was to keep the supplies flowing to the front, a daunting task given the obstacles they encountered at every turn. Time was of the essence for Lawton. If the Americans were to cut off any escape by Aguinaldo into the Sierra Madre, they had to move quickly.

———————

While remnants of the Army of Liberation continued to obstruct Young's advance in repeated engagements, few of which "reached the dignity of combats," the great obstacle to the Americans' progress was the elements. With swamps and jungles on each side of the road, the ten-mile stretch of cart trail to Cabiao was described as "perfectly awful." With "slimy mud-holes six feet deep," the bull carts ground into the mire. According to John Clifford Brown, the soldiers filled the holes with anything they could find, "tearing down fences and houses, cutting down banana trees and bamboos, carrying hay, anything to fill up the mud holes." Knee-deep in the muck, the men got behind the carts and pushed. When that failed, they unloaded the carts and carried the supplies through deep mud and across streams. When the men of the Twenty-Fourth Infantry straggled into Cabiao, they were too exhausted to be concerned about their dismal surroundings, described by Brown as "merely a collection of native huts and tumble-down church."[11]

General Henry Lawton (Marrion Wilcox, *Harper's History of the War in the Philippines* [1900])

Captain John G. Ballance's battalion of the Twenty-Second Infantry swept across the swampy fields and woods toward San Isidro, running General Pio del Pilar's men through the town and scattering them to the east. The former revolutionary capital was soon in American hands.

Lawton had taken San Isidro and was anxious for Young's brigade to push toward Cabanatuan. But the virtually impassable roads refused to cooperate, and now the Rio Grande de la Pampanga compounded Lawton's problem many times over. The river refused to cooperate, its swift current constantly changing course, rising and subsiding as much as fifteen feet overnight, depending on the rain in the mountains. Launches stranded on the sandbars; cascos broke loose from the launches and drifted downstream, stranding below Arayat. Men of the Twenty-Fourth Infantry towed the laden barges against the current with shorelines. Every day saw a new disaster on the river while bull trains and mule wagons sank into the mire and soldiers white and black strove mightily against the elements. It was as if Sinukuan atop Arayat were laughing at them, delighting in making a hash of their grandly conceived plans. From the craggy rim of the volcano, Lawton's three thousand men must have resembled so many disoriented ants floundering amid the mud and greenery.

It was during this furious drive to ensnare Aguinaldo that David Fagen spent his last weeks as a soldier in the U.S. Army. On October 26, Lawton issued an order for seventeen men of the Twenty-Fourth in San Fernando to be rushed upriver to Arayat, where they were to act as guards on the launches. It may have been then that Fagen's time in confinement was ended due to the need for reinforcements in Arayat. On that same day, he received an additional fine of six dollars, no small penalty. It seems that Fagen was either incapable of escaping the wrath of his superiors or, more likely, determinedly unrepentant.[12]

On October 31, Lawton ordered the entire division placed on half rations. His cables to Manila were consistently desperate in tone, furious in one communication, imploring in the next. And all the while, according to Brian Linn, he "drove his overworked men mercilessly."[13]

As Young's flying column pushed north, his men found barrios abandoned except for the wounded left behind. Stranded bull carts soaked in blood attested to the suffering of the peasant fighters and the demoralization of the scattered remnants of Aguinaldo's forces. "Everywhere people report insurgents discouraged," reported Lawton, who added that they were "with not much ammunition, and that home made."[14]

In the midst of this period of intense activity, David Fagen and I Company arrived in San Isidro. Perhaps he had already resolved to join the revolutionaries and was waiting for the right opportunity to make contact with someone he thought he could trust. Spies abounded in the towns and there would have been opportunities for one of them to conduct delicate and highly secretive negotiations with a potential recruit.

In the case of some deserters, a woman served as intermediary between them and the revolutionaries, and by at least one report this was how Fagen took that first risky step toward changing sides. An enterprising Filipino had been doing a bustling business supplying the troops with liquor. Colonel Lyman V. W. Kennon ordered the man arrested and forbade the sale of alcohol in the town. But it seems no amount of punishment could subdue Fagen's boisterous spirit. Even in the midst of his troubles with Moss, the irrepressible young man caroused with the locals, and with a young woman—or so the story goes—who had caught his eye.[15]

"The rain fell incessantly and in torrents," a major reported, "until the entire valley was one vast marsh." Lawton had a supply train loaded but, with the ferry washed away, he could not get it across the flooding river. Young received information that Aguinaldo had left Tarlac en route to Bayombong, Nueva Viscaya, well into the Caraballos Mountains. In desperation, Young proposed cutting loose from the chain of supply. His men would push on in a flying column in a race to cut off Aguinaldo's escape. Each company would bring along five mule-drawn ration carts; otherwise they would live off the land. Lawton agreed, promising to bring the supply trains forward as quickly as possible.[16]

On November 7, Lloyd Wheaton and his two-thousand-man force landed at Dagupan. MacArthur had begun his sweep up the central plain through Tarlac and, after a day of setbacks crossing the river, Young's flying column was on the move. Over the ensuing days Young's three columns conducted a relentless drive through flooded fields and entangling forests, exchanging fire with scattered bands of Aguinaldo's army and scouring the villages for supplies. The ration carts were the first to go when the wheels came off and the wagon bodies sank in the muck. Many of the animals drowned or died from exhaustion. Half the men lost their shoes, sucked off in the mud while their uniforms, muddy and worn for weeks, disintegrated. Some men struggled on, clad only in "cartridge belt and breech-clout."[17]

At each town along the way, Young left a detachment to sustain his supply lines and block Aguinaldo's escape into the mountains. He was counting on Lloyd Wheaton's men to come east from Dagupan, occupying the towns along the way and connecting with his men coming from the southeast. Lawton was effusive in his praise of General Young: "He has swept the country like a cyclone, has scattered and terrorized the enemy and driven them in confusion from every point." Now all that remained to bring the war to a swift conclusion was the capture of Emilio Aguinaldo.[18]

On November 12, Aguinaldo gathered with his retinue of officers and advisers and passed a resolution to disband the Army of Liberation. Soldiers were to return to their home provinces and organize for guerrilla warfare. Aguinaldo had finally adopted a strategy of guerrilla warfare not because it was a superior strategy but because his army had disintegrated. Pantaleon Garcia was appointed "politico-military commander" of the center of Luzon. For the moment, Aguinaldo's only hope was to escape the net being cast by his pursuers.

———

San Isidro was still all bustle, the hub for receiving supplies from down river and moving them north by both land and river. Fagen and three companies of the Twenty-Fourth manned outposts, traveled as guards on the launches, and

On the road to Cabiao (Marrion Wilcox, *Harper's History of the War in the Philippines* [1900])

escorted supply trains. They marched along the gravel streets lined with *sawali* fences, lush gardens, and nipa houses; they purchased food and sundries from thatched *tienda* stalls; they interacted with the locals throughout the day. And at some point Fagen had made contact with the revolutionaries; at some point he had finalized his decision.

The rain fell for thirty hours, continuing all through the night of the six-teenth. Sergeant Patrick Mason and Sergeant-Major John Calloway were both penning their oft-published letters that night in San Isidro, Mason to the *Cleveland Gazette*, Calloway to the *Richmond Planet*. If the article in the *St. Louis Post-Dispatch*, April 16, 1902, can be believed, Fagen spent part of that last rainy night in the company of the woman who would become his wife: "Love for a native Filipino woman was the cause of Fagin's desertion. . . . She held out promises to him of advancement in the insurgent forces if he would desert, and after a protracted 'vino' debauch he left the regiment."

"Love for a woman" may well have influenced Fagen's decision to join the revolutionaries. And the worsening enmity between him and Moss can have played no small part in his decision to clear out. But I would maintain that his desertion was a conscious political act, evidenced by his subsequent unwaver-ing loyalty to the revolutionary cause. Fagen did not desert simply for personal

reasons. He deserted to make war on white Americans in concert with the Filipino revolutionaries.

———•••———

In the morning, the three companies of the third battalion were to cross the
river and proceed north. Did Fagen sleep for even a moment through the long
night?

The rain stopped before dawn. The sky cleared and when the bugler blew
reveille, the soldiers rose in the first light of a perfect, cloudless day. All was
commotion as men formed up in the square before the convent wall. Mules were
harnessed to wagons; officers shouted orders and organized their companies;
the regimental band played a martial tune.

With all the revolvers he could carry in a gunnysack, Fagen slipped away.
In a hidden spot on the outskirts of town, perhaps some backyard garden, a
Filipino officer by the name of Delfin Esquivel, a powerful *hacendero* of the nearby
region of Jaen, sat astride a native pony. He held the reins of another horse,
saddled and waiting.[19]

Soon the young man appeared, hurrying down the muddy path. The officer
handed him the reins of the pony and Fagen mounted up. Perhaps he looked
back, heart pounding, astonished by what he had done, by what he intended to
do. But he had made up his mind. There was no turning back. Let others such
as John Calloway and Patrick Mason register their complaints with a pen; he
would do his talking with a gun.

Renegade

Part Two

70,000 American soldiers fought a counter insurgency war which has seldom, if ever, been surpassed in the ferociousness and barbarity committed by both sides.

George Yarrington Coats,
"The Philippine Constabulary: 1901–1917"

Another Kind of War

16

THE DAY AFTER FAGEN'S DESERTION, General Theodore Schwan in Manila cabled Major General Henry Lawton in the north of Nueva Ecija: "Conditions of affairs among troops at San Isidro will be reported to you probably by Colonel Kennon." What did this mean—"Conditions of affairs among troops"? Did it have anything to do with a black soldier riding away with an "insurgent" officer to join the ranks of the enemy? Perhaps not, but this was the eventuality that many had predicted when the Buffalo Soldiers were ordered to the islands. Would this first desertion be the beginning of a wave of defections by black soldiers? Such a possibility had been a concern of the army leadership from the first, and Fagen's riding away with an "insurgent" officer must have caused quite a stir, both among his fellow black regulars and their white officers in San Isidro.[1]

David Fagen's first eight months with the guerrillas has long been a blank page. In their article on Fagen, Frank Schubert and Michael Robinson wrote: "The censorship imposed on military activity shrouds Fagen's first year as an *insurrecto* officer." While the military declined to share selected reports from the field with journalists in Manila, it is less clear to what extent reports themselves were elided or not filed at all. From my own cross-referencing of documents, it appears that officers in the field were highly selective in what they chose to report. Brian Linn observed that "Funston and the troops under him were guilty of some very harsh policies, especially early in his tenure." One gets the sense that existing reports of harsh measures are only the tip of the iceberg.[2]

Fagen was not mentioned in the press until August 18, 1900, when the *Manila Freedom* identified him as the leader of a devastating ambush on an American patrol. Long before then, the army was aware of his activities—the first reference to Fagen I found in army communications was March 1900—but they were not sharing those reports with the press. I have not uncovered any reference to specific orders, but the careful silence maintained by the army in regard to David

Fagen suggests, in my opinion, that silence on the subject of Fagen was the official policy. Again, the question arises: Were they afraid that word of his desertion and success as a guerrilla officer might prove infectious among his former comrades-in-arms stationed in northern Nueva Ecija?[3]

The simplest escape route from San Isidro was to the east where Pantaleon Garcia, the new politico-commander of central Luzon, had withdrawn with 800 men—250 of them sick or wounded. This was near the foothills of the Sierra Madre, at Papaya, a safe ride of about twelve miles over a patchwork of rice fields and forest where the Americans had yet to venture. The 1902 article in the *St. Louis Post-Dispatch* states that "he left his regiment and joined the insurrectionist force under Col. Padilla. . . . Padilla commissioned him a second lieutenant and gave him a separate command." Subsequent reports support the *Post-Dispatch* story, though by one account he began as a drill instructor with the guerrillas and only later took command of his own company.[4]

————

While the new lieutenant began to adjust to his strange surroundings, to a new language, to a status bizarrely different from any he had ever experienced, the drama to the north continued to unfold at a frantic pace. Otis's grand plan appeared on the verge of success. MacArthur's men swept up the plain into Pangasinan, and Brigadier General Samuel B. M. Young's three columns cut off any escape into Nueva Vizcaya. Captain John G. Ballance's battalion of the Twenty-Second veered west, fought several sharp engagements, and then stalled in the flooded rice lands of Pangasinan. Sick, without shoes or much in the way of clothing, food, or medicine, they could go no farther.[5]

While Ballance's men waited for supplies, General Young's column had practically reached the coast at San Fabian where General Lloyd Wheaton had landed days earlier. Wheaton had only to move a short distance inland, occupy a string of towns, and there was a good chance Aguinaldo would be caught in the three-way pincer. But, for reasons still debated, Wheaton did not seem to understand the mission. The end result was that Aguinaldo and his small entourage managed to slip through the space Wheaton had failed to occupy, then move up the coast with Young's men and an army battalion only several hours behind them. Had Aguinaldo been captured, in all likelihood the war would have been over.[6]

What followed—the escape of Aguinaldo into the mountains—is one of the central episodes in Philippine history. At Tirad Pass, the young General Gregorio del Pilar, with sixty men, held off the Americans for five hours in what has been called the "Philippine Thermopylae." Fifty-one men, including the twenty-four-year-old "boy-general" Gregorio del Pilar, gave their lives to allow their president's escape.

Over the next eight months, Aguinaldo and his escort of twelve officers and 127 men wandered through the rugged mountains of northern Luzon. Densely forested and populated almost solely by mountain tribes—Kalinga, Igorrotes, and others—who lived apart from the hispanicized lowland *indio*, the mountain jungles were both refuge and source of endless hardship for the small party. Eventually, they crossed the Cagayan Valley and traversed the Sierra Madre to the east coast. There, in September 1900, Aguinaldo established his headquarters at Palanan, a remote coastal village in Isabella Province.[7]

From his hideout, the president continued to issue directives; but from the time of his escape into the mountains, he was more important as a symbol of the revolution than as a strategic commander. The irony at the heart of Aguinaldo's presidency was that while revered by the masses, their affection was anything but reciprocated. During a respite in their long ordeal in the mountains, Aguinaldo and his closest followers dreamed of life after a victorious revolution, of a long sojourn in Europe with one million pesos to ensure they would travel in style. They would retire to connecting haciendas over a vast swath of Nueva Ecija. He even promised to bestow titles of nobility on them. It was an oligarchy he had in mind and, unlike Mabini, Aguinaldo seemed incapable of imagining anything else.[8]

As for the former prime minister, Apolinario Mabini had settled for a time in the small town of Rosales in Pangasinan. There he had continued to write essays reflecting upon the revolution, including an open letter "to the People of the United States," which would be published in the January 1900 issue of the *North American Review*. His eloquent defense of the Filipino position would be widely read among intellectual circles in the states. Despite being a civilian and noncombatant (unless one thinks of words as weapons), Mabini remained a wanted man. As the Americans advanced northward in November, he set off in a hopeless attempt at escape, conveyed by hammock and bull cart. At Cuyapo in Nueva Ecija, the Americans caught up with his straggling entourage. The *New York Times* reported on his capture: "The members of the Philippine Commission here declare that Mabini was the head and front of the insurrection. Aguinaldo, they say, is only a figurehead, but Mabini was the brains and directing power behind him. He is an old man and a paralytic, but of extraordinary ability, and his counsels have always been conclusive with the insurgents."[9]

Mabini, hardly an old man at thirty-five, was imprisoned at Fort Santiago, Manila, where, much to the annoyance of the military governor Elwell Otis, he continued to write his provocative essays. For Otis, the debate was over. The Army of Liberation had been crushed, its leader chased to the hills, "a fugitive and an outlaw." Only a mopping-up operation remained. "There will be no more fighting . . . little skirmishes which amount to nothing," he assured the administration in Washington. The other generals, save Lawton, agreed. "Claim to government by insurgents can be made no longer under any fiction," Otis cabled the secretary of war. "Generals and troops are in small bands . . . acting as banditti, or dispersed and playing the role of amigos with arms concealed."[10]

Otis was not entirely mistaken in his assessment. A tradition of banditry had been deeply rooted in the countryside, never successfully suppressed by the Spanish. *Tulisanes* or *ladrones*, as the bandits were variously called, were often those who had rejected the authority of the church and retreated to the more remote regions. These peasants, who had also wearied of the oppression of the *hacenderos*, were called *remontados*; some sought merely to "flee the bells" and live in unmolested solitude; others resorted to banditry. David R. Sturtevant described the changing nature of this phenomenon in the late nineteenth century: "Rural crime began to take on class connotations. Rustlers, highwaymen, extortionists, and cutthroats preyed increasingly upon estate owners, lawyers, usurers, Friars, and itinerant Chinese merchants—all the emerging enemies, in short, of the troubled peasantry."[11]

While many of these traditional bandits would join the revolutionaries, others would not, leaving the countryside overrun with both guerrilla and outlaw bands. It was not always clear where one began and the other left off and provided the Americans a convenient rationale for attributing all resistance to brigandage.

Adding greatly to the confusion were the various quasi-religious cults that had flourished during the years of revolution and economic privation. Having turned away from the church after decades of oppression, many *indios* did not see their salvation in the ilustrado-led revolution whose civil administrators and military leaders had proven as corrupt and abusive as the Spanish. In many cases the beleaguered peasantry turned to charismatic leaders, faith healers, self-proclaimed "popes" and "messiahs" with promises of a divine intercession that would bring a new age of justice and prosperity. In Pangasinan, the Guardia de Honor was led by a faith healer known as Apo Laqui and his lieutenant Valdez. With forty thousand devotees, the Guardia de Honor controlled the barrios while Aguinaldo's administration had never extended control beyond the towns. According to Sturtevant, the Guardia de Honor and other movements such as Cruz na Bituin and the Santa Iglesia were "equally hostile to hacenderos, Spaniards, Filipino revolutionaries, and Americans."[12]

On the northwest coast of Luzon, in the Ilocano provinces, General Manuel Tinio would lead a guerrilla resistance so determined that the Americans would

only overcome it by implementing a program of extreme brutality, a campaign
levelled against the entire population. Manuel Tinio was only twenty-two, the
youngest general in Aguinaldo's army. His family, Chinese mestizos, was
among the most prominent of the hacenderos in Nueva Ecija. When Aguinaldo
returned with Dewey in May 1898, the president had directed Tinio to raise
several companies in Nueva Ecija and travel north to attack the Spanish garrisons in the Ilocano provinces. After the Spanish had been vanquished in short
order, Tinio had remained as military commander of the Ilocos region and was
still there when Aguinaldo and his dwindling escort made their narrow escape
into the Cordillera Central. Manuel Tinio remained in the Ilocos and left the
job of overseeing the resistance in Nueva Ecija to lesser figures, which, in effect,
created a leadership vacuum that would not be filled for a fateful six months.[13]

Pantaleon Garcia may have been a successful military leader in the revolution against the Spanish, but, as the new politico-commander of central Luzon,
the ailing general seems to have lost heart from the beginning. Perhaps the demoralization that followed the thrashing at the hands of Lawton's expedition
had been too much for him. With his forces in disarray, Garcia called a halt to
the fighting while the scattered fighters could recuperate and a command struc-
ture be reorganized.[14]

If the Filipinos had done little damage to the enemy on the battlefield, they
had suffered tremendous losses themselves—in irreplaceable fighters, weaponry,
and ammunition. Future revolutionaries, in China, in Cuba, in Vietnam and
elsewhere, would take careful note. Guerrilla war first, conventional war only
when the imperial power had been sufficiently weakened thus became the first
axiom of revolutionary military doctrine. Aguinaldo and his generals had gotten
it all wrong.

With Aguinaldo's Army of the Republic no longer an organized force, Lawton
wired Otis for permission to turn his attention to the provinces south of Manila
that had been neglected during the fall campaign. The *poblacion* of San Mateo,
only eighteen miles to the northeast of Manila, had remained under Filipino
control throughout the ten months of fighting. Along with the hill town of
Montalban, San Mateo provided a buffer zone that allowed the flow of "insurgent" troops from the provinces of Morong and Bulacan to the provinces
south of the Laguna de Bay. Otis determined that before an expedition could
be mounted against the southern provinces, San Mateo should be garrisoned
and this northern conduit closed off. A relatively minor operation, historians
have puzzled over Henry Lawton's decision to take charge of what Leon Wolff
called "little more than a scout in force."[15]

It seems the soldiers under General Licerio Geronimo had been receiving instructions in marksmanship from a British soldier of fortune. Correspondent William Dinwiddie accompanied Lawton and reported on the action in *Harper's*. When the Americans were thrown back after their initial carefully constructed assault on the Filipino trenches, Lawton came to the line to urge them on. Geronimo caught sight of Lawton in his yellow slicker and white pith helmet far across the flooded rice fields. "General, I believe they are shooting at you," one of Lawton's aides said. "He laughed slightly, more a grim smile." When Lawton's closest aide was struck, the general helped carry him to the rear but then returned. Again he was persuaded to take cover and began trudging across the rain-swept field. Seconds later Lawton was shot through the lungs, collapsed in the arms of his aides, and died after muttering only a few words.[16]

The irony was lost on no one: the man who had run the Apache chief Geronimo to ground twelve years earlier was killed by the *tiradores de muertos*— the death-shooters—of another Geronimo. According to Stuart Miller, "the name of David Fagen, 'a black renegade from the Colored 24th Infantry,' was frequently bandied about as a convenient scapegoat for every American setback, from Lawton's death to the Balangiga massacre." Fagen, a deserter of four weeks, had nothing to do with either "setback," but being associated with both events is indicative of the prominence he would take in the popular imagination.[17]

The effectiveness of Geronimo's marksmen demonstrated the difference the accurate use of the Army of Liberation's Mausers and Remingtons might have made in the conflict with the Americans. Lawton's insistence upon wandering around in full view of the enemy—and in a yellow slicker, no less—was all but standard practice among the American officers, both in Cuba and the Philippines. In the light of a century of high-tech weaponry and overwhelming firepower, gestures intended as gallant and contemptuous of the enemy seem oddly quaint. From the Filipino perspective, the general had received his proper comeuppance. Had Lawton left the minor expedition to San Mateo to his junior officers, he would soon have replaced Otis as military governor and left his own strategic imprint upon the conduct of the war. Unlike Otis, Lawton was popular with the troops, and his loss came as a heavy blow, not only to them but to many in Washington and throughout the country. The long journey of his casket from Manila to Washington was attended at every stage by tremendous pomp and a genuine outpouring of grief.

On Henry Lawton's last night in Manila, *Harper's* correspondent William Dinwiddie told the general that in the opinion of Otis and his staff, the end of the conflict was near. Asked if he shared that view, Lawton said, "The fact is, I do not know whether this insurrection is over or just begun." Weeks earlier he had been reported as saying one hundred thousand men would be required to bring the islands under control. The War Department was not pleased with these kinds of "alarmist" pronouncements, and Otis was furious with him "for making incautious utterances."[18]

But Lawton was nearly right; at its peek seventy thousand men would need to staff more than five hundred garrisons in order to suppress an ongoing revolution begun against Spain and continued against the United States. Though mauled and poorly led, and having suffered irreplaceable losses of men and matériel—the Filipinos were far from done fighting.

————

Despite the unfortunate reality, Aguinaldo remained a beacon of hope as the shattered remnants of his army returned to their provinces. If many simply wanted to return home and pick up the pieces of their ravaged lives under a new master—some even welcoming the Americans—there were many others prepared to continue the struggle, now employing tactics more conducive to their disadvantaged circumstances.

Aguinaldo had issued detailed instructions for conducting a guerrilla war and regional leaders took to the new regime readily. Each province would maintain only five hundred active guerrillas with militiamen on call in the towns. The villagers and townspeople would supply the guerrillas, house them, care for the wounded, and operate as spies to keep them informed of the enemy's movements. Already, in the first weeks of December, bands of guerrillas had ambushed American patrols between Arayat and Cabiao; one patrol had been captured and another had gone missing. In Tarlac and Pampanga "reports of ambuscades and skirmishes came from every section of the country along the railroad. These districts seemed to be filled with small bands. Not only were stray parties of Americans cut off, but a number of the native officials who had shown a friendly disposition toward our troops were murdered."[19]

Guerrilla attacks and reprisals against collaborators—*americanistas*—would characterize this new phase of the war. The Americans would answer with their own kind of reprisals: burning villages, destroying crops and livestock, using the water cure and other tortures to gain information, while simultaneously implementing a policy of attraction—building roads, bridges, more than one thousand schools, and establishing local governments—that is, in the words of journalist John Bass, conducting both "a harsh and philanthropic war" at the same time. In more than 10 percent of the Philippines there would be no fighting at all; in the more cooperative regions the emphasis would be on the carrot, and in the more recalcitrant provinces the response would be an increasingly severe application of the stick. If the Filipinos were ultimately subdued, it was under conditions of such duress that they were left with a stark choice: submit or die.[20]

There are only two accounts of Fagen's activities during his first six months with the guerrillas—one whimsical, the other stark in the extreme. The latter was recounted by General Jose Alejandrino in *La Senda del Sacrificio*, published in 1933 (translated in 1949 as *The Price of Freedom: Episodes and Anecdotes of Our Struggles for Freedom*). Alejandrino, who succeeded Pantaleon Garcia as commander of central Luzon, did not meet Fagen until the spring of 1901. His description of an incident involving Fagen—purported to have taken place more than a year before the two men first met—is all the more disturbing in that it is related in some detail.

> I had heard narrations of the feats of valor and the intrepidity of Fagan, but his most outstanding characteristic was his mortal hatred of the American whites. At the beginning, when our men did not know him yet very well, he asked them for the custody of several American white prisoners. Naturally, not knowing his intentions, they acceded to his petition. But later on he reported to them that, because they were intending to escape, he was forced to kill them all. He was subjected to an investigation, but inasmuch as there were no witnesses of his act, they had to acquit him. From then on they never permitted him to approach the prisoners, and some white deserters who were with Lacuna were warned to be careful when alone with Fagan.[21]

There are no corroborating references to this incident, and there is ample evidence to contradict Alejandrino's statement regarding threats to prisoners, many of whom were under Fagen's protection for weeks at a time. Also, if Fagen bore a general animosity toward whites, there was at least one remarkable exception. An act of cold-blooded murder would be out of character with everything else known about Fagen.

Alejandrino only first met Fagen more than a year after this act purportedly occurred; he would have learned of it secondhand and he may even have been misinformed. Although he would not have made up such a story wholecloth, it would have been helpful had he given us more of the particulars. During the first week of January 1900, five American prisoners on Mount Arayat were shot and boloed as the African American Twenty-Fifth Infantry fought their way up the slopes toward the guerrilla encampment. Two of the Americans survived, despite each man having been shot twice and hacked with bolos, a long machete-like knife, and in the subsequent trial of General Aquino, charged with giving the order to execute the prisoners, there is no mention of Fagen. Aquino was convicted and sentenced to hang, but the sentence was later commuted to life in prison, and in 1904 he was released from prison, the last guerrilla officer amnestied by President Roosevelt.[22]

On December 3, Colonel Kobbé in San Isidro cabled General Schwan, the chief of staff in Manila: "Pantaleon Garcia is undoubtedly at Papaya beyond Peñaranda—directing men to harass patrols & outposts. Small patrols from Arayat toward Cabiao were attacked today, and the patrol from Cabiao to Arayat has not returned at the usual hour." The following day, Kobbé sent another dispatch to Schwan: "I can see no utility in small patrols between garrisons over same routes at stated hours. They become careless with immunity from attack, cannot reconnoiter away from roads, while insurgents can concentrate, or let them pass, or gather them in. The six prisoners at Papaya [a patrol] are now being guarded with guns taken from them." Presumably this is the same patrol that had not returned the previous day. I found no further reference to these men, and they were probably released, or could "several" of them have been the men Alejandrino was referring to? They were in the same camp together with Fagen, but that is all we know.[23]

Adding to the mystery surrounding Alejandrino's account is a telegram from Funston to MacArthur, on February 12, 1900, reporting on the capture of several of Padilla's men by Captain Cushman Rice, Thirty-Fourth U.S.V.: "Captured prisoners state they saw Captain Padilla with his own hand shoot 2 white American prisoners. They showed Rice graves." Padilla denied having given the order for the killing and was acquited after a trial in early 1902. Who these Americans were is not clear, but Fagen and Padilla were together at the time when the crime purportedly took place. Is it possible that both men were involved in the killing of American prisoners? Or could Fagen have been blamed for an act committed by Padilla?[24]

If Fagen in fact committed this act in the premeditated manner described by Alejandrino, one can imagine any number of scenarios, including the possibility that several white prisoners provoked him in some way, perhaps addressing him in racist terms. No longer subject to enforced subservience, still seething with rage, the slightest hint of racist insult from white prisoners might have set him off. And because neither Fagen nor anyone else elaborated further on Alejandrino's account, this potentially seminal event in his life will remain shrouded in mystery.

By the early months of 1900, about 150 Americans had been captured or gone missing. According to General Otis's report, "Many of those captured suffered severely . . . and a few were brutally slain by their captors." While most were recaptured or released, some were never accounted for, leaving a number of potential candidates to run afoul of a young man burning with a pent-up rage.[25]

If Alejandrino's account—true or apocryphal—is suggestive of Fagen the badman, another story from the time of censorship reveals a much lighter side.

Billets-doux

17

At one time Sgt. Walter Cox, Twenty-second Infantry, and Fagin stood up at a distance of less than 50 yards and emptied their magazines at each other. Neither was hurt.

Iola Daily Register,
April 23, 1902

IN HIS AUTOBIOGRAPHY *Memories of Two Wars*, published in 1911, Frederick Funston described the two letters he received from Fagen as "impudent and badly spelled." Noted for his quick temper, Funston may have tossed the letters into a waste basket—if he hadn't wadded them up and hurled them—for there is no sign of them in his papers at the Funston Library in Topeka, Kansas. Other sources refer to letters written by Fagen to the men of his old outfit and to the regiment, calling for them to join him, and to threatening letters to two officers. If any of these letters have survived, they are waiting to be discovered.[1]

Fortunately, an unattributed story from the *New York Herald*, picked up by the *Washington Post* and published on March 17, 1912, provides examples of what may be all we will ever know of the letters. Like Rowland Thomas's *Fagan*, published in *Collier's Weekly* in 1904, "The Charmed Class Ring" is written as a fable, the character of Fagen more fanciful than real. But even with its tone of a medieval morality tale, the story reveals the fascination the figure of Fagen held for the public during those early years after the war. Were the story not framed around an actual visit with Captain James Alfred Moss, the letters would be dismissed as fabrications. The author begins

123

THE CHARMED CLASS RING

Important Part It Played during the Insurrection of the Natives in the Philippines

In the office of Major General Leonard Wood, Chief of Staff of the Army Captain Matthew E. Hanna has quite recently been relieved by Captain James A. Moss of the Twenty-fourth Infantry. Captain Moss is a man of athletic build, excellent address, and striking appearance. As he sits at his desk opposite Major John Hapgood he is frequently interrupted by brother officers who drop in to congratulate him for his present position in the Chief of Staff's office is one of the choice assignments in the army.

A brother officer from the Philippines for example pushes open the door of Room 222 at the War Department and slaps Captain Moss on the back with a show of admiration and affection.

"Congratulations old scout! This is better than the job Fagan promised you, hey?"

"Which one? He promised me several."

"Oh, yes, I remember he had his eye on you," replies the officer. "By the way did Alstaetter ever get his ring?"

He doubtless remembers the weird mysterious messages from the negro American. Fagan, who after deserting from his company, vowed he would make him his valet or give him a job where an American army officer could feel the effects of his own discipline. He doubtless remembers the shots that rang out unexpectedly from the bushes and underbrush that promised him a job in another world. Certainly the part Lieutenant Alstaetter's charmed class ring played in those adventuresome days has never been forgotten.

Captain Moss had Fagan as a private in his company on the isle of Luzon in the Philippines in the days when General Lawton was last advancing north in October 1899.

Military discipline, rigid and severe, caused Fagan to be brought before Captain Moss more than once and each time the negro seemed to feel that his punishment could only be satisfied by vengeance. So that when he finally deserted and disappeared word was quickly passed around that trouble might be expected.

Before long things started to happen around camp to make the Americans worry. Mysterious shots seemed to come from nowhere among the underbrush and bushes and the activity of the Philippine insurrectos greatly increased.

Then one day a group of Americans stumbled upon a dense under-brush that fairly bristled with rifle shots and caused them to seek shelter for their lives. They quickly rallied and sent shots pouring into the clump of underbrush.

Ordinarily a few well-directed shots would scare the ambuscaders away but not this time. The bushes returned the fire as steadily as it came.

Suddenly there arose from the bushes the figure of a tall negro. He bowed as if to begin a speech and waving his hat called out:

"We're off for the day, boys! Ammunition gone! No use peppering away at me like that. You can't hit me! I bear a charmed life!"

With another bow Fagan dropped into the bushes and disappeared. With him vanished his band of insurgent followers.

The news that Fagan was at the head of a band of insurrectos spread like wildfire through the American ranks. Bring him back to his company dead or alive was the watchword. But it was soon apparent that the task was to be no easy one. Fagan, although he lurked about the camp could not be found. At the end of a day's hunt for him he would make known his unwelcome presence by sending what he called a billet-doux to Captain Moss.

"Have decided to make you my valet," came one message. "Need a good valet so will get you before long."

These messages continued to come to Captain Moss at intervals appearing at places they could be easily delivered.

"Wanted—a private in my company to command like you com-manded me. Moss please apply," came another message while shortly afterward the Americans picked up this communication:

"Got to get somebody soon now. Be careful."

The American officers, eager to get a chance at Fagan, redoubled their efforts and gave him every opportunity of "getting some one" if he so desired. But meantime there happened something which bore out Fagan's prediction and sent a thrill of terror through the ranks.[2]

The author of this fable did not meet Lieutenant Frederick Alstaetter or interview him for the story. But he did interview James Alfred Moss, and it appears that Moss shared with him the content of the letters, if not word for word, then certainly the tone of them. Brief as they are, Moss may have quoted them verbatim.

The *Salt Lake (UT) Herald* on October 30, 1900, reported that Fagen "would take every occasion to send threatening messages to the men of the regiment he had deserted." And an article in the *Manila Freedom* on May 12, 1901, noted that Fagen "especially delighted in harassing his old company and regiment, often sent insulting messages to the officers."

Captain Moss left no doubt that he was the primary recipient of these letters. Second Lieutenant Charles E. Hay Jr. would have been the other most likely recipient, but it may have been someone else.

These "love letters," as the author claimed Fagen called them, reveal a subtle sense of humor—playful and menacing at the same time. Fagen wanted to rattle Moss's nerves, as if toying with the lieutenant before the promised hour of reckoning. Did he have Moss looking over his shoulder? Did he disturb his sleep? Moss does not say, but certainly Fagen seems to have enjoyed crafting his "promissory notes."

Funston's description of the letters sent to him as "impudent and badly spelled" suggests they were of a similar tone as those delivered to Moss. In that these "letters" consisted of no more than one or two lines, it is not out of the question that Fagen could have penned them himself. The bad spelling would be in keeping with someone barely able to read or write.

All of this is suggestive of the trickster. Fagen fought with an acid wit as well as with a rifle. He taunted his opponents, he insulted them, he dared them to come out and get him; he even challenged General Funston to a duel. If Funston's reaction is any indication, the colonial authorities found such impudence intolerable, and their desperation to kill him attests to the challenge he posed to the U.S. colonial authority. The leadership in Manila did not, I believe, see Fagen as merely a rogue soldier but as an African American whose rebellion had far-reaching political implications. A peasant-led revolution joined with highly trained black soldiers in revolt seemed a very real possibility.

Did Fagen linger around I Company's station at Aliaga and take the occasional potshot at James Alfred Moss? The guerrillas frequently sniped at American patrols and at night fired into the garrisoned towns, hitting the unlucky villager more often than the soldier on outpost. The first significant ambush of a patrol from the Twenty-Fourth Infantry occurred on December 28, 1899. Five men from Company G were sent as escort for a sergeant from the Signal Corps, and as they trudged along the Talavera Road a small guerrilla band opened up on them. The sergeant and two of the privates managed to escape. Of the other three privates, one was killed and two taken captive, John Quarles and Edward Sanders.[3]

The earliest mention of Fagen after his desertion is in a report by Major Joseph E. Wheeler Jr. on March 20, 1900, which places Fagen and the two prisoners with Colonel Pablo Padilla in the foothills east of Peñaranda, supporting the claim that he had gone in that direction in the first place. "Three

American negroes are with Padilla," Wheeler reported, "one named Davis [*sic*], is a traitor. Others are prisoners. One is named Edward Landers [*sic*]." Fagen was initially called David by the guerrillas and in two following reports Wheeler referred to him as the "Afro-American traitor called David." (A week before Wheeler filed the report, he and a column of riders were ambushed near Peñaranda; Wheeler's horse was struck and Dr. Chidester shot in the back. There is no evidence that Fagen was involved, but Wheeler's report indicates that he was in the area.)[4]

John Quarles and Edward Sanders would not be released for six months and from a camp where Fagen was known to be at the time. If Fagen did not lead the ambush in which they were captured, he spent a good deal of time with them and undoubtedly tried to persuade them to join the guerrillas, an offer they apparently declined.[5]

Moss only participated in one recorded action, a minor affair that took place February 18 near Buloc. The company had been transferred to San Jose well to the northeast of Arayat, and soon Moss was on his way to Tayug, even farther north in Pangasinan. He had been appointed as regimental commissary, and his scouting and fighting days were largely over. If Fagen were going to send letters to Moss and take potshots at him, these actions would probably have taken place in the first three months of 1900, a time when Fagen's activities went without mention.[6]

I Company was left with Second Lieutenant Charles E. Hay Jr. in command of 110 black soldiers.

In the grainy black-and-white photographs of the campaign, the impression is of a drab and colorless landscape. In reality, the fields were of the most vibrant green; buri palms and bamboos grew along the watercourses; coconut palms, banana trees, guava and tamarind, mangos and flowering poincianas shaded the *sitios* and *rancherias*. There remained unsettled areas of acacia-dotted grass-lands and corridors of forest where the *tao*—the peasant farmer—could gather firewood, hunt, and fish. Besides deer, wild boar, and the *timarau*—the smaller and extremely dangerous wild carabao—there were crocodiles, poisonous snakes, pythons, monkeys, fruit bats, and a colorful assortment of tropical birds.

And to the east the rugged chain of the Sierra Madre ran the full length of Nueva Ecija. There, at the higher elevations, hardwoods such as yellow narra and molave, kapok and dalipawen, luaun and banaba, grew in lush abundance. The Spanish had identified twelve hundred species of trees in the islands; over the ensuing decade American scientists would identify another thirteen hundred varieties, as well as nine thousand flowering plants. (The landscape of Nueva Ecija, formerly a region of forest, savannah, swamp, and

Barrio in Nueva Ecija (José de Olivares, *Our Islands and Their People as Seen with Camera and Pencil* [1899])

lake, has been radically altered since 1900. Benedict Kerkvliet reports that from 1900 to 1940, two hundred thousand hectares of forest and savannah were cleared for rice farming.)[7]

This was the varied landscape where the men of the Twenty-Fourth Infantry settled into what would be their routine for the next year and a half: patrolling the surrounding countryside, escorting supply trains, guarding construction crews, establishing a civil government, and succeeding far better than their white counterparts as goodwill ambassadors to the Filipinos who, having been pummeled into at least the appearance of submission, were now to be benevolently assimilated.

This was something new for the American military. After vanquishing the Filipinos in battle, they were then to induce them to accept Americans as their new colonial overseers. This new pacification project wasn't proving a simple matter, especially in Nueva Ecija. The military governor Elwell Otis cast about for an enterprising officer to bring order to this decidedly unruly region. With the recommendation of Arthur MacArthur, Otis found his man.

At the end of December 1899, General Frederick Funston arrived by train at Calumpit from Manila. With him was his aide, Lieutenant Burton

Mitchell—who also happened to be his first cousin—and his acting adjutant, Captain Erneste V. Smith. The three officers mounted native ponies and set off on the two-day ride to their new station of San Isidro. "I thought the insurrection could not last many months longer," Funston wrote years later. But that was not to be the case.[8]

The previous September, Frederick Funston and his Kansas Volunteers had sailed home to a hero's welcome in San Francisco. As was invariably the case with Funston, wherever acclamation went, controversy was not far behind. Shortly after his return, he made a speech at Stanford University where he criticized the friars in the Philippines as "a brutal and licentious lot" and attributed much of the travail of the Filipino peasantry to the friars. A few days later, an article appeared in the *San Francisco Call* in which a former civilian teamster of the Kansas regiment by the name of Thomas Fox accused the general of having taken part in the looting of the Catholic Church in Caloocan. Funston, Mr. Fox claimed, had paraded about in a priest's robe, conducting a mock mass for the amusement of his men, and afterward sent the robe as well as two "magnificent chalices" home to Mrs. Funston. "According to Mr. Fox, it was a common sight to see soldiers carrying away from churches rich vestments, crucifixes, statues, and altar ornaments." When an archbishop in Minneapolis repeated the accusation, Funston retained a law firm from Topeka to take legal action. "The story about my looting a church is a brutal and stupid lie," Funston charged in his usual full-throated counterattack. Fox was nothing but "a worthless camp follower." He attributed this slander to Catholic resentment over his speech at Stanford and said it was nothing more than an attempt to discredit him. He had left the church's treasury locked in a storage room, he insisted, and Chinese looters had broken in and made off with the valuables.[9]

This controversy was still raging when Funston and his volunteers arrived in Topeka. One hundred thousand people gave their native sons a clamorous welcome in a parade that stretched for two miles. Thirty brass bands and various civic organizations took part, and the cheering never stopped until Funston was presented with "a handsome sword" on the steps of the statehouse. He had already been informed that Otis desired his return to the islands; in his brief speech to the gathered throng, Funston proclaimed loudly, "I shall return to the Philippines and remain there until the insurrection is quelled. I predict that within a year the Philippines will be as peaceful as Massachusetts."[10]

After a ten-day visit with his parents in Iola, Funston set off on the return voyage, and by January 1, 1900, he was settled into a wealthy planter's home just off the square in San Isidro. Funston's wife, Eda, would soon join him and she would occasionally write colorful accounts of the quaint and rustic life at an outpost. Ants were everywhere and could be deterred only by islanding the feet of the beds, the table legs, the ice-chest and sideboard, in cups of kerosene; in the rainy season, huge cockroaches, mosquitoes, and flying insects abounded, and a green mold grew everywhere. But servants polished the teak floors and luaun tables, did the laundry, and maintained the grounds; Funston's collection of war trophies adorned the walls; wicker furniture and mosquito bars over the beds provided an atmosphere of tropical elegance to counter the unavoidable discomforts.

"The condition of the country seemed perfectly normal," Frederick Funston wrote years later, "the towns being full of people and the usual work going on in the fields. And yet there was a nasty little war going on all of the time. It certainly was an odd state of affairs."[11]

General Pantaleon Garcia, politico-military commander of central Luzon, had become too ill to direct guerrilla activities, and Pablo Padilla seemed incapable of exercising any meaningful authority over his roving guerrilla bands. Each party seemed to operate largely on its own, and along with the bands of ladrones (Americanization of the Spanish *ladrón*) they had made venturing into the countryside dangerous in the extreme. "Small travelling parties are attacked," the *Times* reported. "Single travelers frequently disappear or are found dead." Traders on the roads and on the rivers were subjected to taxes repeatedly along the way, so that by the time they arrived in San Isidro they had been fleeced of almost the entire value of their goods. Guerrillas seized carriages and bull carts on the road between San Miguel and Gapan while merchants to the north had become too afraid to travel on the river.[12]

More than anything, local guerrilla chiefs were determined to impress upon the populace the necessity of remaining loyal to the revolution. The *Manila Times* reported that eight women bringing bananas to trade with the Americans were beheaded, their bodies left on the road to Peñaranda as a warning to others who might be tempted to engage in commerce with the invaders. In nearby Papaya, guerrillas under the order of Padilla murdered a Spanish farm manager, his wife, and five children. The *Manila Times* reported these "savage acts of Aguinaldo's rabble" in lurid detail: "The surrounding country of San Isidro is alive with armed bands who claim to be insurgents and no doubt were once, but are now nothing but ladrones. They are always found unarmed except when not wanted, and travelling is not permitted outside San Isidro without an armed escort."[13]

The articles in the *Manila Times*, whether true or fictions planted by Otis's propaganda machine, would have the reader believe that the entire populace of Nueva Ecija favored the Americans, and support for the revolutionaries was maintained only by coercion. While there is no doubt of an active campaign against *americanistas*, determining the true disposition of the majority of Novo

Ecijanos toward the revolution remains a matter of speculation. Peasants did not write memoirs or keep diaries, nor did journalists go into the field, conduct polls, or ask their opinion on the matter. It is clear that the revolutionaries did not enjoy the near universal support that other guerrilla leaders did in the more ethnically monolithic regions of southern Luzon or the Ilocano provinces. The population of Nueva Ecija was a blend of Tagalog and Kapampangan in the south, and immigrant Ilocanos and Pangasinenses in the north. The Ilocanos had become alienated from the Tagalog-led Republic after the assassination of General Luna, an Ilocano, leaving their support for the revolutionaries mixed at best. In the south there was no love between the Kapampangans and Tagalogs. And among the peasantry in general there was a widespread disaffection with the elitist policies of Aguinaldo's government (by which the only land reform amounted to transferring the lands of the friars to the *hacenderos*). And if most of the guerrilla officers were members of the provincial elite, there were many other influential citizens who sensed their best interests lay in siding, however discreetly, with the Americans.[14]

Consequently, instead of a unified opposition, the resistance in Nueva Ecija was a chaotic affair with many guerrillas fighting at the behest of their hacendero and inquilino landlord, others out of genuine loyalty to Aguinaldo and the Republic, and still others simply opportunistic ladrones plying their age-old calling. Degrees of collaboration and resistance were so nuanced that loyalties could only be determined, in the words of Brian Linn, "on a case-by-case basis." With these divisions, along with the recruitment of Macabebe and Ilocano mercenaries, the resistance in Nueva Ecija was particularly susceptible to the classic colonial divide-and-rule strategy.[15]

Frederick Funston had 2,400 men to occupy an area that included all of Nueva Ecija and parts of Pampanga and Pangasinan. Two battalions of the Twenty-Fourth Infantry occupied garrisons in the northern half of Nueva Ecija along with companies from the Thirty-Fourth Volunteer Infantry. There, Colonel Lyman V. W. Kennon had begun organizing a company of Ilocano scouts. In the south of the province the vaunted Twenty-Second Infantry as well as companies of the Thirty-Fourth Volunteer Infantry and a single troop of the Fourth Cavalry manned the garrisons. Perhaps the most useful contingent at Funston's disposal was a battalion of Macabebes called Squadron Philippine Cavalry although, as Funston put it, none was ever seen on a horse. Major Matthew Batson, with a specially designed boot for his injured foot (shuttered by a spent ball during the northern campaign), would rejoin them in May.[16]

While Funston expressed every confidence in the men of the various regiments under his command, it seems he had already envisioned a small ancillary force to travel with him as both bodyguard and rapid response unit. He wanted only the best horsemen for the job, men who were dead shots with a rifle and could handle a revolver in close quarters. Upon arriving in San Isidro, he immediately set about assembling this small collection of cowboys and former Rough Riders that he called Headquarters Scouts. They were culled by reputation from the various regiments under his command. There were eventually twenty-five of these men and not more than twenty at any one time. The first man ordered to report to San Isidro was a nineteen-year-old private from Tucson, Arizona: John W. "Jack" Ganzhorn.

As a young ranch hand, Ganzhorn practiced "the draw-and-shoot" with a single action Colt's .44 and was able to get his first shot off in one-quarter of a second. The practice turned out to be time well spent, for Jack Ganzhorn seemed to find himself in one desperate situation after another. As Headquarters Scout, later as monte dealer and guard in Sonoran mining camps, as Arizona Ranger and railroad secret agent he would, by his count, kill forty or forty-two men "only counting six-shooter fights." Years later he would display his riding skills and play the villain in eight silent movies, characters such as Breed Artwell in *The Apache Raider*, Blackie Wells in *Thorobred*, and Frenchy Durant in *The Valley of Hunted Men*. At last, Ganzhorn settled down in Los Angeles to hone his writing skills; he wanted to tell his amazing story. In 1940 his autobiography, with the perhaps unfortunate but accurate title *I've Killed Men*, was published by Robert Hale, Ltd., in London. One of the men Ganzhorn tangled with, but could not kill, was David Fagen. Jack Ganzhorn's autobiography is one of the more important sources of information about Fagen.[17]

With his scouts riding alongside wherever he went, Frederick Funston set about visiting his fifteen scattered garrisons and getting acquainted with his district. The town of Gapan, only three miles east of San Isidro, had yet to be occupied by the Americans and was considered a hotbed of guerrilla activity. Funston had the town surrounded before dawn by eight hundred men who, at first light, set about searching for any sign of "insurgent" activity. According to Funston, "not a house, stable, out-house, well, or even a single room escaped" careful scrutiny. Captured correspondence identified a number of men as insurgent officers; these men were sent under guard to Manila and a company of the Thirty-Fourth Infantry took up residence in Gapan. In this manner, Funston began to take charge in Nueva Ecija.[18]

Pantaleon Garcia and Pablo Padilla had proved incompetent at the business of guerrilla warfare, making Frederick Funston's job much easier. They had squandered the time before Funston's arrival to prepare for a guerrilla war, failing to set up shadow governments in the towns, to form militias, to build supply networks and secret storehouses—in short, to create a guerrilla infrastructure. Pablo Padilla had proved incapable of controlling his guerrilla

bands and their brutal attempts at ensuring universal support through intimidation were counterproductive. From the numbers of the disaffected, Funston
was able to engage spies and build a highly effective spy network. And when
that failed, there was always the use of the water cure to persuade the uncooperative peasant to talk.

At first the Macabebes administered the age-old torture called *timbain*, but soon
enough the Americans got the hang of it. A returning soldier from the Thirty-
Fifth United States Volunteers, John P. Monahan, described the water cure to
his hometown newspaper in Wadesboro, North Carolina.

> I had taken part in so many cases of administering the "water cure"
> that I ceased to pay any attention to them. Everybody did it. Some-
> times one jugful was enough and the victim would tell where the rifles
> and ammunition were hidden. But most of the time it would take three
> jugfuls, and I have seen as many as five used. Then when we'd stand
> them up and if they would not talk one of the fellows would punch
> them in the jaw or the stomach.[19]

Private Edward H. Beal, also of the Thirty-Fifth United States Volunteers,
recounted that he had assisted in giving the cure "to 12 or 15 natives."

> A lieutenant detailed the detachment with which I was connected to
> give the natives the cure. It was our duty to capture a native non-
> combatant and throw him on his back, placing a short bamboo stick in
> his mouth. The stick kept his mouth wide open and then water would
> be poured on him, striking him on the nose and trickling into his
> mouth. Every time he breathed he would swallow and inhale water,
> thus filling his lungs and stomach. In September, at San Miguel de
> Mayumo, the provost marshal inflicted this torture on a 10-year-old
> Filipino boy whose father was a paymaster in the native army. Lieut.
> Hughes first beat the boy in the face until the blood spurted from his
> nose. Then he directed that the water cure be administered, and four
> of us gave it to him. . . . There are few officers who have not dealt more
> or less cruelly with the natives.[20]

Understandably, the American military left mention of the water cure or
other abuses out of their reports, leaving historians to debate just how extensively
such harsh measures were employed. In the files one runs across suggestive
language, such as an instruction from Funston's adjutant to Major Wheeler,

March 16: "If possible, compel natives to guide you to the insurgent rendezvous in the mountains." Diaries are more explicit, such as an entry by a Private Edward E. Brown, Thirty-Fifth U.S.V.: "April 29 [1900] Had a half hours fight near Condaba [*sic*] captured 89 soldiers, guns and ammunition. Gave the prisoners the agua (water cure)." In a letter to his superior, a Captain Charles W. Wadsworth, Forty-First Infantry, complained about a night raid by "a detachment of American soldiers mounted" on a nearby barrio. The town headman, "as loyal and inoffensive citizen as can be found . . . was seized, bound and put through the usual 'water cure.'" The phrase—"the usual 'water cure'"—speaks volumes.[21]

The next town to be garrisoned was Peñaranda, five miles to the east of Gapan. From there and the other garrisoned towns, patrols searched the surrounding areas for guerrilla bands. But encounters were few, the result, in Funston's opinion, of "their habit of passing from the status of guerrilla soldiers to that of non-combatants." He also cited their "knowledge of the country, mobility, [and] their control over the population either through sympathy or fear."[22]

American patrols could not leave a garrison without spies warning of their departure through smoke signals, balloons sailed aloft, church bells, carabao horns, bamboo drums, and runners racing to spread the word. The Americans countered by leaving small detachments in hiding, waiting in ambush, while the main body of the patrol returned to its post. These ploys were rarely successful. "Many and many a swift night march was fruitless," Funston wrote, "as was many a well-laid plan to surprise the enemy, but we had occasional successes."[23]

In the view of Frederick Funston, that "the Filipinos forsook all civilized methods of fighting" justified implementation of equally severe measures in response. This aggressive approach served the general well in the first months of 1900 against a disorganized opposition. While Funston and his Scouts engaged in some dramatic shootouts with small bands of guerrillas—all described in thrilling detail in both his autobiography and in Ganzhorn's—the guerrillas were dealt the severest blow in late March when a force under Major Joseph E. Wheeler Jr., acting on a tip from a spy, caught a combined force of Padilla's guerrillas by surprise. The losses proved so demoralizing to the guerrillas that most of them hid their rifles and returned to their barrios.[24]

In April the War Department changed the organization of troops in the Philippines, dividing the islands into four departments—Department of Northern Luzon, Department of Southern Luzon, Department of the Visayas, and Department of Mindanao and Sulu. Each department was subdivided into districts and Funston's command, encompassing all of Nueva Ecija and the sparsely populated mountain province of Principe, became the Fourth District of the Department of Northern Luzon. A few weeks later Elwell Otis, the military governor, was relieved by Lieutenant General Arthur MacArthur, and General Lloyd Wheaton assumed command of the six districts of the Department of Northern Luzon.

In early May, a bedridden Pantaleon Garcia—in essence delivering himself up to the Americans—was discovered only a few miles from San Isidro. (Aguinaldo later ordered that if Garcia could be apprehended, he should be tried by court martial and shot.) Ten days later Colonel Pablo Padilla, much despised by the Americans for his purported cruelties, was captured along with another chief, Casamirio Tinio (brother of Manuel). The leadership in Nueva Ecija, such as it was, had been eviscerated. It seemed as if Funston had in very short order taken care of the guerrilla opposition in his district.[25]

But before long, with the arrival of Urbano Lacuna and David Fagen in Nueva Ecija, Frederick Funston would learn that his work had just begun.

The Death of Captain Godfrey

18

THE FIFTH DISTRICT of the Department of Northern Luzon bordered Funston's Fourth District on the south and was commanded by General Frederick Dent Grant, son of Ulysses S. Grant. Toward the end of May 1900, fighting along the border of these two generals' districts grew into a series of fierce exchanges between the guerrillas under Colonels Pablo and Simon Tecson, and Funston and Grant's troops.

In their autobiographies, both Funston and Ganzhorn describe the fireworks that took place in the mountains in lively detail, and from their accounts one would assume that Fagen hadn't been involved in the fighting or even been in the area. No one had ever placed Fagen in these engagements; yet, from my first reading of Ganzhorn and Funston's autobiographies, I could not shake the gut feeling that Fagen had been there. But for more than ten years, despite trying to discern Fagen's hand in the action, I could find no evidence to support my hunch. But then, on my third trip to the National Archives and with the advent of digitized newspapers, my suspicions were confirmed.

San Miguel de Mayumo was the northernmost town in Grant's district, just twenty miles south of San Isidro. On June 1, 1900, the *Manila Freedom* ran a front-page story describing a nighttime attack on the garrison at San Miguel. According to the report, five Americans were killed and seven wounded: "Hearing the bugles shrieking the 'call to arms,' each man grabbed his rifle and cartridge belt and rushed out doors. . . . The rebels seemed to be everywhere, yelling and shouting. It was a case of every man for himself. A hand-to-hand encounter ensued, and pandemonium reined in the little barrio."[1]

The *Freedom*'s story left the impression that a captain and two privates had gone missing during the course of the attack, but in fact Captain Roberts and his party had left town early that morning. Why Charles Duval Roberts had requested permission from his commanding officer to scout out a region known to be a hotbed of guerrilla activity is never explained, or why Major Laws thought it a good idea, especially in May, the hottest month of the year. Due to the intense heat, Laws advised Roberts to utilize only mounted men and, with only seven horses available—five native ponies and two American, including Laws' own mount—the scouting party was limited to seven men.[2]

What befell Roberts and his party is of particular interest because there is strong circumstantial evidence of Fagen's involvement in the attack, something never suggested before.

Roberts's party set off at seven in the morning of May 29, rode north to the Bulo River, and then northeast where they stopped for a noonday meal at the abandoned house of a guerrilla officer. They had just finished their meal when a guerrilla force began firing from across the dry rice fields. The ensuing fight was a desperate one and lasted for more than an hour. Roberts and his six men retreated behind a knoll to lure the guerrillas forward, then charged, volley-firing. The guerrillas retreated but quickly returned in greater force. Spaced at fifty-foot intervals, Robert's men fell back firing and took cover behind a rice berm. Private McCourt attempted to ride for help, but his saddle turned and he was dumped on the ground. Sergeant Gallen was struck and killed; two others were wounded, one mortally. Their canteens had long been empty, and they were down to their last shells when Roberts ordered his men to make a run for it. But by then the guerrillas had them encircled. Roberts fired his last round and raised the white flag, a handkerchief stuffed in the barrel of his Krag carbine. He stood up, disheveled and drenched in sweat. Guerrillas rose up, not twenty feet away; they disarmed the captain and relieved him of his valuables, including his watch and West Point ring.[3]

Roberts, Private McIntyre, and Private Akins (Private McCourt was killed) were brought before Colonel Simon Tecson, brother of Colonel Pablo Tecson and cousin of Lieutenant Colonel Alipio Tecson. (In all, eight members of the extended Tecson family would fight against the Americans.) Simon Tecson's force had consisted of fifty of his own men and fifty of Pablo Tecson's men. In light of the action that was to follow over the next four days and the evidence that emerged, I would make the case that David Fagen was the leader of Pablo Tecson's fifty men in this engagement, and probably the shooter doing the most damage. But there is no proof of that, only circumstantial evidence to suggest it as a strong possibility.[4]

The guerrillas had lost one man killed and two wounded in the fight. At the colonel's urging, Roberts wrote a safe-pass for a party of men to take the severely wounded Private Kinger to San Miguel. Then, with Roberts mounted on a carabao and the two privates straggling along, the captives were led into the mountains. At dawn, they climbed the switchback trail through dense forest and arrived at the guerrilla stronghold on Mount Corona. There they were handed into the custody of Colonel Pablo Tecson.

Word of what had happened to Roberts's party reached San Miguel only when the severely wounded Private Kinger, on a horse-litter, was discovered on the outskirts of the post the next morning. In San Isidro, Funston learned of Roberts capture that evening and called out his Headquarters Scouts. In half an hour the party set off at a brisk canter for the Mount Corona region, twenty-five miles to the southeast. A troop of the Fourth Cavalry and a small pack-train laden with provisions followed.

Before sunrise they arrived at a rocky promontory they called Stony Point. At daybreak, Funston, the Scouts, and the cavalry troop engaged in a sharp fight with the guerrillas, who fired from behind boulders on the steep hillside. When the guerrillas retreated into the hills, the Americans pursued them on horseback. The mounted party emerged from the forest and found one hundred guerrillas making a stand atop a grassy ridge.

Funston and his men dismounted and deployed. They advanced by leap-frog rushes, with half of the men combing the ridge with gunfire while the other half moved up the steep slope. Cavalry Sergeant Pogie O'Brien had his hat blown off, and a bullet struck Ganzhorn's canteen, soaking his leg. Thinking he had been hit, Ganzhorn looked down in dread at his leg, then saw Funston grinning at him. At that instant a bullet landed just short of the prone Funston's face, and for several minutes he was blinded by the dirt in his eyes. But his amazing luck held.

Seven weeks later, an article in the *Davenport Weekly Leader* on July 24, 1900, provided details of the fight to take the ridge and described a flanking maneuver of a detachment led by Lieutenant Hanson E. Ely while Funston led the rushes up the grassy slope.

> The rebels were a bit stubborn but they soon found their position un-
> tenable. As Funston and his men pressed forward the insurgents broke
> and ran. In this fight two were killed, six wounded and four captured.
> The Americans secured their rifles and a hat full of cartridges. Some of
> the insurgents were armed with Krag-Jorgensen rifles and had Ameri-
> can horses with them. As the rebels were running away, a bullet from
> the rifle of one of the scouts cut a stirrip [*sic*] strap and caused the stirrip
> [*sic*] to drop to the ground. It was found to be of American make and it
> is believed that it came from the saddle which belonged to Captain
> Roberts. From one of the prisoners which the Americans captured it

was learned that a deserter from the 24th Infantry was in command of
one of the insurgent companies.[5]

This is the first allusion to Fagen in the press, though not by name, and it
probably went no further than the *Davenport Weekly Leader*. The source may
have been a letter from Lieutenant Ely either to his wife, who maintained the
family home in Iowa City, or to his brother, N. D. Ely, a prominent citizen in
Davenport. Ely's letter does not say specifically that Fagen was in command of
the company on the ridge, and even less does it say that he was riding the
American horse taken from Robert's party. But events soon to follow will lend
greater support to that argument.

————•—————

Being low on ammunition and with a number of his men prostrated by the
heat, Funston sent the Scouts to San Isidro for reinforcements. Late on the
night of June 2 they returned, accompanied by forty-one men of the Twenty-
Second Infantry under Captain George J. Godfrey. Godfrey, "a small man, but
of strikingly handsome appearance," was known for his "big, pointy mustache"
and as "a good joker." He had been severely wounded in the head at El Caney
in Cuba and subsequently had spent more time on sick leave than on active
duty, even at his post at Candaba.[6]

Before dawn, the Scouts and Godfrey's forty men were on the move. The
Scouts led the way to the grassy ridge where they had engaged one hundred
guerrillas three days earlier. Again, a guerrilla band of about twelve men fired
down on them. In what Funston described as "a sharp skirmish of ten minutes,"
Captain Godfrey and his men cleared the ridge. The guerrillas faded away with
a haste that aroused Funston's suspicion, but he was determined to force an
engagement, even if it meant risking an ambush. The guerrillas remained in
sight as if to lead them on as they filed along a trail higher into the forested
hills.[7]

After climbing for about two miles, the Scouts emerged from the forest into
a glade of several acres. They continued warily across the glade as Funston and
then the company of infantrymen entered the open space. In his autobiography,
Funston noted that everything about the encounter that followed was unlike
any he had previously experienced: "The fire discipline of the Filipinos was
usually so poor that they almost invariably let fly as soon as our point came in
sight. . . . But this outfit was better handled."[8]

When the guerrillas opened up from the edge of the forest some seventy
yards to their left front, the officers and Scouts jumped from their horses and
hit the ground. "As we later discovered," Funston wrote, "the enemy was in a

Fagen's primary region of operation (map by Moira Hill, moirahilldesign.com)

splendid deep trench that he had prepared months before, and he now maintained on us a very persistent fire."[9]

His men deployed, Godfrey dismounted and called for his striker to take his horse. At that instant he was shot through the heart and fell without a word. Seconds later Private Etheridge—possibly his striker—also fell, shot through the heart. Over the course of half an hour, the Scouts succeeded in flanking the guerrillas who, in the words of Funston, "vanished into the depths of the forest." He also noted that their fire was "remarkably persistent and accurate."[10]

Neither Funston nor Ganzhorn mentioned David Fagen in their accounts of the fight. It was only two years later that the story in the *St. Louis Post-Dispatch* on April 16, 1902, revealed that the "outfit that was better handled" and fired from "a splendid deep trench" was Fagen's.

> No other man that ever deserted from the United States has been so relentlessly hunted by his comrades as Fagin. Particularly have the men of the Twenty-second United States Infantry been after him, as he is believed to have killed Captain Godfrey, of that regiment near Mount Corona. Fagin and his band of Filipinos had entrenched themselves along a road on which Capt. Godfrey and his company were coming. Capt. Godfrey . . . dismounted and was standing by his horse when suddenly his men saw the gigantic figure of Fagin rise from behind the trenches, and, standing, take deliberate aim at Capt. Godfrey, and fire.[11]

Frederick Funston was the most likely source of this information. In February 1902, just returned from the Philippines, Funston underwent an operation for chronic ulcerative appendicitis in Kansas City, where, given his garrulous temperament and habit of speaking freely with journalists, he probably spoke with a number of reporters. It is also possible that another party passed the stories along, such as his father or his cousin and aide, Lieutenant Burton Mitchell.[12]

In a telegram to the Adjutant General in Manila, May 4, Funston described the four days of fighting in brief: "Captain Godfrey was killed within ten yards of me. . . . We do not know wether [*sic*] the prisoners from San Miguel were with this band or not. There was an American horse which we saw several times." In another telegram the following day, Funston again inquired about the American horse.

> On June 3 we had a severe fight of half an hour. . . . The enemy in these various affairs numbered 50 to 100 men and were well armed and had plenty of ammunition. They were using a number of Krag rifles as was

ascertained from the empty shells found on the ground. There was
with them also an American horse. Can you tell me if the detachment
under Capt. Roberts lost one or more animals?[13]

Roberts's men surrendered seven Krag-Jorgensen rifles and rode five native
ponies and two American horses. That Fagen's band of fifty men were in possession of the rifles and Roberts's horse and saddle would raise the intriguing
possibility that Fagen and his men had participated in the fight with Charles
Robert's detachment in which three Americans were killed and two wounded.

Another incident related in the *Post-Dispatch* article and reprinted a week later
in the *Iola (KS) Daily Register* on April 23, 1902, clearly came from the same
source, either Funston himself or someone close to him.

Upon one occasion when Funston was in the field Fagin sent him a
challenge. The deserter asked that Funston place himself at the head
of a given number of men, and that he, Fagin, would do the same with
his men, and they would fight it out. The negro also offered, if Gen.
Funston preferred, to meet between the two forces and have a personal
encounter. Gen. Funston became greatly angered at this, and every
command in his brigade received orders that Fagin was to be killed or
captured at any cost.[14]

When and where Fagen threw down the gauntlet remains a mystery. But
the image of the strapping black man and the pint-sized general facing off in a
duel is both astounding and a bit comical. Funston was known for his volcanic
temper, once drawing his saber and galloping after a prankster who had tossed
a firecracker beneath his horse. Fagen, obviously a man of mischievous instinct,
made a game—a deadly serious game—of provoking the general into impotent
fits of rage. And, in that, he succeeded brilliantly.

"The Afro-American Traitor
Called David"

19

AFTER MARCHING FOR MOST OF THE NIGHT of May 29, a bone-weary Captain Charles D. Roberts, Private McIntyre, and the wounded Private Akins (Roberts had insisted that Akins ride the one carabao) arrived at the guerrilla camp high on the forested slope of Mount Corona. Colonel Pablo Tecson, Roberts reported, "received us with great kindness and during our entire captivity was always considerate and treated us with all possible care, sharing equally with us the few comforts he had." Roberts spoke Spanish and, strangely enough, the two men would become lifelong friends.[1]

While imprisoned in a mountaintop aerie that afforded him a sweeping view of the lowlands to the west, Roberts could climb up to an outlook in a tree where a sentinel kept watch on the trails through a telescope. On May 31, he watched through the telescope as Funston's men fought to take the grassy ridge from what was almost certainly Fagen and his band. Fagen and his company's ambush of Funston and Godfrey three days later, according to Roberts, "was plainly heard not over two miles away."[2]

Unless Fagen had been kept away from Roberts out of concern for the captain's safety, as Alejandrino maintained, the two men would have met and conversed. There is only what appears to be a veiled reference to Fagen in Roberts's report upon his release, July 15, 1900: "I heard nothing of any American or other white renegades or of any artillery." It seems unlikely that Roberts would have stipulated *white* renegade if he hadn't met a *black* renegade. But Fagen, of course, was an American so the sentence is entirely ambiguous. If mention of Fagen in written reports had been forbidden, then that information would have been delivered verbally.[3]

On June 5, two detachments of the Thirty-Fifth Volunteer Infantry ventured into the mountains toward Mount Balubad, another of the Tecsons' strongholds, and it appears that Fagen was there, too. The guerrillas fired down from the mountain and ambushed flanking parties. Pinned down and in disarray, Major Laws could only wait for the guerrillas to withdraw, then, with the body of one man killed and ten wounded men borne on makeshift stretchers, lead the battered company down from the mountains. A telegram to Manila from General Frederick Grant noted: "Could hear an American shouting and taunting the troops."[4]

There is no record of any other American fighting with Tecsons' men at that time but David Fagen.

This was the proverbial last straw for General Grant, commander of the Fifth District, and over the next five days he and Funston assembled a combined force of thirteen hundred men to assault the guerrilla stronghold on Mount Balubad. By the time General Grant had arrayed his unwieldy force some eight hundred yards across an almost impenetrable tangle of brush and forest from the rugged face of Mount Balubad, the guerrillas had long since departed. In his field report, General Grant boasted of snipers shot out of trees, crops and food-stores destroyed, and a position even the Americans thought impregnable taken with a minimal loss. Funston was less sanguine, considering it largely an exercise in futility and was impressed by Pablo Tecson's deft handling of his three hundred regulars.[5]

Sometime after these events, Fagen led his band north into Nueva Ecija. The resistance had languished there after the fumbling efforts of Padilla and Garcia and their capture in early May. That same month, Lieutenant Colonel Urbano Lacuna, arriving from Baliaug in Southern Bulacan, introduced himself to the garrisons along the Rio Peñaranda by having his men fire into the towns during the night, fraying the soldiers' nerves and ruining their night's sleep if nothing else.

News of Lacuna's return to the province spread quickly and along with it went reports that an attack on one of the garrisons was imminent. On the night of June 10, the three split-companies who were not in the mountains with Funston were "put to a severe test" when Major Tomas Tagunton, Lacuna's third in command, led his men in an attack on San Isidro. A number of civilians were killed and several Americans wounded in the hour-long assault. So pressed were the town's defenders that the American soldiers in confinement were armed and, along with the prison guard, helped repel the attack.[6]

Lacuna then turned his sights on his birthplace, the town of Peñaranda. There, Major Joseph E. Wheeler Jr. commanded a garrison of only sixty men. Major Joseph E. Wheeler Jr. was the son of General "Fightin' Joe" Wheeler, the senior general in the Confederate Army of Tennessee and owner of Pond Farm, the largest plantation in northern Alabama. Wheeler Jr., "always of slight physique," was decorated for gallantry in the battle at San Juan Hill, and a year later he was commissioned a major in the Thirty-Fourth Volunteer Infantry. Assigned to Funston's Fourth District, Wheeler was not only commander of the garrison at Peñaranda but also of the southeastern sector of Nueva Ecija. That put him closest to the mountain refuges of the guerrillas and, given his success at attacking them even in their strongholds, it is no surprise that he became a marked man with a price on his head. A two-thousand-peso reward was also posted for the assassination of Funston, lesser rewards for the heads of his Scouts. According to Ganzhorn, these reward posters were signed by "Major Fagan."[7]

The guerrilla strategy was premised on attacks on small parties by overwhelming numbers, the ambush of Roberts's detail being a prime example. Lacuna would have been advised to stick to that model, but he wanted to restore the flagging morale of the Novo Ecijanos and to have captured one of Funston's garrisons would have helped raise spirits in a way that small-scale ambushes would not have.

With the success of the Tecsons against Funston and Grant, Lacuna had become convinced that the Americans were vulnerable in Nueva Ecija. "At this time we find the enemy very feeble," he wrote to a battalion commander a few weeks earlier. His almost dismissive assessment of the enemy and the aggressiveness with which he amassed a large force only several miles from Peñaranda smacks of overconfidence. Lacuna wanted to strike and strike quickly, but like a boxer too eager to land a blow he did not give equal consideration to his defenses.[8]

Nor did he understand the extent to which Funston had developed an elaborate spy network. On the morning of June 14, one of Funston's spies appeared in Peñaranda. Five days later, Wheeler filed an after-action report with Colonel Lyman V. W. Kennon, regimental commander in Cabanatuan: "About noon of the 14th instant information reached me to the effect that Col. Urbano Lacuna, Maj. Thomas Taguntong, Maj. Manuel Ventus, and Afro-American traitor called David and 400 other armed bandits were in the barrio of Papaya."[9]

Wheeler's revelation that Fagen was with Lacuna at Papaya would not be published for another year in the *Annual Report of the Secretary of War* and went unnoticed down to the present. Funston made no mention of Fagen's presence at Papaya, nor did Ganzhorn. The fact that Wheeler included Fagen with the three foremost guerrilla leaders in Nueva Ecija indicates the prominence that he had attained in the guerrilla leadership and the importance the Americans attached to him.

———‥———

According to the spy, Lacuna intended to burn the town that night. Wheeler wired Funston in San Isidro. As quickly as they could gather their accouterments and saddle up, Funston, Captain Koelher's cavalry troop, and the Headquarters Scouts "took up a keen trot for Peñaranda."[10]

The Scouts located Lacuna's force of two hundred men on the Peñaranda River across from the village of Papaya. They took up positions along an old rice dike at the edge of a forest. Funston left the cavalry troop in reserve, hoping to lure Lacuna into an open fight before unleashing the mounted force. Across a rolling field of brush, several of Lacuna's officers sat astride horses, unconcerned that they were giving away the position of their firing line.

Wheeler's infantrymen were still taking up positions when Lacuna's men opened up and a heated exchange continued for several minutes before Funston gave the order to charge. The men rose up with a cheer and swept forward, taking advantage of natural cover to fire and reload, then rush forward again.[11]

According to Funston, "The Filipinos stood their ground well, and fought hard though ineffectively." While many of the guerrillas took to their heels, others fought until the infantrymen were almost among them. Captain Koehler and his cavalry troop burst from behind a screen of trees to the guerrillas' left and the battle disintegrated into chaos as many of the horses, unaccustomed to gunfire, ran wild with their riders. Some of the guerrillas remained to engage, others fled in all directions, and the fighting became almost hand-to-hand while horses bucked in the middle of the melee. Funston recounted his own difficulties in his *Memories of Two Wars.*

> I mounted just as the advance started, and thereafter the most of my efforts consisted of trying to keep the brute from jumping clear off the island of Luzon. Major Harris's horse also bolted with its rider just at the beginning of the fight, and had the bad taste to run under a tree with our energetic medico. Major Wheeler's horse was killed, while those of Admire, Mitchell, and Lyles broke loose and escaped into the woods, being eventually picked up by the enemy.[12]

Sergeant Maurice "Pogie" O'Brien was an old hand in the Fourth Cavalry, much loved by the men in the company. During the charge a bullet shattered his left arm just above the wrist. He cried out to Captain Koehler that he had been hit and Koehler shouted, "Don't fall! Stick to your horse!" But seconds later O'Brien was shot through the heart and tumbled from his horse.[13]

Whoever had sighted on Pogie O'Brien had taken careful aim and, after wounding him, made a deadly correction. David Fagen would be the most likely candidate as marksman, but there is no evidence to confirm that. Were it not for Wheeler's later reference to the "Afro-American traitor called David," Fagen's participation in the fight at Papaya would never have been revealed.

"With reference to the conduct of the enemy," Major Wheeler reported, "their fire was heavy but not accurate, and the greater part of them fled before our advance; but some of them stood their ground and were killed fighting desperately at almost hand-to-hand combat."[14]

The infantrymen and cavalry pursued the fleeing guerrillas for miles. The guerrillas had left twenty-two men dead on the field and thirteen wounded. It was as if little had changed since the first day of battle with the Americans fifteen months earlier. Wheeler attributed the Americans' "light casualties" to "a heavy and accurate fire, an expert use of cover, as well as the wild firing of the enemy." The bravery of the young Filipinos and their willingness to stand and fight could not overcome their inability to make effective use of their rifles.[15]

The fight at Papaya was not an auspicious beginning for Urbano Lacuna and only in retrospect could the enormity of this early loss be fully appreciated.

Urbano Lacuna

20

AGUINALDO'S DETAILED INSTRUCTIONS for waging a guerrilla war ran for many pages, but the essence of the guerrilla strategy could be summed up in a single paragraph.

> The purpose of the guerrillas shall be to constantly worry the Yankees in the pueblos occupied by them, to cut off their convoys, to cause all possible harm to their patrols, their spies, and their scouts, to surprise their detachments, to crush their columns if they should pass in favorable places, and to exterminate all traitors, to prevent natives to sell themselves for the invaders gold.[1]

Urbano Lacuna understood his mission perfectly, but instructions that looked straightforward on paper were not so simple in the implementation. Under Aguinaldo, the Filipinos had only turned to a guerrilla strategy after a disastrous nine months of conventional warfare, and in Nueva Ecija another six months of inept leadership had followed. Lacuna was faced with a steep uphill climb.

To begin with, he assigned to the notorious Lieutenant Colonel Isidoro Carmona the unenviable task of setting up a supply system, collecting taxes, and restoring relations with the prominent citizens in the towns. Isidoro Carmona, in the words of Orlino Ochosa "a vicious man who feared no other man," had served under the notorious General Pio del Pilar in Manila. Carmona "had gained a reputation as an arrogant and cruel officer" who had personally tortured Spanish and Macabebe prisoners. With his face scarred from wounds received in fighting the Americans, the intimidating Carmona was quite successful at securing contributions to the cause. According to Brian Linn, other guerrilla officers worked "to reestablish an infrastructure of partisans, militia, tax collectors, and shadow governments." But while Lacuna was surprisingly successful at reinvigorating the struggle in Nueva Ecija, Funston's spy network and the collaboration of Pablo Padilla and Pantaleon Garcia, along with so many of their subordinates, undermined much of his efforts to inspire a unified resistance in Nueva Ecija. The war in the Fourth District was permeated by an atmosphere of intrigue and dissimulation in which true loyalties were hard to discern. Lacuna, who despised Pablo Padilla, was prepared to do whatever was necessary to regain the full support of the population; if not given freely, then he would have it by other means.[2]

Urbano Lacuna was born in 1862, the third of five sons in a family of "wealthy proprietors." Unlike the Tecsons, who were descended from Chinese mestizos who had become influential landowners in the eighteenth century, Lacuna was, in Funston's words, a "full-blood Malay, very dark, of medium stature, and possessed of the quiet dignity of his race." Like so many of the revolutionary officers, Lacuna had embarked upon a career in the Spanish colonial government, working in various capacities—as a forest ranger, a clerk in the provincial governor's office in San Isidro, and as a public defender of the poor. Finally, he became a captain of the militia under the Spanish military governor Augustin. According to Orlino Ochosa, Lacuna "led the Gapan Volunteers who became famous fighting in central Luzon campaigns."[3]

Years later, in his autobiography, Funston observed that there were many subordinates among the guerrillas "who thought as little of burying a man alive as of killing a chicken." But "Lacuna and Pablo Tecson . . . were of a different stamp, and though they did not hesitate to destroy property, were chary when it came to taking life unnecessarily, both of them being in addition quite humane in their treatment of such Americans as fell into their hands." Other historians have passed along Funston's view of Lacuna; Brian Linn describes him as "a humane and chivalrous commander."[4]

These qualities are stressed to the point that one may argue that they have, perhaps inadvertently, left an idealized picture of Lacuna as a leader. Just as Funston in his autobiography omitted the more unpleasant details of the war in his district, his view of Lacuna seems to have mellowed over the intervening decade. In his long piece in *Collier's Weekly* on April 21, 1902, and in interviews with the press, Funston described a very different Lacuna.

> Lacuna was a man of much greater courage and energy than Padilla, and was at the same time more cruel. A reign of terror now begun throughout the whole district. Every native who was in any way suspected of sympathizing with the Americans or of aiding them, or who

General Urbano Lacuna

neglected or refused to pay the contributions demanded, was assassinated, if a way could be found to do it. Many men were buried alive, others flogged to death, and still others executed with the bolo.

It is probably not an exaggeration to say that three hundred natives were murdered by the insurgent chiefs in this district in one year. As many as thirty of these were women and children, they being killed for the purpose of punishing their relatives.[5]

In the *San Francisco Chronicle* on April 3, 1902, Funston increased the number buried alive in his Fourth District "at not less than four hundred," and elaborated even further: "I want to say that American soldiers have been burned and tortured, mutilated and buried alive by these people. I had the pleasure of capturing and hanging some of the fiends who tied two negroes belonging to the Twenty-fourth to stakes and left them to starve."[6]

These portraits of Urbano Lacuna seem to be of two different men—one ruthless, the other humane. Which account is the more truthful—the 1911 autobiography or the lengthy 1902 essay in *Collier's Weekly*—is open for debate. What can be said is that Urbano Lacuna was not a man to be taken lightly.

As for Funston's stories of "insurgent" cruelty and butchery, one has to take his words with a measure of caution. These sweeping claims were made during his tour on the banquet circuit after his return to America in early 1902. With a few gin-rickeys under his belt as he expounded before his well-fed banqueters, the temptation to regale them with bloodcurdling tales of Filipino cruelty could get out of hand. His numbers veered wildly from banquet to banquet. At a gala at the Lotus Club in New York, he boasted of personally stringing up thirty-five *insurrectos* and, as if that were not shocking enough, "told of 24 American soldiers who had joined the Filipinos and who were afterwards captured and executed as traitors." In San Francisco, the number of executed deserters became six. As for rescuing two "negroes" bound to stakes and left to starve, I found no other reference to that incident, which doesn't mean it didn't happen.[7]

Were these deserters African Americans from the Twenty-Fourth Infantry? Were they strung up in the field, in effect, lynched, as he had promised to string up Fagen if ever caught? Or did they only exist in Funston's imagination? There is no reference in the files or newspapers to executed deserters other than Lewis Russell and Edmond DuBose, two African American deserters from the Ninth Cavalry executed in 1902. But what about these other supposedly executed deserters? The problem with Funston—for both his contemporaries and for historians—was trying to discern when he was telling the truth and when, in his over-the-top exuberance, he was either lying or exaggerating.

Even as the defeat at Papaya might have counseled against any further large-scale assaults, Urbano Lacuna had already turned his sights on another of Funston's garrisons. Manicling, a barrio of San Leonardo, was about six miles to the northeast of San Isidro and only four miles north of Gapan, a little farther than that from Peñaranda. The tiny village had become a rendezvous for Lacuna's men, almost as if they were daring Funston to come after them. The general reacted to the provocation by ordering forty men from the Twenty-Fourth Infantry, Company C, under Lieutenant E. B. Mitchell, to garrison the town.[8]

Funston wrote that the black regulars of Company C didn't set out from San Isidro for their new post until July 4. Upon their arrival they chose a convent facing the town square for their quarters but had no time "to construct anything in the way of adequate protection."[9]

A garrison of only forty men must have looked particularly tempting to Lacuna, especially one without the usual sandbagged perimeter. In calculating how the battle might play out, Lacuna was convinced that the larger garrisons at Gapan and Peñaranda would hear the firing at Manicling and send reinforcements, leading to a potentially chaotic engagement on several fronts. Accordingly, Lacuna—now *Brigadier General* Lacuna—elected to divide his men into three groups. While two smaller detachments attacked Peñaranda and Gapan and kept them preoccupied, Lacuna would lead a larger force of three hundred men in the assault on Manicling.

The attack began at ten o'clock. The guerrillas fired from behind logs and trees, from gardens and even from some of the town's nipa houses. The soldiers lay "close to the ground behind some improvised shelter." The fighting lasted for four hours. Lieutenant Mitchell was hit in the shoulder, Private T. C. Brown shot in the back, and Private Will Webb killed. As the fight raged on, Mitchell began to worry about their dwindling supplies of ammunition. His men had started with four thousand rounds and, after four hours of fighting, only five hundred rounds remained.[10]

Funston wrote that Mitchell was "ably seconded by First Sergeant Walter Washington, a fine-looking old soldier." More detailed accounts of the fight credit Sergeant Preston Moore with shooting out the candles in the convent doorway that had been revealing their position. In his autobiography of 1940, Jack Ganzhorn wrote:

> The Twenty-fourth negroes had made a game fight every foot of the way. Although shot badly early in the attack, Lieutenant Mitchell never weakened. Every one of the men was loud in praise of Sergeant Washington, a white-haired negro grown old in his Uncle Sam's army. They

swore that Washington had refused to lie down, but stood there flat-footed, cursing and taunting the gugus, fighting like a madman.[11]

After four hours, Sergeant Randall Craig, Corporal Nathan Walker, and six privates crawled out and came within ten yards of Lacuna's line before the general ordered his men to withdraw. If Lacuna had persisted for another hour, Mitchell and his men, down to twelve rounds per man, would have run out of ammunition and been compelled to surrender. But Lacuna had lost twenty-one men killed and many more wounded, a frightful toll. He may have been low on ammunition as well.[12]

Lacuna had failed to overrun the garrison and Funston thought his strategy a foolish one. Brian Linn did not fault the strategy so much as the failure of execution. Had Lacuna thrown all seven hundred men at Manicling, could he have overrun Mitchell and his forty men before reinforcements had arrived? The heavy loss of some of his best fighters and precious ammunition discouraged any further large-scale assaults on Funston's garrisons. But even fiercer fighting awaited them in the hills.

———————

Walter L. Washington was undoubtedly "fine-looking" but he wasn't old. Ganzhorn had taken his cue from Funston's autobiography, adding the white hair and creating the sense of an old "before the war" type, the loyal and compliant black looked upon affectionately by whites. In fact, Walter Washington was only twenty-seven years old, born in Washington, DC, in 1873. When he first enlisted in 1895, his occupation was recorded as a "tinner," which may have meant a tinsmith or, more likely, a worker in a cannery. On June 10, 1898, he reenlisted as a corporal and was wounded in the charge at San Juan Hill. When he reenlisted six months later in February 1899, it was as Sergeant Washington. In his first enlistment at age twenty-one, Washington's height was recorded as 5 feet 11½ inches; at his second enlistment he had grown to 6 feet 2 inches, six inches taller than the average black recruit in 1897. His rise to become first sergeant was nothing short of meteoric and he must have been not only impressive in his bearing but also gifted at commanding the respect of more than one hundred spirited young men.[13]

With the army's continued silence on Fagen, one can only say there is a strong likelihood that he was at Manicling that night. If he were not there, he would have been leading the assault on Gapan or Peñaranda. But, given his vow to settle some scores with his former regiment, it seems unlikely he would have missed the attack on Manicling. If that were the case, he might have answered Sergeant Washington's taunts with some of his own.

David Fagen and Walter Washington were to meet up again two months later, September 13, on a muddy road near Manicling, and there they would resume their argument.

―――――――

After the attack on Manicling, Funston ordered out all the mounted men at his post and an all-day scout turned up no sign of the enemy. "We were greatly impeded by the condition of the fields," he reported, "the mud being knee deep to the horses." On July 9 he telegraphed Manila that Lacuna and the main body of his men had returned to the mountains, leaving several small bands that had attacked Cabanatuan that morning. "These bands left down here follow the usual plan of appearing in the daytime in the guise of peaceful citizens only taking up arms at night."[14]

Funston proposed an expedition into the mountains but, much to his annoyance, was ordered to hold off by military governor MacArthur.[15]

A month earlier, the controversial General Pio del Pilar had been captured in Manila. After being denied a role in the resistance by Pantaleon Garcia, del Pilar lingered for a time in Bulacan, then went into hiding in and around Manila, where he was soon betrayed by a spy and arrested by the secret police.

Reputed to be the most notorious bandit leader in the islands, Pio del Pilar seemed almost as much in revolt against the privileged classes as against the Americans. An article in the *American Review of Books* conveys the fascination the rogue general held for the Americans: "General Pio del Pilar represents the objectionable half-breed who inherits the evil tendencies of both races. He is clever and unscrupulous, attractive and treacherous, brave and dishonest. He comes close to the villain of a cheap melodrama and in the last century would have made a capital pirate."[16]

Milagros Guerrero reported that in the province of Morong, del Pilar's men "were more interested in pillaging the countryside and in gambling . . . than in preparing for the conflict with the Americans."[17]

Upon his capture, the seemingly pliant Pio del Pilar immediately took the oath of allegiance to the American flag, and MacArthur set him right to work. Del Pilar was to serve as mediator in trying to persuade Generals Isidro Torres and Urbano Lacuna to accept an offer of amnesty and take the oath of allegiance. Funston thought any peace overtures to Lacuna a waste of time and cabled Manila: "Regarding suspension of hostilities against Lacuna . . . I hope there is no impropriety in my saying that from what I know about Lacuna I do not believe that any effort to make him surrender will be of avail. . . . He is just now revelling in a lot of new found power and I doubt if he will pay any attention to any of the other generals who may attempt to make him give up."[18]

At MacArthur's behest, Pio sent a letter to Isidro Torres encouraging him to surrender. But, in typical del Pilar fashion, he also had another letter secreted to Torres warning that the first letter was just a ruse and to disregard it; as soon as conditions were favorable he planned to return to the field.[19]

Whatever General Torres thought of Pio del Pilar's machinations, he spurned MacArthur's amnesty overture, and del Pilar moved on to San Isidro. After conferring with Funston, Pio and three companions rode into the mountains to Lacuna's camp while Funston fumed to Major Wheeler in Peñaranda:

> It is no use. I am positively prohibited from attacking the camp in the mountains while the present alleged negotiations are in progress. Of course I do not understand the logic of this business, that they can raid the towns and we cannot follow them wherever they may go, but my hands are tied. Pio del Pilar who was in Gapan left there yesterday morning for Lacuna's camp with a letter from General MacArthur. I do not think this will last much longer but in the meantime much damage will be done. It seems that at present we can do nothing except strike them if we can down on the plains. They shot up Cabanatuan last night, killing one soldier.[20]

On July 11, Pio del Pilar and two members of his party returned to San Isidro. Funston wired Manila:

> Pio del Pilar and two companions came in here late last night from the mountains and the former asked me to telegraph General MacArthur that the mission he was sent on was a complete failure. . . . The insurgent lieutenant, Legaspi, who went out with Pilar was killed by Lacuna and Pilar himself had a hard time of it and Lacuna upbraided him and insulted him and with difficulty was induced to allow him to return. Lacuna sent an impertinent letter to me by Pilar without any provocation as I have had no communication with him. Pilar told me that unless Lacuna is thrashed soundly and very soon that he will have this whole province ablaze as his force is increasing as rapidly as he can collect arms. I am ready to administer the thrashing as soon as I am allowed.[21]

Pio del Pilar's near fatal encounter with Urbano Lacuna presents a strikingly different picture of the guerrilla leader more often noted for his restraint and humanity. By all accounts, Pio del Pilar was Urbano Lacuna's mentor in the art of war, and the impression left is one of mutual regard, with del Pilar as the more experienced general and Lacuna as the loyal line officer. That Lacuna would "upbraid" and "insult" his mentor and have to be restrained from killing

him suggests their relationship was not nearly so amicable as previously portrayed. Del Pilar's apparently casual transition from revolutionary general to
turncoat negotiator for the invaders must have infuriated Lacuna, and their
dramatic confrontation reveals the depth of his commitment to the struggle.[22]

In Captain Charles Roberts's report following his release, July 15, 1900, he
added to the conflicting opinions that swirled around del Pilar: "General Pio
del Pilar is hated by all Tecson's men. They say he is a ladrone and was deposed
from command and sentenced to death before his capture by the Americans."
The *Manila Times* painted an even crueler picture of del Pilar, accusing him in a
report of October 31, 1899, of "having gone so far as to compel a Spanish nun
to live as his mistress."[23]

Even if these stories were slanders spread by his enemies, they do not seem
entirely out of character, given Pio's checkered reputation. In a telegram to
Lieutenant Colonel Wilder in Baliaug, Funston again stated that "Legaspi was
killed by Lacuna while Pilar had a hard time of it and although he had an interview with Lacuna was not allowed to enter the enemy's camp." And he added,
"He [del Pilar] has asked me for an escort to San Miguel as Simon Tecson has
issued orders to have him captured on his return."[24]

The Americans soon uncovered del Pilar's duplicity in his communications
with Torres, for he was arrested while returning to Manila. "He is now held
incommunicado in the walled city," various newspapers reported. "The authorities refuse to divulge the reason for his arrest."[25]

Eventually the Americans would decide that despite having taken the oath
of allegiance, played the mediator, and been sentenced to death by Aguinaldo,
Pio del Pilar's loyalties remained with the revolutionaries. He would be deported
to Guam with other captured guerrilla chiefs and influential supporters of the
resistance. And, in one last head-spinning twist—they would elect Pio del Pilar
their leader![26]

Mount Corona

21

IN HIS AUTOBIOGRAPHY Funston made no mention of Pio del Pilar's failed mission. He wrote that before Lacuna's attacks of July 4 he had been inclined to scale down his operations and wait out the rainy season. But now he determined that "mud and quagmires notwithstanding, we again had to take the field." Over the following week he assembled a force of eight hundred men including a cavalry troop, two companies of the Thirty-Fourth U.S.V., a battalion of the Twenty-Second Infantry, and a battalion of Macabebes under Major Matthew Batson. And, as always, Funston's Headquarters Scouts rode with him, now under Lieutenant Richard C. Day.[1]

With the start of the war with Spain, Richard C. Day joined the Rough Riders and distinguished himself at Las Guasimas and in the charge up Kettle Hill, where he was shot in both the shoulder and the arm. Roosevelt described him in the most laudatory terms in *The Rough Riders* in which there is a photo of him. Richard C. Day was 6 feet 4 inches tall, a superb horseman, and even faster on the draw with a Colt .45 than Ganzhorn.[2]

With a full packtrain of rations and ammunition, Funston's eight hundred men set out from Peñaranda at five o'clock on the morning of July 16, 1900. The column wended its way across the rain-soaked plain, through broken forest and field. The Sierra Madre, dark and foreboding beneath the low sky, rose abruptly from the foothills. At Minalungao, the Sumacbao River had carved a deep gap in the mountains, with sheer rock walls pocked with caves on both sides of the river. There, on the crest of a high ridge, the guerrillas watched the approaching column, visible for miles in the distance.[3]

Funston led his men "straight into the mountains toward the insurgent camp." Five days of fighting and maneuvering followed. In sorting through the various versions of Funston's campaign in the mountains, one is left with the impression of a chaotic blend of pursuits, numerous small encounters, and

157

On the hike in Nueva Ecija (Marrion Wilcox, *Harper's History of the War in the Philippines* [1900])

several major engagements. The more differing accounts one reads of the campaign, the more muddled the picture. At one point, Funston thought he had Lacuna trapped, but an overly zealous officer spoiled the scheme before other units could be put in place. As Lacuna and his men vanished, the Americans were left the considerable pleasure of burning twenty-six thatched barracks and a sizeable cache of supplies.[4]

Urbano Lacuna broke up his forces and retreated farther into the mountains; Funston followed suit, sending smaller detachments after the elusive guerrillas. He dispatched a message to be wired to Manila: "Am going to stay at it until the mountains are cleared of insurgents and all camps destroyed."[5]

Batson and his Macabebes came upon Lacuna's largest camp, and the guerrillas made a determined stand. In the sharp action that followed, thirty-six guerrillas were killed and seven Americans wounded. The following day a patrol discovered Lacuna's arsenal. The loss of twenty-four irreplaceable rifles and three hundred pounds of gunpowder was a serious blow to the guerrillas, but far more costly was the loss of their vital reloading machinery.[6]

For days, Funston and Captain Koehler's cavalry troop tracked the guerrillas "up hill and down, across raging streams and through dense tropical forests until we were in the country of the Ilongotes and Negritos, doubtless where no white man had ever been."[7]

A year later, a soldier-cum-journalist who had been with Funston on the expedition described the landscape in the *Los Angeles Times*.

> As one leaves the great valley, the banana, mango and cocoanut groves give way to a dense undergrowth, impenetrable except by narrow trails, while giant mahogany trees, festooned with creepers to the topmost branches almost shut out the light in places. . . . Fantastically shaped peaks rise up, abrupt and precipitous on all sides, and afford splendid sights of observation against the intruder. . . . Everywhere a prodigality and recklessness of nature, unknown in more Northern latitudes, is apparent.[8]

Funston was sure that he was on Lacuna's trail, but in fact Lacuna and most of his men had given him the slip days earlier. With rations growing short and no grass for the horses, Funston finally abandoned the pursuit.

———————

Meanwhile, a column led by Major Joseph E. Wheeler Jr., with two short companies—C of the Thirty-Fourth Volunteer Infantry, under Captain George Gibson, and F of the Twenty-Second Infantry under Lieutenant David L. Stone—ninety-six men in all, wended its way south over tortuous mountain trails. Wheeler's force was in pursuit of Pablo Tecson's two hundred men who had come north to assist Lacuna in the attacks of July 4. The seemingly omnipresent Jack Ganzhorn had some familiarity with the countryside and had been sent along as guide.

Ganzhorn had only partially recovered from a bullet wound in the foot received in the fight at Papaya a month earlier. Walking was difficult, but he could ride and was not one to sit out a campaign. On the afternoon of July 22, Ganzhorn and Major Wheeler rode at the head of the column as it followed the side of a deep ravine. A steep crescent-shaped hill loomed to their right. To their left the ravine fell off abruptly and then rose in a rocky cliff somewhat below them. In his report of August 6, 1900, Lieutenant Stone noted, "There was not a dead angle or dead space in this position."[9]

At 2:30 p.m. a soldier walking point caught sight of a guerrilla on the hillside, swung his rifle into action, and shot him. The guerrillas returned fire from the crest of the hill, and the battle was on. Ganzhorn and Wheeler jumped from their horses, and the entire column scrambled for an almost nonexistent cover.

According to Ganzhorn, Major Wheeler "took in our desperate situation at a glance and yelled, 'Charge!'" Lieutenant Stone wrote, "It was impossible on account of the configuration of the hill and the surrounding country to flank the insurgents' position and the only thing to do was to take it by direct assault." Ganzhorn described the "charge" as more "a snail-like climbing . . . where unless one clung to grass and small brush he slid back farther than he went up." Their situation was rendered even more precarious when a heavy fire was opened from the sheer, rocky cliff across the ravine. "This," Stone wrote, "gave the insurgents a front, left enfilade and reverse fire upon our troops as they advanced up the hill to the right."[10]

According to Funston, "The combat that ensued was the most severe that occurred in the Fourth District. . . . The fight was a desperate one." The *Manila Freedom* concurred: "A desperate and bloody fight ensued. The hill was so steep that our men had to assist themselves with their hands, and those that were hit rolled for some distance down the mountain side."[11]

From Ganzhorn we get an eyewitness account of the charge:

> Scrambling for a foothold and favoring my pet foot, I let go of my carbine for a second. It slid out of reach behind me. I climbed with both hands with the thought in my mind that when we reached the top my .45 would be better anyway. Before we had covered fifty yards in that first rush upward a wounded man rolled back down the hill.
>
> Major Wheeler and Captain Gibson gamely tried to keep ahead of their men, urging them on. Another ten yards, another wounded soldier rolled and tumbled backward. By now I had ceased to breathe, was just gasping. The man on my right screamed, slid from my line of sight.
>
> Twenty yards from the top the withering fire increased. Directly above me, deliberately firing his piece, grinning and mocking us, still wearing parts of the uniform he had disgraced, I saw the leering features of Fagan, the deserter.
>
> In trying to crawl around a projecting hummock, Fryburger had slid over against my left side, his head and shoulders just ahead of mine. He lifted his rifle to shoot at the grimacing black face of the American renegade. I heard Fagan's bullet hit Fryburger's right shoulder. Clinging to the grass with one hand, the wounded man turned his eyes to my face.
>
> "For God's sake, Ganzie," he screamed, "kill that black devil!"
>
> Hanging on with one hand and clawing for my six-shooter, I saw Fagan's Remington carbine level, puff smoke, and heard a sickening thud. Blood and brains from a terrible hole in poor Fryburger's head spattered into my eyes. His body slid back, struck a clump, and tumbled to the bottom of the hill. Sobbing for breath, crazy mad, I wiped the warm sticky mess from my face.

Years have not dimmed that awful picture. I've seen it in the long, dark nights, over and over again. Down through the years, I've heard Fryburger's agonizing cry for me to kill Fagan. God, how I wanted to! But when I could see to shoot, Fagan was not in sight.

Bullets screamed above my head, snipped the dry grass all around me . . . Gripping my six-shooter and dragging Fryburger's rifle, I struggled to keep up with the men still climbing. A soldier between Captain Gibson and me flopped on his side, rolled backward.

On the extreme left, Major Wheeler cried, "Keep going, men! Faster!"

Captain Gibson got on to his feet, waved his pistol and cheered: "Come on soldiers! Give that black devil the hell that's coming to him!" . . . Gibson's arms flung upward and he pitched backwards.[12]

Funston described Captain George Gibson as a Scots Highlander with a "burr" that was a delight to all the men. "Although he finally recovered, his wound was of the most terrible nature, a Remington bullet having struck him under the eye and ploughed its way through his face and one shoulder, coming out the small of his back." The trajectory of the bullet would suggest that Gibson was not standing when he was hit but clawing his way up the slope and looking up toward the ridge.[13]

Private Luther Troxel worked his way back down the slope under heavy fire and administered aid to the wounded captain. Wheeler reported that the "defenders held their ground with unusual persistence, and some were killed at a range of thirty yards" while they "still poured a heavy fire" from across the ravine. And he added, "I think they were slow in realizing we were actually coming up there."[14]

Back down the trail the rear guard clawed its way up the hill and had some success in flanking the guerrillas on the crest. Ultimately the accurate firing of a platoon of Company F under First Sergeant Ole Waloe, a Norwegian immigrant cited for "his coolness, bravery and efficient manner" during the fight, succeeded in driving the guerrillas from their rifle pits.[15]

The men took refuge on the crest while firing continued from behind boulders on the cliff across the canyon. Details went down the hill under fire to look for the dead and wounded. Private William Hunter was hit coming down the hill and died the following morning. Corporal Martin Burkhart dressed the wounds of one of the fallen and then dragged him to a small ravine on the side of the hill: "In doing so he was subjected to the fire of the enemy for over half an hour." Corporal Fred Winter dressed the wounds of three men and helped carry them under fire to the top of the hill. All were decorated for gallantry in action and Doctor Chidester so distinguished himself in tending to the wounded that he was awarded the Medal of Honor.[16]

In the fight, seven were wounded, all serious—stomach, knee, thigh—and one man killed, Private Albert Fryberger. Major Wheeler's report described his wounds: "A. Fryberger Co 'C' 34th Lacerated wound of head with destruction of entire crest of skull."[17] Given the guerrillas superior position, one might expect the American losses to have been significantly greater. According to Lieutenant Stone, "The firing of the Insurgents was low and accurate throughout the engagement." But the lieutenant also offered his theory as to why there weren't more casualties: "I attribute the small loss in the company to the fact that they all wore khaki blouses and trousers and could not be distinctly seen in the grass. I could not see my own men lying or kneeling in the grass fifty yards away from me."[18]

As soon as the guerrilla riflemen had been dispersed from the cliff, Wheeler's men wasted no time preparing for the long trek out of the mountains. They were short of rations, and it was imperative to get care for the wounded. With their dwindling supply of ammunition—they were down to fewer than fifty rounds per man—they were in fear of another attack, and their exit from the mountains was more a headlong flight than an orderly retreat. Each soldier carried a shelter-half, a half of what would now be called a pup tent, and these, along with poles stripped from the woods, were used to fashion makeshift litters for the wounded. Given the urgency of the moment, Fryberger's body was left on the field.

The column struggled on along the precarious mountain trail. At dark it began to rain. Soldiers carried candles to guide the litter bearers, others moved ahead and built fires in the woods on the mountainside "to keep the litter bearers from slipping off the trail and going some distance down the mountain." Wheeler was particularly effusive in his praise of Lieutenant Stone in leading "a column in evacuation of casualties" and using "every endeavor to find a trail to the flat country, to spare no effort that would insure the column against ambuscade." At midnight, they reached the summit of a high hill and collapsed in exhaustion.[19]

The following morning the march continued over the mountains and down through nearly impassable jungle ravines to the foothills. For the next day and a half they waded across swampy rice fields, finally straggling into the barrio of Santa Cruz where ambulances and escort wagons awaited them. Major Wheeler reported theirs "was a task calculated to tax the very limits of human endurance."[20]

In their reports of the fight and the agonizing return to the lowlands, neither Wheeler, Funston, nor Sergeant Williams mentioned David Fagen, though all were fully aware of Fagen's participation in the fight. Ganzhorn's description places a different emphasis on their exodus from the mountains.

> Now came two days and nights of heart-breaking work—battling our way, carrying our dead and wounded over rough mountains, wading shallow streams, chopping a path for the crude litters through entangling jungle. Hatred flamed in the heart of every man of us against that black renegade. . . . During the long, sad trip back to San Isidro the bitterness of our loss seemed greater because we knew it was largely due to the experience and training received by Fagan while a soldier of the United States. . . . Every man in that fight prayed for a chance to kill the traitor.[21]

Days later, the *Manila Freedom* portrayed the fight as a glorious victory and, in the usual spirit of exaggerated body counts, claimed that the Filipinos left "over fifty of their dead in the rifle pits." Major Wheeler reported twelve enemy killed. Funston and the *Manila Freedom* both reported that Pablo Tecson led the rebels. Wheeler described the enemy as constituting the "combined forces of Lacuna and Tecson." In a telegram of August 2, Captain Smith in San Miguel wired Funston: "Padilla [former guerrilla officer] here today and said that Wheeler had fight on 22nd with Lacuna and Torres and not with Tecson."[22] Whether Lacuna or General Torres took part in the actual fighting will probably never be determined. The question of Fagen's participation is not in doubt.

Wheeler's description of the battle contains no reference to Fagen, nor does First Sergeant H. D. Williams's eyewitness account. Funston makes no reference to Fagen's participation, nor does the *Manila Freedom*. There was only Ganzhorn's breathless description of his encounter with Fagen and the death of Fryberger, written some forty years after the fact (though it must be noted that Fryberger's name and the nature of his fatal wound, as well as the details of the fight, were in complete accord with the official reports).

Lieutenant David L. Stone—who in a long and storied career would rise to the rank of major general—filed his report on August 6, 1900. It is so darkly smudged as to be barely legible. On page 4, he wrote, "A prominent figure among the insurgents was David Fagan, a renegade, deserter from the 24th U.S. Infantry. He was plainly seen and shot at by members of Co. 'F' but they were not fortunate enough to hit him."[23]

Forty years would pass before Ganzhorn placed Fagen squarely in the middle of the fight at Mount Corona. And Lieutenant Stone's report, tucked away in a yellowing folder in the archives, would go unnoticed for more than a century. The army had done a good job of keeping Fagen's role in the war a secret. But soon the veil of secrecy would be lifted.

Alstaetter

22

The name most dreadful in the ears of American soldiers in the Philippines during the insurrection was that of Fagan, an Afro-American soldier who deserted the Stars and Stripes and became, according to common belief, the most brilliant and dangerous of the Filipino chieftains, not excepting Aguinaldo himself. How much of this reputation Fagan owed to his exploits, and how much to the mythmaking faculty natural to mankind, we do not pretend to calculate; but his name did excite vividly among our soldiers a superstitious terror similar to that which made awful among the Saracens the name of Richard the Lion-hearted.

New York Age,
April 20, 1905

ACCORDING TO GANZHORN, Fagen was "grinning . . . leering"—as he fired down upon the Americans, who were finding their uphill fight anything but amusing. Men don't typically grin during battle as if enjoying combat as a kind of rough-and-tumble game. Freely parodying black people was the order of the day, and for a black villain to "grin" and "leer" while killing a white man would only further inflame the white reader's sense of outrage, rendering the moment when the villain receives his "just reward" all the more satisfying. Ganzhorn assures the reader that "the cunning Fagan" will eventually get his.

Ganzhorn may well have embellished his story by dressing Fagen in "parts of the uniform he had disgraced" and appearing to be gloating as he shot Fryberger. And yet it does not seem out of the question that an exultant Fagen might revel in the chance to have at a disadvantage those who had held every advantage over him in every waking hour of his prior life. If he had in fact deserted out of desperation and rage at the treatment he had received at the hands of his white "superiors," this opportunity to sight down upon his sworn enemies as they gasped and flailed in the most vulnerable of straits might have inspired a grin of unleashed fury, of pure vindictive joy.

Had Fagen planned and directed the ambush near Mount Corona, as Ganzhorn believed? Events that were to follow shortly after that engagement suggest that if Fagen hadn't led the attack, he had been a central player in its conception and execution.

In the days after the fight on Mount Corona, the indefatigable Funston, along with three companies of the Twenty-Second Infantry and three squadrons of Macabebes, scoured the trails in the Mount Corona and Mount Balubad region. The general's intent was not only to flush the guerrillas out of the mountains but also to destroy their food supplies and sources of shelter as well. On this occasion, he reported: "On the march from Sibul we covered a large section of new country south of Corona burning villages and destroying cornfields. Saw but few insurgents."[1]

While Funston and his men ranged as far as "the Pacific divide," Lacuna's men had come down from the mountains and gathered in the dense forest north of Jaen. Batson and his Macabebes were in search of them in that area but having no luck. A Dr. Shellenberger of the Engineer Corps wrote that according to his notes, "he [Fagen] was engaged in attacks upon our road parties" near Jaen on the thirty-first.[2]

A day later, just nine days after the fight in the Bulacans, a young lieutenant in the Signal Corps, Frederick W. Alstaetter, accompanied by three men of the Signal Corps and an eleven-man escort of the Fourth Cavalry, led a survey party north toward San Isidro on the San Miguel Road. Alstaetter and his party had started from Manila; for five days they had been making an examination of roads and trails leading from Manila to San Isidro via Norzagaray and San Miguel.[3]

On this first day of August the heat was intense and shade scarce, the streams swollen by the summer rains, the derelict patchwork of rice fields, canebrakes, and scrub forest a lush green. At 12:30 p.m., seven miles south of San Isidro, Alstaetter and his party rode along between swampy fields of recently planted rice. With the sweltering heat and the languid motion of the horses plodding through the rain-soaked earth, the party had lapsed into a collective daze. When the large guerrilla force opened up on them, pandemonium ensued. Men yanked their Krag carbines from their saddle scabbards and reeled from their plunging horses. As they scrambled for cover, Private Tischler was hit and killed, Private Long shot in the abdomen. The horses fled in every direction. Within minutes the ambush developed into a battle, with Alstaetter and his men fighting partially submerged in the roadside paddy.[4]

Lieutenant Frederick W. Alstaetter (1897 USMA Class Album, Special Collections, USMA Library)

In the initial panic, no one was probably more confused than Lieutenant Frederick Alstaetter. He had been in the islands for only ten weeks, all but the previous five days spent in Manila. His training was as an engineer and a surveyor; leading men in combat was probably more of an afterthought. Raised in the small town of Golian, Ohio, the twenty-four-year-old Alstaetter was a gifted student, graduating sixth in his West Point class of 1897. As was often the case with the top graduates, he was assigned to the Signal Corps, the beginning of a long and illustrious career as an army engineer.

Alstaetter's men had only 120 rounds apiece in their double-rowed, blue-webbed belts, and as the guerrillas continued to encircle them in a tightening noose, escape was not an option. Nor was help likely to arrive from San Miguel or San Isidro. They would either be killed or be forced to surrender. Neither outcome was a palatable one, especially for an officer. It seems the revolutionaries bore a particular animus toward American officers. They took pleasure in doing cruel things to them. While describing some of the atrocities committed by Americans, Teodoro A. Agoncillo conceded that the guerrillas were just as capable of brutality: "Noses and ears were lopped off and the bleeding wounds seasoned with salt. In some cases American prisoners were buried alive." Some of these stories were the result of overheated imaginations, further embellished with each telling; others were the creation of Otis's propaganda machine, but some of the reports were true. The example fresh in Alstaetter's mind during the long and hard fight was of a recently captured Lieutenant Brewer and a sergeant. The men had been stripped and staked over anthills. As the fight dragged on, Frederick Alstaetter had plenty of time to contemplate Lieutenant Brewer's slow and agonizing death. He had no reason not to expect a similar fate.[5]

The fight went on for one hour, then for two. The men used their ammunition sparingly, picking their shots with care and firing just enough to keep the enemy at bay. The guerrillas crept closer, circling in as the small party's position became increasingly exposed. A private—also by the name of Brewer—was shot in the arm, Private Newman hit in both arms (by the same bullet). After almost three hours, Alstaetter's men were down to their last shells. Their canteens were empty, throats parched, their situation hopeless in the glare and suffocating heat of the midday sun. And then their cartridge belts were empty.

The Fourth Cavalry's Record of Events states that the fight lasted more than two and a half hours, and added, "When they saw that they would be taken, some of the men threw their revolvers and gunbelts into the deep mud and water."[6]

According to a friend's account years later, Alstaetter "thought long and hard before he fired his last cartridge. The temptation to save it for himself was strong." But out of a sense of loyalty to his men, the young lieutenant knew he could not "take the easy way out." When the guerrilla commander sent forward a messenger with a white flag, promising the lieutenant his men would be well-treated if they surrendered, Alstaetter ordered the white flag raised.[7]

The guerrillas rose up and came forward, rifles aimed at them. Desperately thirsty, soaked in sweat and paddy muck, Alstaetter and his men stood and awaited their fate. The young lieutenant, disoriented, his legs unsteady after the long flight, found himself being pushed and prodded along the road. In another minute he was brought face to face with an American black man, his uniform similarly caked in mud.

"Fagin led the attacking party," Alstaetter later recounted. "I was taken to him just as soon as captured. My watch and class ring were taken from me, and the negro took charge of them."[8]

An article in the *Lima (OH) News* stated that Alstaetter's ring "was literally torn from his finger" and that "he protested strongly" and "begged for its return." There is no other mention of Alstaetter being roughed up in the confiscation of his watch and ring or of him making any protest. Certainly these were some anxious moments as he was brought face-to-face with the notorious renegade.[9]

Just what words passed between the two lieutenants upon their first meeting, the tenor of it, would be most interesting to know. Was Fagen gracious in victory? Was he severe or subtly threatening? Or perhaps "impudent," as Funston would have him. One can imagine the mischievous smile of a Cheshire cat as Fagen admired his new ring and looked over his prize catch. Whatever Fagen's disposition, Alstaetter would later report that he was impressed by his captor's demeanor as he watched him giving orders in Tagalog.[10]

While a detail buried the body of Private Tischler in the field, others rounded up the American horses. The occasion must have been a triumphal one for David Fagen, to lead the procession of white captives and deliver the prisoners to Lacuna. "He was made a great deal of by the Filipinos," Alstaetter recounted, "and was in command of from 350 to 400 insurgents when my party was captured." With these two ambushes in quick succession, it is no surprise that the guerrilla leadership should hold Fagen in high regard.[11]

Once in the foothills, Lacuna dispatched a small detachment of men to bear the wounded—all wounds "severe"—to San Isidro. A short time later he sent a letter to Funston, "purported to have been written from Corona," promising that the prisoners would receive good treatment.[12]

With his captives safely handed over to Urbano Lacuna, Fagen and his band took their leave. He and Alstaetter would not meet again for three and a half months, when they would have occasion to become much better acquainted.[13]

None of this sounds like a man who so hated the whites that his trigger finger became itchy when in proximity to one. Alstaetter, as well as others who met Fagen, stress a vivid personality, a sense of humor, and a general affability that seem in conflict with Alejandrino's account of a man who asked for the charge of some white prisoners and, under a dubious pretext, shot them. Whatever the explanation, Alstaetter made clear that Fagen was at no time a threat to him. "They treated me kindly enough, only once one who was not in authority indulged in threats."[14]

Had Lieutenant James Alfred Moss fallen into Fagen's hands, it is easy to imagine that his reception might not have been so cordial.

The following morning at seven o'clock the wounded were brought into San Isidro, and at 8:30 a.m. Acting Adjutant Captain E. V. Smith wired the news to Funston, who was away in San Miguel: "Wounded says 3 and ½ companies on authority of Fagin. Many still there." Three days later, on August 5, the *New York Times* reported on the capture of Alstaetter and his men.

> The first serious check which the Americans have met in the past two months is recorded in a dispatch received this morning from Gen. MacArthur. It is assumed that the little American command which suffered so severely was completely trapped, and it was obliged to surrender or be exterminated.[15]

Funston's Great Roundup

23

Fagin soon became a hero in the eyes of the Filipinos, and was eventually the last to leave the trenches after his men had taken flight.

St. Louis Post-Dispatch,
April 16, 1902

FUNSTON'S MOUNTAIN EXPEDITION in late July and early August had ranged from the Peñaranda River to Mount Balubad and as far back as the Pacific divide. On August 12, he reported to General Wheaton, "There is nothing left in 500 square miles of mountain country, all barracks and camps having been destroyed." Now, in his latest scheme, Funston envisioned a force of two thousand men in a great sweep of the lowlands between San Isidro and San Miguel. "Am arranging a big movement to clean out the country north of San Miguel which since we chased the enemy out of the mountains is very badly infested."[1]

With Batson and his Macabebes cutting off any retreat to the mountains, a cordon of men would have Lacuna's fighters corralled. David Fagen, with his direction of two recent ambushes, had gotten the general's fullest attention. Funston was eager to set his grand scheme in motion, but the elements would not cooperate: "The whole country is impassible the rivers all being out of their banks the troops are being held in readiness."[2]

While the rain turned the sodden landscape lush and green and the rivers flooded, the intrigue and double-dealing of a guerrilla war continued in the garrisoned towns. A directive to Funston from the adjutant in Manila reveals the deep involvement of the citizens in the resistance and also how thoroughly their activities had been penetrated by Funston's network of spies. Fourteen prominent citizens were ordered arrested and confined in San Isidro prison, all charged as contributors in aiding and abetting the revolution. "Supplies are

171

sent out from Barrio of Gapan at night on backs of carabaos also from San Isidro and Peñaranda."[3]

Many of these men were thought to have been solidly in the American camp. American officers throughout the islands were encountering the same phenomenon, and the Manila papers were full of references to the "wily and treacherous Filipino." MacArthur, only months into the job of military governor, had concluded that the entire population supported the *insurrectos*, while Funston maintained that the townspeople supplied the revolutionaries out of coercion. Whether cooperation willing or coerced, Captain John R. M. Taylor backed MacArthur's assessment: "the pueblos, regardless of the fact of American occupation and organization, were the actual bases for all insurgent activities, not only in the sense of furnishing supplies to the guerrilla bands, but also as affording their members secure places of refuge."[4]

The guerrillas, even officers, came and went in the guise of amigos, and those townspeople who collaborated with the Americans were never safe. Lieutenant Burton Mitchell, Funston's aide and cousin, wrote to the *Iola Daily Register*, describing San Isidro as "one of the best towns in Luzon" with a *presidente* who had much more power than a typical American mayor: "He is well educated, intelligent and foxy as can be, seems perfectly loyal to us, furnishes reliable information about the movements of the enemy. . . . His life has been threatened time and time again and he never sleeps in the same house two nights in succession, for fear of assassination."[5]

To Funston, the people had flocked to the garrisoned towns to escape the depredations of marauding guerrilla and ladrone bands. While there is no question the villagers were hard-pressed by the guerrillas for food, for care for the wounded, and for replacement fighters for those lost, Funston never acknowledged his own contribution to the influx of people into the towns—the burning of crops and villages, punitive night raids by mounted patrols, and the not infrequent abuses committed by detachments on the hike. Private Edward H. Beal's description of the methods his company of the Thirty-Fifth U.S. Volunteers used to extract information would suggest that however extreme the reprisals committed by the guerrillas, the Americans resorted to their own brand of harsh measures as well.

> Once we caught a Filipino major. The officers are the worst of the lot to get information out of. They put him on the rack until I thought he'd die, but they could not get him to talk. Then they threw him into an old deserted bamboo shack and went off. I don't suppose he ever got out of there, though. He was too far gone.

Another time we caught six Filipinos about 7 o'clock in the morning outside of San Miguel. We knew they had rifles hidden, but they wouldn't tell, so we tied them into a crouching position, took them to a little creek and pushed them in until they were immersed. Five men stood on each Filipino until they could tell from the bubbles that the captive had enough. Then they would let him up long enough for air, and down he'd go again.

We found out where the rifles were hidden.[6]

Almost daily, Lacuna's men cut sections of telegraph wires, carting away a half mile of wire at a time and chopping down poles as well. Funston burned the houses and even entire barrios nearest the scene of the cut and summarily executed the perpetrators on the rare occasions one could be apprehended. For instance, a cable from Funston to Manila stated, "Man who has had charge of work of cutting telegraph lines captured and shot yesterday." Or, "man who cut wire . . . expired very suddenly same day so it will not be necessary to try him." There were also casual mentions of barrios burned: "Buluarte is a barrio or rather sitio southeast of Santo Cristo which I burned some weeks ago." These reprisals seemed to have no effect on Lacuna's resolve to wage war on the invaders, however limited his means.[7]

Lacuna commanded anywhere from eight to twelve guerrilla companies, each from ten to fifty men and assigned to a sector of Nueva Ecija. Among his foremost captains or *jefes de guerrilla* were Pedro Panungao, Dionisio Santos, Sixto Francisco, Pedro Villaroman, Diego de Guzman, Eugenio Lazaro, Cornelio Mendoza, and David Fagen. Their assignment was to secret themselves in the woods, maintain contact with other companies by patrols, and, though they were never to fight the enemy "from the front," they were directed to "never let him pass unmolested." More than twenty other officers were in charge of such activities as supplying the troops in the mountains, gathering intelligence, and enforcing tax collection. The town leaders, outwardly friendly to the Americans, were usually in charge of collecting taxes, with the threat of a midnight visit from the guerrillas for the reluctant contributor. The guerrillas also stopped travelers at makeshift checkpoints on the roads. These coercive fund-raising activities did not endear the guerrillas to many of the impoverished people of the towns and barrios and, given Funston's disruptive spy network, Lacuna's overall success at mounting an effective guerrilla resistance in Nueva Ecija was mixed at best.[8]

Because so much of their ammunition was nearly worthless, especially when the powder became damp in the rainy season, Lacuna's men used it to fire into the towns at night to disturb the Americans' sleep and keep their nerves on edge. Colonel Clarence Edwards described the Filipinos' inventive way of filing cartridge casings and modifying the reloaded shell to fit a variety of rifles. "The ammunition that is used in the Remington is just as ingenious. They use anything from an old .45 shell or the shell of a .30 caliber to a home-made shell of a tin can. Except in the Mausers, of which they have only a few, they use black powder and not very good at that."[9]

In the grainy images of old photos we see the rows of peasant fighters in their *rayadillo* uniforms, rifles with stiletto-thin bayonets, *balanggot* hats with the front brims molded in an upward sweep. In the histories of the war, they remain largely ciphers, pawns in a chess game, casually expendable. We rarely, if ever, see the war from the Filipino footsoldier's perspective, or that of the peasant caught in the crossfire. In guerrilla bands such as Fagen's, the peasant conscripts and volunteers fought and suffered largely in anonymity, the wounded left in outlying barrios to die or recover with little or no medical assistance, the dead often abandoned where they fell as outgunned fighters fled for their lives. The ordinary peasants were the Filipinos that Fagen knew best; aside from the guerrilla chiefs of the region, he had no association with the Filipino elite.

It seems the prevailing view among American historians has been that most peasants participated out of obligation to their *patrons* and, in the words of Glenn Anthony May, "were essentially indifferent to the conflict." Resil Mojares takes strong exception to that contention, while agreeing with May's general analysis of why the Filipinos eventually lost the war. Reynaldo Clemeña Ileto argues that while the peasants he calls *los pobres y ignorantes* may have fought ostensibly at the behest of their *patrons*, they were also motivated by a vision of *kalayaan*— of a kind of liberty neither the Americans nor the Filipino elite was prepared to offer. In the companion novel of his *Noli Mi Tangere*—*Il Filibusterismo*, Jose Rizal wrote: "The peasants of that day kept alive a legend that their king, imprisoned in chains in the cave of San Mateo, would one day return and free them from oppression . . . the natives called him 'King Bernardo.'"[10]

Andres Bonifacio, founder of the Katipunan, attached a great deal of importance to the legend of King Bernardo, the warrior-king whose spirit was trapped in the mountains, as a motivating symbol for the indio. According to Ileto, "Not only was Bernardo Carpio the man in the mountain who would come down to free his people from oppressors, but as Bonifacio and his compatriots in the Katipunan saw it, each lowly *indio* could *be* Bernardo Carpio."[11]

Just what motivated Lacuna's men to fight on against such daunting odds is difficult to say. Many had been swindled out of land they had pioneered and worked for generations, and had gone from landowners to powerless sharecroppers, the *kasama*, in many instances all but a slave to the *hacendero* and

The Revolucionarios

inquilino. Perhaps they still clung to the belief that in driving out the Americans, the victorious leaders of the Republic would restore to them what was rightfully theirs. Perhaps they still believed in the promised return of King Bernardo.[12]

Gauging the level of commitment of the peasant fighters as the "nasty little war" dragged on, understanding why they kept fighting in what appeared increasingly to be a hopeless cause can only be guessed at. But their tenacity and loyalty were not to be taken for granted, nor their sacrifice trivialized. Ileto quotes an early commentator, Isabelo de los Reyes: "the people speak little and perhaps think little . . . but the little that they think is intense, forms their second nature, and that which they believe is their faith, is fanaticism in them and works miracles, moves mountains, creates new worlds and other prodigies."[13]

On August 14, Pablo Tecson paroled the ten enlisted men captured by Fagen. They were brought down from the mountains on a difficult two-day march that avoided all trails. Alstaetter, the prize catch, remained a prisoner.

On August 16, Funston received word that one hundred armed soldiers were in Pajo and that with them was "an American negro Insurrecto . . . Lacuna is with them." The next day, Major Wheeler in Peñaranda sent a telegram to Funston, confirming that these men were gathered in the Santo Cristo area south of Gapan: "Agent reports that Lacuna, Taguntong, Ventuce, Delfin, David and four hundred men were in Santa Cristo Wednesday afternoon and are believed to be there now. . . . The insurgents have seized four women in Gapan accused of being spies for the Americans. One of the women given to David."[14]

The last line must have come as a shocker to Funston. The image of Fagen being given a woman—presumably as punishment for her and reward for him—played into all the stereotypes regarding black male sexuality that white males, in a volatile mix of fear, outrage, horror, and envy, dwelled upon to the point of obsession. Wheeler, the future owner of the largest plantation in northern Alabama, saved the choice bit of news for last, knowing that the revelation would set Funston's imagination reeling as it had his.

Like many a soldier, Fagen took his pleasure when he could, knowing the next day might be his last. That he was both fond of carousals and also a terror in battle would hardly be unique in the history of warfare.

———•———

At last, at the end of August, Funston was ready to set his latest grand plan in motion. On the twenty-eighth he wired Major Wheeler in Peñaranda: "on the evening of the 26th Lacuna was in Pajo with many armed men. Fagan is with him and there is no prospect of their departure. He [Lt. Admire] says 17 American prisoners are concealed in woods near Pajo. I am able to account for but 14 men who ought to be with him."[15]

This telegram, like so many others, lets slip what the authors of subsequent field reports were careful to omit—the name "Fagan." Information as to who the captives were, where they had been captured, and how they were finally accounted for is not clear. That Lacuna had collected so many prisoners would suggest that his guerrillas had been more successful in their ambuscades than Funston's reports would indicate.

As with many a well-laid plan, the general's great sweep of the lowlands did not go quite as envisioned. After floundering about for hours in the swamp, some companies gave up and returned to their posts. Colonel Keller's men waded five miles in mud and water over their knees and "frequently into arm pits." Others reported having to swim at times, struggling across rivers on rope-lines, and fighting through thick growths of cane leaf. Lacuna's men broke into smaller units while others did their usual disappearing act, hiding weapons and blending into the populace. The seventeen prisoners disappeared with them.[16]

The one notable success in the general's grand sweep was the wounding and capture of Lieutenant Colonel Ventuse, second in command to Lacuna. "He [Ventuse] was a man of much influence locally and had much prestige among the insurgents. . . . The capture of Ventuse was well worth all the work,"

Funston claimed in his report, trying to put the best face on his failed operations. "I regret exceedingly that the expedition was not more successful but the difficulties of the region at this season have to be seen to be appreciated."[17]

Thus ended Funston's latest attempt to strike a decisive blow against Urbano Lacuna and see the upstart renegade hanging from a picket rope. The "nasty little war" would go on.

Sergeant Washington and Captain Fagen

24

ON SEPTEMBER 10, 1900, an informant brought in a report to Lieutenant David P. Wheeler, Twenty-Second Infantry, at Cabiao: "Gen. Lacuna with all the troops he had taken from this side of the river returned Monday. . . . Three American negroes, armed, were with the insurgents and they had three American horses."[1]

This is the first mention of any other deserters joining Fagen. Two more black deserters hardly constitutes the wave of defections Fagen had hoped for and the army had feared.

But, if nothing else, Fagen must have enjoyed the companionship of these two African Americans in what may have begun to feel like an increasingly lonely rebellion. He was just beginning to be known back in the states but was probably unaware of his growing notoriety, having only recently garnered small mention in the *Manila Freedom*. The day Lieutenant Wheeler reported Lacuna on the move with a large force including the three black men, the *Pittsburgh Daily Post* and a number of other newspapers published the same brief report, dated September 9 in Manila: "David Fagin, a deserter from the Twenty-fourth Infantry, is leading a band of Filipinos in Nueva Ecija. This band is very active in raiding the quartermasters' wagons and in robbing peaceful natives."[2]

I found no accounts in the files or in the Manila papers of raids on quartermaster wagons led by Fagen prior to September 9, nor of raids led by any of Lacuna's other *jefes de guerrilla*. It would seem that official reports of raids by Fagen and his "very active" band had been suppressed. And did he and his company rob peaceful natives? The distinction between being willingly supplied by hard-pressed villagers and unwillingly supplied was probably a cloudy one, with the inhabitants of one barrio more enthusiastic supporters of the cause than those of another. Or perhaps he and his band did in fact engage in a little plunder at the expense of the hapless villagers, not unlike their American counterparts. The accuracy of this brief report is impossible to ascertain, but obviously Fagen and his men were making some kind of trouble to draw this attention.

As for the three black men riding American horses, there was no way the guerrillas could acquire American horses other than by stealing them. Or, perhaps, they had come by them in these unreported raids on supply trains. A week earlier, Acting Adjutant Smith had cabled the commanding officer in Cabanatuan: "A number of American horses are concealed in the woods in place known as 'Sitio de Manoag' between Zaragosa and Jaen. Make effort to recover." The Sitio de Manoag was only several miles from where the three "American negroes . . . had three American horses."[3]

General Jose Alejandrino signed Fagen's promotion to captain September 6, 1900, and ten days later Lacuna added his signature to a second document. Fagen received his commission at San Leonardo, where Urbano Lacuna had established his headquarters on September 11. This was almost within shouting distance of Funston's garrisons at Manicling and Peñaranda, and the guerrillas wasted no time in setting to work.[4]

On September 13, Lieutenant Edward B. Mitchell, with nine men out sick, had thirty-one men of the Twenty-Fourth Infantry at Manicling. Mitchell himself had just recovered from the moderate wound to the shoulder he had received in the fight of July 4. In August he had petitioned for more men from Funston to replace the men out sick, but Funston had none to spare.[5]

That morning a detachment of eight men under Sergeant Walter L. Washington set out for San Isidro in escort of a mule-wagon. They were to pick up rations as well as an additional wagonload of provisions and return that afternoon. This was during the rainy season, ten days after a massive storm had flooded the streets of San Isidro, destroyed nipa houses, knocked down telegraph poles, and collapsed a new hospital that had been near completion. The Twenty-Second Infantry had limited their patrols "on account of flooded conditions of the country. It was nearly impossible to go anywhere except on the principal roads." The fields and tangled woods would have been a lush green and extremely swampy.[6]

At 2:30 p.m. Mitchell received an urgent message that "a force of insurrectos" planned to attack Sergeant Washington's wagon party upon its return. The lieutenant called out thirteen men—leaving nine soldiers to guard Manicling against attack—and led them hurriedly four miles down the muddy cart trail toward San Isidro.

But instead of meeting up with Sergeant Washington and his men, the would-be rescue party ran into a large guerrilla force estimated at four-hundred strong. Mitchell's men quickly fired "several very effective volleys," but the surprised guerrillas soon recovered and within minutes the small party of regulars was taking fire from all sides. Mitchell and his thirteen men plunged into the forest and escaped across a lake five to six feet deep. "The insurrectos followed us," Mitchell reported, "but were unable to find the direction we had gone." Muddied and exhausted, the detachment hurried on the mile and a half to Gapan.[7]

One would think that would have been enough excitement for one day, but Major Wheeler called out thirty-eight men of the Thirty-Fourth U.S. Volunteers to accompany Mitchell, and back across the river they went.

In the meantime, the large guerrilla force under Captain Fagen ambushed the returning wagon party. Sergeant Washington's detachment, which now included two mule drivers and a Hospital Corpsman, Private Patrick Shea—twelve men in all—held off the overwhelming force until nearly surrounded, then "became badly scattered." Walter Washington was wounded in the first volley but not severely; either he was unable to run, or he chose not to. He was last seen standing by one of the wagons. Whether he was returning fire and taunting the enemy is not known. But it is not hard to imagine the famously combative first sergeant and the equally vocal guerrilla captain engaging in a war of words in the midst of battle.

Six of Washington's men escaped, four of them wounded. Hours later, three of the escapees straggled into Manicling; a fourth was found alive by a search party the following day. Two of the escapees were tracked down by the guerrillas and killed, and four of them were taken captive, among them Private Patrick Shea of the Hospital Corps. One of the mule-wagons, laden with rations, was led away, presumably in the direction of San Leonardo. Captain Fagen ordered the other wagon set afire in order to lure a rescue party to the scene, or so our old friend Jack Ganzhorn maintained.[8]

A short time later, Lieutenant Mitchell, now with fifty-one men, arrived back at the road and proceeded eastward where a column of smoke rose from the site of the ambush. He was overtaken by Lieutenant Richard C. Day and sixteen of Funston's Scouts, dispatched when news reached San Isidro of the attacks. Funston had also directed Lieutenant Morrison in Gapan to take all the men available and to cross the river into Manicling country. As soon as the firing had been heard in Peñaranda, Lieutenant Dietrick set off along the river with forty men of the Thirty-Fourth Volunteer Infantry.[9]

Day's mounted men raced ahead where smoke billowed from the second wagon that had been set on fire. As they came upon the site of the ambush, a guerrilla force estimated at 150 men opened fire, killing two horses in the first volley. Day's men leapt from their horses and scrambled for cover. The guerrillas came on, driving the Scouts down toward the bank of the flooding Rio Peñaranda (often referred to as the Rio Chico). Three hundred yards to the west, Mitchell ordered his men "to clear the road on both sides" but found the guerrillas just as intent upon holding their ground.

With their backs to the flooding Rio Chico, Day's sixteen scouts fought to hold off the guerrillas moving closer behind cover of brush and trees. If Jack Ganzhorn can be believed, Fagen announced himself to the Scouts and, while creeping forward through the undergrowth, exchanged insults and taunts with Lieutenant Day.

Both Mitchell and Day reported that the engagement lasted for two hours, during which time Mitchell's fifty-one men made little or no progress inching their way forward from the west. According to Ganzhorn, the Scouts "had fired their last Krags and had their six-shooter shells in their hats beside them, waiting for the end," when, as night came on, Lieutenant Morrison's detachment and Lieutenant Dietrick's forty men converged on the scene. Funston reported that "quite a hot fight" took place in a last exchange in which Private Edward C. Johnson was "mortally wounded and died a short time later." Funston expressed his regret that with night approaching, the guerrillas slipped away, leaving seven of their dead on the field.[10]

In their reports of the day's wild events, neither Funston, Mitchell, nor Day mention Fagen or any other guerrilla leader.[11] We have only Ganzhorn's rendering of the action in his autobiography and strong circumstantial evidence to make the case for Fagen's participation. A cross-referencing of the various reports makes clear that Ganzhorn conflated Lacuna's attack of July 4 on Manicling and the attack of Sergeant Washington's wagon train on September 13. This blending of the two engagements was almost certainly intentional with the idea of introducing the notorious Fagen in a fight in which Ganzhorn was *not* present, then following with his dramatic face-to-face encounter with Fagen near Mount Corona on July 22.

Still getting around on crutches, I missed the fighting on the night of July 4. Taking advantage of the rainy season, and wanting revenge for his defeat at Penaranda, General Lacuna attacked the garrisons of Penaranda, Gapan and Manacling [*sic*] simultaneously.

Penaranda had no trouble repulsing the enemy, but the fight in Manacling was different. That very day, July 4, forty negro soldiers of the Twenty-fourth, under a Lieutenant Mitchell (not the Mitchell on General Funston's staff), arrived to garrison the town. While General Lacuna with four hundred men attacked the handful of negroes in Manacling, Fagan, a deserter from the Twenty-fourth, now an officer under Lacuna, ambushed two four-mule wagons under escort of a few negro soldiers. After killing all but one of the escort, the ambushers burned the wagons in the road. The only mounted troops in San Isidro at the time were the Scouts and under the command of Lieutenant Richard C. Day they crossed the Rio Chico and raced for Manacling.

Fagan, the American renegade, cunningly waited in ambush near the burned wagons.

As the nine Scouts with Lieutenant Day galloped up to the scene of the ambush, the gugus met them with a volley. Quickly hitting the ground and deploying, their backs to the swollen river, the Scouts made their fight. Death by gunfire or drowning was their only choice.

Driving his gugus to the attack, creeping closer behind shelter of brush and trees, the renegade Fagan kept up a string of taunting boasts.

"Captain Fagan's done got yuh white boys now," he jeered. "Less'n you all surrender, my little gugus is gonna chop on yuh with their meat-cutters!"

Lieutenant Day leaped to his feet. Hartzell and Bates pulled him back down as he shouted, "Go to hell, you black scum! A million of you yellow-bellied rats couldn't whip Funston's Scouts!"

When other troops arrived to support the Scouts, they found the boys had fired their last Krags and had their six-shooter shells in their hats beside them, waiting for the end. In the vicious fight of the next few minutes Private Johnson was killed. Fagan got away with a few of his men, but many lay on the scene of the murdering ambush.[12]

Ganzhorn's account comports with the three military reports in all but a few details: "ten" Scouts rather than "sixteen," "killing all but one of the escort" when only three were killed. After Mitchell's men had initially engaged the enemy and narrowly escaped across a lake, Fagen and his men would have had plenty of time to ambush the supply train. After overwhelming the escort party, there was time for a guerrilla detachment to unharness the mules that hadn't been shot and make off with the rations and captives. This might account for the discrepancy between Funston's report of 150 guerrillas and Mitchell's of four hundred; certainly a large number of men would have been required to get away with their big haul: four prisoners, the provisions from the destroyed wagon, the surviving mules, and the other wagon laden with supplies. By the time Mitchell and his men arrived back at the road and encountered Day and his Scouts, Fagen and his smaller contingent would have been ready for them. The Scouts rode ahead and into the ambush.

———

Three days later, the guerrillas again attacked the garrison at Manicling but apparently to little effect as no details were provided. On that same day a patrol found Walter Washington's body in the same place he had last been seen by his men. "I saw his body which was beyond identification," Mitchell wrote. "I recognized his blue shirt and chevrons on his arm." The lieutenant also reported that "Privates Benjamin, Lee Brown, Thomas Brown and Pvt. Shea, Hospital Corps, are now in the hands of the Insurrectos."[13]

Thomas Brown had been wounded in the fight of July 4. Several days passed before the bullet was removed from near his shoulder blade. Now he was a captive, his shoes confiscated and, with the other prisoners, made to march throughout the night in hip-deep water.

The references to Fagen's presence in the immediate area of Manicling by both Lieutenant Wheeler and General Lacuna, along with Ganzhorn's account, all but confirm that Fagen did indeed lead the attack of September 13. An additional piece of circumstantial evidence linking Fagen to the attack near Manicling comes from Private George Jackson's letter to the *Manila Times* on May 14, 1901.

The Renegade Fagan

Dear Sir—Will you kindly publish this letter in the columns of the *Times* for the benefit of all who may be interested about Fagan the great renegade. The article published in the morning (May 12th) *Freedom* concerning him says . . . "Unhappy was the fate of any American prisoners who fell into Fagan's hands. He was shot, and tried afterwards." To that last statement, I will say that there are (or have been very recently) patients in every hospital in Manila who were captured by or been in Fagan's custody as prisoners and each one of them claims that Fagan treated them all right and would not let the natives harm them. I have been captured twice by the insurgents. The last time I was put with Private Morgan [Michael] of Company E, 9th Infantry, and Private Patrick Shay [*sic*], of the Hospital Corps, both of whom were prisoners at the time and had been under Fagan for weeks at a time. They both say that Fagan treated them the very best he could under the circumstances.

I did not write this letter to vindicate the great renegade. I only wish to correct a few of the many mistakes that the *Manila Freedom* published concerning him.

Private Geo. W. Jackson,
Co. I, 24th Inf.[14]

George Jackson, captured by Fagen October 10, and Patrick Shea were captives together during the middle two weeks of October, less than a month after the fight of September 13. It is unlikely that Shea would have been "under Fagan" all that time if he hadn't been captured by him.

Captives had a rough time of it. Thomas Brown told of an officer who, in the absence of Lacuna, had taken him out and had him flogged. Alstaetter's health was reported to be "broken." And Patrick Shea may not have survived the ordeal. A communication from Manila to San Isidro on January 11, 1901, directs that "Pvt. Patrick J. Shea . . . be sent to 1st Res. Hospital, Manila, for treatment provided [he] can bear the transportation." Private George Jackson had not fared well with his wounds either, and he and Shea must have renewed their acquaintance while in a hospital in the early months of 1901. And while there, George Jackson, clearly an admirer of "the great renegade," had conducted his own survey of men who had been captured by Fagen as to how they had been treated.[15]

As all indications point to Fagen as the leader of the ambush, the question again arises: why the determination to keep any mention of Fagen's participation out of the official record? If they were no longer afraid that he might inspire a full-scale revolt among his former comrades-in-arms, what were they afraid of?

On September 10, Lieutenant Wheeler's report of "three American negroes," armed and on horseback with Lacuna, raises the distinct possibility that three days later, all three African Americans participated in the ambush of Sergeant Washington's detail and later held off Lieutenant Mitchell's force, which included thirteen regulars of the Twenty-Fourth Infantry—African Americans fighting African Americans in the marshy jungles and fields of Nueva Ecija. These two deserters who had joined Fagen would fight with the revolutionaries; in two weeks, one would be wounded in the arm, his name and fate unknown. The other, name unknown, would die in an engagement with Lieutenant Jernigan and his Ilocano Scouts on December 4, 1900.[16]

Did David Fagen and Walter Washington exchange words on that fateful day of September 13, 1900? And if they did, what did they say to one another—the revolutionary and the patriot—as the bullets flew?

Fall Offensive

25

IN MIDSUMMER 1900, Emilio Aguinaldo issued a call for guerrilla leaders throughout the islands to step up their attacks in the hopes of influencing the American presidential election in the coming November. The leadership's thinking—a case of *wishful* thinking bordering on the fanciful—was that if the revolutionary forces could inflict enough bloodshed upon the invaders, it might cause the American electorate to lose its appetite for nation-building and elect the antiwar Bryan. In a captured letter from Aguinaldo, the revolutionary president prayed to "God that he may grant the triumph of the Democratic Party in the United States." The McKinley administration wasted no time in making the letter available to the press. Funston himself wrote to a congressional candidate in Kansas, advising him that he held captured guerrilla documents "that would make fine Republican campaign matter," including one that contained "instructions transmitted by Aguinaldo to his subordinates to keep up the fight hoping that it might bring about the defeat of McKinley."[1]

Fagen's attack on September 13 was part of a concerted offensive throughout the islands with a wave of ambushes and acts of sabotage that unnerved the authorities in Manila and in Washington. Subduing the Filipinos was proving far more difficult than anyone had imagined. On that same day, September 13, a patrol led by Captain Devereaux Shields met with disaster on the island of Marinduque. Of the sixty men ambushed, six were wounded, four killed, and the remaining fifty captured. A few days later in Laguna province, General Juan Cailles outmaneuvered a force of 130 Americans, killing or wounding 57 of them. From the Ilocos to Albay, on the islands of Samar, Panay, Cebu, Negros, and Leyte, American patrols were ambushed, miles of telegraph line cut down, garrisoned towns assaulted, the countryside made unsafe for travel without heavily armed escort. Even Funston allowed that "exterminating the enemy" was not proving a simple matter.[2]

Nowhere did the guerrillas mount so vigorous an offensive as in the Ilocos Provinces of northwestern Luzon. Under General Manuel Tinio, the Filipinos laid siege to the towns along the Abra River, cut off the Americans' supply lines and communications, and ambushed patrols whenever they ventured out from their posts. Finally, General Samuel B. M. Young ordered that detachments of fewer than one hundred men were not to be sent out. Young pleaded for more troops and advocated the implementation of the harsh tactics employed by the British against the Boers in South Africa: summary execution, burning of crops and homes, detention camps for civilians in hostile zones. MacArthur was not quite ready to go that far and instead sent more troops. But as conditions worsened, the general's thinking began to evolve along the lines of General Young and the vast majority of the officers and enlisted men in the field.[3]

"This disaster to American arms is considered the worst since the outbreak of the war," reported the *San Francisco Call* in September. WAR ALL OVER THE ISLAND OF LUZON: *The Rebellion Growing in Magnitude* shouted the headline in the *Mobile Weekly Monitor*: "Army officers insist that the situation no longer admits of pacificatory treatments: that the insurgents must be taught a sharp lesson, or, emboldened by the success of their guerilla warfare, they will mobilize in sufficiently strong force to annihilate detachments now holding small towns."[4]

MacArthur grudgingly acknowledged that this islandwide offensive could have been accomplished only with the support of the general population: "'The skulking bands of guerrillas,' as the remnants of the insurgent army have been called, are a mere expression of the loyalty of the towns. They could not exist for a month without urban support."[5]

But while this strategy led to short-term gains against the Americans and a boost to morale, it undermined the long-term goal of wearing down the enemy in a protracted war of attrition. Expectations of a Bryan victory were raised to absurd heights, leaving the ultimate outcome an all but assured and crushing disappointment.

William Jennings Bryan's chances of defeating a popular William McKinley were slim at best. Under McKinley the country had pulled out of one of the worst depressions in American history and won "a splendid little war" in Cuba. And the wildly popular hero of that war, Theodore Roosevelt, had joined McKinley on the ticket.

At first glance the Democratic Party platform seemed to hold great promise for the revolutionaries. While careful not to criticize the war and risk being accused of disloyalty (which they were anyway), the Democrats proposed first to establish a stable form of government in the islands and afterward to grant the

Filipinos their independence. Furthermore, they would protect the new nation from outside interference. But even had Bryan pulled off an upset, it is not likely that he would have presided over independence for the Philippines any time soon. The Filipinos had in mind a more immediate independence; the Democrats favored a period of tutelage rather than "abrupt disentanglement."[6]

Early in the campaign, Bryan declared imperialism the "paramount issue" and then, seeing that this tack wasn't going to play well, largely dropped the subject. The issue dear to his heart was the exploitation of the farmer by the corporate and banking interests in the East. But more strident antiwar comments by other Democrats, as well as members of the Anti-Imperialist League were like raw meat for Roosevelt. He barnstormed the country, delivering fiery speeches about the men "who had made the ultimate sacrifice for their country" and deriding his opponent's position as "treasonable." Aguinaldo's ringing endorsement of Bryan was especially discomfiting to the Democrats and one they would gladly have done without. After all, this was the same Aguinaldo who had called for his fighters to "give such hard knocks to the Americans that they will set in motion the fall of the Imperialist party, which is trying to enslave us."[7]

McKinley, campaigning largely from his porch in Canton, Ohio, ran on "the full dinner pail," and scoffed at the Democrats' plans for the islands: "We are required to set up a stable government in the interest of those who have assailed our sovereignty and fired upon our soldiers."[8]

To William Henry Scott, in casting the Filipinos as the aggressors, the Americans had conveniently turned reality on its head: "The horrors of war were thus being inflicted not by American aggression but by Filipino obstinacy." From McKinley on down, American officers and officials professed bafflement at the Filipinos' continued resistance in the face of America's "benign" intentions. "Hostilities will cease," McKinley asserted, "when those who commenced them will stop."[9]

"Our sons were in the Philippines," the president proclaimed, "because in the providence of God, who moves mysteriously, that great archipelago has been placed in the hands of the American people." Walter Karp all but ridicules the inscrutable McKinley's nonsensical but effective circumlocutions: "America's possession of the Philippines . . . was attributed to the workings of 'destiny.' It was deemed not the design of men, but of 'Providence.' It was ascribed to 'the natural outcome of forces constantly at work.' Having happened through destiny, happenstance, providence, or historical determinism, America's control of the Philippines . . . brought distasteful but unavoidable 'duty' in its train, namely the duty to rule the islands."[10]

The military leadership in Manila was just as confident that McKinley would be reelected. In their view, when the guerrillas understood that there would be no change in policy they would lose heart and finally give up their hopeless quest for independence. With the rainy season making activities in the field difficult in the extreme and the desire not to stir controversy before the election, any grand plan for bringing the revolution to an end could wait a few months. One could argue that these two factors—the coming election and the unfavorable weather conditions—had the effect of prolonging the inevitable. Meanwhile, military governor MacArthur began to devise a new plan, one that would call for less emphasis on the carrot and a much heavier application of the stick.

In the last weeks of September, after Fagen's ambush of the wagon train, Lacuna and his men seemed to have had the run of the countryside in the region around San Isidro. The day after the attack, General Wheaton admonished Funston in a telegram: "the Dist. Comdr. directs that proper escort be furnished to trains moving with supplies in your district. Small detachments unable to resist one hundred guerrillas must not be sent on the roads. Your attention is directed to this matter which has been the subject of instructions heretofore." This last line would seem to refer to those previously unreported raids on quartermaster trains; that is, why would the authorities in Manila be admonishing Funston unless the guerrillas had conducted earlier successful raids? The area around Manicling had become so dangerous for Funston's patrols that he was ordered to send only one large shipment of supplies to Mitchell's garrison and otherwise avoid venturing into the "Manicling country." When Mitchell received word that the bodies of two soldiers killed in the ambush had been located, he suspected another ambush in the making and informed Funston that he did not deem it safe to retrieve them. The bodies, left in the wagon taken away after the September 13 attack, had been found on the road from barrio Pantabangan to Gapan. Funston ordered Lieutenant Morrison in Gapan to "send a strong detachment" to recover and bury the bodies.[11]

Everything about the communications between Funston and Manila during that month of September seems tinged with alarm. Lacuna had put a scare into them, even if he couldn't overwhelm the smallest of Funston's garrisons at Manicling. Just what Lacuna's thinking was at this critical stage of the war in Nueva Ecija would be interesting to know for he seemed to be at a loss as to how to proceed, that is, how to build upon his recent success. It was as if he and Funston had achieved something of a stalemate, with the Americans in control of fifteen garrisoned towns and the guerrillas able to move about with relative impunity in the countryside. Rather than press his advantage, if it truly was an advantage, Lacuna's next move seems almost arbitrary, as if, unable to devise a well thought-out strategy, he simply chose to wander north with his two hundred regulars with no clear purpose in mind.

Northern Nueva Ecija was the region garrisoned by the Twenty-Fourth Infantry, detachments of the Thirty-Fourth United States Volunteers, and some four hundred Ilocano Scouts. Colonel Lyman W. V. Kennon was the commanding officer for the northern half of the Fourth District. Under the leadership of intrepid officers such as Lieutenant Frank Jernigan and Lieutenant Henry Ripley, the Scouts were an effective force for Funston in the Fourth District. The Ilocanos knew the countryside, could pick out "active rebels" from a crowd all "protesting their innocence," and were not above terrorizing the non-Ilocano populace.[12]

After taking a swipe at Santa Rosa the evening of September 21, Lacuna and his men moved into the region east of Cabanatuan. On the twenty-third, Lacuna's two hundred armed men and "200 without," most of them impressed from the local barrios, squared off against fifty men of the Thirty-Fourth U.S.V. under Captain Cushman A. Rice. The fight lasted for more than an hour. The twenty-three-year-old Rice received a mild shoulder wound and had his horse shot out from under him; a private was killed. Rice reported seven guerrillas killed and many wounded. (The mysterious Cushman Rice later became the inspiration for two adventure novels, both made into silent movies.)[13]

After the fight, the Americans apprehended a boy who claimed he had been impressed "as a herder" by the guerrillas. Colonel Kennon passed along that information in a telegram to Funston. The boy reported that Major Delfin Esquivel and Colonel Teodoro Sandico had been in camp with Lacuna as well as a "negro captain" and two white prisoners. The prisoners, Privates Patrick Shea, Hospital Corps, and Michael Morgan, Ninth Infantry, were passed into the custody of Colonel Teodoro Sandico. (Funston, correctly, suspected Michael Morgan of being a deserter serving with the "insurgents" rather than a prisoner.)[14]

Lacuna lingered in the area, engaging in small and pointless scraps, before crossing the Rio Grande de la Pampanga and establishing a headquarters in the forests north of Jaen.

Fagen and his men passed many an uncomfortable night in jungle and swamp, avoiding American patrols, in travel to and from mountain camps, or scouting for a potential ambush. Staying in the same barrio was too dangerous to chance for more than a night or two; Funston's spies seemed to be everywhere. Often Fagen and his men ate little, if anything, while on the move. They slept exposed to the rain, to devouring mosquitoes, to the wet ground and drenched foliage. Monkeys chattered all night in the trees; geckos repeated their cacophonous song a half dozen times before dawn. Several giant fronds of the buri palm might be fashioned into a rain cape, but these offered little more protection than the American soldiers' despised ponchos and shelter halves. Events of the first week of October 1900 give one a sense of the precarious conditions under which Fagen and his men lived, beginning on October 2, when a spy informed Lieutenant David P. Wheeler in Jaen of Lacuna and Fagen's presence in the area. At four o'clock in the morning Wheeler and forty men of the Twenty-Second slipped out of town and marched to the barrio of San Pablo. At first light they encountered Lacuna's outpost and drove it back in a running fight of about a mile where they struck the main body of Lacuna's force, about one hundred men. The guerrillas mounted a "stubborn resistance" for twenty minutes before Lacuna and his men fell back, some moving upriver and others escaping across the fields.[15]

Wheeler located the house Lacuna had been using as his headquarters and found "a number of valuable papers, implicating natives in San Isidro and here [Jaen], as well as revealing a well-organized spy system." In the same house, Wheeler found Fagen's rubber raincoat and tin cup with his name inscribed on it. Wheeler and his men had come close to catching both Fagen and Lacuna.[16]

But the most severe loss was the cache of valuable papers. The loss of secret documents and spy lists was an all too common event among Lacuna's operatives. Recurring blunders like this made Funston's job much easier.

If Lacuna's men were no match for Wheeler and his company of the Twenty-Second, they could at least take out their frustrations by tearing out telegraph lines, three hundred yards of which came down that morning several miles north of Jaen.[17]

After the near miss with Lacuna and Fagen, Funston sent out numerous patrols. As the patrols returned from their hikes, small detachments broke off and remained in hiding "in reasonable supporting distance of one another." Two days later, a spy again tipped off Wheeler as to Lacuna and Fagen's whereabouts. At four o'clock in the morning, Wheeler and thirty men slipped out of their post and marched for the barrio of Sapang. Lacuna's spies had frustrated American attempts at night raids, and in this case a runner reached Lacuna and Fagen only minutes before Wheeler and his men crept up on the barrio. In another close call, the guerrillas vanished into the forest.[18]

Just what Lacuna and Fagen were trying to accomplish in remaining around Jaen after these two narrow escapes is not at all clear. Only hours after the near miss in the barrio of Sapang, a spy reported to Wheeler that he had located Lacuna and Fagen in hiding "south of the Post." David Wheeler—who

did not seem to be getting much sleep—called out his men and by midafter-
noon had "succeeded in surrounding 29 natives in the jungle and underbrush."
(In arriving at that specific number, it would appear the spy had done a head
count.) Wheeler sent word to San Isidro, informing Funston that he had Lacuna
and Fagen trapped. Funston, his Scouts, and Company M of the Twenty-Second
Infantry, under Captain Jacob F. Kreps, mounted up and spurred their horses
in a rush to join Wheeler and his men. They forded the Rio Grande and made
an interior move back toward the river, where Wheeler was waiting for them.[19]

From here we have only the last words of the report from the Twenty-
Second Infantry's Record of Events: "Lacuna and the deserter Fagan . . . could
not be located on account of dense underbrush" and "succeeded in escaping
after nightfall."[20]

With those few but telling phrases, we are left to imagine just how this intense drama played out. In my imagination I see Funston, Wheeler, and Kreps
creeping forward and crouching low to contemplate the forbidding tangle of
forest and underbrush. The two men they most wanted to capture or kill were
lurking in there somewhere. They were trapped, and there were fewer than
thirty of them. Several hours of daylight remained. All they had to do was go in
after them. They confer in low voices, perhaps whispering. If ever the hunt for
the guerrillas resembled "tiger shooting," as Funston called it, this was the
moment, with the light fading, the forest still and foreboding. Did they debate
whether to venture into the woods? Did they decide to lead their men into the
forest one cautious step at a time, rifles held ready, hearts pounding? Or did
they determine that closing with an unseen enemy in such dense undergrowth
was too dangerous?

Given Funston's reputation for aggressiveness, I find it surprising that he
didn't lead his men straight into the tangle of underbrush. He had Lacuna outnumbered four or five to one. This was the chance he had been waiting for
since the previous May. But on this occasion, it appears the usually recklessly
bold Funston decided to stand pat. With the cordon of soldiers around the
trapped guerrillas, they could wait until daylight, and perhaps bring even more
troops to the scene before flushing the guerrillas from their hiding places.

But when daylight came, Lacuna and Fagen and the twenty-nine men were
gone.

Old Scores

26

FAGEN HAD NOT ONLY issued calls for the men of his former regiment to desert; he had also sent letters threatening them with harm should he capture them. Was his motivation in attacking his old company and other elements of the Twenty-Fourth Infantry driven by ideological passion or personal grievance? Was he out to punish them for persisting in the service of their white oppressors? Was he out to get even for the way they had treated him during the ordeal with Lieutenant Moss? The answer would seem to be both.

At eight o'clock on the morning of October 10, 1900, a detail of twenty African American soldiers from Company I of the Twenty-Fourth Infantry set out from San Jose, its mission to locate and repair a break in the telegraph line between San Jose and Cabanatuan to the south. With a "native lineman" accompanying them on horseback, Corporals William J. Burns and Charles "Cash" Henry led the eighteen privates, among them George W. Jackson, a 5 foot 4 inch fireplug of a man from Mountain Top, Virginia. These were men from Fagen's old company, men he knew well.[1]

By eleven, the party had marched ten miles and had still not come upon the break in the line. On they trudged, the only sound the rising and falling screech of the cicadas, the intense heat and humidity discouraging conversation. To their right, an open expanse of grass two to five feet high stretched away to a line of forest. To their left, grass five to seven feet high crowded the road.

The morning's dull routine ended when Private Henry Clay glanced to his left to see a sentinel crouched in a carabao trail in the grass. Clay swung his rifle into action and shot the guerrilla before the sentinel could put his own rifle to use. With that, from farther up the road, guerrilla riflemen rose up from the roadside ditch and blindly opened fire through the wall of grass. The twenty men of I Company plunged in confusion into the field to their right. Four of the men ran back toward San Jose, ignoring Corporal Burns, who shouted after

192

them, "Steady, men. Lie down!" The remaining sixteen soldiers rallied and "fell back firing, but owing to the high grass were unable to see each other or the enemy."

Over the ensuing half hour of fighting, two more of the men broke off and ran. That left fourteen men, scattered throughout the field, to hold out singly or in pairs. George Jackson was hit early on but continued to return fire. After fifteen minutes Private Skinner was wounded in the leg.

If the fight was a desperate one for the black soldiers, the guerrillas were finding it no less unnerving. Like their American counterparts, seven of Fagen's men also took flight. In another twenty minutes most of the men of the Twenty-Fourth were down to the last of their 120 rounds. The long line of guerrillas left the ditch and swarmed in an encircling maneuver. For a few minutes they crept forward and then came on quickly.[2]

The fighting ended "in an almost hand to hand conflict" in what the investigating officer called "one of the most stubbornly contested little fights of the war." One by one the men of the Twenty-Fourth Infantry were surrounded and overwhelmed by superior numbers. George Jackson was hit a second time, a severe arm wound, while three guerrillas were killed and seven wounded in the final charge. Two more men of the detail had crawled away in the grass and avoided capture; the other twelve were not so fortunate.

If the guerrillas were in a celebratory mood, it was of a sanguinary nature. The native lineman had been shot through the head in the early part of the fight: "His head was subsequently dissevered from his body." The grisly spectacle and scene of pandemonium that followed had to have been a harrowing experience for the captives. Private James became "crazed with fright, tried to escape and was shot in the back, falling instantly."

When Colonel Lyman Kennon arrived at the site of the ambush two days later, he found the body of a "colored soldier" "horribly mutilated . . . face beaten to a pulp and unrecognizable." Private Eugene Young, one of the four who had initially run back down the road, was presumed captured. Weeks later, Young's body was found "horribly mutilated."[3]

Corporal Cash Henry, who had lost his hat during the fight, collapsed and died two days later of heat stroke. Subsequently, the hats and shoes of all the prisoners were confiscated.

And what did the guerrilla captain make of this ghastly celebration and seeing his former comrades brought so low? Did he speak to them? It is hard to imagine that nothing was said. Fagen and William Watson had been in the guardhouse at San Fernando together. For months, he had issued threats against his former company, and now he had delivered.

And yet, no matter how complete the victory, the success must have been tinged with disappointment for Fagen that no white officer had accompanied the twenty black regulars. Lieutenant Charles Hay Jr. may have been Fagen's primary target, but certainly another white officer from the Twenty-Fourth—any officer—would have done splendidly.

"It is my opinion," Hay wrote in a telegram, "that the disaster was due to a well laid plan to cut the wire and then to await the detachment sent out to repair it." And again he reported that "Surviving members all agree in saying that commands to insurgent forces were given in good English."[4]

In the tumultuous scene after the fight, Fagen was probably hurrying to consult with the other officers, organizing his men, determining the disposition of the prisoners. The sizeable guerrilla force divided into three detachments and dispersed, each taking some of the prisoners. About five miles south of the scene of the ambush, the procession passed through the village of Baloc. No one, it seems, was more inflamed in the hours after the victory than Fagen. While riding through Baloc he left an ominous message to be delivered to the Americans when they came in pursuit, as surely they would.

Two days later, Colonel Kennon passed through Baloc with a large force and wired Funston from Talavera the following day: "Left San Jose 7 am arrived here five ten. Met no enemy. From all I can learn party ambushing colored men numbered not more than one hundred. They are believed to have gone to Santo Domingo, reported that two hundred went through Baloc Wednesday also that colored insurgent will hereafter take no American prisoners. Shall round up Santo Domingo tonight. Men stood by hard march with great fortitude."[5]

Colonel Kennon found the telegraph lines cut in six places, requiring a half mile of wire to replace it. None of the telegrams and later reports refer to Fagen by name. Aside from Hay's report of "commands in good English," there is only Kennon's veiled reference to the "colored insurgent."

Kennon's reference to Fagen—"colored insurgent will hereafter take no American prisoners"—places Fagen not only there but in charge. It also makes clear the extent to which Funston and his superiors in Manila wanted to conceal Fagen's role in a devastating ambush of his former company. And it suggests that Fagen was not at all disturbed by the harm inflicted on his former comrades-in-arms, in fact quite the contrary, having sent messages to his former comrades "threatening them with special vengeance."[6]

Soon after passing through Baloc, Teodoro Sandico proceeded southwest to Santo Domingo, taking with him some of the captured soldiers from I Company, including Private George Jackson.[7]

If George Jackson had any sort of exchange with Fagen in the short time after the fight, it was probably brief. Jackson had been shot twice, and perhaps

Fagen spoke to the wounded man, whom he could not have known well during their brief time together in I Company a year earlier. Most likely George Jackson simply observed Fagen in action and whatever he saw must have made quite an impression, given that Jackson would be so bold as to refer to Fagen twice as "the great renegade" in his letter of May 12, 1901.[8]

——————

Fagen and his band stopped for the night of October 10 in the barrio of San Francisco, near the Rio Chico de Pampanga, and about four miles south of Baloc (probably not the barrio of San Francisco near San Antonio). Five days earlier Funston had dispatched Captain C. C. Crittenden with two companies of the Twenty-Second Infantry to Jaen, to arrive by the seventh. "Shall . . . give them no garrison or escort duty but have them constantly and systematically hunting insurgents. I hope to keep those two companies as a mobile column that can at once pull up and go anywhere." Late the night of the tenth, Crittenden received word that Fagen was in Barrio San Francisco, fourteen miles from Jaen. He called out his two companies, and in a driving rain they set forth.[9]

This night appears to be the one described by Jose Alejandrino in his memoir, which began as follows: "Fagan was very fond of carousals and drinking. In some of his escapades he arrived in a small village on the banks of the Rio Chico of Pampanga. He looked for a guitar, and, with some members of his guerrilla, he began to drink and serenade the women of the place."[10]

The celebration carried on until well into the night before Fagen retired to a nipa house for a few hours' sleep. In the meantime, Captain Crittenden had to feel good about his chances of catching the renegade. No one would expect two companies to be out in such foul weather marching fourteen miles in the dark. A reporter from the *Manila Freedom* quoted Crittenden in an article several days later: "We left at midnight, and I think the worst hike we have had on the island, was that night march through the swamps, through water waist deep, mud to the knee, surrounded by tall grass and brush that one could not penetrate three feet away from the trail."[11]

In Alejandrino's account, a guerrilla sleeping in the same room as Fagen was awakened by sounds just before dawn. He shook Fagen by the shoulder and whispered for him to wake up. He was certain that he had heard footsteps and the voices of American soldiers. A groggy Fagen finally stirred. When he peeked out of the window opening, he heard the Americans whispering nearby. According to Alejandrino, "He lost no time in jumping out the window and, taking advantage of the circumstances that the Americans could not fire for fear of wounding their own men in the dark, he selected the site nearest to the forest and with a revolver he shot his way out and escaped."[12]

Crittenden's account, a very disgruntled one, makes no mention of Fagen shooting his way out, and it may have been another episode that Alejandrino is referring to; in any case, as always, Fagen proved uncanny in his ability to elude the Americans. Crittenden told the reporter:

> We marched and surrounded the place just at day light, but found Fagan had gone, but we captured fifteen of his men, some armed, though most were without arms. They found that Fagan was only thirty rifles strong and he put in his time robbing the natives and dodging Americans. He is simply a "fake," and his only followers are the worst class of "ladrones" that infest this province. I do not think that he had any connection with the main army, and it is only a matter of time until we land him, then I do not think any kind of C. M. [court-martial] would be in order.[13]

Captain Crittenden, his nose seriously bent out of joint, was sputtering nonsense, but it was a purposeful nonsense. In discrediting Fagen, he could both vent his frustration and also further remove the idea that Fagen might have led the previous day's attack or otherwise be a central player in the guerrilla resistance in the Fourth District. If the military could not expunge Fagen's name from the record entirely, they could portray him in the worst possible light. Crittenden also reaffirmed Funston's later assertion that "it was mighty well understood that if taken alive by any of us he [Fagen] was to stretch a picket-rope as soon as one could be obtained."[14]

After news of the ambush near Muñoz, Funston's spies were looking everywhere for Fagen, and one of them had located him in Barrio San Francisco. Fortunately for Fagen and his men, the guerrillas had runners of their own. If fifteen of Fagen's men were captured, then the guerrillas must not have had much warning before the arrival of Crittenden's companies. Fagen and many of his men probably escaped at the last second while others didn't make it, and he very well may have shot his way out.

—————

In their memoirs, Funston and Ganzhorn made no mention of the renegade's ambush of the detail from his former company. The army also deleted any reference to Fagen from the record, and for more than a century accounts of the ambush of October 10, 1900—telegraphic and after-action reports, Regimental Returns, War Department Reports, the Manila newspapers, and later references to the engagement such as Brian McAllister Linn's—leave Fagen out of the picture (curiously, Linn writes as if Fagen never existed).[15]

But there is ample evidence to confirm that Fagen led the devastating ambush, beginning with a previously untranslated letter from Lacuna buried in the Philippine Insurgent Record (PIR) files in Manila. News of the successful attack reached Lacuna quickly over the "bamboo telegraph." The following day he penned a letter to "Sir Captains Dionicio and Lovero Santos" directing the brothers to prepare their soldiers for the return "immediately to General Quarters." He then addressed the misbehavior of some of his soldiers, once again revealing a ruthlessness that isn't typically associated with Lacuna: "Execute this order and don't get distracted, take Giron prisoner or kill him right there and also the two accomplices in the robbery, as well bring those who were looting, like Paningit and Pedro, because they have charges to answer to and what's more they are useless people and a dishonor to everyone."

And in closing, Lacuna left a final instruction for his two captains:

> Also bring the 7 deserter soldiers who were in the Company of David, and who left in the line of fire, abandoning their compañeros.
>
> Quartel General of Operations on October 11, 1900
> The General 1st Chief of Operations
> Urbano Lacuna[16]

On November 2, a newspaper in Pennsylvania, the *Wilkes-Barre Record*, published a story, saying that "David Fagan, a white soldier, had deserted and been made a Filipino general." The report went on, "Some time ago Fagin captured forty Americans, seven of whom subsequently made their escape" and concluded, "If reports be true this deserter exceeds the worst Filipino insurgent leaders in cruelty and general brutality."[17]

Upon reading the story at his station at San Quinton, twenty miles from San Jose, Sergeant Winfield S. Solomon of the Signal Corps wrote to correct the newspaper. On March 21, 1901, the *Wilkes-Barre Record* published Sergeant Solomon's letter, dated January 3, 1901. "David Fagan is not a white man, as you state, but a colored man," the sergeant began and continued with this account: "It was Fagan, with a company of insurrectos, who captured twelve men of the company from which he had deserted several months ago, one of whom tried to escape and was cut to pieces. Two others died and the remainder were allowed to return to their company several weeks ago. . . . They told tales of severe treatment and were warned that the next time it would be still worse for them."[18]

Sergeant Solomon's last line is in agreement with Colonel Kennon's message to Funston, "that colored insurgent will hereafter take no American prisoners," and reports that Fagen "had sworn special enmity towards his former company." The *Wilkes-Barre News* on November 8, 1900, went even further in stating specifically that "David Fagin . . . is one of the most daring and bloodthirsty of the Filipino Generals. He is charged with torturing American prisoners." In fact, there is no evidence that Fagen took part in torturing prisoners, American or Filipino, which is not to say that he didn't. But the newspaper's claim, as well as others, reflects a good deal of jounalistic license.[19]

If Alejandrino was indeed describing the night of October 10, Fagan's celebratory mood would suggest a man who was feeling no qualms about having ambushed and inflicted great harm on twenty members of his former company. Fagen's devotion to the revolutionary cause is unquestioned, but a burning desire to settle some old scores seems clearly in the mix.

"General Fagan"

27

Fagin knew that he would never be allowed to surrender, as were the Filipinos. Even though some officer had been present to protect him, the troops would have killed him without the formality of a trial.

St Louis Post-Dispatch,
April 16, 1902

FREDERICK FUNSTON'S FREQUENTLY VOICED reservation about the abilities of the black regulars was particularly in evidence after the ambush of I Company's detail on October 10. In the days following the attack, telegrams flew back and forth between Funston and various officers in the north who had set out with large detachments to find the "insurgents" and rescue the prisoners. Funston was particularly concerned about the garrison at San Jose and asked Colonel Freeman to rush two companies of the Twenty-Fourth south to "strengthen the garrison." "It is feared that the recent success of the enemy may lead to an attack on that place which might result in the already decimated company being overcome . . . all available troops at Cabanatuan are to be at once sent to the scene of the disaster."[1]

The haste with which seven men of I Company's detail had abandoned the field prompted an investigation, resulting in charges of violations of the Articles of War: losing their accouterments, "misbehavior toward the enemy," and failure to heed a command.[2]

Lieutenant Hay tried to put a positive spin on a bad situation: "From the appearance of the men's cartridge belts, quite a resistance was put up but our men were too greatly outnumbered to hope for a victory."[3]

Funston would have none of it and wired Manila the following day: "I do not think Lieut. Hay at San Jose can be censured for sending out a detachment of that size. He has only one company and ordinarily 20 men ought to be able to take care of themselves if well handled." And to that point, he lamented the scarcity of officers in the regiment, with so many on special duty. And he concluded: "In view of the recent happenings it is impossible to arrive at any other conclusion than that the negro soldiers here will not fight unless led by white officers. They go to pieces as soon as attacked. This does not arise from lack of loyalty but because they have no iniative [*sic*]." That same day, he cabled Colonel Freeman, commanding officer of the Twenty-Fourth, stating that "recent affairs show the necessity" of sending white officers to accompany all details: "While the colored troops do not lack either loyalty or individual bravery they seem to go to pieces when attacked from lack of knowing what to do."[4]

In his investigation, the Twenty-Fourth's adjutant, Captain Bachelor, strongly disagreed with Funston's assessment. The captain recommended certificates of merit for all the men, noting "the heaps of shells where each man had fought" and the overwhelming odds they had faced, estimating the attacking force at four hundred men. Apparently, George Jackson had distinguished himself in particular in the fight as Bachelor recommended him for the Medal of Honor. Bachelor offered in conclusion: "Had a commissioned officer of experience been in command and had led his men gallantly and skillfully, the result, in the face of such odds and under the circumstances, in my opinion, would have been about the same."[5]

Funston replied in a scathing letter, saying that the guerrilla force couldn't have been more than 150 men and that Jackson had merely done what a soldier was supposed to do.[6]

Two weeks later, on October 24, George Jackson and Edward Skinner, barefoot and hatless, straggled into San Jose. They had been released because their wounds were in bad shape, and the guerrillas had no means of taking care of them. A few days later all but one of the remaining prisoners were released, some seriously ill. William Watson was the last prisoner released and did not come in until December 4. There is no evidence that Watson and Fagen, who may have spent fifteen days together in the San Fernando guardhouse, were renewing an old acquaintance, but such a scenario does not seem out of the question. Certainly, Funston had his suspicions about just where the captives' loyalties lay.[7]

On October 14, Lieutenant Hannay in Jaen received word from an informer that two of the privates who had been captured on September 13 near Manicling were being held in the swamps south of Zaragosa. Lieutenant Hannay called out his company of the Twenty-Second Infantry and led them on another "all night march through swamps." While it was still dark they "surrounded the small group of houses occupied by the prisoners and guard." Funston, relaying Hannay's report to Manila, goes on: "It was not yet light and I regret to say that in the scrimmage that took place one of the prisoners, Pvt. Benjamin was killed by the fire of our own men. The other Thos. Brown was recaptured and is now here. . . . All of the four prisoners captured near Manicling are now accounted for except Private O'Shea [*sic*] of Hospital Corps who is a prisoner with Sandico."[8]

Private Thomas C. Brown's luck was holding; he had been wounded during Lacuna's assault on Manicling the night of July 4, captured by Fagen on September 13, and survived a rescue mission that his fellow prisoner did not. In the eagerness of Lieutenant Hannay's men to kill Fagen, the soldiers may have mistaken James Benjamin for the renegade. According to the *Manila Times*, Hannay's soldiers also mistook Brown for Fagen and were dealing with him "severely" when they discovered they had the wrong man. Brown told the reporter of the hardships he had faced as a captive, moving continually on long hikes with water up to his hips, no shoes, and very little to eat. The reporter concluded: "That Fagan is very popular with the insurgents is evident as Brown states his name is very frequently spoken, but more often he is referred to as General Fagan."[9]

Private Brown's story led to a front-page headline in the *New York Times* two weeks later, AMERICAN DESERTER A FILIPINO GENERAL / DAVID FAGIN OF TWENTY-FOURTH INFANTRY AN INSURGENT / IS ACTIVE IN THE FIELD / HAS PARTICULAR ENMITY TOWARD HIS FORMER COMPANY— RECENTLY CAPTURED TWENTY AMERICANS: "Fagin, who holds the rank of General among the insurgents, has sworn special enmity toward his former company. Of the twenty men he captured a month ago seven have returned. One was killed in a fight, his body being mutilated. Fagin sends messages to his former comrades threatening them with violence if they become his prisoners."[10]

It seems that Fagen was waging two wars, one in service of the Filipino revolutionaries, fighting to evict the American invaders, and his own private war, a war of retribution against his former regiment. On both counts, he was proving very successful. That his men held him in such high esteem, promoting him to "General" Fagen in their enthusiasm, and that his name would be heard everywhere among Lacuna's fighters would put the lie to Captain Crittenden's disparagement of Fagen as nothing but a criminal.

———————

While Funston had called out "every available man from Aliaga, Cabanatuan, Talavera and San Jose" to try to apprehend Sandico, Fagen and his band had already joined Lieutenant Colonel Joaquin Natividad in a barrio called Campo Batasan on the edge of the Candaba Swamp, not far from Cabiao. Natividad, only twenty-four, had returned from service with Tinio in the Ilocos provinces and become Lacuna's adjutant. From a prominent family and a member of Aguinaldo's core group of exiles, Joaquin Natividad would later do very well under the Americans in San Isidro.[11]

And while at Campo Batasan, Fagen and Natividad hatched a scheme, something quite different from the usual ambush.

Early on the afternoon of October 25, 1900, Fagen and a company of seventy-five men settled in along the east bank of the Rio Grande de la Pampanga. Stands of pandanus and thick brush provided cover along the edge of the steep bank, a sheer drop of twenty feet in places. Across the river, Mount Arayat loomed, green and lush, cloaked in forest giants.[12]

At last the distant chugging of an engine carried from downstream. The men stirred and took up their rifles. Soon the steam launch *Stonie* rounded the river bend and came into view. The *Stonie* towed a casco loaded with merchandise bound for San Isidro.

When the launch drew within range, the line of riflemen rose from the undergrowth. This must have been an almost festive occasion for Fagen's men; they did not have to shoot at a dodging and darting target that was also shooting back at them. All they had to do was hit the *Stonie*. And hit it they did, blasting away for ten minutes. Bullets pinged and ricocheted off the metal hull, shattered the wheelhouse windows, and sent the native crew and passengers shrieking in all directions. The crewmen jumped over the side and swam for the far shore, the passengers took cover in their cabins. "The launch was literally filled with holes." The frantic captain, hunched behind the bullet-riddled wheelhouse, pleaded with the attackers to cease firing.

Fagen called a halt to the firing, and the captain guided the *Stonie* close to the shore where it came to a grating stop near the bank. The guerrillas dropped down the steep embankment and swarmed over the launch and casco. The three passengers—a French merchant, a "*Chino*," and Señora Padilla, wife of the former "insurgent" colonel—had all been wounded, Señora Padilla severely in the shoulder. They were hauled up on deck and greeted by the "notorious renegade" who, Colt .38 in hand, relieved them of their valuables. While the guerrillas worked in a frenzy to grab everything of value, others set about demolishing the launch's machinery. There was no time to waste, and in a matter of minutes Fagen and his men cleared out, bringing the captain and his mate along as hostages and leaving the three passengers on the stranded launch.

The following day the *Manila Times* ran the story, "obtained through official sources," on the front page. The official source was Frederick Funston, in a wire to the adjutant in Manila. In Funston's imaginative telling, when the firing was heard "troops came out so quickly from Arayat and Cabiao that the insurgents did not have time to loot the cargo or seriously damage the boat, and fled." The article stated that Natividad and Fagen led the attack with 125 men. Lieutenant Whitfield had "recaptured" the captain and mate.[13]

This was the account that appeared on the front page of the *New York Times* on October 29, 1900. Three days later, a follow-up report appeared on page three of the *Manila Times*.

> We are now in receipt *from our own correspondent* [emphasis added] at San Isidro the following account of the attack. . . . The steam launch "Stonie" . . . was attacked . . . by seventy-five men under command of the notorious Fagan. The launch was literally filled with holes. They surrendered and steamed for shore where the boat was boarded by the ladrones and all on board of her were relieved of what valuables they had at the point of a gun. Everything that could be conveniently carried away was taken and the machinery demolished to such an extent that it made further progress impossible. The master of the boat, who is part owner, and one other employee were taken prisoner. . . . The steam launch "Sterling" . . . towed what was left of the Stonie and cascoes to Cabiao.
>
> From later reports it was learned that the owner of the Stonie had been released and is at present in Arayat.[14]

A comparison of the "official" account of the ambush and the "correspondent's" version offers one of the more glaring examples of the unreliability of military reports to the press. One gets the sense that the need to show the army in a favorable light and minimize any damage inflicted by the guerrillas led some over-zealous officers—in this case General Funston—to fabricate as much as report.

While Lieutenant Quinlan and his fifty Macabebes came down river from Cabiao, Lieutenant Whitfield in Arayat received word that the *Sterling*—the rescue vessel—had also been fired upon. He quickly assembled a detachment of thirty men and set off at four in the afternoon. Quinlan found the *Stonie* and casco stranded in the river. A woman and a boy identified Fagen as the leader of the "insurgents" and pointed to the direction they had run with the contraband.[15]

Lieutenant Whitfield and his thirty men hiked seven miles along the river-bank and camped for the night. The next morning, they encountered two men crossing the rice fields; they turned out to be the captain and mate taken from the *Stonie*. They had been released at four o'clock and reported they had been robbed of their gold watches and two hundred dollars in gold.[16]

The lieutenant and his men trekked across miles of rice paddies and as they entered a barrio, a large band of guerrillas fled into the forest. Whitfield and his men tracked the guerrillas into the swamp until, knee-deep in mud and with night coming on, they returned to the village called Pala Pala. There they settled down for the night. In the morning the women told the lieutenant that Fagen had been there and that guerrillas stayed there often. "Therefore upon this information I burned the barrio consisting of twenty-one houses," Whitfield reported. After spending the day in a fruitless and muddy search of the swamp, the lieutenant and his men returned to Cabiao.[17]

In a telegram to Funston, Keller wrote, "The insurgents were under Fagan 75 men with rifles." He also reported in an earlier telegram that the captain of the Stonie had "a letter to give to Gen. Funston." Possibly this was one of the two "impudent and badly spelled" letters Fagen sent to the general. It could be that after making short work of the *Stonie*, Fagen couldn't resist penning a few gibes for good measure.[18]

As noted above, on October 29, 1900, the "official"—that is, fabricated— version of the raid on the *Stonie*, with the headline AMERICAN DESERTER A FILIPINO GENERAL, ran on the front page of the *New York Times*, introducing Fagen to the citizens back home and confirming the attack on his former company several weeks earlier.

The authorities in Manila had done their best to suppress word of Fagen's involvement in previous engagements, most recently the ambush of members of his former company on October 10 and of Sergeant Washington's supply train on September 13. Now, in a complete reversal, here was the renegade on the front page of the *New York Times*. Either the leadership in Manila had loosened their restrictions on the press or, more likely it would seem, the cat was out of the bag. Too many people had spread the word about Fagen for his activities to remain a guarded secret. More than one hundred newspapers picked up the story, making the raid on the *Stonie* the most publicized of the renegade's exploits.

The *Salt Lake (UT) Herald*'s interview with several of the soldiers who had known Fagen in his time at Fort Douglass provided the most vivid description of young Fagen as a freewheeling gambler and fast talker. Retired Sergeant Alexander Williams had declared that Fagen "never would make a soldier. He was just naturally too lazy and had too much book learning in his head." By the time Sergeant Williams spoke with a reporter from Salt Lake's other major newspaper, the *Tribune*, that same day, he had moderated his opinion of Fagen and offered a somewhat different account.

Fagin came here as a recruit, I think, from Tennessee, and was here but a few months. He was a bright young fellow and was a graduate of Wilberforce college, near Cincinnati. Fagin's downfall came from lack of discipline. He was unruly and disobedient and for that reason he could not obtain the promotion that his qualifications would otherwise have obtained for him. . . . I did not see him often in the islands, but I knew before I left that he had deserted.[19]

With one year of schooling at most, Fagen was not a college graduate, whether from Fisk or from Wilberforce. More accurate, as numerous other accounts would affirm, was Sergeant Williams' characterization of Fagen as "bright" and "unruly." Sometime in that month of October 1900, the unruly young man from Tampa celebrated his twenty-second birthday.

"Negritos Soldados"

28

No one "boasted of the supremacy of the Anglo-Saxon" more stridently than Frederick Funston. Steeped in half-baked theories of Social Darwinism, the general only needed a few Gin Rickeys to set him off, especially if there was a member of the press nearby. Of the Filipinos, he opined: "They are, as a rule, an illiterate, semi-savage people, who are waging war, not against tyranny, but against Anglo-Saxon order and decency." Once on the subject of the Anglo-Saxon, Funston was hard to stop: "After the war, I want the job of Professor of American History in Luzon University, when they build it, and I'll warrant that the new generation of natives will know better than to get in the way of the band-wagon of Anglo-Saxon progress and decency."[1]

And so it went in one intemperate broadside after another.

Many years later, one of Funston's officers related an "amusing" story of those early days to a reporter for the *Lincoln (NE) Daily News* on June 8, 1914. The story typifies the white Americans' preferred view of the black man as harmless and childlike, superstitious and buffoonish. But beneath the humiliation of the black soldier, the article reveals how eager Funston was to capture Fagen. Funston concocted several schemes to entrap Fagen and one can sense his mounting exasperation as these schemes came to nothing.

> Brigadier-General Frederick Funston is a soldier, every inch of him, and he has a sense of humor which is lots bigger than he is. So it came about that a negro soldier in the company from which the renegade David Fagan had deserted, furnished some fun for the officers of General Funston's staff.
>
> Every effort had been made to capture the negro who had joined the rebels and was giving them valuable military training and the example of a dare-devil spirit. He had every member of his old company, brave soldiers under fire, so scared they would not go out after dark. He was

206

their voodoo. They were afraid they would wake up with a slit throat if they stirred from the lines or even put their heads out of their tents.

One day a letter from David Fagan was intercepted by a sentry. It was addressed to a private in the negro regiment, who was a messmate of Fagan. "Come out," it said, "and join us," and then it went on to tell of the wild debauches and good times ahead.

Funston sent for the negro, had him smuggled in by the back door, hoping that he might prove of sufficiently stern stuff that he could be used in capturing the renegade. One glance put the idea up in the air. He was one of the superstitious ones, who could face bullets, but would never do for a secret mission of danger.

"Are you a friend of Fagan?"

"Ye-es, sar, I done know Fagan, Marsa Gen'l, but Ise no friend o' that man, suh, deed I ain't."

"This letter is written to you by him. He wants you to join him," the general said looking the negro in the eye.

"I don't want nuffin' to do wid that man, Marsa Gen'l," the negro tremblingly stuttered. "I ain't goin' to 'sert no soldiers hea'bouts, nohow, not ef I can help it."

"Would you if I ordered you to?" the general asked, leaning across the table. "Are you a brave soldier?"

"Yes, sah, Ise a brave soljer, Marsa Gen'l, but I ain't lost no black desertah, sah, and I don't reckon I wants to find him, nohow."

"When you enlisted you wanted to be a soldier, and you have to obey orders if you are a soldier. Now, I am going to order you go out with this letter and get Fagan."

The general had not cracked a smile. His officers were convulsed with mirth. Some had to leave to keep from spoiling the fun.

The negro seemed, all at once, to crumple up at the knees. He slid to the floor in front of one of the staff officers. Tears streamed down his cheeks and his voice choked as he sobbed his plea.

"Please, Marsa Captain, please jest tell the Gen'l t-t-that I ain't that kind o' a soljer."[2]

The writer's tone in rendering the story tells more about white attitudes in this deeply racist time than it does about the real thinking of the black regulars in the Philippines, many of whom wrote articulate and thoughtful letters to family and hometown newspapers. Blacks were fair game for white ridicule, ridicule that reinforced stereotypes that virtually every white American grew up with at the time.

Like the *New York Herald* piece of 1912—"The Charmed Class Ring"—and Roland Thomas's earlier short story, "Fagan," so embellished is this extended anecdote that one may question how much, if any of it, is true. All three sprang from the myth of the deserter Fagen and affirm, if nothing else, that he had captured the popular imagination in those first years of the new century. We know that he was fond of carousals and, if there is any truth to that part of the story, it would seem he was having a fine time when he wasn't out "with his guerrilla," as Alejandrino phrased it. And, even caricatured, the depiction of the black soldiers' superstitious fear of Fagen may not have been that far off the mark. At the end of 1901, Lieutenant Frederick Alstaetter described his time in captivity to a reporter from the *Leavenworth Times*: "Wonderful tales were told about Fagin by the Filipinos. I heard that the American soldiers feared his powers to some extent. I was told that the negroes of the Twenty-fourth Infantry gave him extraordinary powers and that had a whole company come upon him suddenly they would have broke and run."[3]

Also, in response to Rowland Thomas's award-winning story, a critic at the *New York Age*—possibly editor T. Thomas Fortune—wrote of Fagen that "his name did excite vividly among our soldiers a superstitious terror."[4]

The emphasis was not only on the fear Fagen instilled in his enemies but on a fear heightened by the possession of supernatural powers. Regardless of how Fagen thought of himself, to his foes he was the badman—the "supernatural trickster." Like the gifted poker player that he was, with his ability to "read" his opponents and to bluff when necessary, Fagen may have cultivated the image and taken pleasure in inspiring a quaking terror in his enemies. One can see him laughing at the thought.

The complex subject of Fagen as badman and trickster and how his connection to the southern American / West Indian trickster tradition relates to the Filipinos' own trickster and badman myths is a subject for a scholar with greater knowledge of both Filipino and American folkloric traditions. But, as with Eric Hobsbawn's studies of primitive rebels and social bandits, Fagen could arguably be placed, at least partly, in those traditions.

———•∙•———

That the black regulars found themselves, as John Calloway put it, "between the devil and deep blue on the Philippine question" should hardly come as a surprise, and the concerns of the authorities in Manila and of Funston as to just where their deepest loyalties lay do not seem unfounded. But these men had families, had savings, had careers, and most emphatically had as much claim to America as their homeland as any white person. Regardless of their sympathies for the Filipinos, desertion was too extreme a step for all but a few.

But certainly they were conflicted in the role they were asked to play in the war. "I want to say right here that if it were not for the sake of the 10,000,000 black people in the United States," an anonymous writer from the Twenty-Fourth Infantry confided to the *New York Age*, "God alone knows on which side of the subject I would be." (The anonymous author may have been John Calloway, who later cited T. Thomas Fortune as a character reference.)[5]

Others criticized American policy as "a gigantic scheme of robbery and oppression" cloaked in talk of benevolence and democratic ideals; they complained of the brutality of white soldiers, having witnessed acts of torture and looting and been themselves subjected to the same abusive language heaped on the Filipino peasant. After a time, the white officers began to suspect the sympathies of the black regulars lay more with the long-suffering Filipinos than with the policies of the country they were sworn to serve. In the words of Willard B. Gatewood Jr., "What troubled many of them was the idea that, by shouldering the white man's burden in the Philippines to prove their own loyalty and patriotism, they were put in the position of suppressing freedom for the Filipinos. . . . This dilemma bred all kinds of ambivalence."[6]

Throughout the year 1900, the regulars of the Twenty-Fourth Infantry carried out their duties escorting supply trains, guarding construction projects, performing outpost and interior guard duty, managing the civil administrations of their towns, and patrolling the countryside. There they engaged in several fights of significant scale and were constantly sniped at and drawn into small scraps: "bushwhacking and skirmishing is the work of the American soldiers," Sergeant Preston Moore, stationed at Manicling, wrote to the *Richmond Planet*. "This might be called the bloody field, from daily skirmishing." And Private S. T. Evans wrote to a friend: "Temple, words cannot tell you the hardships I have been through since we have been here. I have been in nine battles and have escaped injury in all of them. . . . I have got so used to hearing Remingtons whiz by my head that they don't bother me a bit."[7]

Racial tensions would only increase wherever black and white outfits were stationed at the same post. When detachments of the Twenty-Fourth Infantry traveled through towns occupied by white troops, the whites in some instances refused to provide shelter or food, leaving them to buy food from the locals and find accommodations with them. The Filipinos, seeing the blacks disparaged and treated with contempt in the same manner they were, felt a natural affinity for the "Negritos Soldados."[8]

One can track the deteriorating morale in the regiment through the company rolls, with increasing numbers in confinement, punished for the smallest of infractions, and accused, in the slang of the day, of "going bamboo." And, indeed, many of the black regulars found the company of the Filipinos far more agreeable, some becoming attached to young women and learning the language with a facility that astounded the educated whites. (According to Alejandrino, "Fagan spoke Tagalog very vividly.") The reenlistment rate plummeted to below 20 percent. At the heart of this discontent were the strained relations between white officer and black enlisted man. According to Willard B. Gatewood Jr.: "Black soldiers complained bitterly about the treatment at the hands of those with a prejudice against Negroes . . . they charged such officers with cursing and abusing enlisted men and with subjecting them to inhuman treatment for even minor infractions of military regulations."[9]

Lieutenant James A. Moss later became captain and regimental adjutant. When a soldier complained of being called "nigger" and struck by an officer "with a six-shooter," Moss dismissed the charge as "a malicious prevarication." Jonathan Dentler stated, "He [Moss] also explained the large number of soldiers locked up in the guardhouse and tried by general courts-martial with the argument that the regiment 'contains a large number of scoundrels.'"[10]

At the end of 1900 there were seventy thousand American soldiers in the islands and six thousand of them were from black regular and volunteer regiments. Nearly one thousand of the African American soldiers would remain in the islands when their tours of duty were done, many of them marrying Filipinas, starting a family, and trying their hand at farming or working in Manila.

In considering whether to remain in the islands or return to America, the thinking of many of them seemed to run along the lines of Edward A. Johnson's observations, penned the year before in *History of the Negro Soldiers in the Spanish-American War*: "The Negro soldier in bracing himself for . . . conflict must needs forget the cruelties that daily go on against his brethren under that same flag he faces death to defend; he must forget that when he returns to his own land he will be met not as a citizen, but as a serf."[11]

One of the men who found himself in sympathy with the Filipinos was Battalion Sergeant Major John W. Calloway. Calloway had become involved with Mamerta de la Rosa, a young woman from the garrisoned town of Santa Rosa, just north of San Isidro, and they probably met when Calloway was stationed there briefly in early 1900. In April, Mamerta joined Calloway at his station in San Jose where they carried on an affair—discreetly for a time, but ultimately not discreetly enough.[12]

The previous February, Calloway had been sent down to Manila as escort to some prisoners. When his detachment stopped for the night in San Fernando, he looked up his friend Tomas Consunji, with whom he had worked at the Provost Marshall's Office. Consunji and his father, a wealthy merchant, invited Calloway to their home for dinner. As they had before, they talked frankly about the war and about the oppression of the black race in America. Calloway expressed his misgivings about American policy. They agreed that the war was grossly unjust but that there was little to be done about it. Calloway, an ardent supporter of Booker T. Washington's gradualist approach to race relations, advocated patience for the Filipinos; above all he emphasized the vital importance of education in uplifting the masses.[13]

After he had returned to San Jose, Calloway responded to a letter from Consunji, thanking him for his hospitality and once again voicing his unhappiness with the prosecution of the war: "After my last conference with you and your father, I was constantly haunted by the feeling of how wrong morally we Americans are in the present affair with you. . . . Would to God it lay in my power to rectify the committed error and compensate the Filipino for the wrong done! . . . The day will come when you will be accorded your rights. The moral sensibilities of all America are not yet dead."[14]

Calloway had served under Lieutenant Colonel Charles Keller, whom Funston described as "a rather stout man, past middle-age" with "a most pronounced German accent." Calloway was on the best of terms with Keller, but on August 20, 1900, Keller was transferred to the Twenty-Second Infantry, taking command of the garrison as Arayat.[15]

In October, John Calloway and Mamerta de la Rosa were married. They had been living together in San Jose for most of the year, and Mamerta was seven months pregnant. Cohabitation, however frowned upon, was common throughout the regiment; even many white officers openly consorted with a "querida"—a mistress. Lieutenant Colonel Keller had not objected to Calloway's domestic arrangement, "a matter of common knowledge at the station."[16]

But after Keller's transfer to the Twenty-Second Infantry, Calloway came to the attention of regimental commander Colonel Henry B. Freeman, whom he hardly knew. Freeman was sixty-three years old and nearing the age of mandatory retirement. The *Salt Lake (UT) Herald* described him as "a tall, handsome officer, with a bearing decidedly military."[17]

Perhaps Calloway counted on his usefulness in managing the myriad details of regimental business to ensure him the same latitude with Colonel Freeman that he had enjoyed with Keller. But that was not to be the case. In late October, Freeman had him charged with bigamy, accusing him of "occupying the same house and living in illicit cohabitation" with a native woman.[18]

When Calloway reenlisted on March 7, 1899, he was recorded as married, but in the June 1900 census he was listed as single and never before married. One of the entries had to be incorrect.

At his trial, Calloway defended himself ably and was acquitted "on account of lack of technical proof," which still didn't resolve the question of his marital status. Later, Moss would denounce Calloway as "a thorough scoundrel," who "shamefully abandoned his American wife, who from all accounts is a very respectable woman."[19]

Though acquitted, Calloway knew he would have to tread lightly around Colonel Henry B. Freeman. Nonetheless, he had escaped disaster and by late October had returned to his administrative duties. As stressful as the trial must have been, Calloway may have found something oddly thrilling about it as well. It seems as if he took pleasure in knowing that he was brighter and better read than the white officers over him, that he was capable of besting them in a duel of wits. Some of the more thoughtful black soldiers did the same—they wrote letters and spoke out while still attending assiduously to their duties—but none, while trying to remain within the fold, took risks as audaciously as John Calloway.

It was during this tense period, while defending himself against the bigamy charge, that Calloway would have read about or heard of Fagen's raid on the *Stonie*. From the first, Calloway must have seen that David Fagen was incapable of walking that fine line, of juggling those two worlds. With his volatile nature, his inability to finesse his way around the whites' impositions, he could only have seemed destined for court-martial and years in confinement at hard labor. But Fagen had refused to accept his assigned role. Rather, he had transformed himself into a larger-than-life figure, a singular and uncompromising character. This wresting control of his own fate may have been awe-inspiring to many of the black soldiers—disturbing, intimidating, an act alien to them in its open defiance. But no matter how critical Calloway may have been of the war, never would he have dared what Fagen had done: it was suicidal, it was traitorous and magnificent all at the same time.

Others believed Fagen's act of disloyalty reflected badly on the African American regiments, making it that much harder for their loyal service to bring credit upon the black soldier and on African Americans in general. Like Walter Washington and others, many were uncompromising in their loyalty to the flag and Fagen's treasonous act was something to be lived down. Calloway himself may have deplored Fagen's actions; we'll probably never know what he thought of Fagen, or what Fagen thought of him. We only know they were well acquainted and that the association would have decidedly negative consequences for John Calloway.

The same day the *New York Times* ran the front-page account of Fagen's raid, Captain Arthur Williams, the Provost Marshall in San Fernando, arrested Antonio Consunji, accusing him of acting as a political agent for the insurgents after having taken the oath of amnesty. In searching Consunji's home for evidence, they had come across John Calloway's letter to Antonio's son, Tomas. "The writer is, to say the least, very indiscreet," Williams wrote to Colonel Freeman. "He is John W. Calloway, Sgt. Major 24th Infantry, and I think it would be well that the Colonel should see the letter."[20]

Henry B. Freeman was, apparently, delighted to receive the letter, and he penned one of his own to General Wheaton.

> Respectfully forwarded to Headquarters Department of Northern Luzon, to the Adjutant General Division of the Philippines. Battalion Sergeant-Major Calloway is one of those half-baked mulattoes whose education has fostered his self-conceit to an abnormal degree. He has shown himself to be without principle by abandoning his legal American wife for a Philippino woman, and in my opinion he is likely to step into the Philippino ranks should a favorable opportunity occur. . . . I recommend . . . that he be immediately sent to Manila for safe-keeping until he can be discharged without honor and deported.[21]

White officers, married and single, carried on affairs with Filipina mistresses, as well as visited houses of prostitution reserved for officers. Lieutenant R. C. Corliss, whose career is associated with Fagen, would eventually marry a Filipina, to the embarrassment of his father in Denver. Lieutenant Frank Jernigan, leader of the Ilocano Scouts, would suffer public humiliation when, just as he was boarding a transport to return home to wife and family in America, his Filipina mistress stood on the docks, holding up their infant child and screaming after him in reproach as he sailed away. Jernigan was not the only American soldier to slink out of the islands, leaving mistress and child behind. But the act of consorting with a Filipina was not typically seen as a step toward desertion, an association that Colonel Freeman makes in Calloway's case. Perhaps Fagen's example and the close relations many of the black soldiers had established with Filipinas influenced the colonel's thinking. Or perhaps Freeman, the obviously racist commander of a black regiment, was just looking for an excuse to put the "uppity" Calloway in his place.[22]

With Freeman's recommendation, General Wheaton took little convincing. He passed the report on to General MacArthur, adding: "In my opinion he will desert to the assassins infesting this Department if he has the opportunity." MacArthur concurred on November 22, and two days later Wheaton ordered Calloway arrested and brought to Manila where he was confined to Bilibid prison.[23]

From prison, Calloway wrote an impassioned letter in his defense.

> The only meaning which I can now conjure up for that clause of the letter [expressing sympathy for the plight of the Filipinos] is a heart-expressed pity for all the wrongs the race of the young man had suffered for centuries at the hands of the Spaniards. . . . I probably remembering

that I too was a member of an oppressed race, and a cord of sympathy
for conditions was felt . . . that we as a people in America have few
rights that any one is bound to respect is perfectly plain to every colored
man.[24]

In order to make a final determination in Calloway's case, Major Inspector
General Wills conducted extensive interviews with him. He concluded that
Calloway was "a bright man, with an adroit mind, a very good command of
language, and a marked skill in evading a question and misconstruing words."
Calloway asserted that the letter "had no bearing on the struggle of the time
and was nothing more than a friendly, sympathetic missive to a person who,
though Filipino, had been friendly to the Americans."[25]

Major Wills saw it differently: "In discussing relations likely to exist between
the Filipino and American races, Tomas Consunji refers to the negro in America
as an example of an oppressed race. Tomas Consunji, Captain Williams tells
me, is like Calloway in that he is very fond of talking pseudo sociology and racial antagonism. It would seem probable that his views on the oppression of the
negro by the Americans are derived from Calloway." Wills found it "impossible
to assume that" Calloway's letter expressed "anything save sympathy with the
Filipino insurrection."[26]

On the matter of Calloway's "bigamy," Wills pointed out that Calloway's
wife had arrived in Manila in an attempt to bring about his release and that
they were on good terms. Even if Calloway had an American wife, she would
not have had time to travel to the Philippines. It would seem that Wills is referring to Mamerta de la Rosa, but his report is no help in resolving the mystery.

Major Inspector Wills further noted that with fifteen hundred dollars in
savings, it was unlikely that Calloway would desert. Nevertheless, Wills regarded
him as a dangerous man and recommended deportation under restraint and
discharge without honor.

John Calloway, now a private, fought frantically in his own defense. He
cited his years of meritorious service; he presented letters of recommendation
from white officers and Chaplain Allensworth; he explained time and again
that he had merely been engaging in banter when he spoke in sympathy to
young Consunji. The whole thing was laughable, an absurd misunderstanding.
How could they possibly construe these few words of consolation to an acquaintance as evidence of treason? Overnight the militant John Calloway evaporated,
leaving the devoted soldier repudiating, denouncing, denying the very existence
of that other troublesome person.

But General Arthur MacArthur was not moved and passed on his opinion
to the War Department: "It is very apparent that he is disloyal and should he

remain in these islands, he would undoubtedly commit some act of open treason and perhaps join the insurrection out and out. One man of the 24th Infantry by the name of David Fagin has already done so and as a leader among the insurrectos is giving great trouble by directing guerrilla bands."[27] Without waiting for the War Department's response, Private Calloway was subjected once again to a humiliating strip search before being locked in the hold of the transport *Sherman* and returned to the Presidio. Two months later, without court-martial or hearing, John Calloway was turned out of the Presidio guardhouse, a free civilian, discharged without honor.[28]

"The Courage of His Convictions"

29

AT THE END OF THE *Manila Freedom* article about Captain Credenden's near miss at capturing Fagen, the reporter closed with a curious aside: "I think our trouble will end with the election." The military establishment shared this belief, confident that a McKinley victory would deal a body blow to the "insurrection" and bring about the collapse of guerrilla activity islandwide. On August 31, MacArthur reported to Washington: "Captured papers contain convincing evidence that insurgent leaders are making strenuous effort to hold together until after election; indications also strong that disappointing result will induce many surrender."[1]

As expected (by everyone except the "insurgents"), McKinley won in a landslide over Bryan. But in the weeks following the election, while there was a noticeable diminution of guerrilla activity, the revolution showed little sign of the collapse the Americans had anticipated. It was as if the true import of the revolutionaries' loss had yet to sink in, and throughout the last two months of the year they sustained the fight with enough vigor to raise the army's growing impatience to a boiling point. In Manila, MacArthur chafed at this continued defiance of American authority. "Expectations based on result of election have not been realized," he reported to Washington. It seemed to him that no matter what benevolent civic projects the Americans undertook—schools, civil administrations, roads, clean wells, and the like—the great majority of Filipinos went right on supporting the revolution.[2]

And if MacArthur's patience had worn thin, it paled beside the darkening mood of the soldiers in the field and the frustrations of their officers. In the last months of 1900, reports of widespread American misconduct, at first only whispered, soon became too loud to be ignored. The abuses were not just those committed on the quiet by small detachments on the hike but also those actions condoned and encouraged by their superiors. When MacArthur finally announced his get-tough policy in late December, Brian Linn noted, "It may be argued that the general's action was a classic example of the adage that those who wish to lead must rush to the front of the crowd."[3]

An article printed in the *New York World* and elsewhere described the increasingly harsh American response to Filipino intransigence.

> It is now the custom to avenge the death of an American soldier by burning to the ground all the houses and killing right and left natives who are only "suspects." . . . To compel information as to where they have secreted their arms, the natives are often strung up by their thumbs, or nooses put around their necks and they are partly strangled.
>
> If many actual occurrences were literally told, the people would refuse to believe that such barbarities take place under our flag.[4]

Newspapers that supported the administration were just as strident in their denunciation of critics of the war. The historian Richard Welch wrote, "Most blameworthy were those opponents of the nation's Philippine policy who would charge our soldiers with brutality. Such men were the enemies not only of the army but of the truth."[5]

"The chief fact about the Philippines," the *New York Evening Post* countered, "appears to be that if you lay any disagreeable truth before the administration you are a liar and a traitor."[6]

Even William Jennings Bryan was castigated as a traitor. A journalist for the Rochester, New York, *Democrat and Chronicle* compared Bryan's perceived disloyalty to that of Fagen.

> It seems there is one American friend of the Filipino insurgents and bandits who has the courage of his convictions, however despicable his conduct may be. His name is David Fagin and he is a deserter from the Twenty-fourth United States Infantry. This unmasked traitor is especially ferocious against his former company of the Twenty-fourth Regiment and threatens to torture any of them who may fall into his hands. He is now a "general" among the Filipino robbers and cut throats.
>
> It is obvious to every candid mind that this fellow Fagin is doing openly and with arms in his hands on the field of action precisely what Bryan and his party are doing with voice and pen, if not in a more substantial way, to this country. Fagin is simply campaigning for Bryan in the Philippines instead of in the United States.[7]

Fagen was not campaigning for Bryan, and one may wonder to what extent he was aware of Aguinaldo's strategy for influencing the coming election, or if he had any sense of the larger political arguments beyond wanting to defeat the Americans and send them packing. How he might have expressed himself as to his convictions is impossible to know; in political terms, he was a man of action, not of words. But whatever Fagen's convictions, there was no question of his courage or commitment to the revolutionary cause.

In branding Bryan a coward and a traitor for criticizing the McKinley administration's conduct of the war, the article provides an example of just how rancorous the presidential campaign of 1900 became. The Anti-Imperialist League, in the words of Russell Roth, "a high-level assemblage of Brahmin blue bloods, business and professional people, former government officials, university presidents, clergy, and writers" was an outgrowth of the abolitionist movement a half century earlier. In the fall of 1898, as the McKinley administration's imperialist intentions in the Philippines became increasingly apparent, these influential intellectuals formed the league in Boston. They soon established offices in thirty states and gained the backing of a number of prominent newspapers. Moved by the Filipinos' fierce determination to win their independence and by reports of atrocities committed by American soldiers, opposition to the war spread. Many Americans, remembering their own war of independence against an imperial power, identified with the Filipino cause. By the presidential campaign of 1900, the league had achieved its greatest influence across a broad spectrum of the American populace. According to Daniel B. Schirmer, the league's impassioned anti-imperialist arguments found traction with "labor, farmers, middle class, blacks, whites, native-born, foreign-born, all political parties and beliefs, radicals, liberals, and conservatives." The anti-imperialists were adamant in the belief that to acquire colonies ran counter to everything the country stood for. America could not be a republic at home, they argued, and an imperial power abroad.[8]

The antiwar opposition made for a clamorous campaign, but it was not enough to defeat William McKinley and his imperial ambitions in a time of militaristic patriotic fervor and an improving economy. Unlike the later war in Vietnam, there was no television beaming home images of the horrors of war to American living rooms. Instead, there was one single cable from Manila to Hong Kong, and the American military governor had control of it. Nor was there a draft to compel young men to fight in a war they might believe unjust; young Americans in 1900, brimming with patriotism, marched off to war enthusiastically. The anti-imperialists, largely represented by the older generation (not unlike the loudest voices against the 2003 Iraq War), were no match for the youthful exuberance—personified by the figure of Teddy Roosevelt—of a nation sensing itself on the verge of international greatness.[9]

Alstaetter Revisited

30

FREDERICK ALSTAETTER'S CHILDHOOD must have been an interesting one, surrounded as he was, the only male, by five doting sisters. In a letter dated September 15, 1900, Alstaetter reassured his sisters that "he was still meeting with the most kindly treatment from his captors. . . . But I must admit to tell the truth, that it is a cage even if it is gilded, and just the chance to carry on a conversation in English would be considered a great boon."[1]

The lieutenant was not to remain in "good health" much longer. Captives suffered from an inadequate diet and exposure to the elements, to mosquitoes and days of incessant rain. In his boredom Alstaetter began work on a calendar cane, a carved work of art with each day of his captivity duly notched.

He had been warned that escape was hopeless; all the mountain trails were guarded, and should he attempt to escape through the jungle he would only become lost and die of hunger and exposure. And should he try to escape, they warned that he would be shot. But that didn't keep Alstaetter from planning his escape. His guards kept a close watch on him and whenever he went out of the little nipa house that was his cell, several guards went with him. Finally, with his pockets full of hardtack, Alstaetter waited until the guards had become distracted, then he plunged into the jungle. They tracked after him as he struggled all through the day, trying to keep ahead of his pursuers. He followed the course of a ravine, fighting through the undergrowth, making his way down toward the lowlands. After a lonely sleepless night, he pressed on and happened on a trail. He tramped on, thinking he had made his escape. But after thirty hours on the run, his hopes were dashed when a band from Tecson's camp cut him off on the trail.[2] The guerrillas did not, as promised, kill Alstaetter, and nothing was said of any punishment. This may have been the time when "one who was not in authority indulged in threats."[3]

Funston continued to work on a prisoner swap, and by late November he and Lacuna were on the verge of an agreement.

Why Fagen left Lacuna and joined Tecson on Mount Corona in the last days of Alstaetter's captivity is a mystery. The two men had not seen each other since the day of Alstaetter's capture on August 1, but Fagen's appearance in Tecson's camp was tied to Alstaetter's pending release. One possible explanation was that Alstaetter hoped for the return of his West Point class ring and his watch. But that doesn't seem to fully explain Fagen's arrival on the scene. Alstaetter told the reporter from the *Piqua Daily Call*, "We were taken into the interior and I did not see any more of Fagin until four days before I was exchanged, the last of November, 1900. Those four days I saw him all the time. We slept side by side together in a little hut and ate out of the same dish."

Alstaetter had begun to suffer from the stomach ailments that would affect him for the rest of his life. "They were in extreme poverty and we did not get much to eat," he reported. Whatever he and Fagen dined upon from their single bowl was probably not all that appetizing and certainly insubstantial, mostly rice and, if they were lucky, some dried fish. They were left to talk. "Fagin was a typical Southern negro," Alstaetter recounted, "with no education and ignorant, but he possessed good common sense." "He was often amusing," he added. "He would get out his Filipino commission as a Captain and show it to me and say: 'We are way above these ignorant Filipinos; we are equals; we amount to something.'"

Alstaetter first insulted the Filipino generals, saying they were invariably to be found a half mile in the rear during an engagement, and then he has Fagen insulting his own loyal fighters. Of course, Alstaetter's quote reads like a paraphrased conversation recalled from more than a year earlier. Fagen's actual words may not have been so disparaging of his fellow fighters as the quote makes him sound. Then again, maybe Fagen felt ambivalent toward his new "adopted countrymen," if he ever thought of himself that way at all. It would seem that he had fully embraced the revolutionary cause, and that is my belief. But we can't be completely sure. Perhaps he felt more alone than anything, a man without a country, fighting to survive in a hostile world.

But whatever Fagen's wording, it seems clear enough that he meant to place himself and Alstaetter in the same class. For a former black private and a deserter to boast of his equal worth to a white officer in the year 1900 is refreshing in its boldness. To Alstaetter's credit, he did not seem to find Fagen's claim offensive, as most officers of the day would have. After all, he had observed that "his way with the natives was wonderful" and reported that Fagen had "treated him very kindly." Fagen had impressed him, and one gets the sense from Alstaetter's description that unlikely as it would seem, they had formed something of a friendship. He may have found Fagen's assertion outlandish and even comical, but he seemed to appreciate the flair, the boldness, with which the renegade repeatedly brought out his commission and made his case for their shared high standing.

"Then again," Alstaetter told the reporter, "he would forget himself when I spoke to him and he would jump to his feet and say: 'Yes, sah,' the way he had been in the habit of replying to his American army officers."

Here again, did this really happen? And if something like it did occur, did it happen more than once? Or was Alstaetter, speaking off the cuff to a reporter, shaping his account to achieve a desired effect? Perhaps he did not want to sound too much in admiration of a "lowly" black man as he went on, "Wonderful tales were told about Fagin by the Filipinos." It seems Alstaetter, in his "almost unbearable solitude," appreciated the occasion to talk to someone, even a black man and a "traitor." At least he was an "amusing" black man, one who "possessed good common sense." These small observations by Alstaetter, however meager, are useful in establishing that Fagen was not some wild-eyed zealot, mentally unbalanced, or recklessly violent. And certainly not the man of criminal instincts or limited intelligence as the army would have it.

As for Fagen's unfortunate disparagement of his fellow revolutionaries—if Alstaetter had quoted him accurately—it is likely that he felt the strain of living in another culture, one he could never fully be a part of, even as he identified with the Filipinos' oppression by the whites. In addition, having to speak in a new language must have been wearing. The gulf between him and Alstaetter was that vast chasm that separated black and white America in 1900. But in the broadest sense they were of the same culture. It is possible that even as Alstaetter represented that world of American whites that had caused Fagen so much pain, he still felt a cultural affinity, a connection that he could not feel with the quite different Filipino culture.

"He feared capture by the American soldiers," Alstaetter recounted, "and imagined the whole army was after him. He would proclaim that the Filipinos were sure to be victorious and that the American soldiers were about to give up. He did this to buoy up his own courage and that of the Filipinos. His influence over the natives was wonderful. . . . He repeatedly stated he would never be taken alive. He said once: 'The American army wants me bad. They won't get me.'"

The record makes clear that Fagen was not imagining things. From Funston to the lowliest white private in the Fourth District, every man dreamed of being the one to kill the "notorious renegade." "They [the authorities] allege that next to Aguinaldo there is no man whom they are so anxious to capture," the *Manila Times* reported. This desire only increased as Fagen continued to prove maddeningly elusive. As the article in the *Iola Daily Register* later noted, "No other man that ever deserted from the United States has been so relentlessly hunted by his comrades as Fagin . . . it was generally understood that the regiment that killed or captured him would stand high with the commanding officer, and for this reason Fagin was sought as never was a deserter before."[4]

It would hardly come as a surprise that Fagen would feel the pressure of being a hunted man. One can sense the undercurrent of desperation, the forced merriment, in his carousals. Death was stalking him and yet he remained defiant. Alejandrino reported of a nightmare Fagen had that he was being seized by a white mob. It would not be surprising if such visions haunted him on many a night.[5]

Alstaetter and Fagen passed four days together, and out of those four days of close proximity came these invaluable crumbs of conversation but maddening in their brevity. One can see the two officers sitting cross-legged on woven mats, the light on the ground beneath the hut visible through the split bamboo flooring, their shared bowl between them. Perhaps a gecko clung to the thatched wall high up in a shadowy corner; a tiny green lizard scampered about; a column of colorful termites filed up a sapling post. Maybe the rain pattered on the roof of woven palm leaves. There they sat. So, Lieutenant Alstaetter, what did you talk about for four days? Did you ask Fagen why he deserted? Did you discuss the war? Did you talk about your lives back in the states? There you were, lying a few feet apart through the long nights. What did you talk about over those many hours spent together?

Frederick Alstaetter lived to the ripe age of ninety-three, dying in 1966. It would be nice to think that somewhere among his effects there is a reminiscence—a few yellowed pages perhaps—describing his encounter with Fagen, something besides the two exchanges with reporters. But I doubt it.[6]

Captain Charles Roberts was required to write a lengthy report after his release from captivity, explaining in detail how he was captured and what happened in the six weeks that followed. I searched in vain among the files for a similar report from Alstaetter. That account and other reports may exist; if so, hopefully someday they will turn up.

————•••————

At last Funston and Lacuna finalized their plan to secure Alstaetter's release. During his sweep of the lowlands the previous August, the highly regarded Major Ventuse had been seriously wounded and captured. After more than two months in the hospital in San Isidro, Ventuse had nearly recovered. Funston sent a letter to Lacuna, offering to release Ventuse in exchange for Alstaetter, and Lacuna accepted the offer.

Fagen escorted Alstaetter down from the mountains. The night before his release the two men spoke for the last time. "On leaving Fagin I asked him about my ring," Alstaetter told the reporter, "and he said that he had loaned it to a friend who was away on another island."[7]

This was complete nonsense and both men knew it, but Alstaetter seemed to bear no rancor toward Fagen for that bald-faced lie. Fagen himself must have squirmed while casting about for some plausible excuse and coming up so painfully short. He could have—and should have—simply said he was keeping it and cited any number of reasons. But put on the spot, he did himself no credit, though it is easy to understand the significance the ring held for him.

The following day, escorted by a "native who was also carrying his few effects," Frederick Alstaetter, calendar-cane in hand, made his way across the rice fields and down corduroy cart roads into Gapan. The garrison in Gapan had not been expecting him, and he was greeted with jubilation when he and his escort walked into town. His long ordeal was over.[8]

A Christmas Souvenir

31

AFTER PARTING WITH FREDERICK ALSTAETTER, Fagen and his band ranged to the northwest, crossing the Rio Pampanga and passing near Jaen. Several days earlier, on November 15, Lacuna's men, probably under the notorious Tomas Taguntun, had burned much of the *poblacion* to the ground as payback for the aid some of the locals had provided to Lieutenant David P. Wheeler and his forty-man garrison. The spies' tips to Wheeler had led to the capture of Delphin Esquivel, the region's most powerful *hacendero*, and had on several occasions nearly resulted in the capture or killing of Fagen and Lacuna.[1]

In further retaliation, the guerrillas kidnapped four citizens of Jaen who had served as spies for Wheeler and took them off to the swamp. Funston promptly had four members of Esquivel's family imprisoned and put on bread and water. He threatened to have them shot if the spies were not released. How this tit-for-tat was finally resolved is not clear, probably with the release of the hostages all around.[2]

On November 26, not far to the northwest of Jaen, Fagen and his men engaged Lieutenant Ivers P. Leonard and forty men of the Twenty-Second Infantry in a fight near San Francisco. No casualties resulted from this skirmish, but Leonard reported the capture of a horse with saddle and bridal. Fagen had recounted to General Alejandrino that when pursued by the Americans he frequently "had to leave the horse because his feet are faster than those of his horse. Besides, he could squeeze himself into and pass places, which a horse could go into only with great difficulty."[3]

Leonard must have stayed after Fagen because on December 2 he reported to Lieutenant Colonel Keller in Arayat who passed the information on to San Isidro: "Am informed that Fagan has orders from Lacuna to report to latter at Santa Cruz mountain Tuesday and that Lacuna is making a general concentration there. Fagan has been impressing men for Lacuna between here and Chico for several days and expects to cross Rio Grande below here tonight or

Tuesday morning at Bulieron, San Julian or Libertad as proves most convenient. Has train of five or six carabaos carrying supplies."[4]

The news that Fagen was returning set off a near frenzy of activity over the next few days as various outfits swarmed over the area in the hopes of intercepting him on his return across the river. In conjunction with Leonard's company, Lieutenant Day and the Scouts, along with a mounted detachment under Lieutenant Sheldon, scouted through "the country east of Cabiao in search of Fagen's band." Other outfits did the same, all without success.[5]

But that night, Lieutenant Leonard received word that Fagen was in the barrio of San Francisco, near San Antonio. In the early morning hours, Leonard's company, coming from the southwest, and David P. Wheeler's company, advancing from Jaen, converged on San Francisco. They charged into the barrio before dawn but once again found themselves grasping at thin air.[6]

In some barrios it seems Fagen and his band were more welcome than in others. Young men feared being conscripted; the impoverished villagers were pained to share food from their meager stores; some of Lacuna's bands took what was not offered and had engendered a growing resentment among the beleaguered peasants. And there was always the danger of an American detachment charging into the barrio at the first hint of dawn, stabbing their bayonets through the walls of palm leaf, rousting out the villagers and herding them to the center of town, bringing the threat of the water cure and the torch. Fagen would have outpost guards in place for such an eventuality, but even if he were enjoying a game of poker by the light of candlewicks floating in coconut oil, drinking *tuba* from a polished gourd, or playing a guitar in the company of the village musicians, he had to remain on his guard; he had to sleep lightly.

On the night of December 5, Frederick Funston received word from a spy of the "exact location of Tagunton's band." Well after dark, the general set out in a steady rain with Lieutenant Day and the Scouts, including Ganzhorn, and Troop A of the Fourth Cavalry under Lieutenant Morrison—seventy men in all. Instead of riding along the river and revealing their intentions to spies, they rode to the northeast all night in a pouring rain, eventually curving south in a twenty-five-mile loop that brought them to the east of the barrio of Rio Chico.[7]

As it turns out, Tagunton was not in Rio Chico . . . but Fagen and Lacuna were. At daybreak, Funston's party spurred their horses and rode quickly along the south bank of the river, hoping to overrun Tagunton's camp before the guerrillas' outposts could warn them. But when they arrived at the village, also called Rio Chico, Lacuna's guerrillas, estimated at one hundred men, were waiting for them.

The Rio Chico was a good forty yards wide, the water clear and swiftly flowing. Funston's men dismounted and charged through the village gardens, streaming around the nipa houses and firing as they went. "'A' Troop's top cutter, First Sergeant Alexander, fell badly wounded," Ganzhorn recounted, "but got up fighting like a spitting panther and stumbled ahead with the charge." Sergeant Schwartz, running with Funston and Ganzhorn on either side, went down, a Mauser bullet striking him just below the eye and passing cleanly through his head. Miraculously, he survived.[8]

Funston's seventy men halted at the edge of the river. There they "poured in a rapid fire in exchange for the hail of bullets coming across at them from the rebels." The general gave the order to charge, and with a roar the men dashed into the river. "Under that withering fire, through water waist deep, we charged," Ganzhorn wrote. "While struggling to keep our feet against the swift current which made accurate shooting impossible, we again glimpsed the renegade, Fagan."[9]

"The rebels did not flinch until our men were within 75 yards of them," the *Manila Times* reported a few days later. At last Fagen ordered a retreat and one hundred men faded away into the thick brush.[10]

Four Filipinos were left dead on the field, and one man was captured. "The prisoner gave the information that General Lacuna and the notorious Fagan were in command of the rebels on this occasion, and several of our men say they heard an American negro plainly giving commands during the skirmish."[11] "In this fight I got a fairly good look at the notorious Fagan at a distance of a hundred yards," Funston wrote in his autobiography, "but unfortunately had already emptied my carbine."[12]

While neither Funston nor Ganzhorn were able to get a shot at Fagen, one of the men did. Sometime during the fight, he received a wound, first reported as moderate, then upgraded by overzealous journalists to severe. The wound was at best moderate, possibly even superficial, as he was soon back in action.[13]

Funston may have been telling the truth about his empty carbine, but his account has the ring of a "likely story," leaving the suggestion that with a loaded carbine he would have drawn a bead and dispatched his nemesis, something he obviously longed to do.

Once again Lacuna and Fagen had thwarted Funston's attempt to bring the fighting in the Fourth District to a decisive end. But clearly, as the fight at Rio Chico indicated, the Americans were increasingly the ones on the offensive, and the guerrillas were on the run. As the new year approached, that trend would only accelerate.

----·×·----

In the islandwide American offensive that followed the election, guerrilla actions fell by half in November and December. Surrenders soared from 54 in September and October to 2,534 in the last two months of the year. With all that, what was most maddening to the Americans was that the guerrillas and their supporters—arguably the overwhelming majority of the population— would not acknowledge the obvious: their cause was lost. They could not win, and yet they kept fighting.[14]

And back home in Washington the powers-that-be had become no less frustrated. General Lew Wallace, a former governor of New Mexico, advocated sending "every hostile Filipino captured to Guam," in effect turning it into a penal colony. "It will take a thousand years to pacify the Philippine Islands at this rate," he predicted. Clarence Edwards, chief of the Insular Division of the War Department, wrote to a friend serving in the islands: "The yellow journalists are jumping on us fearfully. . . . A little throttling is necessary. General killing." With the election over, the administration no longer had to worry about a backlash at the implementation of harsher tactics. The time had come to take off the gloves—that is, as a matter of stated policy.[15]

On December 19, the military governor MacArthur issued his proclamation. Printed in English, Spanish, and Tagalog, this tract of military legalese—the Lieber Code—put the Filipinos on notice: the rules had changed. The proclamation announced the implementation of *General Orders 100*, a manual of warfare drawn up in 1863 by Frances Lieber and signed by Abraham Lincoln, detailing rules for every contingency faced by an occupying army—ten sections and 157 provisions. MacArthur informed the Filipinos that they were in violation of any number of these rules. This, of course, was news to the Filipinos or even that such a "thing" as *General Orders 100* existed or that an invading army had the right to hold them accountable to its own self-serving set of standards. MacArthur's proclamation was printed in bold type and appeared every second day in the *Manila Times* and elsewhere, an ominous warning to the people: cooperate or else.[16]

Previous practices by the revolutionaries and their supporters that had been treated with leniency would no longer be tolerated. MacArthur sent out instructions to his departmental commanders: "one of the most effective means of prolonging the struggle, now left in the hands of the insurgent leaders, is the organized system by which supplies and information are sent to them from occupied towns." The general's aim was to destroy this system. Filipinos not actively supporting the Americans were to be classed as enemies. The proclamation authorized the confiscation and destruction of property, deportation of prominent citizens, reprisals in the case of assassination, summary execution of spies and fighters not in uniform. Even *suspected* guerrillas were subject to arrest.

"Whatever action is necessary," MacArthur directed his commanding officers, "the more drastic the application the better."[17]

Throughout much of the archipelago, a de facto implementation of *General Orders 100* had been in effect for some time. MacArthur's official proclamation and detailed instructions to his departmental commanders now gave his officers legal cover to do what many were already doing, only now they were to do it with even more vigor.

Among those commanders, Funston was hardly one who had to be encouraged. But some officers voiced concerns, pointing out that it was outrage at Spain's use of these very same tactics—torture, summary executions, "reconcentrado" camps—that had sent America storming off to "liberate" Cuba only two years earlier. But as Gregg Jones observed, if some officers were troubled by this obvious inconsistency, "Others, like Frederick Funston and Lloyd Wheaton, suffered few moral qualms, and they summarily executed guerrillas, burned villages and tortured suspects as a matter of course."[18]

In the last weeks of December, Frederick Funston seemed to be wholly consumed by a determination to capture and string up David Fagen. If the general was not leading a search party of Scouts and mounted infantry, other patrols of infantry, cavalry, Macabebes, and Ilocanos were in the field hunting for the deserter who seemed always to be only one village away, close by in the swamp, or just across the river.

And when Funston came home after another hard day or fruitless night in the saddle, he at least had the consolation of having a wife to greet him and provide some of the comforts of home. Eda Funston was one of only four American women in San Isidro, the others being her sister, Magdalene, and the wives of two captains. In 1906, six years after these events, Eda provided a colorful account of the women's improvised Christmas party for the December 24 edition of the *Iola Daily Register*. First, the local prominent citizens invited them to a "Filipino hop." The band was very good, Eda Funston noted, but the weather too hot and humid for dancing. Then came the Christmas dinner party for the officers stationed in San Isidro.

> All that sweltering hot afternoon we "manufactured" souvenirs and prepared "dainties." I had brought with me a roll of crepe paper, and from this we made little heart-shaped favors, but our souvenirs were our masterpieces. . . .
> General Funston was at that time hunting diligently for a negro deserter by the name of Fagan. What, then, could he wish more than the capture of Fagan for a Christmas present?

From black cloth we made a doll with black darning cotton for hair, dressed it as a soldier and, with a rope suggestively tied around its neck we presented the deserter, with all becoming formality, to the general for his Christmas gift. It is needless to say that he was delighted with the "capture."

For each guest we made something similarly appropriate and for all wrote jingles to suit.[19]

Eda Funston did not repeat any of the "jingles," but her sister, Magdalene, continued the story in a letter to her mother:

I had forgotten Fred's verse and the joke on him. For some time he and his men have been trying to capture "Fagan" a colored man, who deserted from the 24th Inf. and has joined the insurrectos;

By Jimminy Christmas Fred
What's that I see?
Poor old Fagan
Hanged to a tree?
How did it happen
This is queer
Tell us about it
We're dying to hear.

After the laughing had subsided we went into the dining room for the refreshments.[20]

The party over, Funston resumed the hunt, and on the night of the twenty-ninth he almost succeeded in making his Christmas "jest" a reality. But for a letter written by a soldier of the Twenty-Second Infantry, one would think that Funston's sole objective that night was the capture of Lieutenant Colonel Joaquin Natividad. His telegram to Manila states tersely that they had attempted the capture of Natividad: "Information being faulty, he escaped."[21]

In a letter to the *Evening News* of Jeffersonville, Indiana, Sergeant Homer Bailey provided a more detailed picture of the attempted capture, an elaborate movement of five companies, converging on a barrio from three directions.

The surrounding country is very swampy, making it difficult to follow, but since the election the Insurgents have not had much rest. Fagin, the negro deserter from the 24th Infantry, operates in this province, Nueva Ecija. . . . A short time ago a movement was made which nearly resulted in his capture as follows. General Funston . . . moved south

with infantry and cavalry while we came north. Two companies from
the west surrounded a Barrio, a small village, rounded up every body.
Fagin, with his chief, Col. La Tividad [Natividad], were there all right,
but managed to escape.[22]

These close calls were taking their toll on Natividad, and with this last
narrow escape it appears the lieutenant colonel had begun to contemplate the
"unthinkable."

On the night of January 2, 1901, a large guerrilla force under the command
of Major Tomas Tagunton attacked San Isidro and burned two hundred
houses. This was meant as punishment for the townspeoples' refusal to continue their contributions to the struggle, a sign of the flagging support of much
of the populace and the growing desperation of the revolutionaries. Fagen and
his band probably took part in this raid, or perhaps it was Fagen's band that
carried off nearly a mile of telegraph wire earlier that day near Cabiao where
he and his men had been located the night before.[23]

On the evening of January 4, Funston received word from Natividad that
he was ready to discuss terms of surrender. Funston and his "numerous staff"
mounted up and rode for the arranged meeting place, a barrio of San Isidro.
The following day, the general reported to Manila, "he was perfectly willing
to bring in all men he could get his hands on 25 with rifles, comprising his
personal escort, but I thought that hardly enough and persuaded him to do
better."[24]

What Funston wanted was Fagen, and he made the capture or killing of
Fagen a condition of Natividad's surrender. "So early this morning," Funston
continued in his telegram, Natividad "left Calaba barrio where I had told him
to concentrate his men, with all armed men in his command for the region
south of here to try to round up and bring in Fagan's band. He is acting in good
faith. Before the 7th at least I hope to be able to report a good surrender. Please
do not allow this to become public at present."[25]

That capturing Fagen was foremost on Funston's mind is evident from the
telegrams his adjutant, Captain E. V. Smith, sent on January 4, the night of
Natividad's proposed surrender: "For the present do not disturb the band of
insurgents collected near San Fernando. The General had a talk with Natividad
last night. He has collected forty of his men with rifles in Calaba and is to surrender them within four days. The delay is because he is trying to work a ruse on
Fagan and capture him and bring in his company."[26]

The next morning Captain Smith wired Major Yeatman, the commanding
officer of the Twenty-Second in Arayat: "Natividad . . . is now in Calaba with
some of his men" and "promises to bring in Fagan."[27]

It is possible that Fagen got wind of Natividad's treachery, or that Natividad secretly had Fagen warned. In any case, after three days of plotting and intrigue, Funston abandoned his scheme. On January 6, he wired Manila:

> This evening . . . I received the surrender of the Insurgent lieutenant-colonel Joaquin Natividad with his lieutenant Gregorio Cadhit and eleven soldiers of his personal escort. . . . Yesterday he had sent to their homes the remainder of his escort, keeping their rifles which were surrendered this evening. This was done because he had not confidence in some of his men and feared they would prevent the carrying out of his plans to surrender. . . . As a result of the interview I had with him three days ago he planned to kill Fagan and bring in his company but was unable to do it as Fagan's men are badly scattered and the whereabouts of that individual unknown.[28]

As it turns out, if the reports later that evening were correct, Fagen and his band had been nearly within shouting distance of Funston the previous night. In another letter to her mother, dated January 6, Magdalene Blankert wrote: "After dinner Capt. Smith came in to tell Fred that Fagan and his men had planned to attack the town that night and, too, that he thought it best to send some men out to watch." Magdalene and Eda packed a few things and went to bed in their clothes in the event Fagen and his men might set fire to the town, as Tomas Tagunton had done four days earlier. But Fagen, perhaps alerted by his own spies that Funston was on to his plans, decided against an attack. In any case, the night passed without incident.[29]

Did Natividad actually intend to help Funston "work a ruse" on Fagen? It seems doubtful; with so many loyal fighters around him, Fagen almost certainly would have been tipped off, if his own acute instincts hadn't told him some sort of plot was afoot. That Lacuna's men would have gone along with a scheme to betray Fagen seems far-fetched. Natividad probably had no intention of carrying out such a plan or even considered it possible but went along with Funston's game in order to secure his own surrender and avoid assassination by his men. It appeared that in surrendering Natividad feared for his life, an indication that many of his men were incensed by his act of disloyalty and also of their resolve to fight on.

Joaquin Natividad went over in a big way, poring over captured documents, decoding them, confirming and adding details, naming names. "To all of the above he is willing to testify before military commission," Funston reported to Manila. On January 12, Natividad accompanied Funston on an expedition in search of Pablo Tecson. On that same day, Lacuna promoted Tomas Tagunton to lieutenant colonel and assigned him to replace Natividad as zone commander. The loss of Natividad came as yet another severe blow for Lacuna.[30]

If others like Natividad and Simon and Alipio Tecson could negotiate their surrender under generous terms, surrender for Fagen meant certain death at the end of a picket rope, or worse.

The Revolution Falters

32

M ACARTHUR'S GET-TOUGH POLICY, coming on the heels of the disillusionment following McKinley's reelection, appeared to be having the desired effect. Seventy-nine guerrillas charged with atrocities were executed, hundreds more imprisoned. In the Ilocos Provinces, the people were essentially being burned out of their homes and starved into submission. Throughout the island, the most severe measures went into effect. Intent on avoiding criticism at home, MacArthur reinstituted censorship of the American press while Filipino newspapers "were forced to publish U.S. handouts and fill their remaining columns with trivia."[1]

On January 16, adding a different kind of punitive measure to the mix, MacArthur ordered the deportation of forty-nine prominent Filipinos to Guam, accusing them of actively supporting "the insurrection and the irregular guerrilla warfare by which it is being maintained." Foremost on the list was Apolinario Mabini. Deported along with him were Simon and Alipio Tecson, both of whom had recently surrendered; Artemio Ricarte—known as "the viper"; Maximo Hizon, Mariano Llanera, and Pio del Pilar. The party, along with eleven of their servants, sailed into exile on January 17, 1901.[2]

After Lacuna and Fagen, Funston was most eager to capture and hang Major Tomas Tagunton, now second in the chain of command and active in the vicinity of San Isidro. Tagunton was a giant by Filipino standards, nearly six feet tall and heavyset, a frightening figure to his men and more so to his enemies. Noted for his cruelty, Tagunton was, in Funston's words, "the most notorious" of the guerrilla "assassins." "This man murdered scores of people," Funston claimed, "and burned a number of towns to punish the inhabitants for giving information to the Americans, or for neglect to pay insurgent taxes."[3]

On January 25, 1901, while scouting along the Malimba River, Funston and his Scouts surprised a band of thirty guerrillas in a *cogon* field. Traveling with

Funston was a Major Brown, who had acquired a newly invented Colt automatic pistol. Among the fleeing guerrillas they saw a large man wearing an officer's shoulder straps. Major Brown, firing multiple rounds from his new weapon, shot and killed the notorious Tomas Tagunton. "We were mighty jubilant over the result of this little skirmish," Ganzhorn wrote. "We now needed only the chance to line our sights upon Fagan to make our satisfaction complete."[4]

The death of Tagunton capped Funston's most successful month in the long year of fighting; his men had captured more than 150 rifles, as many as they had won during the previous four months. Lacuna had started with fifteen hundred rifles; now he was down to four hundred, virtually the only serviceable ones were captured Krags. Funston reported that Sandico's "entire following has dispersed, and the men are individually surrendering."[5]

An article in the *Scranton Republican* on January 1, 1900, described the salutary effects of MacArthur's new get-tough policy. Throughout the islands, American patrols were on the move and giving the "insurgents" no rest. "The daily bulletins chronicle the burning of hundreds of native barracks and shelters and many hostile villages are burned and their destruction never reported." Rather than release captured guerrillas after disarming them and administering the oath of allegiance, MacArthur ordered "the wholesale retention of rebels" and "every available building is being used as a jail."[6]

In February and March, Funston's men in the Fourth District and General Grant's in the Fifth District pushed deeper into the mountains. Everywhere they went they burned or confiscated corn and rice stores and cut off supply trains. On February 25, General Grant reported: "Almost no rice has gone to the mountains and the insurgents cannot live in the mountains during the coming rainy season. All rice belonging to the insurgents has either been captured or destroyed."[7]

But even as the opposition in northern Luzon crumbled, the resolve of the people in other areas only seemed to be increasing, particularly in Batangas and other provinces farther south. It seemed to Funston that the bloody business of counterinsurgency might go on for years before the Americans had gained full control of the islands. The key, in his estimation, was Emilio Aguinaldo, who was still exhorting his scattered generals to carry on the struggle and deal ruthlessly with those who showed signs of weakening in their resolve. The president-in-hiding was the symbolic cornerstone of the revolution. Funston was convinced that if Aguinaldo could be removed, the resistance would collapse. But where was the *presidente*? And how to get at him?

On the morning of February 26, 1901, Manila was abuzz. According to the *Manila Times*:

RENEGADE FAGAN IN TOWN
—**Police Tried Capture, but the Bird Had Flown**—

> Fagan the renegade has added another chapter to his notorious career
> and apparently is as daring as he is unscrupulous. Sunday he visited
> one of his old haunts in Manila, and was identified; but during the
> interval between his identification and his attempted capture, he gave
> his pursuers the slip.[8]

Fagen was not in town, as the editors of the *Times* soon discovered, but the idea of the "daring" renegade coming into Manila and carousing right under the noses of the authorities was too good not to let the story run. Supposedly, a man who had shipped with "Fagan" aboard the *Sheridan* recognized the deserter in a "house of ill-fame." Fagen was in conversation with a woman when he noticed the man and his teamster friend eyeing him. He stood up, glaring at them, and the two men scurried out in search of the police. But when they returned with two members of the guard, Fagen had disappeared. The women of the place directed them to another establishment down the street, but Fagen was not to be found there either. They discovered he had returned to the house of ill-fame, but before they could get there, he was gone again. This Keystone Kops routine went on for some time when, an hour later, Fagen was spotted gambling in yet another saloon. The word was he "had plenty of money and was spending it freely." With a cohort of policemen scouring the streets and bars in search of him, the renegade still gave them the slip.

In the morning, all of Manila was on the lookout for "the notorious renegade Fagan": "The men at San Fernando station are on alert, and assert that if Fagan or any man resembling or representing Fagan is still around that district, that it will be but a short time till he finds himself in the hands of the authorities. They allege that next to Aguinaldo there is no man whom they are so anxious to capture."

The *Manila Times* had learned that the man mistaken for Fagen had been located and his identity determined to the satisfaction of the police. But the *Times* did not report this, leaving its readers to believe the "notorious renegade" had actually been so bold as to come to town and cavort directly under the noses of the authorities.

This picture of a daring black rogue was just too good a story to let go. In this depiction of a brazen and nattily dressed rascal, we are the beginnings of the mythic Fagen, the black badman reviled for his perceived wickedness but secretly—if not openly—admired for his defiance of the white man, his noose and the burning stake. This story is suggestive of the 1890s badman: the man

who could appear and disappear as if by magic, baffling his pursuers, a dangerous and rough character with a devilish sense of humor. In that, the story was
not entirely wrong.

In February 1901, six men from the Ninth Cavalry, stationed in the southern
Luzon province of Albay, deserted and joined the revolutionaries. Like Fagen,
they were noted for teaching the guerrillas how to handle firearms, the improved accuracy of the men under the black deserters being frequently re-
marked upon. In November 1901, a newspaper in Hawai'i picked up an article
from the *Manila Times* headlined DEVILTRY OF U.S. DESERTERS:

> The authorities recognize the fact that deserters from the Ninth Cavalry
> led the insurgents during the fight near Lipa in July, at which time Capt.
> Wilhelm and Lieut. Ramsey of the Twenty-first Infantry, Lieut. Lee of
> the Engineers, and several enlisted men were killed. It was remarked at
> the time that the shooting had been too accurate for natives to render
> such dire results. Later it was ascertained definitely that deserters had
> led the natives and fired the shots that killed the Americans.

The articles also reported that black deserters were operating on Samar
and "in the Camarines there are a number of deserters from the colored cavalry
regiments, who have caused untold trouble for the Americans." On July 4,
1901, General Belarmino, with 217 of his men, surrendered to Colonel Wint at
Legaspi. The Regimental Returns of the Ninth Cavalry state that William Victor
and Fred Hunter, deserters from Troop G, "with carbines, belts, ammunition,
were brought into Legaspi by officers of Belarmino's command and turned
over to Colonel Wint." Soon after, perhaps the same day, Fred Hunter was
shot and killed, reportedly trying to escape. The phrase "turned over" leaves it
unclear whether the two men voluntarily surrendered or were brought in
against their will. On July 8, Private Garth Shores from Troop H "was brought
in wounded and surrendered to Colonel Wint at Legaspi, by Colonel Bober of
Belarmino's staff." Shores and Victor, as well as Edmond DuBose and Lewis
Russell, who may have been the men doing the damage at Lipa, were sentenced
to death. Roosevelt commuted the sentences of Shores and Victor to life in
prison at hard labor. Russell and DuBose were hanged before a crowd of three
thousand in February 1902. The records only indicate six deserters from the
Ninth Cavalry, but the *Manila Times*'s assertion that there were black deserters
active on Samar and in the Camarines makes one wonder if there weren't more
than those six and, if so, whether some of them might never have been apprehended. African Americans would remain active in the guerrilla resistance to
American occupation of the islands long after Roosevelt declared the war over

in July 1902, a fact never acknowledged by colonial authorities but substantiated elsewhere. Of the fate of Dubose and Russell, E. San Juan maintains, "Records prove that their execution was deliberately agreed upon by the military to serve as a warning to soldiers not to emulate Fagen."[9]

San Juan's article states, "We know the names of seven of about twenty-nine African-Americans who deserted—their names have been expurgated from ordinary historical accounts . . . only Fagen of Company I seems to have survived in civic memory." Willard Gatewood puts the number of black deserters at "a dozen or so." Stephen Bonsal, writing for the *North American Review* in 1907, claimed that "the negroes deserted in scores for the purposes of joining the insurgents, and many of them, like the celebrated Fagan, became leaders and fought the white troops and their former comrades with zest and ability."[10]

"Scores?" "About twenty-nine?" "A dozen or so?" Perhaps we'll never know the precise number for sure. One can find the stories of the deserters from the Ninth Cavalry in the *Record of Events*, though the impartiality of the citations is questionable. As for the others purportedly erased from the record, I wouldn't know. But Funston's claim to have strung up a number of deserters in the field makes one wonder. As for desertions from the Twenty-Fourth Infantry to the enemy in Nueva Ecija, conflicting reports place the number anywhere from 150 to one. The claim that there was only one desertion to the enemy is of particular interest because of other information imparted in the report. With Funston away somewhere, the acting assistant adjutant, Erneste V. Smith, was left to make a "report of desertions to the enemy that have occurred within this district."[11]

Smith listed six or so desertions from the Twenty-Second Infantry, none suspected of serving with the "insurgents." Then Smith followed with a dubious assertion: "The commanding officer, 24th Infantry, reports that but one desertion to the enemy has taken place in that regiment." He continued:

> Private David Fagen, 24th Infty, deserted at San Isidro, N.E., taking no
> arms with him. The desertion was planned and aided by an insurgent
> officer. (It is reported to Dist. Hdqtrs. that one Delfin Esquivel was that
> officer. He is now serving sentence of military commission at Bilibid.)
> Fagen was of the criminal class, a ruffian and an insubordinate soldier
> with seven previous trials and convictions. It is well-established that
> Fagen has served actively with the insurgents. (It is said that he has
> reached the grade of Major but is now almost without command owing
> to certain acts of cowardice on his part.)[12]

"Certain acts of cowardice?" Reading that phrase brought me to a full stop. After a moment's consideration, my reaction was to completely dismiss Smith's claim. For more than a year, Captain E. V. Smith had to sit at his telegraph, sending reports to Manila either skirting around the knowledge of Fagen's involvement in one engagement after another, or perhaps sharing that information in code. This passive role must have been frustrating as the tally of the renegade's exploits mounted up. Now, at this late date of February 19, 1901, here was his chance to get in a dig at the traitorous upstart. This report would go into the files as the last word on desertions in the Fourth District. What better opportunity to smear Fagen's reputation as a bold fighter for all time?

In just three weeks after this report, Fagen will prove himself again in battle, striding in full view as he taunted the enemy. Alejandrino and Lacuna would continue to hold Fagen in the highest esteem, praising his "feats of valour," and even Funston, in an article in *Collier's Weekly* exactly one year later, would write of the "courage and ability" of the renegade who had been "a cause of unending trouble."[13]

And yet there is no way to prove that Smith did not make this statement based upon reliable, or perhaps not so reliable, intelligence. Could Fagen have actually committed "certain acts of cowardice"? More than one? In the unlikely event that he had, it's conceivable that he was suffering from what is today called PTSD, or post-traumatic stress disorder. He had been in fight after fight for more than a year, relentlessly hunted by Funston's troops. That he might have "cracked" for a time does not seem unreasonable. Yet Smith's accusation of cowardice remains the only one of its kind and is arguably suspect.

That Fagen would be promoted to major makes complete sense. With the death of Tagunton, he would be the officer in line to take his place as zone commander of southern Nueva Ecija. But I have found no other reference to a promotion to major other than Ganzhorn's claim that reward posters for Funston, Wheeler, and the Scouts were signed "Major Fagan."[14]

As for Freeman's claim that there had been only one desertion to the enemy from the Twenty-Fourth Infantry, Colonel Keller of that regiment had reported five desertions, Wheeler reported three, and Funston two. One man, a Private Snyder of the Twenty-Second Infantry, wrote home to his father in Nebraska that 150 black deserters had killed 75 white men of the Twenty-Second Infantry in battle. Snyder's father took the letter to the hometown newspaper, which printed the shocking story. This, in turn, prompted the War Department to order an investigation, ending with Snyder's groveling apology and revision of his estimate of black deserters to a measly 4 in total. Which are still three more than Colonel Freeman could come up with.[15]

Whether there were twenty-nine desertions from the black regiments or twelve, those numbers would represent a miniscule fraction of the six thousand African Americans serving in the islands. If Fagen had hoped to inspire a wave of defections, by the fall of 1900 he must have understood that his would be a lonely rebellion.

In January 1901, another group of *principales* in Manila formed the Federal Party. With an eye to becoming incorporated into the United States, including eventual statehood, they swore allegiance to the American flag and encouraged Filipinos everywhere to do the same. The cause was lost, they proclaimed, and it was certainly not in their interest as prominent landholders and businessmen to see the war linger on: that part, of course, went unmentioned. Alejandrino, writing years later, was especially bitter in his criticism of these men: "The great majority of the rich and educated elements who had been attracted to the cause of the Revolution during its successes were in no manner capable of following up in times of adversities." These same men who had so enthusiastically backed the revolution had now formed a party devoted to its defeat and total surrender to American colonial rule.[16]

The Federal Party sent out spokesmen everywhere to persuade their countrymen to give up the fight. At considerable risk, emissaries traveled to guerrilla strongholds to make their case, and with some success. In late February, twelve *principales* in Nueva Ecija, backed by the Federal party, signed a letter to Urbano Lacuna. The time had come to end the conflict; if he didn't surrender, they would mount a vigilante movement against him led by "the former insurgent General Padilla." Pablo Padilla bore a particular animus toward Lacuna because of his association with Fagen, who had led the attack on the *Stonie* in which Padilla's wife had been wounded in the shoulder. Lacuna, in turn, despised Padilla for having betrayed the revolution.[17]

During the month of February and into March, guerrilla officers and regulars came in daily, swore the oath of allegiance to the American flag, and handed over their rifles for the promised thirty pesos. In Nueva Ecija, Funston's adjutant, Captain E. V. Smith, cabled Manila: "Federal Party pushing Sandico and Lacuna hard. Alejandrino seems to be the one that is holding back. It is not however certain that Alejandrino is in direct communication with Lacuna."[18]

Alejandrino was, in fact, with Lacuna in the Buloc Mountains. Sandico and Villacorta were in hiding in the north of Nueva Ecija, dressed as peasants. With MacArthur's threat to hold officers accountable for the assassination of *americanistas* and other purported crimes, many felt the need to cut deals before they were captured, and the chance to negotiate their surrender on more favorable terms was lost. This would become the case for Alejandrino, whom Funston was eager to see tried, convicted of murder, and hanged. On January 1, Funston wrote to Crittenden, who had been chasing Alejandrino on Mount Arayat: "Both General MacArthur and General Wheaton are extremely anxious to

have him gotten rid of. I hope you will make [it] hot for him and . . . if possible
ascertain names of all people in Arayat . . . who have been aiding him and confine them preferring charges in all cases where convictions can be secured."[19]

Jose Alejandrino, just thirty years old, was not a military leader by nature
or training. He was a chemical engineer thrust into the role of general. His
loyalty to General Luna during the early period of conventional warfare with
the Americans had put him at odds with Aguinaldo and his supporters. In May
1900, when Funston captured Pantaleon Garcia, Alejandrino, as second in
command under Garcia, had taken over as commanding general of central
Luzon. Aguinaldo did not learn of this change of command until October—
which gives one an idea of just how out of touch the president was during the
height of the guerrilla war. The president was furious and ordered Alejandrino
arrested. But no one seemed inclined to enforce the arrest order—one more
occasion when Aguinaldo's commands went ignored—and Alejandrino remained the "titular head of Central Luzon."[20]

Throughout 1900, Alejandrino was kept constantly on the run by units of
the Twenty-Second Infantry and hounded by Macabebe scouts. He remained
almost exclusively in the Mount Arayat region, accompanied by his aides and a
small guard, and took part in no action. Beyond ordering collaborators punished,
as directed by Aguinaldo, Alejandrino was unable to organize a coherent resistance on the central plain of Luzon, and yet the American leadership in Manila
considered him of the utmost importance. Alejandrino seemed bemused by all
this interest: "In spite of the fact I played a very secondary role in the war, the
Americans nevertheless conceded me certain importance and were anxious to
capture me, dead or alive, believing that I might even substitute Aguinaldo in
case the latter were captured or killed."[21]

In the last week of the year 1900, with more than a thousand men scouring
the Arayat region, Alejandrino was forced to take flight. In a forty-eight-hour
ordeal, he and his small staff managed to crawl through the American lines and
join Lacuna and his last holdouts in the Buloc Mountains. This was when he
first met Fagen, the man about whom he had heard so much.

Also joining Lacuna was General Isidro Torres, from the south of Bulacan,
and a white deserter by the name of Alfred E. Nelson. Nelson had fallen in love
with a Filipina, one who also happened to be actively recruiting for the resistance. Nelson was "a foreigner," and he deserted from Gapan on the late date
of January 6, 1901.[22]

Using Federal Party representatives as a go-between, Funston pushed hard
to induce Lacuna to surrender. On March 1, he received a letter from Lacuna
putting off any surrender until he could bring his "chiefs" together. "From the
tone of the letter sent by Lacuna to members of Federal Party here in reply to
their manifesto," Funston wrote, "I think he will prove stubborn."[23]

Over the next few weeks—while Funston absented himself on some mysterious mission—Captain Smith and the Federal Party members went back and
forth with Lacuna. Finally, Smith concluded that Lacuna was stalling for time
by adding new conditions whenever an agreement seemed close. On March 15,
Smith proposed to "name a time when he is to meet me without further discussion. If he answers in the negative or fails to come troops will be at once put
after him."[24]

Lacuna was not persuaded and a few days later Lieutenant Moses with two
troops of the Fourth Cavalry and fifty Macabebes wended their way into the
Buloc Mountains. After they had penetrated nearly twenty miles into the rugged
hills, the trail became so steep they were forced to dismount and proceed on
foot, dragging their supplies after them. Up and up they climbed, another seven
miles, the trail snaking up a deep ravine.

Lacuna's men awaited them, peering from rocky outcroppings down on
the steep slopes of brush and high grass. "With Lacuna were the renegades
Fagan and Nelson," the newspapers later reported, "and the prospects of
squaring accounts with those two traitors gave a peculiar zest to the cavalrymen's pursuit." At a place the guerrillas called Fort Rizal, Lacuna's men opened
"a withering fire" from the ridgetops on three sides. Captured Krags were almost the only serviceable weapons remaining in the guerrillas' arsenal, but
with these fifty or so rifles Lacuna's men were able to keep Lieutenant Moses's
men pinned down and inflict substantial damage. The battle began at ten in
the morning and lasted for four hours.[25]

All the talk was of a Macabebe who was shot in the face, the bridge of his
nose gone and one eye left hanging out. He "coolly tore out the eye and continued the fight." A report in the *St. Louis Post-Dispatch*, not published until
January 19, 1902, elaborated on the incident: "A private in the hospital corps . . .
said that a renegade named Fagan was in command of a company of insurgents
that day and in plain view of the scouts. He walked up and down in front of his
line and called upon the Macabebes to come and take him."[26]

This was the same man that Captain E. V. Smith had accused of "acts
of cowardice" only weeks earlier. Either Smith was mistaken or Fagen had re-
gained his nerve. In the fight, three Macabebes were killed and twelve wounded,
while Moses also reported four members of Troop A wounded. After four
hours, the guerrillas broke off and withdrew. "Very difficult country," Moses
reported, "and further pursuit with wounded on hands impossible." With sixteen casualties on stretchers, an exhausting two-day exodus from the mountains
followed.[27]

While Lieutenant Moses's men rested, other detachments pushed up all the
mountain trails. With almost no food and little serviceable weaponry, Lacuna's
ragged force could only retreat deeper into the mountain forests.

On March 22, a *Manila Times* correspondent in San Isidro reported on the engagement in the Buloc Mountains and closed his account with a few words of praise for San Isidro, for its well-kept gravel streets, and the pleasant feeling of security one had while moving about General Funston's town. As to where the "little General" was, the reporter could only speculate, and he ended by saying, "as he is always busy, it is easy guessing that he is on some exploit again."[28]

Funston was indeed on another of his exploits, a mission of such secrecy that only a handful of senior officers had a vague notion of where he was. After years in his quest for glory, years of proposing perilous missions and gallant ventures to his superiors, one of them had finally given Frederick Funston his official blessing. Arthur MacArthur, it seemed, had nothing to lose. Frederick Funston had everything to lose—or to gain.

The Road to Palanan

33

O N THE PARTICULAR DAY that the reporter in San Isidro speculated as to
Funston's whereabouts, the general and his men were on the northeastern side of the Sierras, staggering through the jungles of Isabella Province;
Funston and his aide, Burton Mitchell, were near collapse from hunger and
exhaustion. The general's grand scheme was still on track but had repeatedly
been in danger of unraveling in a way that would likely have proven fatal for
everyone in his party.

On February 9, 1901, Funston received a telegram from Lieutenant J. D.
Taylor, commanding the company of the Twenty-Fourth Infantry that garrisoned Pantabangan, a hill-town in the northeast of Nueva Ecija. One of Taylor's
patrols had intercepted a courier from the north coast; the courier had in his
possession a packet of twenty encoded dispatches. In two days, the prisoner
and his documents were delivered to San Isidro. It quickly became apparent to
Funston that the messages were from the highest level, from Aguinaldo himself,
and had been destined for Lacuna, Alejandrino, and several other generals.
But what did the messages say? The courier, Cecilio Segismundo, declined to
translate at first but finally succumbed to the general's noted powers of persua-
sion. Torture? Aguinaldo later claimed that Segismundo told him he had only
talked after two applications of the water cure. David Bain writes that Funston
"only noted that they used forceful means. He declined to go into detail."[1]

The documents contained a wealth of information about the revolutionaries' operations. More importantly, the whereabouts of Emilio Aguinaldo was
finally revealed. He was with a small group of officers and a guard of no more
than fifty in the village of Palanan, an isolated hamlet on the rugged northeast
coast of Luzon. Supposedly, the townspeople and even most of the guard were
unaware of his identity.

At first, Funston thought only of forwarding this valuable acquisition to the
high command in Manila. But he was unable to sleep with all this exciting

information jostling around in his head. And as he mulled it over hour after hour, as was Frederick Funston's nature, a plan began to take shape. A ruse! At four o'clock in the morning, too impatient to wait for dawn, the general roused his aides and the hapless Segismundo, and then he began setting his plan in motion.

Among Aguinaldo's missives that had been decoded was one to Lacuna, ordering him to gather four hundred guerrillas from the surrounding commands and send them north to Palanan. It was this particular directive that had inspired the general's scheme.

Funston and his Scouts had narrowly missed capturing Lacuna the previous October and had recovered much of his correspondence and quantities of his official stationary. Using Lacuna's *Brigada Lacuna* stationary and forging his signature—the handiwork of the ever-useful Ramon Roque, a master forger— they prepared a confirmation of his request for men that would be sent ahead to Palanan when the time was right.

It was a grand charade the general had in mind, with most of the prospective players unaware of the nature of the roles they were being conscripted to play. Aguinaldo's "reinforcements" would actually be Macabebes posing as guerrillas. Three turncoat Tagalogs would lend the enterprise credibility; chief among these was Hilario Talplacido, an officer Funston had captured with Pantaleon Garcia the previous May. Lieutenant Gregorio Cadhit, who had surrendered with Joaquin Natividad, as well as another captured officer, would fill out the officer complement. The bewildered Cecilio Segismundo, who had been maneuvered from loyal rebel courier to active *americanista* in a matter of days, was to be pressed into service as a guide. Five American officers would come along as well, pretending to be prisoners of war, along with a dashing Spanish soldier-of-fortune, Lazaro Segovia, who had worked as a secret agent for Funston and was an expert in Tagalog. Funston, of course, was not about to miss the excitement and required the assistance of his aide, Lieutenant Burton Mitchell, who also happened to be his cousin. That took care of two of the "prisoners." Captain Harry Newton was brought up from Manila because he had some familiarity with the north coast. Captain Russell Hazzard and his brother, Lieutenant Oliver Hazzard, had organized a Macabebe battalion and knew their charges well. The Hazzard brothers, both quite tall and strikingly handsome, were sharpshooters with a well-demonstrated taste for action.

It was a wickedly brilliant scheme, devious and unsporting, and one fraught with danger—just the kind of swashbuckling exploit Funston had been trying to arrange for years. As a man who, like Theodore Roosevelt, was the very embodiment of his age, an age of melodramatic theatricality and shameless self-promotion, Frederick Funston was not unappreciative of the accolades that would come his way were he to be successful. He was out to cover himself in glory or die trying.

Funston traveled to Manila and petitioned to have his scheme approved by Arthur MacArthur, then to work out all the operational details. But there was no rush; Aguinaldo would not be expecting the reinforcements for some time, as they had to be gathered from as far south as Cavite Province and undertake a long and dangerous trek over the Sierra Madres. The party was assembled in Manila under the greatest secrecy. They sailed the night of March 6 on a gunboat, the Vicksburg, rounded the Straits of San Bernardino, and moved up the east coast of Luzon. It was only when the party was well out to sea that Talplacido and the other two former rebel officers were informed of the plan. They were astounded. They were already branded as traitors; did Funston really think they would commit this most duplicitous act of all? Participate in the betrayal and capture of Aguinaldo?

Yes, he did. They were reminded that they had taken the oath of allegiance to the United States; they could decline if their conscience absolutely demanded it, but with the cheerful option of stretching hemp as soon as they were returned to Manila. Under those conditions, the three former "insurgents" decided to go along. Segismundo, given the same unhappy choice, also capitulated.

During the night of March 14, the party of eighty-nine men slipped ashore in Casiguran Bay, from which point they would pretend they had been traveling over the mountains from Nueva Ecija. A courier forwarded the letters to Aguinaldo, explaining that an American survey party had been ambushed in the mountains and five prisoners were being brought along. What followed was a perilous march through 110 miles of inhospitable enemy territory, all of which was later recounted in thrilling detail by Funston in a serialized form that kept readers eagerly awaiting the next installment. The numerous missteps and close calls almost exposed their true identity and required some quick thinking. Struggling through mangrove swamps and dense forests, the retinue of fake guerrillas very nearly disintegrated as their rice supplies ran out and the rigors of the hike brought them to the verge of collapse still miles from Palanan. When, finally, Funston and his men were too weak to go on, the general sent a scout ahead to ask that food be sent out to them. Given sustenance by the enemy they were intent upon attacking, they pressed on the last miles. Later, this act of double-dealing struck Funston's critics as being particularly disgraceful, if not a violation of the laws of war.

But the ruse worked, and at last the column of "reinforcements" straggled into Palanan and was greeted with jubilation by Aguinaldo's small contingent, a jubilation that turned to shock a moment later when the Macabebes, feigning a celebratory rifle salute, opened fire on their welcoming party instead.

After a brief flurry of gunplay and fisticuffs in the president's thatched headquarters, Aguinaldo and his staff had been taken into custody, his guard scattered to the hills. The Vicksburg dashed into Palanan, the prisoners and their
captors were whisked aboard. On March 28, 1901, Frederick Funston, in effect,
deposited Emilio Aguinaldo on Arthur MacArthur's desk in Manila. Mission
accomplished.

For once General MacArthur, feared far and wide for his endless and in-
comprehensible monologues, was speechless. And the order was that Funston,
himself no paragon of verbal economy, was to keep his mouth shut as well,
awaiting further instructions from Washington. But the general's publicity staff
had already leaked news of the mission to the press as far away as Boston, rendering the War Department's orders irrelevant.

Overnight, the news was splattered in huge letters on every front page
from Manila to Iola, Kansas. Frederick Funston had done it again. While some
decried the use of trickery in the capture, noting that a similar act on the rebels'
part would have been denounced as treacherous and beyond the pale of civilized
warfare, most thought it as spectacular as any made-up exploit of Kit Carson
or Carl Greene in the dime novels.

Many of Funston's long-standing soldier-critics left off with their carping
and sidled over to the ranks of his admirers; there was no use fighting it, not after
a stunning feat of this magnitude. But among other military circles, Funston's
astounding achievement met with a notable lack of enthusiasm. Where there
should have been a mood of celebration, an air of gloom pervaded the halls of
the War Department in Washington. Finally, in a plaintive groan, someone had
to come out and say it: "Anybody but Funston."[2]

Frederick Funston was perfectly aware of his hypocrisy, as he was to later
admit, saying, "The whole affair was not clean." He had continually complained of the "'insurrectos'" violations of the rules of civilized warfare, and in
stringing up two guerrilla officers caught torturing Macabebe captives, he had
cited a provision of *G.O. 100* as his defense. Of atrocities reportedly committed
by Lieutenant Henry Ripley's Ilocano Scouts, Funston wrote "addicted, as
they are, by reason of their untamed natures, to brutality, it is necessary to
personally direct their smallest movements and establish by example a high
ideal of American humanity."[3]

In *Lincoln's Code*, John Fabian Witt noted the concern Funston's actions
raised among both politicians in Washington and at the highest levels of the
military: "President Roosevelt quietly asked the international law expert Theodore Woolsey of Yale University to defend the legality of the ruse in the pages
of the popular press, but the use of enemy garb was clearly unlawful. Lieber's
General Orders No. 100 had said so unequivocally, and in other contexts

American officials said as much themselves. Funston's daring gambit was an impetuous breach of the basic laws of war."[4]

In defending themselves against accusations of brutality, both military and civilian officialdom fell back on a single argument: in a war against savages "with no claims on the laws of war" all bets were off. Savage behavior had to be met with retaliatory measures severe enough to bring hostilities to a swift end. Witt cited that argument as "Woolsey's ultimate defense of Funston's otherwise unlawful ruse to capture Aguinaldo."[5]

But certainly a little bending of the rules seemed a small price to pay for having Emilio Aguinaldo under wraps at last. There was nothing to do but bear up as best one could while "Fighting Fred" spent the next months savoring the limelight and crowing over his latest act of derring-do. The *Manila Times* started off the coverage with a flattering sketch of a tough-as-nails, bearded Funston and a breathless account of the capture: "A Graphic Description of the Daring Expedition by the Brilliant Soldier who has struck the Final Death-blow to the Insurrection." The general was the toast of the town.[6]

A week later, Funston was promoted to Brigadier General in the regular army, not a bad trick for a man who had skipped West Point and any other formal military training to go straight to work as a Cuban guerrilla. Dozens of the most prominent officers in Manila, including his hero General Lloyd Wheaton, threw a banquet in his honor at the Luzon Cafe. The diminutive Funston relished a stroll down a cordon of his beaming contemporaries, then sat with cigar and snifter as one speaker outdid the other in singing his praises.

Undoubtedly, Funston was well aware that most of them were gnashing their teeth the entire time they were making a great fuss over him, but that only made his victory all the sweeter. He hadn't steamrolled over and past all of them on the basis of popularity or even native intelligence and ability. No, he knew there was something else that had driven him to exceed his peers, perhaps—as much as anything—a small man's determination not to accept bigger men's presumptions of superiority, in fact, to stuff those presumptions back down their throats. After taking the measure of his seemingly manifold liabilities—short stature, desultory youth, and lack of military credentials—Frederick Funston had compensated . . . and then some.

Surrender

34

O N MARCH 29, while Funston recovered aboard the Vicksburg, posing for photos and chatting amicably with the captured president, Captain Smith reported, "It is reasonably certain that we have Lacuna and his people hemmed up. I think Moses attacked him yesterday or certainly this A.M." Lieutenant Moses had gone so far into the mountains and into such difficult country that his whereabouts had become a mystery. Eventually, Lieutenant Day and his Scouts managed to track him down. Lacuna was not "hemmed up," but he was on the run and his men all but played out.[1]

The American officers drove their charges to exhaustion, allowing them only a day or two of rest before leading them back into the mountains. Their orders were to "stay out as long as possible." They were to carry as many rations as they could carry and "still do the work," and if needed they were to impress bearers to carry rations. "Will keep Ilocanos out indefinitely and supply them with pack train from Peñaranda," Smith reported. Eventually Lieutenant Moses became ill and was barely able to carry on; in his weakened state, his troopers from the Fourth Cavalry fell into dissension, causing Funston to cite the "lack of discipline among his troops" and to reassign Moses to Peñaranda. By then there were at least eight columns out at a time, like long lines of ants wending their way over mountain saddles, down into another ravine and across another frothing river, always deeper into the trackless forests until several columns found themselves at the Pacific Coast. Somewhere in those mountains, Urbano Lacuna and his remaining fighters managed day after day to elude their pursuers.[2]

They were in the rugged high country of dipterocarp forest, great hardwoods with massive buttresses and clinging vines, the air heavy with the smell of dampness and decaying vegetation. Rattan lianas and strands of pink freycinetias draped from limbs encrusted in a hoary moss. Ferns and giant vanda orchids flourished in the crotches of the trees. The dense canopy high overhead left the forest floor in a green gloom where Lacuna's men, on the verge of collapse, straggled forward, up and down mountain switchbacks covered in snaking tree roots, the forest floor thick with humus and fallen trees overgrown with coiling vines. A soldier who had served with Funston described his foray into the mountains.

> An incessant buzzing proclaims the existence, if it were not made manifest in more disagreeable ways, of winged insects. In every conceivable color they are here, and in some places almost render life unbearable. In the deeper and more remote recesses of these mountains, where great trees and parasitic growths form almost a solid roof, even at midday a semi-twilight prevails and the moisture drops from the trees almost like rain. The ground is like velvet, dark and yielding, and damp almost to saturation.[3]

All rice shipments from the lowlands had been cut off. Even Lacuna's own "chiefs of the guerrillas who were in charge of providing them with food" could not locate them. They were reduced to eating tubers, the shoots of wild palms, and catmon and other wild fruits, all bitter or sour and doing little to appease their gnawing hunger.[4]

"Malaria was preying upon us," Alejandrino wrote, "and in the absence of quinine we were able to combat the disease only by drinking a decoction of *dita* [a sour fruit]."

Of Fagen, whom Alejandrino had only recently met, he wrote: "He was very affectionate and helpful to me, going to the extent of carrying me in his arms and on his shoulders when I, weakened by fevers and poor nutrition, had to cross rivers or to ascend steep grades. The services which he rendered to me were such that they could only be expected from a brother or a son."[5]

To convey not only himself up steep hillsides but also to carry another man on his shoulders, day after day, attests to Fagen's strength and amazing durability. Equally admirable is the loyalty he showed to the revolution and to Lacuna who, despite suffering from a kidney ailment and aware of the hopelessness of their situation, could not bring himself to surrender.

For Fagen, the odds had never been good, but he must have begun with the belief that the Americans could be driven out. Perhaps he had at one time imagined the "good life" after the invaders were gone, the prestige and honors that would come his way. But by the time he and Lacuna's last diehards had been driven to the mountains, he must have long known victory would not be theirs. Did visions of the hangman's noose, of the burning stake, plague his nights? Only a disturbing account by Alejandrino touches on the subject.

As previously noted, almost nothing is known of Fagen's "wife." We know she lived in camp but do not know whether she ever accompanied him with his guerrilla. Alstaetter makes no mention of her. We know that she was Tagalog and remained a faithful companion long after the war ended. The story recounted by Alejandrino is a troubling one.

> Fagan spoke Tagalog very vividly and lived in the camp with a woman. One morning this woman presented herself to me crying and showing one cheek bitten off and saying that Fagan had done it.
>
> I sent for Fagan and asked him what happened.
>
> "I was only dreaming," he answered.
>
> He related to me that he had dreamed that he was being surprised by the Americans and, not having the intention to be caught alive, he resisted as much as he could with punches, kickings and bitings, but his fury against the enemy had been rained on his woman companion.[6]

It is possible that Fagen was engaging in some fast talking to squirm out of an uncomfortable situation, but Alejandrino seems to have taken him at his word. That Fagen might actually have had a nightmare and struck out violently in reaction is entirely conceivable given the imminent threat of a southern-style lynching that he had lived under for a year and a half.

In early April, Teodoro Sandico and twelve fighters managed to find Lacuna in the mountains. In negotiations with Captain Smith, Sandico had arranged for his own surrender, but Smith had inveighed upon the zone commander "to try and persuade Lacuna and Alejandrino to also come in." Sandico found Lacuna unreceptive and he may not have even broached the subject. Alejandrino wrote: "Physical sufferings, however great they were, were less than the moral sufferings that we endured in seeing the effects of the campaign of pacification undertaken by the Federal Party which subtracted daily from us men and resources. Officers and soldiers abandoned us."[7]

One who cleared out in the night was Teodoro Sandico. Funston, having returned from his epic adventure, wrote to Manila: "Sandico . . . says reason he did not present any men was because he had been with Lacuna with what was left of his former command for some days and as Lacuna was not willing to surrender he, Sandico had to steal away quietly in order that Lacuna would not stop him."[8]

In another telegram, Funston reported that Sandico's twelve men "were taken away from him by Lacuna."[9]

With so many defections and with Aguinaldo's call for the revolutionaries to lay down their arms, Alejandrino and Lacuna agreed that it was time to negotiate their surrender. Alejandrino "offered to discuss the conditions of our surrender with the Americans. If they would guarantee our lives and personal liberty, I would return to notify Lacuna and his men."[10]

In the third week of April, Fagen and his band accompanied Alejandrino down from the mountains. "Flat country is being scouted constantly to prevent bands coming out of mountains," Funston had reported. Despite these elaborate measures, the guerrillas dodged the patrols and crossed the lowlands to the Arayat region.[11]

The Americans soon got wind of Alejandrino's presence in the area and of his intentions. They were determined that Alejandrino should not surrender—in which case, in Funston's words, "their hand would be stayed"—but be captured or killed. At the same time, a survey party encountered Fagen and his band on the mountain, and his presence there, as well as Alejandrino's, brought out American detachments in full force. On the eighteenth, a Lieutenant Mitchell of the Twenty-Second Infantry led three companies in a sweep of the western slope of Mount Arayat while Funston and his troops, including Macabebes, canvassed the eastern side. On April 26, E. V. Smith wired Manila, "Alejandrino will if possible be killed or captured and made to answer for his crimes."[12]

The one thing Funston did not want was Alejandrino's surrender—apparently surrender offered the only chance of avoiding the hangman's noose, though nothing was assured—and certainly Alejandrino understood this. The trick was how to surrender without getting shot or captured. After eluding Funston's detachments for ten days, Alejandrino, accompanied by one aide, both men armed with revolvers, slipped past the outpost guard at 4:30 a.m. and presented himself at Major Baldwin's headquarters in Arayat.[13]

Baldwin, roused from his bed, was livid—at the inattentiveness of his guard and at Alejandrino. But he could hardly turn the general away. He wired Funston in San Isidro. Funston was, if anything, even more incensed. After conferring with Manila, Captain Smith wired regimental commander Major Yeatman in Arayat: "It has been ordered by General Wheaton that Alejandrino cannot surrender except unconditionally. He will undoubtedly have to stand trial for murder."[14]

After communicating with Manila, Funston, his aides, and a contingent of Scouts mounted up and rode at a brisk pace for Arayat. Judging by Alejandrino's description of their first meeting, Funston was not cheered by the prospect of the general's surrender: "A few hours later, General Funston arrived and without much ado and in a brusque and authoritarian manner, told me: 'You cannot surrender yourself without first delivering Fagan.'" Jose Alejandrino drew himself up and answered, "The surrender of Fagan is an infamy which I cannot commit because I know that if you catch him in your hands, you would be capable of bathing him in petroleum and burning him alive. You have soldiers. Why don't you catch Fagan yourself?" "Then, you will remain a prisoner," General Funston said.[15]

When Funston threatened Alejandrino's arrest for refusing to deliver Fagen, Alejandrino remained unmoved. He knew the Americans were bent on trying and hanging him and was probably hard-pressed to conceal his anxiety as he faced down a very hostile Frederick Funston. But Alejandrino stood his ground. The translation from here is garbled, but the general's argument is plain enough: "I came here because of my confidence in the honor of the American Army and because I believed that you will permit me to return to our camp as what General MacArthur did in case we did not arrive at an agreement."[16]

This seems like a stretch, as no conditions had been set for his surrender before he had delivered himself, but then the general played his last and most important card: "If I was mistaken and you insist on my remaining a prisoner, I will, of course, have to resign myself to force, but you should know, General, that neither Lacuna nor his men will surrender once they come to know the unjust treatment that I have merited from you."

Funston was not moved and ended the negotiations abruptly: "You are under arrest."

Were it left to Funston, he probably would have charged Alejandrino with murder and kept him under arrest. But this was a decision for the leadership in Manila, given that Alejandrino had invoked the name of MacArthur and mentioned the supposed trust that had been established between them in previous negotiations.

Alejandrino was escorted to the house of Don Clemente Santos. Two sentinels with fixed bayonets remained in the room with him throughout the night. In the morning, orders arrived from General MacArthur. Alejandrino was to be released and allowed to return to Lacuna to arrange the conditions of their surrender.[17]

In his autobiography, Frederick Funston took care to make no mention of Alejandrino's surrender at Arayat, especially of his demand that he hand over Fagen. Fagen was to be a minor character in his epic tale of adventure, a "wretched man" who wrote him several "impudent" letters, not a deep thorn in his side, a foe whose capture and execution had become an obsession. Only thirty-three years later would Alejandrino's account attest to the general's fixation upon the figure of David Fagen.

With MacArthur's order, Alejandrino and Fagen journeyed back to the mountains. As the small party made its way across the sweltering flatlands, this being the driest and hottest time of the year, Fagen must have reflected on his fate. Alejandrino "had heard narrations of the feats of valor and intrepidity of Fagan," and now he was to abandon the man who had carried him on his shoulders up steep hillsides and across raging streams.

Alejandrino took with him a "lengthy letter, in which was set forth a statement of conditions as they then existed, the surrenders of several prominent leaders being cited, and a copy of Aguinaldo's proclamation being enclosed." Lacuna remained noncommittal, requesting further clarification from Funston. Finally, after a back-and-forth exchange of letters, with Alejandrino as go-between, an agreement to surrender was reached. Lacuna was to gather all his men at the barrio of Papaya, where he and Funston would parlay. Funston would confine his men to their garrisons and allow Lacuna's men free passage through the countryside.

When Lacuna's men were convened at Papaya, Funston, his aides, and an escort of the Fourth Cavalry rode to the barrio to discuss the final terms of surrender. "The curiosity of all of us to see and talk with the man who had made things so warm for us during the past year made us quite impatient to cover the ten miles," Funston wrote. Without a white flag or a man riding point, Funston and his entourage rode quietly into Lacuna's camp. At last Lacuna appeared. After shaking hands with each of the officers, the general ordered cake and coffee served. "We found him to be an apparently full-blood Malay, very dark, of medium stature, and possessed of the quiet dignity of his race." They spoke in Spanish and soon the negotiations began.

> And then came up the question of Fagan. It was made clear that this man could not be received as a Prisoner of war, and that if surrendered it would have to be with the understanding that he would be tried by court-martial, in which event his execution would be a practical certainty. Lacuna recognized the fact that any other solution was out of the question, and it was finally agreed that with the exception of Fagan all of his men were to march to San Isidro, deliver their arms, and take the oath of allegiance to the United States.[18]

A young soldier of the Fourth Cavalry, Frank Snowden Sholl, who was in attendance, reported, "The insurgent chief permitted many relics like buttons and insignias to be clipped from his uniform when the khaki-clad cavalrymen surrounded him." Sholl got for himself "the acorns that adorned Lacuna's hat in lieu of tassels."[19]

Four days later, Lacuna and his men marched through Gapan and down the dusty cart track to San Isidro. Corporal George Athey of the Twenty-Second Infantry wrote home: "The surrender was a very impressive sight, with the torn and tattered clothed Philipino soldiers as they filed into town in column of twos . . . what happiness it brought to some homes as wives and children circled about their fathers and brothers for the first time in two years." The men stacked their rifles in the town plaza and stood at attention while Funston administered the oath of allegiance to the United States. Lacuna was the last general to surrender in the Northern District of Luzon. Although the most controversial and bloody episodes of the war would take place over the next twelve months in Batangas and on Samar, and savage fighting would continue for years afterward, the war against the Americans was effectively lost with the capture of Aguinaldo and the collapse of the revolution in the Northern District.[20]

Funston's Fourth District has been called a "backwater" in the war in Luzon; the resistance in the Ilocos region in the far north and in the southern province of Batangas was more unified and sustained with greater intensity, which, in turn, led to a much harsher American response. But even as something of a sideshow—a lost cause from the beginning—the commitment the Filipinos under Lacuna brought to the struggle in the Fourth District should not be trivialized. And if Fagen's role in the overall war was one of relative insignificance, his contribution to the struggle in Nueva Ecija was central to the resistance there. David Fagen led virtually every successful engagement against the Americans under Frederick Funston. Fagen was in command in the fight with Funston on June 4, 1900, resulting in the death of Captain Godfrey; in the fight with Major Wheeler near Mount Corona on July 22, 1900; the capture of Lieutenant Alstaetter on August 1, 1900; the attack on Sergeant Walter Washington's wagon party and subsequent fight with Lieutenant Day and his Scouts on September 13, 1900; the attack on Company I, Twenty-Fourth Infantry, with the capture of twelve on October 10, 1900; the attack and looting of the steam-launch *Stonie* on October 25, 1900; the fight with Funston at Rio Chico on December 5, 1900; and the engagement at Fort Rizal on March 15, 1901. And there were undoubtedly other ambushes, attacks, and incidents never reported. David Fagen had given all he could to the revolutionary cause.[21]

For more than a year, Fagen and Lacuna had been all but inseparable and now the time had come to part. Alejandrino wrote: "When our surrender was effected, I really felt sorry in having to leave Fagan. I left him some twelve rifles for his defense."[22]

In Alejandrino's autobiography, he spoke of engaging in pleasant conversation with Funston as they waited for Lacuna and his men to arrive. Funston talked of his time as an artillery officer with the Cuban rebels and then described in some detail the capture of Aguinaldo:"He finished the story by telling me that the whole affair was not clean. He asked me about my opinion and I answered him that if I had resorted to a similar ruse against the Americans, I would have been hanged for being a forger. . . . My answer drew from him a frank and loud laughter."[23]

Funston was not nearly so kind to Alejandrino: "It is a fact beyond dispute that Alejandrino . . . carried out a most relentless policy in his treatment of those of his unfortunate countrymen who were so unlucky as to incur his displeasure, and the scores of executions by our own military authorities of men who had carried out his orders are matters of record, the instigator of these hideous crimes saving his own skin by avoiding capture, and finally surrendering after the government had all but stayed its hand."[24]

As for the suffering and death inflicted upon civilian and combatant alike under Funston's direction, summary executions, crops and houses burned, livestock killed and suspects tortured, there was nothing but the deep satisfaction of a job well done.

Only one small, nagging task remained: to see David Fagen hanging from a picket rope. "Whatever he had been before," Funston wrote, "he was now a bandit, pure and simple, and entitled to just the same treatment as a mad dog; which is what he got."[25]

Or was it?

Ladrone

Part Three

While the smoke of battle still hung over the hills and valleys of the Philippines and every town and barrio in the islands was smoking hot with rebellion, she [the United States] replaced the military with a civil regime and on the smouldering embers of insurrection planted civil government.

Governor-General James F. Smith,
1907,
quoted in Blount, *American Occupation*

Outcast

35

D ID FAGEN EVER REGRET the course he had taken? After serving the revolutionary cause so faithfully for a year and a half, he had nothing to show for his sacrifice. Lacuna had gone home to manage his "large rice interests" on his farm near Santa Rosa. Alejandrino had taken a job with the city of Manila as the assistant chief engineer, saving up money to return to his hacienda near Arayat, which had been destroyed by the Americans. But Fagen had nothing to return to; he had been cast out, consigned to the life of a fugitive. Did he feel betrayed, abandoned? Did he see himself as a pitiable figure, as the sergeants of the Twenty-Fourth Infantry professed, or did he remain defiant? Did he become "a bandit, pure and simple," as Funston phrased it, or did he think of himself as still at war with the Americans? Events that were to follow suggest the latter.[1]

In May, reports came that Fagen had been captured near San Fernando and placed in double-irons. In denying the report, the *Manila Times* referred to "the renegade's *robber* band," turning him from *jefe de guerrilla* to bandit even before the surrender had taken place. In June, a soldier of fortune calling himself "Filipino Bill" advertised that for $1,000 in gold and with three scouts provided by the army, he would "deliver one Fagan, now in the mountains of Nueva Ecija." It seems no one took up Bill's offer and nothing more was heard from Fagen through the summer of 1901. With him were his common-law wife and probably a small band of associates. It is doubtful that he took part in any farming activity, even working a garden patch, but he may have hunted. The forest was home to deer, wild boar, and *timarau*—the wild carabao. There were monkeys, fruit bats that dangled like enormous papayas in the trees, and giant hornbills whose squawk echoed through the forest—all fair game to supplement a diet of fish, rice, squash, beans, and taro. There were cigars to buy from the Negritos, the tiny aboriginal tribesmen who lived in the mountain forests. There was *tuba*, made from the sap of the coconut palm, and *basi*—sugarcane wine. Perhaps he had a guitar to while away the evenings.[2]

259

Then, in September, came a report that he had turned up in Los Angeles, having stowed away aboard a troopship returning to the states. Although the story was quickly discounted, the article prompted the *Manila Times* to send a reporter out to interview the officers and noncoms of Fagen's former company. One officer heard it from the "natives" in Peñaranda that he had joined the deserters from the Ninth Cavalry in Batangas; by another rumor he had been shot and his right arm paralyzed. A third officer, and the one probably closest to the truth, maintained that he was living with his wife in the jungles east of Santa Rosa. One of the officers scoffed at the reports of Fagen's reputation as fearsome leader of a guerrilla band, dismissing them as "so much moonshine" and Fagen as a "good-for-nothing whelp." The noncommissioned officers were more sympathetic and "thought he was more to be pitied than censured." A sergeant said: "Fagan had a pretty hard time of it in his company. He was made to do all sorts of dirty jobs and from the treatment he got, I don't blame him for 'clearing out.' . . . I certainly condemn the course he has taken and the bad repute brought upon the regiment, but the public doesn't know all that an enlisted man has to put up with or they would not be so quick to judge."[3]

In his *Memories of Two Wars*, Frederick Funston wrote that Fagen had dropped out of sight for a time "but now he began to be heard from, he having in some way obtained two or three rifles and with a couple of unreconstructed natives, taken to the *bosque*, whence he had made a few forays for the purpose of committing a few robberies." Funston's use of the expression "unreconstructed natives" is both chilling and revealing as to how he viewed the American project in the islands. And, as for Fagen in "some way" obtaining rifles, we know that Alejandrino had left him twelve of them.[4]

With the renegade's reappearance on the scene, Funston, still smarting from his failure to settle with the man who had led him in circles for more than a year, traveled from his new headquarters at San Fernando to Manila. There he met with his mentor, General Lloyd Wheaton, "and came back with the authority to offer a reward of six hundred dollars for Fagen, dead or alive."[5]

With reward posters in Tagalog and Spanish posted throughout Nueva Ecija, Funston's scheme was an ideal way to separate Fagen from the Filipino population that had protected him. All that was needed was for one traitor, tempted by the reward, to turn on him at an unguarded moment. And so the story goes that, with a price on his head, Fagen and his wife withdrew into the jungles of Principe Province until, in rags and accompanied by only two Negritos, they descended to the remote east coast of Luzon where the Umiray River flows into the Pacific. It was as if they had been hounded to the edge of the world, the windswept sea blocking any further progress, the forbidding jungle-clad mountains at their backs.

On the morning of December 5, 1901, Lieutenant R. C. Corliss returned from a scout in the region of his headquarters at Bongabong, a remote outpost of about ten nipa houses in the foothills of the Sierra Madre. Corliss's small command consisted of one American sergeant and a platoon of Philippine Scouts. Unlike the constabulary, which served as a separate police force, the scouts were attached to the American army.

R. C. Corliss's relatives back home in Denver probably got a good laugh at the name of his station and the picture of the young man exiled to the middle of nowhere. At midday, the villagers had returned from their morning labors in the rice fields, and Bongabong had taken on that deserted feel in the hours of siesta. The entire populace seemed to go into a daily period of hibernation, with not a whisper of a breeze to rattle the drooping palm fronds or banana leaves. Even the animals—the pigs snorting in the shadows beneath the huts, the little dogs scratching at their fleas, the carabaos submerged to their nostrils in their mud wallows—settled into a villagewide torpor.

But soon a disturbance outside brought the lieutenant to the door of his headquarters. Villagers began to gather as a small party came down the road into the barrio; the group of men and boys was led by a well-known figure in the region, the hunter Anastacio Bartollomé. Bartollomé carried a sugar sack, slung on one shoulder, and a rifle on the other. Several young men carried two more rifles and more sugar sacks.

Corliss waited as the bustling crowd stopped before him. Bartollomé opened the sacks and, one by one, began pulling items from them: a U.S. Army Colt .38 revolver and holster, a pair of saddlebags, a torn and faded army-issue blue shirt, a pair of field glasses, a Spanish trumpet, a frayed pair of gauntlets, three coats—two insurgent, one civilian—a vest, insurgent-style shoulder straps, and two photographs.[6]

Then Bartollomé reached into a sack and brought out his prize, holding it up by its wiry black hair. The moldering head he held before Corliss, he claimed, was that of David Fagen.

Corliss wasted no time telegraphing the news to San Fernando. Then he sat down to depose Anastacio Bartollomé. The following day the lieutenant sent his report along with Bartollomé's sworn statement to the headquarters in San Fernando. The official investigation begins simply: "Makes report of the supposed killing of David Fagan, deserter, by natives. Gives list of things found in his possession." Then comes Corliss's report of Bartollomé's appearance in Bongabong and a description of the head "partly decomposed Teeth—good & regular; nose, large and flat; forehead, reclining [sic]. . . . Features seemed to correspond with photograph brought in, presumably Fagen's."

In listing Fagen's effects, Corliss noted that Alstaetter's ring was found inside the field glasses. Then he took down Bartollomé's story: "The time of the killing was December 1st 1901 about ten a.m. Circumstances are given in report of Anastacio Bartollomé herewith enclosed." Corliss related more of Bartollomé's story: The hunter and five companions had traveled over the mountains from Irurulong to hunt, fish, and "buy 'bejucos' from the Negritos," the tiny tribesmen who bore sub-Saharan African features and were the original inhabitants of the islands thousands of years before the ancestors of the lowland *indios* arrived. When Fagen and his wife appeared on the morning of December 1, Bartollomé, who had served with the guerrillas in the north of Nueva Ecija, recognized the wanted man. Out of fear of Fagen and thinking of the reward, Bartollomé invited Fagen, his wife, and their two Negrito companions to share in their meal of sweet potatoes and fish. At a prearranged signal, Bartollomé and his men set upon Fagen and his party with bolos. Corliss wrote, "Fagan was mortally wounded and ran about 100 yards and dropped dead. Both Negritos escaped badly wounded. Fagan's wife ran for the ocean and jumped in and drowned herself."

They then cut off Fagen's head, buried the body beside the Umiray, and with his effects set out on the five-day trek over the mountains to Bongabong.

On December 7, 1901, the *Manila Freedom* and the *Manila Times* announced the death of the "notorious Fagan." Over the ensuing days, hundreds of newspapers covered the story. The *Manila Freedom*'s account began, "Fagan has been reported killed time and time again, some soldiers on the line declaring that they had sent the fatal bullet during some engagement in which the negro was known to be participating and others have gone so far as to state the location of his grave."[7]

According to the *Manila Times*, General Bisbee "wired instructions to Lieutenant Corliss to make a complete and satisfactory investigation . . . and instructed him to note any marks about the head and especially the teeth" (which Corliss had already described as "good & regular"). In Manila, General Wheaton instructed Corliss to pay Bartollomé for the arms he had brought in. There is no record of Bartollomé ever receiving the six-hundred-dollar reward.[8]

Wheaton's aide de camp, Captain F. D. Webster, sent a telegram to Captain James A. Moss, now regimental adjutant of the Twenty-Fourth Infantry, asking him to send all the information he could about Fagen. "The evidence is very good that he has been done away with," Webster concluded. Moss responded by sending an "information slip" and wrote that "additional information" was on its way. (There is no trace of this additional information in the files.) He also noted that Captain Gose, the new commanding officer of Company I, had "taken no action in the case."[9]

The enclosed information slip, presumably written by Moss, the white officer most familiar with Fagen's case, reads in part:

> Eyes: brown #1, Hair: dark, Complexion: Black. Height: 5 feet, 10 inches,—curved scar ¼ in. on chin. . . . Weight when last seen: about 163 pounds,—Was loud mouthed and given to slang and profanity.
>
> He was a rowdy soldier and a "bad man." One who thought it smart to "buck" the 1st Sergeant. At the time of his desertion he had seven (7) previous convictions and was almost constantly doing extra fatigue duty.[10]

A month passed before the 2nd Endorsement whereby General Wheaton charged Colonel David Craigie with disposing of Fagen's effects as per Army Regulation 176. Included in the file is a meticulously detailed report of the proceedings. A panel of three officers, headed by Colonel Craigie, met on January 18, 1902, examined Fagen's effects, and made a list of them. Alstaetter's ring had been given to Funston to deliver to the lieutenant in the United States.[11]

In describing the head, Corliss had noted that the "features seemed to correspond with photograph brought in, presumably Fagen's." Aside from noting the photograph's disposal at auction for fifty cents, there is no other mention of it in the files. It seems the photograph was never shown to members of Fagen's company for confirmation or, if it had been, the authorities did not get the response they were looking for. That the photo was disposed of at auction without further mention would suggest that it had been determined not to be of Fagen.

The total value of Fagen's effects came to four dollars. That concluded the work of the Board of Officers. On February 14, Wheaton's aide-de-camp sent an inquiry to "Commanding Officer, Co 'I,' 24th Infantry, for information whether he has fully complied with A.R. 175 and 176 and for prompt action in case he has not done so." A week later, on February 27, 1902, Captain Gose was finally heard from: "No action has been taken by the Company Commander as it was not known that that [sic] it had been decided that Fagan had been killed."[12]

Bisbee forwarded Gose's response to Wheaton in Manila; Wheaton forwarded it to the commanding General Adna Chaffee, who in a 9th Endorsement, forwarded the collected information to the adjutant general of the army In Washington.

And that is the sum total of the investigation into the "supposed killing of David Fagan": Bartollomé's deposition taken by Lieutenant R. C. Corliss and the lieutenant's accompanying report; an exchange of telegrams between Moss and Webster; a single "information slip"; a detailed account of the disposal of

Fagen's effects; a query by Wheaton's aide-de-camp to Captain Gòse; Gose's explanation as to why no action had been taken; and then the forwarding of this paltry collection of odds and ends to Washington. Case closed.

And more than a century later, this is where Fagen's story was thought to have ended. But a forgotten and long-unnoticed article from Manila's third English-language newspaper, the *Manila American*, made a mockery of the investigation when it was only two days old. The report came on December 7, the same day as the headlines in the *Manila Times* and *Manila Freedom* announced Fagen's death. But the reporter for the *Manila American* seems to have taken the extra time to investigate the army's claim of Fagen's beheading more thoroughly.

FAGAN REPORTED DEAD ONCE MORE
Has Been Killed About a Dozen Times
Officers Take No Steps
His Head Brought in by a Native Head Hunter
—It is not identified—

Manila, P.I. Dec. 10.—Fagan is dead—maybe. He has been killed again. The fact that he has been killed twelve times in the last ten months makes no difference. He goes on being killed with a regularity that is surprising. There can be no doubt that he is really and truly dead this time because the man who killed him brought his head in to the commanding officer of the post and said it had recently belonged to Fagan. What better evidence could one want? It might be said by way of parenthesis, that Fagan had been killed just as dead several times before. The commanding officer at Bongabong is so positive that the man who brought in the head of an American negro actually slayed Fagan that he threw him in the guard-house as a reward, and right away began an investigation to learn how many American negro soldiers have failed to answer roll call lately.

The truth of the matter is that the military authorities do not take a bit of stock in the story told by the native who brought in the head, but are inclined to believe that the head was sent in by Fagan himself. According to a report that was received in Manila yesterday, the head was so decomposed that those who had seen it were quite undecided whether it was the head of an African or a Negrito.

It is generally known that a small but very determined detachment of scouts and members of Fagan's old company, left a certain post in the northern part of the island about three weeks ago for the purpose of bringing in the notorious renegade. This party is under the command of a very able officer, and one in whom the authorities have the utmost confidence. He has been pressing Fagan very closely, and it is believed that so closely is he pressed that he sent in the head that was delivered at Bongabong for the purpose of throwing the soldiers off his trail.

An officer on duty in Manila, who knew Fagan, told a reporter for the *American* last night that Fagan can be easily identified by certain dental defects. This fact is well known to the officers throughout the section to which Fagan had been operating, and if the severed head ever formed a part of his anatomy, there would be no difficulty in identifying it.[13]

The article then recounts Bartollomé's tale and concludes: "The whole story is decidedly fishy, and unless the detachment that is now out after Fagan succeeds in bringing him in, the public may hope to be regaled with the details of Fagan's death again in the near future."[14]

Either the *Manila American*'s reporter was a gifted storyteller and decided to keep Fagen alive awhile longer, or maybe he was onto something. Yet, if the *American*'s story was true and Fagen was still alive, how could that have escaped notice all these years?

In the United States, only the *Leavenworth Times* picked up on the *Manila American*'s story. The story appeared on January 19, 1902, about six weeks after appearing in the *Manila American*, and it was probably mailed by someone in the army to Leavenworth, site of a major military post. Until our own time of digitized newspapers, the article has remained buried in the archives of the *Leavenworth Times* and on a rarely viewed microfilm roll of the *Manila American* in the Library of Congress.

Some may choose to believe the *Manila American*'s story a fabrication and stick with the account of Fagen's death on the beach at Dingalan Bay on December 1, 1901. That cannot be discounted as a possibility, even if the *Manila American*'s story puts it in doubt. The Record of Events of the Twenty-Fourth Infantry does indeed refer to a patrol of twenty men of Company I away on detached service. The corporal in charge of that detail was none other than William Watson, who had spent fifteen days in the San Fernando guardhouse with Fagen and had been captured by him a year later on October 10, 1900. Why members of Fagen's old company would be on the hunt for him—if the *Manila American*'s account is true—would be very interesting to know. Were they out to restore the good name of the Twenty-Fourth Infantry, and Company I's tarnished reputation in particular, by killing the traitor who had brought dishonor to the regiment? I find it hard to think of another plausible explanation for their involvement.[15]

And if the *American*'s story was not a fabrication and if Fagen was indeed still alive, then the question becomes—what happened to him?

———•·•———

Only four and a half months after the *Manila American* ridiculed the report of Fagen's death came a second report, this one in the *St. Louis Post-Dispatch* on April 16, 1902, that would seem to not only confirm the *American*'s contention that Fagen had survived but also announce his murder and beheading all over again. Is it possible that Fagen's new lease on life had been no more than a brief reprieve?[16]

In January 1902, Frederick Funston returned from the Philippines to Kansas City and in February underwent an operation for chronic ulcerative appendicitis. He had brought with him Alstaetter's West Point ring and, as Alstaetter was stationed only a short distance away at Fort Leavenworth, it would be interesting to know if the two men met and if Funston personally handed over the ring. If that had been the case, the two men would undoubtedly have spoken of Fagen, and one can only imagine how such an exchange might have gone.

It also seems, as mentioned earlier, that while recovering from surgery, Funston had spoken freely with a reporter from the *St. Louis Post-Dispatch*. The other possibility is that his cousin, Lieutenant Burton Mitchell, his father, or another close associate had related the stories to the reporter.

After recovering for several weeks in the hospital, Funston visited the family in Iola, Kansas. Then he embarked on a nationwide speaking tour. "The Filipino doesn't love us a bit," he announced at one lavish banquet after another. "He doesn't know what gratitude is. He has no sense of appreciation, and I believe he'd like us better if we dealt more severely with him."[17]

When he boasted of having personally strung up thirty-five Filipinos without trial, the crowd roared its approval. "We cannot punish the Filipinos as they deserve to be punished," Funston lamented before cheering banqueters. "If we did we would never get through hanging them!" Hanging was the theme of the day, the off-the-cuff numbers dependent upon the whim of the moment.[18]

The standing ovations that greeted calls for stringing up critics of the war emboldened Funston to add to the list of candidates ripe for hanging. Consigned to the ranks of the treasonous were senators, prominent citizens, clergymen of all denominations, newspaper editors, and college presidents, in essence, anyone who disagreed with Frederick Funston about the conduct of the war.[19]

Finally, in Denver, Funston turned his sights on Senator George Frisbie Hoar of Massachusetts, the Senate's most relentless critic of the war. Ridiculing

Hoar for "an overheated conscience," Funston requested permission from Washington to attend a banquet in Boston where, it was widely rumored, he would recommend stringing up the highly respected septuagenarian. Several reporters, eyebrows raised, questioned Funston as to whether he might have gone a little too far in his criticism. Funston scoffed at the notion: "The idea that an army officer must keep his mouth always shut is a hallucination. I have a mouth. I use it for two purposes. One is to eat and the other is to talk, and when I talk I mean what I say, because I know what I am talking about. I cannot see that an army officer must wear a gag just because he is an army officer."[20]

But President Roosevelt could see that and ordered Funston to don his gag immediately. The headline read MUST CEASE HIS CRITICISM. "I am directed by the President," the acting Secretary of War wrote, "to instruct you that he wishes you to cease all further public discussion of the situation in the Philippines." TEDDY AND FREDDY: A WAR TRAGEDY, Joseph Pulitzer's *New York World* headlined gleefully. *Freddy Talked About the Philippines; Teddy Says He Musn't.* CAN'T I SPEAK IN BOSTON?" ASKS FREDDY; "NO!" SAYS TEDDY.[21]

The day that the newspapers broke the story of Funston's censure, the *Iola (KS) Daily Register* ran not only that startling news on its front page but also the article it had picked up from the *St. Louis Post Dispatch* that had been published a week earlier.

FUNSTON'S ENEMY
David Fagin, Who Challenged Him to a Duel, Is Dead.

> David Fagin, the gigantic negro who deserted from the Twenty-fourth United States Infantry, joined the Filipino forces and fought with desperation, has been killed. He successfully eluded the regular forces of the United States, and the honor of his killing rests with the native troops, who shot him and then brought in his head as a trophy to substantiate their story.[22]

When I first came upon this article, I assumed the *Daily Register* was simply recycling old news, both to relate these new fascinating details of Funston's encounters with Fagen and also to soften the embarrassing impact of the news of Funston's censure blared on the other side of the front page. After all, when Fagen was first reported killed on December 7, 1901, the *Manila Freedom's* headline read: NOTORIOUS FAGAN KILLED / *Native Scouts, Shoots Him and Brings in His Head.* And the *Manila Times* headline ran THE NOTORIOUS RENEGADE FAGAN'S CAREER IS ENDED / *Anastasio Bartolome, a Native Scout, Brings in the*

Head of the Deserter. A number of other newspapers, from Texas to Pennsylvania to North Carolina, had all reported in December that Fagen had been "shot" by "native scouts" who had subsequently brought in his head. When I later discovered the original article in the *St. Louis Post-Dispatch*, published a week earlier, it still seemed as if the paper had resurrected the old news of Fagen's death in order to share the new details about Fagen and Funston. Funston was making headlines all over the country with his reckless pronouncements and riding a wave of notoriety, if not of popularity. Anything about the controversial hero who had captured Aguinaldo made for good copy.

Only later, as I came across additional clues, did it occur to me that the story in the *Post-Dispatch* might have actually been reporting *new* news. This was a dismal thought but could not be brushed aside. Could Fagen have been shot in April 1902 by members of the fledgling Philippine Constabulary? The constabulary had been founded the previous August 1901 and had been judged hopelessly inept in its fumbling attempts at becoming a credible police force. And yet the article stated "native *troops*" rather than "native *scouts*." If Fagen had faked his death and lived on for a few months, Funston certainly would have been aware of that fact. Yet, in his autobiography, published in 1911, he stuck with the story of Fagen's beheading by Bartollomé. Was Funston hiding the true story, or had he understood the *Post-Dispatch/Iola Times* piece to be simply a rehash of the original report of December 1901?

And, as it turns out, the latter is the case. In reading the article more closely, I came across this line: "The men who brought in Fagin's head also brought in Lieut. Alstaetter's ring, which is regarded as proof that Fagin was killed as the natives reported." Of course, Anastacio Bartollomé brought in Alstaetter's ring on December 5, 1901, of that there is no doubt. Frederick Funston sailed home with the ring in mid-December 1901 and returned it to Alstaetter. So indeed, the *St. Louis Post-Dispatch* story was simply a retelling of the original account of Fagen's supposed beheading on December 1, 1901. The *Manila American* had convincingly portrayed that initial report as a sham, and subsequent evidence will support the *American*'s claim. It seems that David Fagen was very much alive in the year 1902.

The Renegade Comes to Town

36

WITH THE CAPTURE OF AGUINALDO and the surrender of almost all of the guerrilla chiefs in the Northern District, the Americans were confident that organized resistance in the south of Luzon and in the Visayas would soon collapse. The administration in Washington was eager to have the messy business of "insurgency" behind them (and off their conscience) and get on with their "civilizing" mission, as if further resistance could be wished aside in a wave of good intentions dubbed "benevolent assimilation."

Now there were two American authorities in the islands, with Governor General William Howard Taft in charge of civilian affairs (in the regions deemed pacified) and General Adna Chaffee in command of military operations in those areas still in organized revolt. Taft remained convinced that any continued resistance would melt away before the policy of the carrot. Chaffee and the regional army commanders were under no such illusion. The tension and back-biting between the military and civilian authorities would continue over the ensuing decade and lead to a pattern of mixed messages that left the American people confused as to the true state of affairs in their newly acquired colony. Were the Filipinos happily accepting a new era of American tutelage, or were they persisting in revolt?

While the resistance had always been fragmentary and only nominally under the control of Emilio Aguinaldo, the president's capture has been likened to cutting off the head of an octopus, leaving the Americans to contend with the writhing ganglia of a failing revolution. As the fighting moved south to Batangas and its bordering provinces, and then to the island of Samar, conditions in central Luzon were anything but settled. There, more than ever, the revolution had devolved into a chaotic blend of diehard guerrilla resistance, banditism, and religio-political cultism, all hostile to both the Americans and their Filipino minions in Manila.

The ravages of more than a decade of upheaval had left even the less-contested provinces all but prostrate. On February 17, 1902, the Chicago *Inter Ocean* reported that "five years of war . . . have destroyed the best and most necessary aids of the splendid agriculture of the Philippines by exhausting the money of the pueblos, the majority of which have been burned." Even worse was the loss of carabaos, reduced to one-tenth of their former numbers by epidemics of rinderpest and overuse by the warring parties. The carabao was essential to the *tao*'s survival. Added to the misery were plagues of locusts and periodic outbreaks of cholera, diphtheria, tuberculosis, dysentery, and typhoid. David R. Sturtevant wrote, "Intense hunger—verging, at times, on wholesale starvation—compounded the agonies of peasant survivors. In many districts, food became a far more precious commodity than human life." Under such duress, the peasants found no relief from their hacendero landlords. According to the economic anthropologist Brian Fegan, "The landowners reacted to all these threats to their economic interests by squeezing tenants harder." This trend would continue without interference from the American authorities.[1]

In their eagerness to move from a military to a civilian control of the islands, the Americans established a Philippine Constabulary, a rural "police" force made up of Filipino regulars under the command of American officers, aptly described by Paul Kramer as "a colonial army in police uniform." This force was to take the lead in quelling the continued disturbances in the countryside, freeing up the American army to contend with the provinces still in organized revolt.[2]

On September 14, 1901, the assassination of William McKinley by an immigrant anarchist elevated Theodore Roosevelt to the presidency. Two weeks later, on the island of Samar, four hundred guerrillas under General Vicente Lukbán set upon a company of the Ninth Infantry while the men breakfasted at an outdoor mess area. Of the seventy-four men in the company, forty-eight were killed in the initial bolo assault; others managed to fight their way to longboats on the beach and escape across the channel to the island of Leyte. Of the twenty-six survivors, all but four had been wounded.[3]

Following the "Balangiga Massacre," the military governor Adna Chaffee assigned General Jacob H. Smith the task of pacifying Samar. The brutality of the campaign that followed created a national scandal and would lead to Smith's court martial and forced retirement. Conservative American historians have complained, perhaps with some justice, that the story of "Howling" Jake Smith's campaign on Samar has become the enduring and distorting image of the war, as if to say that Samar was uniquely horrific and should not be taken as representative of the broader war. This argument, however unintended, has the effect of downplaying the severity with which the war was waged in other regions of the islands.[4]

Newspapers were soon filled with rumors of atrocities on Samar, leading to public outrage. Cartoons depicted army firing squads executing blindfolded children. "The water-cure atrocities and the kill and burn method of warfare in vogue in the Philippines have punctured a hornets' nest," the *Bedford (PA) Gazette* reported. "Many letters from officers, surgeons and enlisted men describing the tortures of Filipinos have been published."[5]

In the opinion of Brian Linn, the "Balangiga Massacre" had "panicked Chaffee into authorizing the most extreme measures against the remaining centers of armed resistance." The other region to be subjected to "extreme measures" was the province of Batangas where General Miguel Malvar was leading the fiercest resistance the Americans had yet encountered. For some military historians, General J. Franklin Bell's operation conducted over the first four months of 1902 was "a master-piece of counter-guerrilla warfare" that stands in glaring contrast to "Hell-Roaring" Jake Smith's universally condemned assault on Samar. Other American and Filipino historians take the opposite view, some even declaring Bell's operation in Batangas genocidal.[6]

In the first phase of the operation, Bell ordered the general population to relocate to zones within the towns, the very system of "reconcentrado pens" that General Valeriano Weyler had resorted to in Cuba and which had provoked such outrage in America. Any person outside the designated zones would be considered an insurgent, to be shot unless immediately surrendering. By concentrating the entire civilian population, the general had, according to Glenn Anthony May, "turned most of Batangas and Laguna into virtual free-fire zones."[7]

The next phase was to eliminate the guerrillas' food sources. In the first expedition, on January 1, 1902, approximately 1,800 soldiers spread out over a designated area and proceeded to destroy everything in their path, burning 500 tons of rice, killing hundreds of hogs and chickens, 200 carabaos, 800 head of cattle, 680 horses, and burning more than 6,000 houses. Another wave of soldiers did the same in an adjacent zone. This was just the beginning as Bell's men methodically laid waste to Batangas sector by sector. In May's words, "The predictable result of such behavior was ecological destruction on a massive scale."[8]

While the tons of rice destroyed, the numbers of livestock killed, and houses burned were all recorded in detail, there are no statistics for the numbers of Batangueños, civilian and guerrilla, killed or abused by the soldiers "in officially sanctioned wrath." May can only report, "In addition to ravaging the countryside, the U.S. troops were guilty of more than a few other outrageous acts." And he concludes, "The commission of abusive acts by U.S. military men was anything but rare in the final battle for Batangas. The evidence about their occurrence is simply too extensive to discount."[9]

The phrases "more than a few" and "anything but rare," as opposed to numbers in their stark specificity, point to the difficulties faced by the historian when so much information was either not recorded, suppressed, or dismissed out of hand should a report come to light. Whatever the degree of atrociousness of the operation, the end result was a countryside laid waste, with malnourished villagers confined in squalid and disease-prone conditions while the army tracked down the remaining guerrillas. In April, holding out almost alone, Malvar surrendered, convinced the Americans would resort to mass murder if he didn't call for an end to the struggle.

According to Governor General Taft, "The severity with which the inhabitants have been dealt would not look well if a complete history of it were written out." Bell was stung by the harsh criticism that came his way and, compared in the press to "Butcher" Weyler of Cuban infamy, he was subjected to several official investigations. Not surprisingly, the inquiries led to the exoneration of Bell and the officers under him. The public soon grew inured to stories of atrocity and death on a mass scale; they had heard enough and were ready to move on.[10]

On July 4, 1902, with the end of resistance in Batangas and Samar, President Roosevelt declared the "insurrection" over. In a case of wishful thinking and shrewd politics, he assured the nation that the islands had at last been pacified.

———————

While Bell's operation was underway in Batangas, and a scandal brewing over Smith's campaign on Samar, much of central Luzon remained anything but pacified. Instead of an organized guerrilla resistance directed by the provincial elite, the countryside was overrun with irregular bands, some led by former insurgent officers, others by avowed bandits or self-proclaimed popes and messiahs—all in opposition to the Americans and, in particular, to their new indigenous "police" force, the constabulary.

After having declared the islands pacified, the leadership in Washington did not want stories of unrest and continued rebellion "noised about" in the press. But, as good journalists will, some persisted in challenging the administration's rosy narrative of peace and cooperation meant for home consumption. "Whatever official reports may say of the pacification of the Philippines," the *Pittsburgh Daily Post*'s Frederick W. Eddy wrote, "accounts of conditions are misleading which leave the impression that the islands are orderly. Order prevails in very few of them."[11]

To the Americans, these "ladrones" (Americanization of the Spanish *ladrón*) who numbered in the thousands were not diehard revolutionaries but misguided souls suffering from a cultural "disease"—in General Fred Grant's words, the irresistible "tendency to brigandage." In fact, a large portion of the rural peasantry viewed these afflicted malcontents as Robin Hoods and as revolutionaries, and their material support was indeed a form of taxation, that is, contributions to the ongoing cause of getting rid of the Americans. The chief of the Philippine Commission reported, "The greatest obstacle encountered by the constabulary in their pursuit of ladrones is the sympathy of the natives of almost all climes with robbers." Many of these so-called bandit leaders were former guerrilla officers who had refused to take the oath of allegiance and withdrawn to the mountains and wilder places. Renato Constantino wrote, "The people, minus the ilustrados, now confronted the Americans."[12]

"Filipinos generally have little faith in the American talk of self-government," the journalist Frederick W. Eddy observed. "The notion commonly prevailing is that self-government can be brought about only by making life so uncomfortable and disheartening for Americans that they will be glad to give up the islands to native rule." And, indeed, there was little or no distinction made between banditry and revolution; the people of the rural regions were out to oppose the Americans in every way, to disrupt their attempts to impose a stable colonial rule and, most immediately, prevent their native police force from taking control of the countryside.[13]

Out of this teeming chaos—what David Sturtevant describes as "a demoralizing half-world of fading guerrillas and jaded bandits"—a former guerrilla chief, Faustino Guillermo, emerged to consolidate the various bands around Manila under his leadership. All swore fealty to a New Katipunan, their purpose to continue the revolution. Guillermo operated out of the town of Diliman, on the outskirts of Manila, and his formidable organization soon became known as the Diliman Gang.[14]

In September 1902, General Luciano San Miguel, a former revolutionary general for the provinces of Bataan and Pangasinan, assumed command of operations in Rizal and Bulacan; Faustino Guillermo became his second in command with prominent ladrone leaders such as Julian Santos, Ciriaco Contreras, and Apolonio Samson as leading officers. San Miguel had refused to take the oath of allegiance, and in the coming January he would become the acknowledged commanding officer of the revolution, "recognized as chief of all the troops," and carry on the fight under the Katipunan flag.[15]

"It continues to be the official fashion to attribute to ladrones acts of the character for which insurgents formerly got credit," Frederick Eddy wrote in the *Pittsburgh Daily Post*. Virtually every American official, civilian or military, would insist upon applying the words "ladrone" or "bandit" to any person deemed opposed to American authority. "They masquerade at times as 'revolucionarios' in order to win assistance," Governor Taft explained, which was as close as he could come to admitting there might be more behind the unrest in the countryside than mere banditry. In November 1902, he would back the passage of the Bandolerismo Statute, also known as the Brigandage Act, by which any group of three or more Filipinos caught engaging in "criminal" activity would suffer death or a minimum of twenty years in prison. In addition, any "person knowingly aiding or abetting such a band of brigands" would be subject to ten to twenty years' imprisonment. By this measure, all resistance to American authority after November 1902 was classed as brigandage.[16]

Under Captain William Warren, the constabulary established a headquarters at Novaliches, twenty miles from Manila, and sent patrols into the surrounding countryside in search of Guillermo and his men. Guillermo, in just one day, ambushed two patrols, killing a number of policemen, then attacked Captain Warren's camp that night, killing five more men and wounding Warren. Major Allen, chief of the constabulary, then sent out a force of two hundred well-armed men against the "gang of cutthroats," but Guillermo and his men simply disappeared, disbanding and blending with the civilian population or moving deeper into the mountains.[17]

After several weeks of guerrilla inactivity, the constabulary command, with Taft's blessing, proposed an offer of amnesty to Guillermo and his men. The initial negotiations seemed promising and Guillermo agreed that if granted immunity from past offenses, he and his men would consider surrendering. In his dissertation on the history of the constabulary, George Yarrington Coats wrote, "As a result the outlaws were permitted to rest while being generously fed and subsidized with secret service funds."[18]

Taft had given Guillermo until November 15 to accept the amnesty offer. But Guillermo did not wait to answer, and on October 30, three hundred of his men attacked a constabulary patrol near Novaliches and laid siege to the town. It seems that Faustino had never intended to accept the amnesty offer but had used the truce period to reorganize and rebuild his forces.[19]

The inspector in charge at Novaliches was Charles J. Bates, formerly a captain in the African American Twenty-Fifth Infantry. In the fight, Bates and his men were ambushed by a band of three hundred "ladrones" and driven back to Novaliches. With his post under siege, Bates sent an urgent, scrawled message to Lieutenant De Rubio in nearby Polo (Bignay).

> Novaliches 30 Oct 1902
> Lieut. Rubio Polo
> I had a big scrap this afternoon I want you to come over here with all your men and plenty of arms I am out, have four wounded and 2 of my men captured come over at once I am about surrounded.
> Bates Insp

A photocopy of Bates's handwritten message appeared in Vic Hurley's *Jungle Patrol: The Story of the Philippine Constabulary*, published in 1938. Below the photocopy of Bates's note, Hurley added a descriptive sentence: "Despatch sent by Inspector Bates to Lieutenant De Rubio during pursuit of insurgents under Fagin, American deserter."[20]

And for more than a century this has been the only citation put forth to suggest Fagen might have been alive after December 1, 1901, the *Manila American*'s article and other evidence having gone unnoticed until now.

Had Inspector Bates referred to Fagen by name in the dispatch, the evidence would have been overwhelmingly persuasive, but we have only Vic Hurley's undocumented and therefore dubious attribution thirty-five years later. Did Hurley simply pull the name out of a hat, having heard of the famous "Fagin" and hoping to liven up his account? Or had he been privy to some insider information?

In 1925 Vic Hurley worked his way on a tramp steamer bound for the Far East. He wound up in Zamboanga, Mindanao, and decided to try his hand at farming coconuts. After barely surviving a disastrous year in the wild, he went to work for a large-scale coconut grower in Zamboanga. Three years in the employ of Goodyear Rubber followed, during which time he married. In 1934, he and his wife returned to the United States, and in 1935 Hurley published an account of his misadventures as a would-be coconut farmer. While in Mindanao, he had met old hands from the Philippine Constabulary, men familiar with the wild early days of the American regime. He was even made an honorary Third Lieutenant of the Constabulary. Under the pseudonym Charles L. Clifford he wrote the screenplay for *The Real Glory*, starring Gary Cooper and David Niven, based on the war against the Moros on Mindanao. After another screenplay and two more books, *Zamboanga, Men in Sun Helmets*, and *The Swish of the Kris*, Dutton published *Jungle Patrol: The Story of the Philippine Constabulary*.[21]

Hurley did not supply footnotes for *Jungle Patrol*. In a two-page bibliography at the end of the book, he described how he came by his sources. With a dearth of military records and little else written about the constabulary and their soldier-of-fortune officers, Hurley was left to other devices: "A systematic attempt was made, therefore, to get into personal correspondence with retired officers, and to compile, from other personal accounts, the data concerning the corps." His information, Hurley explained, was almost entirely derived "from personal memoirs" contributed by some "forty odd officers."[22]

At the end of his introduction to *Jungle Patrol*, Hurley wrote: "I am proud of the confidence with which they [the officers] have turned over to me the combat orders, diaries, and personal memoirs of this most neglected chapter of American military history."[23]

Vic Hurley's papers are archived at the University of Oregon. Among the small collection of letters and manuscript copies, there is no sign of the "combat orders, diaries, and personal memoirs" shared by those men. Perhaps his correspondence with former constabulary men still exists and may someday be located, but it is hard to imagine where to look. Vic Hurley and his wife were childless, and he died in 1978.[24]

The first indication that Vic Hurley may not have been simply throwing out the name of "Fagin" comes from a report that created a brief stir two weeks after Inspector Bates's near-disaster at Novaliches. A number of American newspapers published a shortened version of an account obtained from the *Manila American* on November 14, 1902.

AMERICAN NEGROS REPORTED IN LEAGUE WITH LADRONES
**Reports Received Indicate That the Lawless Elements
Are Being Drilled and Led by a Number of Renegades
Were Formerly Soldiers of Colored Regiments**

Stories from different parts of these islands are arriving here frequently of late pointing out that a number of American negroes, evidently formerly belonging to the Army, have joined the ladrones and are not only leading bands of these highwaymen in fights against the officers of the law, but are also using their knowledge gained in the army in drilling the ladrones and in organizing them in a crude military way.

From the province of Bulacan comes information of the effect that there are about 300 ladrones led by an American negro who propose to wipe out the Constabulary and that a few miles out from the town of Caloocan four American negros are actively engaged in teaching a large number of highway men the rudiments of military tactics and how to handle firearms.

These stories, while lacking official confirmation, come from what are considered reliable sources and so often have they been repeated lately from various provinces that there seems to be as no doubt but that a number of discharged soldiers formerly of some colored regiment have taken to the highway and are now members of ladrone bands.[25]

If Vic Hurley was right about Fagen leading three hundred men in the attack on Inspector Bates and his constabulary detachment, could Fagen then have been the "American negro" leading a band of three hundred ladrones in

Bulacan? This is the first hint to support, at least circumstantially, the *Manila American*'s contention that Fagen had faked his death. And if Fagen was that "negro" leading three hundred "ladrones" in Bulacan, it would seem he had not gone into the business of banditry but had remained intent upon making war against the Americans.

Over a period of three days, from December 19 to December 22, 1902, a number of American newspapers, including the *Los Angeles Times* and the *Chicago Tribune*, ran the *Manila American* story: NEGROES LEAD LADRONE BANDS, ending with the following: "The story is not officially confirmed." In a flicker of light, the story flashed across the pages of several dozen newspapers and was gone, having scarcely been glimpsed. Officials neither confirmed nor denied the story; they simply ignored it. Over the four-month campaign that followed, with scores of detailed accounts of the pursuit of Luciano San Miguel and his men, one finds not a word in official reports of any involvement of "American colored men" or "an American negro" leading three hundred ladrones in Bulacan. As quickly as these "American negroes" appeared on the scene, they vanished.[26]

In the aftermath of the attack on Bates and his men, Major Allen was so incensed by the resumption of hostilities by the "ladrones" that he persuaded a reluctant Taft to call out the army as well as units of the Philippine Scouts in a large-scale joint operation. On November 9, word came from Manila that "General Davis has strengthened the garrison in Rizal province and will co-operate with the constabulary in exterminating the Ladrones. A big campaign is expected." The annual report of the Philippine Commission for 1903 relates the events of this period in detail. But there is no mention in these reports of renegade ex-soldiers from the "colored" regiments.[27]

On February 5, 1903, a report came from Manila that four hundred "ladrones" had attacked and sent thirty-five men of the constabulary near Polo into a headlong retreat: "The engagement was reported to be sharp and the ladrones more like insurrectos than thieves." The *Manila Times* noted that the small bands of "ladrones" in the outskirts of the city had grown tenfold. These forces were unmistakably under the command of San Miguel, Guillermo, and Santos and fighting under the banner of the New Katipunan: "We have threats and mutterings in the city, and blood and pillage and proclaimed revolution outside the city. It would seem to be time for somebody to wake up."[28]

On February 8, Inspector Keldily led more than one hundred constabulary men in a "fierce encounter" with more than three hundred men under San Miguel and Guillermo. The revolutionists, as they called themselves, fought for two hours; an American inspector and a constabulary man were killed while

Keithly had the pleasure of blowing up the revolutionaries' arsenal. The following day, the army dispatched several companies of "natives scouts" to join the constabulary in pursuit of the attackers and laid plans for cordons, north and south, that would prevent the "ladrones" from fleeing to other regions. Blockaded by Philippine Scout and constabulary companies, San Miguel's men would be driven toward Manila and captured as the net closed in on them.[29]

The maneuver seems to have had at least some partial effect, judging by the numbers of "ladrones" snared in the net, although with their ability to disband and coalesce virtually overnight, most of San Miguel's men did their usual disappearing act. At the start of this campaign, the *Leavenworth Times*, drawing from what was almost certainly one of the missing articles from the *Manila American* (more than twenty issues over that period of several months did not survive to be microfilmed), dropped a bombshell.

RENEGADE FAGANS LAST SEEN IN MANILA

Manila, P.I., February 10, — Fagan, the notorious renegade, whose death has been reported times without number, has turned up again. This time he has been reported seen in Manila. A former member of the 25th [*sic*] Infantry, the regiment from which Fagan deserted, claims that Fagan was in Manila for several days last week. In fact, he does not deny that the notorious bandit was at his house, remained there two nights and ate several meals there. He was accompanied by the woman who is supposed to be his wife. When he left the home of his friend, Fagan did not return to the north where he has been for so long, but instead went to Batangas province. It is understood that he is making his way to the Camarines, and expects eventually to reach Cebu or Iloilo and engage passage on some sailing vessel sailing direct from these ports to Singapore or Hong Kong. If he succeeds in getting away he will be able to reach the United States, and probably will never be made to pay for his many crimes. The man who claims Fagan visited him, says the once bold and daring renegade seemed hopelessly broken down; that he was nervous and restless and seemed to be in constant fear of capture.

When asked why he did not inform the police of the presence of Fagan in Manila, the fellow said that Fagan had been good to him on several occasions when he was a "rookie" and that he did not mean to go back on him now that Fagan needed friends.[30]

Was this yet another fabrication by the *Manila American*? Did some imaginative editor decide it would make for good copy to bring Fagen back to life every once in a while? Or did a veteran of the Twenty-Fourth living in Manila have some fun pulling a reporter's leg? The reader will have to decide.

If the story was in fact true, as I believe it was, Fagen's decision to sneak into the city must have come as a result of the pressure the constabulary had put on him; perhaps he had come close to being captured. Perhaps he'd had a bad time of it in the fight near Polo on February 5, for it is at about that time this story places Fagen and his wife in Manila. The former soldier's description of Fagen as "broken down," "nervous and restless," and in fear of capture seems reasonable. To have come into the city, his situation appeared to have been a desperate one. In Manila, crawling with Americans and Filipino collaborators, he had ventured into the lion's den. More than anyone, Fagen the gambler would have understood that the most charmed poker player's luck runs cold sooner or later. How could he not, at times, have had visions of the approaching end of his death-defying odyssey? A fugitive for nearly four years, he is the mythical black man on the run, the bloodhounds on his trail.

If the newspaper account was true, Fagen's supposed plan to travel to the Visayas in order to sail away to Hong Kong or Singapore was probably meant as a feint to throw the authorities off; otherwise his host would not have revealed his planned itinerary. Did he and his wife ever plot to escape the islands? Did they dream of it? Would it have been possible? If he had hoped to survive to an old age, escaping the islands was his best chance.

A People's War

37

Throughout the entire Archipelago, during the period 1901–1917, no other single area surpassed central Luzon in the production of malcontents, fanatical leaders, intrigues and rebellions against the authority of the United States. This turbulent area was, in fact, the epicenter of the resistance movement to American suzerainty.

George Yarrington Coats,

"The Philippine Constabulary: 1901–1917"

IN THOSE EARLY YEARS OF COLONIAL RULE, the Americans were not just preoccupied with the brutal suppression of resistance in the countryside but had continued in ever more sophisticated ways in the "harsh and philanthropic" dual mode that journalist John Bass had earlier characterized American policy. Elections at the municipal and provincial level brought Filipinos into a growing colonial bureaucracy, encouraging collaboration across a broad spectrum of Filipino society. A free press flourished largely uncensored, and the 1903 census held out the promise of the creation of a Filipino National Assembly, a lower legislative body working in conjunction with the Philippine Commission. The election date for the assembly was dependent upon achievement of "a general and complete peace" throughout the islands, save the regions of the "Moros or other non-Christian tribes." By 1905 the projected year for the election was 1907, and this undoubtedly gave provincial officials and members of the Manila elite, many of them former revolutionaries, added incentive to aid in the suppression of any further armed resistance in the countryside. All these inducements held out the promise of eventual independence, and many Filipinos saw it in their best interests to go along, at least on the surface, with the American's long-term project of the Filipinization of the colonial government.[1]

Even before Roosevelt declared the war over in 1902, a shipload of young American schoolteachers, men and women, arrived to take up the task of educating Kipling's "new-caught, sullen peoples, half devil and half child." Flushed with the missionary impulse, they named themselves the Thomasites, after the USAT *Thomas*, the ship that had brought them on their mission of benevolence. By 1904 the administration had established more than four hundred new schools.[2]

MacArthur's "wily and treacherous" Filipino had disappeared. Roosevelt's references to the Filipinos as "cutthroat Comanches and renegade Sioux," to "Tagal bandits," were to be forgotten. The gugu and the nigger, object of extermination, had become America's little brown brother, to be uplifted and Anglosaxonized. An explicitly racist conception of the Filipinos gave way to one of paternalistic condescension, a people in need of American guidance and supervision. Paul Kramer, in *Blood of Government*, best describes the shifts in racial attitudes as the American colonial project took hold.

> More than any other, the new colonial state's defining metaphor would
> be tutelary and assimilationist, one that cast the colonial state in its
> entirety as a school and made its task the active transformation of
> Filipinos in an unsteady and necessarily indefinite movement toward
> "Americanism."[3]

But this process of benevolent assimilation—of indoctrination—was not going nearly so smoothly as American officials would have the citizens back home believe, particularly in the countryside where the fighting continued right up to the outskirts of Manila. Only ten days after commencing their grand sweep of Rizal and southern Bulacan, the constabulary suffered an embarrassing defeat at the hands of Luciano San Miguel and Faustino Guillermo. The *Manila Freedom* described the fight as a disastrous rout, with a constabulary officer captured and many enlisted men wounded. The *Manila Times* reported: "It is not yet known who the leaders of the ladron forces are, but there is a rumor that the American renegades who have identified prominently with the ladron-insurrecto movements recently are at the bottom of this attack."[4]

As always, the authorities had nothing to say about these "American renegades" and the extensive reports of the Philippine Commission make no mention of them. If the description of Fagen as broken down and intent upon escaping the islands was true, then he may not have rejoined the fight. But all that can be said for sure is that after a brief sojourn in Manila, Fagen and his wife vanished—at least from the public record—not to be heard from for several years.

On March 28, 1903, after three months of almost constant warfare, constabulary and Macabebe Scout detachments caught up with General San Miguel at Corral-na-bato in Rizal Province. LUCIANO SAN MIGUEL DIES FIGHTING CONSTABULARY LIKE A DEMON, the *Manila Times* headlined. On June 10, 1903, Faustino Guillermo, "the jungle fox," was captured along with many of his men. Eventually more than three hundred of San Miguel's fighters were either hanged or sentenced to long terms in Bilibid prison. In Guillermo's much-publicized trial, the court sentenced him to be hanged. In the extensive testimony during the trials of Guillermo and of other defendants, there is not a single reference to the American blacks.[5]

If San Miguel, Faustino Guillermo, and the Diliman Gang had been vanquished, the result was more a dispersal of the opposition than its defeat. No sooner had the constabulary put down an uprising in one province than another would break out elsewhere. By the end of 1904, the unrest was islandwide and resistance so intense that the civil government could claim only nominal control of rural areas. For the Americans and the constabulary leadership, opponents to American authority could only be termed bandits, which they divided into three categories: ladrones, ladrones *politicos*, and ladrones *fanaticos*. If those considered mere bandits or political bandits were more easily suppressed, the many militant secret societies continued to flourish. The Pulahans of Samar, Cebu, and Leyte, still little understood to the present, waged a savage fight from 1904 to 1907. Other self-proclaimed popes and messiahs led guerrilla movements, such as Papa (pope) Faustino Ablena on Leyte and Papa Isio on Negros. Secret religio-political organizations such the Colorum of Batangas and Tayabas, the Guardia de Honor of Pangasinan and the Ilocos, and the Santa Iglesia of Nueva Ecija and Bulacan attracted the almost universal loyalty of the peasant masses in their respective regions.[6]

An implacable foe of the Americans, Macario Sakay, sought to revive the New Katipunan and found popular support throughout central Luzon. When his guerrilla bands invaded towns within twenty miles of Manila, the alarmed civil authorities were yet again forced to call out the U.S. Army. "For one cause or another," Governor Taft mused, "the Filipinos have become suspicious of the Constabulary and resent its use as a colonial army." Taft understood perfectly well the causes of the hostility of the rural masses, but he feigned bewilderment when it suited his purposes. Alfred W. McCoy provides the most straightforward explanation: "Led by officers detailed from the army, the constabulary patrolled Luzon's countryside like an occupation force and persisted in merciless tactics used at the peak of Philippine-American War—burning crops, maltreating civilians, and torturing suspects."[7]

And under another of Taft's personally crafted pieces of legislation—the Reconcentration Act—tens of thousands of rural peasants were forced from 1902 to 1906 into relocation camps. Several years would pass before Macario Sakay and his senior officers were lured into surrendering under false promises of leniency, then promptly tried and hanged.[8]

Farther north, in the region from southern Bulacan to Pangasinan, a charismatic figure known as Apo Ipe—Felipe Salvador—led the Santa Iglesias, a militant and religious sect that dominated the region for years. To a Filipino official, Salvador was "the most skillful, astute, witty, and eloquent of all the outlaws which formed quasi-religious sects."[9]

For years Salvador remained at large, adored by the people and moving openly through the barrios of Nueva Ecija and northern Bulacan. According to George Coats, "Salvador preached a socialist doctrine and promised his followers ownership of the land and many other benefits if they overthrew the government." Unlike most of the bandit-insurrectionists, Coats noted, "in many respects Salvador used the tactics which were later perfected by Mao Tse-tung. He deliberately treated the people of the barrios very well and did not rob or harm them."[10]

Felipe Salvador maintained his headquarters atop Mount Arayat and, when pursued, disappeared into the Candaba Swamp. Protected by the barrio people and careful to limit his attacks on the constabulary, he evaded capture for years, dropping out of sight for months at a time. But on April 16, 1906, he overplayed his hand. Eighty of his men attacked the constabulary headquarters in Malolos, killed three constabulary men, and made off with rifles and ammunition. Similar attacks took place in other provinces that same night, and the *Manila American* warned of "Alarming Disaffection Spreading in Northern Luzon" in a wave of "Fanaticism, Outlawry, and Insurrection."[11]

Salvador's attack on Malolos brought the constabulary out in force. Every available man was sent north from Manila. Salvador's strategy had always been to withdraw after an attack, but this time he elected to fight. For two months his followers took on the constabulary in "running battles" that, according to Sturtevant, "flared across the length and breadth of seven provinces." On May 10, 1906, dozens of newspapers picked up a report from Manila: "Salvador's fanatical ladrones on Monday night raided and looted Malasiqui, a town of 9,000 population in Pangasinan province, Island of Luzon."[12]

It was during this period of turmoil in central Luzon that—if the story is true—the renegade Fagen, who had not been heard from for more than two years, reappeared on the scene.

"The Old Arch-Renegade Fagan"

38

T HE SALVADORANS' ATTACK ON MALASIQUI was not the only disturbing news coming from Pangasinan during that period of turmoil in 1906. On May 5, a correspondent for the *Manila Times* warned of "*A Black Peril Threatening Some Northern Towns.*"

GANGS OF NEGROES INSTITUTE REIGN OF TERROR

> With the closing of the Benguet Road and the abandonment of what was known as Camp Boyd, a gang of about 500 American negroes, who had been discharged from the army, were left without work. A considerable proportion of these swarmed to the lowlands and are now said to be preying upon the inhabitants. . . . They (the negro soldiery) seem to get closer to the Filipinos and learn more easily native ways and the native language, which, combined with their superior physical strength, is said to make them more dangerous than the same element among the white soldiery. The natives of Bayombong and Bautista are calling for protection.[1]

The constabulary dispatched its inspector general, Captain Herman Hall, to investigate the *Manila Times* report. Hall returned to Manila and, in the constabulary leadership's customary manner of dismissing reports of unrest in the countryside out of hand, informed the paper that there were only about thirty-five "Afro-Americans in the province." They were "living quietly, although there are a few who do some midnight marauding."[2]

To the Americans, the turmoil that continued after Roosevelt declared the war ended in July 1902 was the result of "ladronism," particularly in the form of carabao rustling, and to the fomentations of "bogus popes" and "saints" who kept the superstitious peasantry worked into a state of pseudo-religious excitement. No matter what evidence the colonial authorities might encounter to the contrary—that among the bandits were revolutionists still intent upon ousting the Americans, or that many of the so-called popes or fakirs were preaching a form of socialism, a proletarian sharing of the islands' bounty and a return to true Christian simplicity—they could see only bandits and religious fanatics. No other interpretation was acceptable and the constabulary reports and the reports of the Philippine Commission are consistent in their bias, resulting in a mix of half truths and a skewed interpretation of events at best.[3]

The competing narrative, that the masses were continuing the revolution without the support or the guidance of the elite, was true enough; but however lofty the intent, the result was a campaign marked by wanton cruelty and destruction and even by widespread carabao rustling. This last seemed to have had only the most tenuous connection to the ongoing revolution—that is, raising funds to carry on the fight, but raising the funds at the expense of the starving peasant in whose name the struggle was being waged. The Americans might be excused if they found this state of affairs a bit confusing.

If there were some truth to both narratives, trying to weave the two together into one impartial account of those chaotic years is probably impossible.

It seems, if a subsequent report be true, that Fagen had become the carabao rustler par excellence, as always the leader, and had been joined by as many as fifty of the African American soldiers who had elected to remain in the islands after mustering out. His "gang" was in league with Filipino carabao rustlers and supposedly lived in something approaching rural splendor in a mountain resort on the Pangasinan-Zambales border. This region of twisting jungle ravines and mountain caves had been the hideout of Roman Manalang, a diehard ex-revolutionary general and his band, for more than a year before he was killed in 1903. And again, if the report was true, Fagen and his wife and the band of thieves had taken up residence in Manalang's old abode.[4]

In 1906, in his report of conditions in the province of Pangasinan, Governor Isabelo Artacho referred to both revolutionists and carabao rustlers in the region, and of one gang in particular. If the article soon to make the front pages in Manila, and even in the states, is true, then David Fagen was still very much alive and chief carabao thief of the region.[5]

Inspector General Herman Hall's report to the *Manila Times* insisting that only a handful of blacks were causing trouble in Pangasinan would seem to have put an end to an unfounded rumor. But three days later, on May 19, 1906, readers of the *Times* were greeted with a startling headline.

FAGAN COMES TO LIFE

**Reported Leader of Desperate Gang of Cattle Rustlers
Carry off Pangasinan Cattle Worth P12,000–Manage to
Evade All Pursuit—
Said to Play Starlight & Have "Pen" in Heart of Mountains**

If reports be true Fagan, who, like Felizardo, has already been em-
balmed, has come to life.

In spite of having his head cut off and identified "beyond all per-
adventure of a doubt," and in spite of a five thousand dollar piece of
fiction published in *Collier's Weekly*, it is said the notorious renegade of
the Twenty-fourth persists in walking the earth for a while longer.

And not only is he reported to be alive, but active—nothing less
than the "big chief" of a band of cattle rustlers of his own color, who
are running things in the Province of Pangasinan in a way which has
baffled the authorities by its cunning. Unless the band can be stopped
soon, that province bids fair to be denuded of all its cattle.[6]

A photo of Fagen accompanied the front-page article. Unless the editors
simply picked out a photo of an African American soldier and passed him off
as Fagen, then this is the only photographic likeness of Fagen to be discovered
to date. The lengthy story continues with a detailed account of the gang's
operations, noting the theft of valuable carabaos of Australian stock. Farmers
in Pangasinan were "at their wits end" and "the Constabulary and the police
are also said to be worked up over the situation, as thus far all their efforts to
run down and break up the rustling gang have proved futile." According to
the reporter from the *Times*, "The methods they pursue are suggestive of Rolf
Boldrewood's stories of Starlight and other cattle raiders and highwaymen
famed in the bushranging annals of Australia." Rolf Boldrewood's *Robbery under
Arms*, published in 1888, was a popular novel of the time; its anti-hero Captain
Starlight, "a renegade from a noble English family," was likened to Robin
Hood and Jesse James.[7]

The reporter finally got to the shocking news announced in the headline.

And the head of this daring gang of rustlers, if the reports be true, is the
old, arch-renegade Fagan, of the 24th Infantry.

The officers of the law deny the Fagan reports when put up to
them, but there may be a reason for this. In any event, the story as told
in Pangasinan is that Fagan is "out again."[8]

The author of the piece then assays to fill in the background of Fagen's story for the unfamiliar reader: "The history of Fagan is generally well known. Having a grudge at one of his officers he deserted from the 24th and turned renegade, hanging on the track of those who had incurred his wrath and picking them off as occasion offered. He took up with a native woman and placed himself at the head of a band of desperadoes, carrying out a career of deviltry extending over two years."[9]

Rather than place Fagen as commanding officer of a guerrilla company serving under Lacuna and waging war against the Americans for one and a half years, the article's author moves Fagen straight from desertion to leader of a band of "deperadoes" convened for the purposes of committing "deviltry." The impression conveyed is that Fagen had been an independent operator from the first and had never engaged in combat operations as a revolutionary officer. This distortion of Fagen's history will add to the difficulty of trying to make sense of a later account. The author goes on to describe the story of Fagen's supposed beheading in the mountains of Bongabong and concludes: "After the Felizardo episode, however, this sort of postmortem identification has lost some of its assurance, and there appears to be fair reason to believe that Fagan, like Felizardo, will have to be killed again."[10]

A year earlier, Cornelio Felizardo, a brilliant and ruthless leader for three years under Sakay, threw the constabulary off his trail for a time by faking his death. For months the Manila papers were abuzz with reports of Felizardo's supposed death followed by the discovery of his return to life, and finally with his assassination by undercover constabulary men posing as *revolucionarios*.[11]

Five weeks after the *Manila Times* announced Fagen's return from the dead, the *Washington Post*, Thursday, June 28, 1906, picked up the story: "FAGAN AGAIN ON THE WARPATH—According to reports received at the Bureau of Internal Affairs, Fagan, the renegade negro who deserted the Twenty-fourth Infantry in the Philippines, is at large again, causing a new reign of terror." Numerous other newspapers picked up the story of Fagen's return to life.[12]

But, as happened repeatedly, there does not appear to have been any follow-up on these reports. It is telling that the article cites the Bureau of Internal Affairs as its source; this would be the only time the authorities would acknowledge Fagen's continued existence, if indeed the newspaper accounts had it right. Whatever the reasons "the officers of the law" had for denying "the Fagan reports," the constabulary's leadership never stated them explicitly. That the Manila papers went silent on the subject of Fagen suggests either pressure from the highest levels of American authority to suppress any further news, or possibly the report of Fagen's continued existence had been determined to be a fabrication. But if the latter were the case, why wouldn't the newspapers announce—with the blessing of the authorities—that they had gotten it wrong? But I found no retraction of the story. It seems there is simply nothing.[13]

I could find no further mention of Fagen until 1909, and if the article is to be believed, Fagen had been "silenced" by that time. But that is not a certainty. If Fagen had in fact been done away with, how, when, and where this took place remains a mystery. The reader will have to decide which of several scenarios seems the most plausible.

With the report by the *Times* of Fagen and his band's activities in Pangasinan, the authorities sent a company of Philippine Scouts to join the constabulary in the hunt for the rustlers. And they may have had some success, at least in one instance. In Governor Isabelo Artacho's report of July 27, 1906, to the Philippine Commission in Manila, he wrote: "Municipal police and rural guards have been able to bring about the death of one thief in the hills of Nueva Ecija; the facts in this latter instance have already been reported to the central government."[14]

That this thief went unnamed and a separate report was sent to Manila hints at the possibility that the man whose death had been "brought about" may have been Fagen. If the thief was so important that his death merited a special report, then why not state the man's name? Or did the authorities prefer not to confirm the *Manila Times* story that Fagen had come back to life? Without a name this is all conjecture, and unless Artacho's report lies gathering dust in a file in Manila, it and similar provincial reports were probably destroyed in the firebombing of the city in February 1945.

Colonel James G. Harbord was the assistant chief of the Philippine Constabulary from 1903 to 1909; he filed summaries of the constabulary's activities for the years 1907 and 1908, describing the actions and fates of numerous bandit leaders and their men. Among these reports there is no mention of Fagen and his band.[15]

But in 1909, at the close of his long tenure with the constabulary, Harbord penned a lengthy article summing up the constabulary's decade of struggle and the ultimate eradication of "ladronism." This article seems only to have appeared in several small-town newspapers in Kansas, Harbord's home state, one paper in Texas and one in Alabama, and has only recently become available with the digitization of old newspapers. According to Harbord, with the exception of Felipe Salvador all bandit leaders of note had been killed, hanged, or imprisoned by 1907. "Robbery and pillage was the business of these gangs," Harbord wrote, "and cattle stealing their principal and most lucrative occupation." He attributed the ability of these gangs to thrive to the "timid disposition of the average native" who, fearful of losing life and property, put up little or no resistance when their towns were raided. "The organized insurrecto forces had been broken up and dispersed by the American troops, but guerrilla warfare succeeded and a number of guerrilla bands were still scattered about the islands." By that sentence, Harbord appears to refer to outlaw activity that occurred after the end of the war in Northern Luzon in June 1901, but that is not entirely clear. He then moves on to describe Mario Sakay's revival of the Katipunan, ending with the executions of Sakay, Mantalon, Villafuerte, and "some few others." Throughout the article Harbord provides no dates, but Sakay and his compatriots held out from 1904 until their execution in 1907. Harbord then follows by describing the brutality and ruthlessness of the various ladrone bands.

> In the towns where the people showed any friendship for the Americans, these night raiders were wont to visit, and their departure was generally marked by the firing of the residences of the poor peaceful natives, and the carrying off of the wives and daughters of those who were known as the Americanistas. . . . In the northern part of the Island of Luzon, a band of ladrones held forth for some few years, and gave the constabulary great trouble. This band was supposed to have been headed by a renegade negro named Fagan, who had deserted from the Twenty-fifth [*sic*] Infantry, U.S.A. Fagan was a hard man to kill, but after the Manila papers had reported his death in 25 different places in the space of two years, the constabulary finally succeeded in silencing him.[16]

Harbord's reference to Fagen's "band of ladrones" holding out "for some few years" would seem, if nothing else, to confirm that Fagen was not killed by Anastacio Bartollomé at Dingalan Cove on December 1, 1901. Harbord says it was the constabulary that "silenced" Fagen after "the ladrones had held out for the space of two years." There is no way to know whether Harbord was referring to the guerrilla years (1900–1901)—which seems the least likely—or to a period immediately following the end of the war in Northern Luzon, say 1902–3, or to the middle years of the decade, as suggested by the *Manila Times* article of May 19, 1906, the first time Fagen was identified as leader of a gang of carabao thieves. Given the two references to Fagen still being alive in 1903 and 1906, with no reports to contradict those claims, it is my belief that Fagen lived at least until the summer of 1906. Harbord wrote that the Manila papers had reported Fagen's death in twenty-five different places over the space of several years. In examining Manila's three English-language papers from 1902 through 1907, I found no report of Fagen being killed. There were about ten Tagalog and Spanish-language newspapers in Manila where reports of Fagen's purported death might have appeared. Possibly, Harbord was confusing rumors of Fagen's killing with actual newspaper accounts.

Colonel Harbord singles out Fagan and his gang as the most troublesome in Northern Luzon, yet in none of the half-dozen histories of the constabulary is there any mention of Fagen aside from Vic Hurley's single and unsupported reference in *Jungle Patrol*, a descriptive sentence below a photo of Inspector Bates's scrawled plea for help. Yet, as frustrating as Harbord's account is in its lack of specificity, his report makes clear that for several years Fagen's band was the most formidable in Northern Luzon and gave the constabulary (which was not formed until August 1901) great trouble. But the question remains— where, when, and how did Fagen die, if, in fact, he was killed as Harbord claimed?

Eventually, that question may be answered with some certainty, or perhaps David Fagen's ultimate fate will forever remain a mystery. The fate of his wife and whether they had any children will be even harder, if impossible, to determine. In this last phase, David Fagen may best be described in terms of the social bandit, a man wronged and forever at odds with the powers of the state, an outcast left no choice but to fight on. A bandit? A revolutionary? Or some blend of both, with neither term sufficient to describe a man engaged in a life and death struggle against a force bent on his annihilation and determined to consign him to oblivion? However cruel or ruthless he may have been, however fair or wise, we know that he was a flamboyant and charismatic leader of men, a man who delighted in bedeviling his white would-be masters, a guerrilla fighter of extraordinary skill and courage.

Perhaps Fagen was killed early on after faking his death; perhaps he lived on for some five or six years. And the possibility still remains that in his article of 1909 Colonel Harbord decided simply to kill him off on paper and be done with him, and that he slipped away into the mountains with his wife to disappear forever. Whatever his fate, the ultimate significance of David Fagen's revolution was not as a fighter for Filipino independence but as an African American who took up arms against a country bent on empire at the expense of a dark-skinned people and rotten to the core with racism at home. In turning his back on his country, he chose freedom, a perfectly American thing to do.

Afterword

O F THE APPROXIMATELY ONE THOUSAND African Americans to remain in the islands, some fared well, and many did not. According to Willard Gatewood, most took jobs in Manila, working in restaurants and hotels or as clerks and small business owners. There were a few schoolteachers, a field largely closed to blacks despite many qualified applicants, and there was one lawyer and one physician. The physician, William Warmsley, an army surgeon, achieved perhaps the greatest success of any of the remaining blacks, becoming a civil court judge and wealthy tobacco farmer. Others took up farming, including former members of the Twenty-Fourth in Nueva Ecija and Pangasinan. In 1905 Captain James Alfred Moss rode through the old Fourth District and spoke with a number of the veterans who had married Filipinas and begun raising families. They voiced few complaints, other than being gouged for the price of goods and seed.[1]

In the summer and fall of 1902, Governor General Taft had engineered the transfer of the black regiments back to the states out of their order in the rotation. Although the soldiers' service had been judged exemplary, Taft was disturbed by the easy rapport of the black soldiers and the Filipinos in their provincial communities and the many offspring the friendliest of those liaisons were producing. In Brian Linn's words, the black soldiers "responded with justifiable heat" that white soldiers had been just as active on that count, pointing out the number of illegitimate children their white counterparts had left behind. Taft went even further in his bias, excluding even the most qualified blacks from employment in the civil service. The home-style discrimination the mustered-out veterans had hoped to escape from had followed them to the islands. A letter writer—possibly John Calloway—who signed himself "an old soldier" wrote to the *Manila Times*, "It is true that many discharged soldiers have failed to make good here; but this has been caused by their inability to get employment. Many of this class are men of good character but can find none to do."[2]

The success stories, large and mostly small, are typically what one reads of the fortunes of the black regulars who remained in the islands. But even as early as the autumn of 1902, the Manila papers were telling a different story. In December, the *Manila American* headlined an article WORTHLESS RENEGADES / *Discharged Soldiers and Worthless Characters in the Provinces*: "Reports have reached Manila to the effect that certain parts of the archipelago are being terrorized by worthless discharged soldiers, and other renegades with white and black skins . . . it might be said that most of these evil doers are negroes discharged from the 24th and 25th infantry."[3]

According to the reporter, many of the soldiers, as well as packers and teamsters, blew their "finals" carousing in Manila and then drifted back to the towns in the provinces where they had been stationed. They started out on friendly terms with the people in these towns but soon began to sponge off the community. The reporter noted, "Most generally they lived off the female population." As they wore out their welcome, they began ranging in groups of two, three, and four about the countryside, intimidating the people of the *barrios* and exacting "tribute." They were not considered ladrones but simply public nuisances.[4]

Early in 1903, the Bureau of Insular Affairs established the "Dissolute Americans and Vagrancy Act," citing the large number of "dissolute, drunken, and lawless Americans who are willing to associate with low Filipino women and live upon the proceeds of their labor. They are truculent and dishonest." The law provided for the deportation of these alleged miscreants and presumably many of them, white and black, were shipped back to America.[5]

But what about those ex-soldiers who, rather than creating a minor nuisance, had joined the Filipino revolutionists and were actively waging war on the constabulary? Despite the scattered newspaper accounts of their involvement with the revolutionists, there appears to be no mention of these men in the reports of the Philippine Commission. It wasn't just Fagen who went unacknowledged by the authorities, but all of the blacks the Manila papers had reported were very much alive and active in the ongoing resistance to American occupation. If Fagen wasn't the "American negro" leading three hundred ladrones in Bulacan intent upon wiping out the constabulary, then who was this person? And who were the four former soldiers training Filipinos in army tactics right on the outskirts of Manila? In 1905 an article from one of the Manila papers found its way to a small-town newspaper in Kansas with the headline RENEGADES THERE / *American Negroes Aided in Attack*: "Additional details regarding the attack by ladrones on the town of San Francisco de Malabon last night, in which Contract Surgeon J. A. O'Neill was killed, show that the Ladrones numbered 300. They were led by the famous outlaws, Montalon and Felizardo, who were aided by two American negroes."[6]

It is doubtful that we'll ever know who any of these men were or their fates. In 1906, when the *Manila Times* reported that Fagen had come to life and was leading a band of fifty black ex-soldiers, there was no follow-up report on Fagen or on his band. The constabulary had nothing to say about this gang in its official reports or any of the other black revolutionists or ladrones, and yet the Manila papers insisted year after year that they were there. The omission of the blacks from a decade of reports makes it more plausible that Fagen had lived on, his continued existence obscured by what seems to have been a blanket censorship adopted by the civil authorities.

One of the men of the Twenty-Fourth Infantry who managed, in a roundabout way, to remain in the islands was former Sergeant Major John W. Calloway. Three months after Calloway had been discharged without honor and released from the Presidio guardhouse in February 1901, he was back in Manila, reunited with his wife, Mamerta, and daughter Juanita. He found employment as a watchman for the quartermaster's department and continued writing anguished letters to the army requesting a fair hearing. His appeals were uniformly denied. In August, the seemingly omnipresent Captain James Alfred Moss ran into Calloway on the street and advised the authorities that he was a "bad man" and should "be arrested." Calloway was locked in the Cuartel de España and soon again deported. A year later, in 1902, the War Department warned the commanding general that John Calloway, "a dangerous character," had once again returned to Manila. But now, with the city under civilian control, the army let the matter drop. Calloway went to work for the Bureau of Public Printing, and he and Mamerta settled in the Quiapo district. In all, they had fourteen children. In 1934, at the age of sixty-three, he died of what was probably a stroke. The *Manila Tribune* noted his passing: "Old Timer Dies."[7]

Curiously, for all the pain and humiliation he had endured, John Calloway's devotion to the Twenty-Fourth Infantry and his love of country seems to have never waned. On January 17, 1918, at the age of forty-six, he tried once again to enlist, hoping to join his old outfit in the trenches of France. His request was denied.[8]

By 1918 the Philippine census counted only 185 black veterans remaining in the islands, out of the roughly 1,000 who had mustered out there in 1902. America was engaged in another war, a war that dwarfed the Philippine-American conflict in scale and relegated it even farther to the historical back pages. As the years went on, the so called Philippine Insurrection was reduced to a cursory paragraph in the history textbooks, if it was mentioned at all. Finally, there was little remembered of the era but Teddy Roosevelt and his Rough Riders charging up Kettle Hill.[9]

As the war was forgotten—or, more accurately, "swept under the rug"—so was Fagen. The raid on the *Stonie* on October 25, 1900, and the report of his supposed death on December 1, 1901, had garnered the widest coverage in the press, both accounts appearing in hundreds of newspapers. Throughout August 1900 through January 1901, one finds enough mention of him in the press to suggest his name had become something of a household word. More than a year later, in 1903, the *Manila American*'s story of the supposedly dead Fagen's appearance in the city made it no farther than the *Leavenworth Times*. Either other newspapers dismissed it as journalistic mischief, or it had gone unnoticed. It seems likely that someone with army connections in Manila was mailing articles to a journalist friend in Leavenworth, site of a major army post, because both articles appeared about six weeks after they were printed in the *Manila American*. Rowland Thomas's prize-winning story "Fagan," appearing in *Collier's Weekly* in 1905, brought Fagen again into the public eye, and his reported return to life as a cattle rustler in 1906 created a small stir, appearing in at least several dozen newspapers, if not many more. In 1907, Stephen Bonsal's reference to "the celebrated Fagan" in the *North American Review* suggests that the mention of Fagen's name was sufficient to identify him to the reader, and no further elaboration was needed. Harbord's reference to Fagen and his band in 1909 seems to have been printed in a scattering of small papers in Kansas and gone unnoticed elsewhere.

The *New York Age* review of Rowland Thomas's "Fagan," possibly written by its editor T. Thomas Fortune, complained that Thomas had rendered Fagen as a "man-child" and had "deprive[d] him of heroism to make him pathetic." The writer closed, "We wish, for the sake of the story, that Mr. Thomas had made Fagan a 'magnificent criminal' instead of a soft-hearted simpleton; one who would revenge unmerited wrongs with violence instead of suffering himself to be broken by them."[10]

In 1911 the Thomas Y. Crowell Company published *Rainier of the Last Frontier*, a novel by John M. Dean. Dean, in 1902, had served in the army on the island of Cebu in the capacity of something like a chaplain, a kind of unofficial spiritual advisor to troubled soldiers. As Cebu was the place Dean knew best— and describes in vivid detail—he decided to move Fagen and his band there as well for the purposes of his story. And, as if in response to the *New York Age*'s complaint, he did his best to make Fagen a "magnificent criminal."[11]

This fictionalized Fagen speaks "without a trace of dialect" and, "devil-driven as he was," cares only for gold and women. Dean wears himself out trying to nail down his subject, describing him as "a forceful, cool, utterly selfish, vicious, greedy, lustful, childish, fearless outlaw." Fagen's band holds forth in the crater of an extinct volcano, conducts raids, and evades American search parties with ease. Meanwhile, Rainier, the protagonist, has fallen for the lovely Miss Benicia Royce, who had arrived on the island to work as a nurse. When Miss Royce, out for a Sunday carriage ride, is captured by Fagen, Rainier negotiates a prisoner swap, taking Miss Royce's place. Fagen keeps Rainier as a prisoner for the next six years, wandering from the islands of Mindoro, Panay, Negros, and back to Cebu; in his loneliness, he becomes attached to Rainier as someone to philosophize with over games of chess. In their discussions, the deeply religious Rainier works on Fagen's conscience, intent upon converting him. But he finds the work frustrating: "The ethics of Fagan! What a contradiction in terms! The world knows now what only a few in the old army knew then, that Fagan is a name that never mixes with any virtue, unless mere brute courage be counted as such." Finally, as the army closes in on Fagen's mountain hideaway, he releases Rainier. When the soldiers arrive, they find Fagen dead, a bottle of poison at his hand and a note for Rainier.

> Rainier, you sometimes speak to me of religion. Be satisfied to know that death by my own hand alone prevents my surrender to your Christ. I have come to the place where the old memories of the flag are mingling with the old memories of a woman's prayers. It is not safe to live longer. Adios. Fagan.[12]

Whether Dean's Fagen would have satisfied the editors of the *New York Age* is doubtful, but they would have probably given him credit for the effort, if nothing else.

In that same year of 1911, Frederick Funston published his *Memories of Two Wars* in which, as some self-chroniclers will, he was highly selective in relating the exciting events of his war experiences, including his frustrated pursuit of David Fagen. Had he included the full account of his long game of wits with Fagen, the young man from Tampa would have crowded the author much too closely for center stage in the general's tale of heroism and adventure. Although he stuck to the story of Fagen's beheading on the beach at Dingalan Bay, it is hard to believe that he hadn't been made aware that the "rowdy" young man's career had gone merrily on for some time. Like the army's decision-makers on high, Funston seems to have decided to leave well enough alone.

Funston's and Dean's books kept the public fascination with Fagen going awhile longer. The following year, "The Charmed Class Ring" appeared in the *New York Herald* and several other major newspapers. With James Alfred Moss's description of Fagen's taunting letters, the story of Frederick Alstaetter's capture, and Fagen's supposed beheading by mountain tribesmen, the author added a last touch to the Fagen legend. We don't hear of him again until Jack

Ganzhorn's *I've Killed Men* in 1940, followed by Leon Wolff's mention of Fagen in *Little Brown Brother* twenty years later. With Michael C. Robinson and Frank N. Schubert's scholarly essay in 1975, we had the first attempt at a separation of the real Fagen from the mythic Fagen, and there has been growing interest in him ever since.

As much as I can claim to have advanced our knowledge of the real Fagen, he has remained elusive at the most elemental level. Perhaps, that is as it should be. If nothing else, we know that his exploits were not the product of journalistic fantasies. On that count, he was very much for real. And as a mythic figure, he was every bit worthy of his legend.

Acknowledgments

After working on *Fagen* for some years, I knew that if I was going to continue with the project I had to go to the Philippines. I contacted Dr. Leny Mendoza Strobel at Sonoma State University. Leny is on a first-name basis with virtually every shaker and mover in the Bay Area Filipino community and beyond, as well as with a host of historians and intellectuals in the Philippines. Professor Strobel very kindly provided me with connections to many of these knowledgeable people. In the Philippines, my journalist-novelist stepson, Michael Levitin, and I met with Leny's sister, Roxanne, and her husband, Ernesto Gorospe. The welcome they extended to us is something we will never forget and we cannot thank them enough for their kindness. Roxanne and Ernesto took us to meet with Leny's friend Robert "Robby" Tantingco, director of the Center for Kapampangan Studies, Holy Angel University in Angeles. Robert put me in contact with Marcos Calo Medina, great-grand-nephew of Jose Alejandrino. A social anthropologist studying at Oxford, Marcos shared via email colorful stories of his great-great-uncle "Lolo Pepe" as well as set us up for a visit to the family home in Arayat. Marcos's sense of humor, his friendship, and his enthusiasm for the Fagen project are very much appreciated. I am especially grateful to Robert Tantingco for introducing us to Dr. Lino L. Dizon of Tarlac. We were moved by Lino's warmth and passion for Philippine history and thank him for making two outsiders feel so welcome. Asti and Marvin made our stay at Bill's Inn in Gapan nothing short of sublime. And thanks to Erwin for driving us to the edge of the mountains on rocky, narrow roads in a futile search for Mount Corona. I also want to thank Dr. Strobel for introducing me to the esteemed historian Dr. Jaime Veneracion and to Luis Zamora Tecson, grandson of Simon Tecson. Meeting Luis was a great pleasure and I thank him for his encouragement and interest in the project. To the many unfailingly kind and welcoming people we met in our travel in the islands, I offer our sincerest thanks.

The research assistants at the National Archives and Reference Administration put their considerable skills to work in helping me search for the proverbial needles in the haystacks and I thank them for their patience and their expertise. I thank the research assistants at the Library of Congress, particularly Gary Johnson, who did his best to bring the grainy newspaper photo of Fagen into clearer focus. In the end, Anthony L. Powell Jr. offered a clearer, non-newsprint, copy of the same photo from his collection and I thank Anthony for sharing that with us. Jennifer Levine at The Lab in Santa Rosa did a superb job in making the photos and maps book-ready. I am very grateful to Moira Hill for her creation of the map of the Nueva Ecija region, and to Ward Eldredge, Curator for Sequoia and Kings Canyon National Parks, for locating James Alfred Moss's notes from his tour of the parks in 1899. And a thanks to my life-long pal Bill George for accompanying me to Sequoia in the hunt for one more tiny piece of the puzzle.

Before sending out a query, I sent the manuscript to two close friends who had offered to give me their unvarnished opinion. Jim Mascolo, in Colorado, shared his views in a number of phone chats, offering a full measure of constructive criticism as well as encouragement. John Schak, in New York, worked through the manuscript line-by-line and with his usual acute insight recommended changes large and small. Michael Levitin also went over the manuscript with a red pen and my wife, Barbara, with long experience as an editor, was of extraordinary help in tightening and reshaping the work. I owe an immense debt of gratitude to all four readers.

With my initial batch of queries, I received a particularly kind and thoughtful rejection from Yuval Taylor at Chicago Review Press. Mr. Taylor recommended I try a university press and, to my great good fortune, I took his advice. Dr. Gwen Walker, acquisitions editor at the University of Wisconsin Press, is the person most responsible, in innumerable ways, for shepherding the project from query, through proposals, and repeated revisions to a completed book. I will be forever grateful to Gwen for her skill, her sharp wit, and her wise counsel in overseeing the process from submission to publication. The staff at the University of Wisconsin Press could not have been more supportive at every phase of the publishing process: Anna Muenchrath, Sara Kapp, Terry Emmrich, Jennifer Conn, Ryan Pingel, Sheila Leary, and managing editor Adam Mehring. To all of them and others on the staff, I would like to convey my deepest appreciation. I would especially like to thank Sheila McMahon, senior editor, for her meticulous oversight of the manuscript, as well as freelance copyeditor Mary Sutherland, who also gave the work the most rigorous going-over. Alfred McCoy, whose work has been such an important influence on me, gave the manuscript a green light in an internal review, offering suggestions for further research and recommending areas for increased emphasis. I thank Professor McCoy for the support and for the excellent advice. I would especially like to thank the three external reviewers retained by the press. Reader A, whose name I don't know, was penetrating in his or her detailed analysis of the work, offering constructive criticism and suggestions for improvement. I would also like to thank Dr. Jennifer D. Keene, professor of history and chair of the history department at Chapman University, for her thoughtful analysis of the work, her suggestions for improvement, and much-appreciated words of praise. Her input was enormously helpful. I owe a special debt of gratitude to Professor Paul A. Kramer of Vanderbilt University. As well as render a profoundly insightful critique of the work, Professor Kramer marked up the manuscript with full commentary in the margins. This guidance was invaluable—I would say priceless—in seeing the manuscript through its final revisions. I cannot thank Professor Kramer enough for the extra lengths he took on my—and David Fagen's—behalf.

Lastly, I owe the greatest debt of gratitude to my stepson, Michael Levitin, and my wife, Barbara Baer. They have been a rock of support throughout the years and without their encouragement, indulgence, and understanding, *Fagen*'s long journey to publication would never have taken place.

A Note on Sources

When I set out to learn more about David Fagen, I quickly came across Michael C. Robinson and Frank N. Schubert's essay "David Fagen: An Afro-American Rebel in the Philippines, 1899–1901," in the *Pacific Historical Review*, February 1975. This is the source most often cited in articles about Fagen.

Willard B. Gatewood Jr.'s *Black Americans and the White Man's Burden 1898–1903* also came out in 1975. While citing the desertion of four soldiers from the Ninth Cavalry, he wrote, "The greatest publicity was lavished on David Fagen of the Twenty-fourth Infantry." In all of two paragraphs, Gatewood gave a brief rundown of Fagen's desertion and, without a word of his guerrilla career, jumped straightaway to the story of his purported death at Dingalan Bay. And yet, if Gatewood was disinclined to make much of the "dozen or so Negro deserters," his work remains the most comprehensive history of the black soldiers' experience in that era.[1]

In 1982 Stuart Creighton Miller devoted a paragraph to Fagen in *Benevolent Assimilation*, his principle sources Robinson and Schubert's 1975 essay in the *Pacific Historical Review* and an article in the *San Francisco Call-Bulletin*.

> The name of David Fagen . . . was frequently bandied about as a convenient scapegoat for every American setback, from Lawton's death to the Balangiga massacre. The incidents were much too far apart geographically and chronologically for Fagen to have been involved in all, if any, of them. Indeed, it is unlikely that he ever strayed much beyond the Mount Arayat area. . . . Nevertheless, his military exploits and infamy continued to grow in editorial fantasies.[2]

Knowing next to nothing about Fagen's guerrilla career, Miller attributed his reputation as a guerrilla leader to the "editorial fantasies" of the Manila papers, as if confident that further investigation would reveal there was little of substance to Fagen's story. One need not bother looking.

In 1911 Frederick Funston published *Memories of Two Wars*, in which Fagen is remembered as a formidable and loathed adversary. Jack Ganzhorn, one of Funston's scouts, published *I've Killed Men* in 1940; in this account Fagen also comes off as both fearsome and villainous. Jose Alejandrino, the commanding general of central Luzon in the Army of Liberation, published his autobiography in 1933, and it came out in English translation in 1949 as *The Price of Freedom*. Alejandrino, who shared Fagen's company for several months in 1901, wrote of "the feats of valor and intrepidity" of Fagen, and stated that "the services which he rendered to me were such that they could only be expected from a brother or a son." Alejandrino's vivid portrait remains the most important firsthand description of Fagen.

I studied microfilm rolls of the two English-language newspapers in Manila at the time and began to work up a chronology of Fagen's war record. From the National Archives I acquired copies of his enlistment papers; in phone conversations with Leland Hawes, the history columnist for the *Tampa Bay Tribune*, I learned most of what little is known about Fagen's early life in Tampa. That proved about as far as I could go without setting forth on a larger quest, which I had neither the time nor the wherewithal to do. I dropped the subject of Fagen for nearly ten years, expecting to see a book about him come out any day. But none appeared, and in 2007 I decided to go in search of David Fagen.

I traveled to Washington, DC, where I had never been. The National Archives, I soon learned, does not give up its secrets all that readily. After poring over company rolls, Records of Events, enlistment records, after-action reports, the Philippine Insurgent Records, and more, I left feeling more frustrated than encouraged. I had learned a good deal about Fagen but not nearly as much as I had hoped to discover. Over the next few years, I made three more trips to Washington, the third trip being the most productive, when I hit on Telegrams Sent and Received in the Fourth District, 1900–1901. The telegrams, both handwritten and typed on yellowing, crumbling paper, came bundled by the month. And there, month after month, were multiple references to Fagen in action. It seems that in their initial communications, often within hours of a fight, officers revealed information that was later omitted from official reports.

In my forays to the Archives and the Library of Congress, I slowly developed a fairly thorough history of Fagen's war record, but at that time I was a semi-skilled researcher at best. On my first visit, I immediately asked to look at the after-action reports from Funston's Fourth District. But when the worn, artbook-size volumes arrived on the cart, they turned out only to be registries. In the most elegant handwriting from more than a century ago, the reader was informed that a particular after-action report existed and provided the date, the name of the officer, and a four- or five-digit number that promised to lead the researcher to the actual report. But, repeatedly, when the requested files—such as Letters Sent in the Fourth District—arrived, several of the reports were there while many others were not. In my subsequent visits, I persisted in hunting for reports in Record Group 395—Records of the United States Overseas Operations and Commands, 1898–1942—and every now and then hit the jackpot. And sometimes detailed reports turned up in Record Group 94—Records of the Adjutant General's Office: Orders, Muster Rolls, Regimental Returns, Records Relating to Regular Army personnel, Correspondence, and more. But there also, it was very much hit and miss; for example, in the muster rolls of Fagen's former Company I, I found a fifteen-page report of an ambush that I suspected—and later confirmed—had been led by Fagen. When I requested the muster rolls of Company C in search of another report of an ambush I also suspected of being led by Fagen (it was), the two relevant months of the muster rolls simply weren't there—the rolls from August and September 1900 had gone missing. I encountered this sort of thing frequently, left to wonder whether missing rolls and reports had been lost, misplaced, had deteriorated to the point of being illegible, or had for whatever reasons never made it into the files.

But even with Fagen's war record documented, that still left the larger question of who he was aside from a skilled guerrilla leader. In 2014 my journalist stepson and I flew to the Philippines; after five days in Manila, we set out on Fagen's trail, traveling by jeepney, pedicab, and the occasional hired driver. We headed north through Bulacan and Pampanga, and then into the beautiful rice lands of Nueva Ecija. When I attempted to interview local officials, they had no idea what I was talking about. They had no memory of the war with the Americans, either in general or in their local region, and there were no records to examine. But of far greater importance to me was the chance to get a sense of the people, who could not have treated us more kindly, and a feel for the countryside, the great sweep of the lowlands and the rugged Sierra Madres to the east. My regret was that I could not afford to stay longer than a few weeks and, in particular, conduct more than a few days' research in Manila. My study of the war from the Filipino side is derived almost entirely from secondary sources, fine works by Agoncillo, Majul, Constantino, Ileto, Scott, Shumacher, Mojares, Ochosa, and Guerrero.

Back home, I soon hit upon another invaluable resource: the various digitized newspaper collections. They yielded scores of references to Fagen, some quite detailed. War Department reports and a vast array of official documents are also now available online as well as many out-of-print books of the period, available on Google Books and in PDF form. And for less than fifteen dollars a copy, the Forgotten Books Classic Reprint Series now provides digitally re-mastered copies of rare and long-out-of-print books. These new digitized sources, particularly the digitized newspaper collections, provide an invaluable new tool for anyone engaged in historical research.

The search for David Fagen was as frustrating as it was rewarding. A major disappointment was to find that General Urbano Lacuna, the man who knew Fagen best over his guerrilla career, left nothing in writing. Lacuna died in 1911 of a kidney ailment he had contracted during the war, only forty-eight years old. Lieutenant Richard C. Day, who had exchanged taunts with Fagen and pursued him as head of the Scouts for more than a year, died of a kidney disease in 1902. In 1904 Captain David P. Wheeler, who had come close to capturing Fagen on a number of night marches, was stabbed to death in a fight with the Moros. Had these men survived, they might have written about their exploits and about Fagen.

The records of the constabulary seem not to have survived the bombing of Manila in February 1945, or perhaps they are tucked away in a library there somewhere. Early copies of *Khaki and Red*, the official organ of the constabulary, if they still exist, also remain well hidden. The thirtieth anniversary edition, a 232-page review of the constabulary's history published in August 1931, held out great promise. But the two-page review of the constabulary's first years in Northern Luzon, which would have included the names of all the chief bandits and revolutionists killed or captured by the constabulary from August 1901 through 1907, were missing. Detailed reviews of constabulary achievements in the other three sectors of the islands hint at what those two pages—the only pages missing from the entire volume—might have had to tell us. Perhaps the best potential source for learning Fagen's fate would be in examining the Spanish- and Tagalog-language newspapers on microfilm at the Library of Congress.

There is more to be uncovered about David Fagen in what Glenn Anthony May calls "the mountain of files of the National Archives" in Washington, in the libraries of Manila, and in the collections of correspondence and diaries housed in various libraries around the country. Hopefully, some young scholars will undertake the challenge of digging deeper into that mountain of files. I am confident that the information I have collected for this account will significantly advance our knowledge about this little-known African American revolutionary, a most singular and remarkable figure in American history.

Notes

Abbreviations

AG	Adjutant General
AGO	Adjutant General's Office Document Number
DNL	Department of Northern Luzon
INF	Infantry
LOC	Library of Congress
LR	Letters Received
LS	Letters Sent
LSR	Letters Sent and Received
L&TS	Letters and Telegrams Sent
NA	National Archives Records Administration, Washington, DC
PIR	Philippine Insurgent Records, National Archives
RG	Record Group, in National Archives
RPC	Report of the Philippine Commission
SO	Special Order
TS	Telegrams Sent
TSR	Telegrams Sent and Received
USV	U.S. Volunteers
WDAR	War Department Annual Reports, 1899–1908

Preface

1. Charles Chestnutt, quoted in Woodward, *Strange Career of Jim Crow*, 96.
2. John S. Bassett, quoted in Litwack, *Trouble in Mind*, 324.
3. Full account of Charles's "fight to the death": Hair, *Carnival of Fury*, 119–76.
4. Wells-Barnett, *Mob Rule in New Orleans*, 10.
5. Wolff, *Little Brown Brother*, 249.
6. George Breitman, ed., *Malcolm X Speaks: Selected Speeches and Statements* (New York: Grove Weidenfeld, 1965), 26.
7. Derrick Bell, "Racial Realism," *Connecticut Law Review* 34, no. 2 (Winter 1992): 373.

Introduction

1. Kramer, "Decolonizing the History of the Philippine-American War," ix; O'Connor, *Pacific Destiny*, 256.

2. Linn, "The Impact of the Philippine Wars (1898–1913) on the U.S. Army," in McCoy and Scarano, *Colonial Crucible*, 461.

3. McCoy, *Policing America's Empire*, 8.

4. San Juan, "An African American Soldier in the Philippine Revolution," 19, estimates "twenty-nine" black deserters; Gatewood, *Black Americans*, 287, gives "about a dozen deserters."

5. Funston, *Memories of Two Wars*, 314–15.

Chapter 1. The Twenty-Fourth Infantry Comes to Tampa

1. United States Census, 1880, the name spelled Fagan; Florida Census, 1885, the name spelled Fagin; Schubert, "Seeking David Fagen," 19–34; Eric Foner, *Nothing but Freedom*, 51. Much of Fagen's Tampa history I learned (in 1994) from phone conversations with the late Leland Hawes, a historian and journalist for the *Tampa Tribune*. Schubert's excellent article added even more details.

2. Jahoda, *Florida: A History*, 82.

3. United States Census, 1870, 1880.

4. Trask, *War with Spain in 1898*, 183; Tebeau, *A History of Florida*, 285.

5. Schubert, "Seeking David Fagen," 22, 28; Fagen background: Leland Hawes, phone conversations, 1994.

6. Tebeau, *History of Florida*, 286.

7. Florida Census, 1885.

8. *Salt Lake (UT) Herald*, October 30, 1900, 8; information slip on David Fagan, deserter, AGO 431081, NA, RG 94.

9. McKay quote per Hawes, phone conversation; Meltzer, *In Their Own Words*, 100.

10. Kennedy, *Palmetto Country*, 169.

11. Information slip on David Fagen, deserter, AGO 431081, NA, RG 94.

12. Roberts, *From Trickster to Badman*, 185–86.

13. Schubert, "Seeking David Fagen," 25; Chandler, "Harmon Murray."

14. Levine, *Black Culture*, 410–11.

15. Jahoda, *Florida*, 91–93; Leland Hawes, conversation; Schubert, "Seeking David Fagen," 24–25.

16. NA National Personnel Records Center, David Fagen enlistment papers No. 901; *Salt Lake (UT) Herald*, October 30, 1900, 8; Alejandrino, *Price of Freedom*, 175.

17. Woodward, *Strange Career of Jim Crow*, 23; Frederickson, *White Supremacy*, 214.

18. Blackmon, *Slavery by Another Name*, 92.

19. Meltzer, *In Their Own Words*, 143; A. H. Taylor, *Travail and Triumph*, 47.

20. Schubert, "Seeking David Fagen," 27.

21. Jahoda, *Florida*, 98.

22. Musicant, *Empire by Default*, 50.

23. Perez, *War of 1898*, 10, 12, 18.

24. Musicant, *Empire by Default*, 70; Karp, *Politics of War*, 58.

25. Perez, *War of 1898*, 49–50.

26. E. Thomas, *War Lovers*, 70–71.

27. Karp, *Politics of War*, 72, 30, 58; Perez, *War of 1898*, 30, 35; Walter LaFeber, "The Business Community's Push for War," in Paterson and Rabe, *Imperial Surge*, 48.

28. Explosion: E. Thomas, *War Lovers*, 210–11, 213–14, 221–22; Steward, *Buffalo Soldiers*, 93.

29. Perez, *War of 1898*, 21.

30. Millis, *Martial Spirit*, 166; Jahoda, *Florida*, 92.

31. Letter from Sgt. M. W. Saddler to *The Freeman* (Indianapolis), quoted in Gatewood, *"Smoked Yankees,"* 248.

32. Letter from Saddler to *The Freeman*; letter from George Prioleau, Chaplain, 9th Cavalry to *Cleveland Gazette*, 28; letter from John E, Lewis, 10th Cavalry, 32, to *Illinois Record*, all in Gatewood, *"Smoked Yankees"*; Ray Downs, "Florida Lynched More Black People Per Capita Than Any Other State, According to Report," *New Times Broward-Palm Beach*, February 11, 2015, quoting Bailey and Tolnay, *Lynched*.

33. Woodward, *Strange Career of Jim Crow*, 44.

34. Bain, *Sitting in Darkness*, 38.

35. Tolnay and Beck, *A Festival of Violence*, 255; Litwack, *Trouble in Mind*, 477, 312.

36. Tolnay and Beck, *Festival of Violence*, 55.

37. Brundage, *Lynching in the New South*, 54.

38. Brundage, *Lynching in the New South*, 72.

39. "Departure," *Weekly Tribune* (Tampa, FL), May 5, 1898, 1.

40. Gatewood, *Black Americans*, 47–48.

41. Gatewood, "Negro Troops in Florida, 1898," 14.

42. Schubert, "Seeking David Fagen," 27; David Fagen enlistment papers, No. 901, 1898, NA, National Personnel Records Center.

43. Fagen enlistment papers.

44. Fagen enlistment papers; information slip on David Fagan, deserter, AGO 431081, NA, RG 94; Alejandrino, *Price of Freedom*, 174; Fletcher, "The Black Soldier."

45. Steward, *Buffalo Soldiers*, 221.

Chapter 2. Santiago

1. Dupuy, *Compact History of the United States*; Cashin, *Under Fire with the Tenth Cavalry*, 121.

2. Millis, *Martial Spirit*, 348.

3. Gatewood, *Black Americans*, 22–26.

4. Richard Hofstadter, "The Depression of the 1890s and Psychic Crisis," in Paterson and Rabe, *Imperial Surge*, 36; Michael H. Hunt, "American Ideology: Visions of National Greatness and Racism," in Paterson and Rabe, *Imperial Surge*, 19, 20, 23.

5. Jones, *Honor in the Dust*, 72; Steward, *Buffalo Soldiers*, 172.

6. Bonsal, *Fight for Santiago*, 300.

7. Gatewood, *"Smoked Yankees,"* 68, 53.

8. "Unparalleled: A Tribute to the Heroes of the Twenty-fourth Regiment," *Piqua (OH) Daily Call*, September 20, 1898, 1.

9. Bonsal, *Fight for Santiago*, 455.
10. Bonsal, *Fight for Santiago*, 466.
11. Parker, *Gatlings at Santiago*, 171–72.
12. Millis, *Martial Spirit*, 329, 352.
13. Parker, *Gatlings at Santiago*, 202; Bonsal, *Fight for Santiago*, 466.
14. Names of soldiers of regiment who performed duty as nurses or cooks in camp at Siboney: AGO 215561, NA, RG 94.
15. AGO 215561, NA, RG 94; Bonsal, *Fight for Santiago*, 436.
16. Bonsal, *Fight for Santiago*, 457.
17. "Tribute to the Regiment," *Salt Lake (UT) Tribune*, September 30, 1898, 8.

Chapter 3. The Far Side of the World

1. Blount, *American Occupation*, 35; Wolff, *Little Brown Brother*, 52.
2. Kramer, *Blood of Government*, 217.
3. Constantino, *The Philippines: A Past Revisited* (hereafter, *A Past Revisited*), 74, 80; Guerrero, *Luzon at War*, 149.
4. Constantino, *A Past Revisited*, 63.
5. Vicente L. Rafael, "Introduction: Revolutionary Contradictions," in Guerrero, *Luzon at War*, 5.
6. Kramer, *Blood of Government*, 40–43.
7. Agoncillo and Guerrero, *History of the Filipino People*, 156; Constantino, *A Past Revisited*, 177–78, 174, 165.
8. Blount, *American Occupation*, 41; Wolff, *Little Brown Brother*, 73; *Hearings before the Committee on the Philippines of the United States*, vol. 3, January 31, 1902–June 28, 1902, Senate Document 331, pt. 3, 2959.
9. The *Boston Evening Transcript* was the first newspaper to capitalize the word "Negro," starting in 1899. All quotations are left as written.
10. Blount, *American Occupation*, 22.
11. Wolff, *Little Brown Brother*, 40.
12. Blount, *American Occupation*, 58–59.

Chapter 4. Westward

1. Steward, *Buffalo Soldiers*, 224–25.
2. Letter of recommendation—Capt. Black, 24th Inf., RG 94, AGO 294879.
3. Record of Enlistment John W. Calloway, No. 1261, 1899, NA, National Personnel Records Center; Gil Boehringer, "Imperialist Paranoia," 323–58.
4. "Our Black Heroes," *Evening Herald* (Syracuse, NY), September 26, 1898; "Colored Heroes," *Oakland (CA) Tribune*, September 27, 1898.
5. Regimental Returns, Twenty-Fourth Infantry, Co. H, September–October 1898.
6. *Broad Ax*, October 8, 1898; *Salt Lake (UT) Tribune*, October 1, 1898, 1.
7. Clark, "Improbable Ambassadors," 235; Calloway file, AGO 356799, NA, RG 94, filed with AGO 17043. According to Chaplain Allen Allensworth, "Calloway was a teacher in the Post Military School under my supervision, and gave entire satisfaction. He

is prompt, faithful and efficient. He will give satisfaction to any one who may wish his services" (May 21, 1899).

8. Calloway file, AGO 356799, NA, RG 94, filed with AGO 17043.

9. "They Knew Gen. Fagin," *Salt Lake (UT) Herald*, October 30, 1900, 8.

10. "Record of Events," Regimental Returns, Twenty-Fourth Infantry, Co. H, November 25, 1898.

Chapter 5. The Waiting Game

1. Guerrero, *Luzon at War*, 76, 90.

2. Wolff, *Little Brown Brother*, 130.

3. Wildman, *Aguinaldo*, 92–98.

4. Majul, *Mabini and the Philippine Revolution*, 64–65, 111.

5. Agoncillo, *Malolos*, 223.

6. Guerrero, *Luzon at War*, 258.

7. Karnow, *In Our Image*, 124.

8. Jones, *Honor in the Dust*, 97.

9. Miller, *Benevolent Assimilation*, 58; Wolff, *Little Brown Brother*, 143; Sexton, *Soldiers in the Sun*, 82.

10. Karp, *Politics of War*, 98–99, 107.

11. Palmer, "White Man and Brown Man," 80; "Bateman on Drunkenness," *Manila Times*, February 26, 1900, 1; Fiske, *Wartime in Manila*, 105.

12. Majul, *Mabini and the Philippine Revolution*, 45; letter from Mabini to Buencamino, August 17, 1898, quoted from "The Philippine Tariff" speech, Hon. John C. Spooner (R-WI), February 21, 1902.

13. Majul, *Mabini and the Philippine Revolution*, 193.

14. Agoncillo, *Malolos*, 308.

15. Agoncillo, *Malolos*, 241, 376.

16. Wolff, *Little Brown Brother*, 141; Blount, *American Occupation*, 89.

17. Blount, *American Occupation*, 139.

18. Wildman, *Aguinaldo*, 192.

19. Alejandrino, *Price of Freedom*, 111–12.

20. Constantino, *A Past Revisited*, 154, 175, 228.

Chapter 6. Permissions to Hate

1. Litwack, *Trouble in Mind*, 313.

2. Ayers, *Promise of the New South*, 301.

3. Taylor, ed., "Editor Manley's Predicament," *Broad Ax*, December 12, 1898.

4. Curt Eriksmoen, "Black Editor Got Started in Fargo," *Bismarck Tribune*, February 26, 2012.

5. Gatewood, *Black Americans*, 105.

6. Steward, *Buffalo Soldiers*, 252.

7. Gatewood, *Black Americans*, 111.

8. Gatewood, *Black Americans*, 112.

9. Gatewood, *Black Americans*, 111.

10. Taylor, ed., "Race Troubles in the South," *Broad Ax*, November 12, 1898, 1.

11. Eriksmoen, "Black Editor."

12. Gatewood, *Black Americans*, 116; Blount, *American Occupation*, 145.

13. Woodward, *Strange Career of Jim Crow*, 81–82.

14. "Record of Events," Regimental Returns, Twenty-Fourth Infantry, Co. H, January–February 1899; "Twenty-fourth Unsettled," *Salt Lake (UT) Tribune*, January 13, 1899, 7; "Will Reduce the 24th," *Salt Lake (UT) Tribune*, January 26, 1899, 8.

15. "Record of Events," Regimental Returns, Twenty-Fourth Infantry, Co. H, January–February 1899.

Chapter 7. Benevolent Assimilation

1. Blount, *American Occupation*, 147–50.

2. Mabini, *Philippine Revolution*, 46.

3. Blount, *American Occupation*, 45.

4. Miller, *Benevolent Assimilation*, 61.

5. Linn, *Philippine War, 1899–1902*, 53–54; Welch, *Response to Imperialism*, 24. Miller, *Benevolent Assimilation*, 63–64, maintains that Otis took it upon himself to provoke the fighting without consulting Washington. Schirmer, *Republic or Empire*, 128–32, argues for a larger conspiracy. See also *San Francisco Chronicle*, February 5, 1899.

6. Linn, *Philippine War*, 62, 64.

7. Hunt, *Colorado Volunteer Infantry*, 156.

8. Wolff, *Little Brown Brother*, 213–14.

9. John F. Bass, "With Wheaton's Flying Column," *Harper's Weekly*, March 29, 1899, 151.

10. Jones, *Honor in the Dust*, 112–15.

11. Constantino, *A Past Revisited*, 228–29; Alejandrino, *Price of Freedom*, 133–34.

12. Linn, *Philippine War*, 61.

Chapter 8. Snowbound

1. Enlistment, David Fagen, no. 901, 1898, no. 232, 1899, NA, National Personnel Records Center.

2. NA, National Personnel Records Center; "Fever," *Salt Lake (UT) Tribune*, May 1, 1899.

3. Linda Lam, "The Coldest Temperatures Ever Recorded in All 50 States," https://weather.com/news/climate/news/coldest-temperature-recorded-50-states.

4. File on Captain James Brett, AGO 301568, NA, RG 94.

5. "Record of Events," Regimental Returns, Twenty-Fourth Infantry, Co. I, March 1899.

6. "Lt. James A. Moss," *Riders of the Bicycle Corps* (blog), http://bicyclecorpsriders.blogspot.com/2009/01/lt-james-moss.html.

7. Sorensen, *Iron Riders*, 106 pp., mostly photos.

8. "They Knew Gen. Fagin," *Salt Lake (UT) Herald*, October 30, 1900, 8.

9. *San Francisco Chronicle*, March, 14, 1899; list of soldiers who served at Siboney, AGO 215561, RG 94.

10. "Negro Troops to the Rescue," *Salt Lake (UT) Herald*, March 12, 1899, 1.

11. "Record of Events," Regimental Returns, Twenty-Fourth Infantry, Company I, March 25, 1899; Robinson and Schubert, "David Fagen," 74.

Chapter 9. "Fighting Fred" Funston

1. Funston, *Memories*, 185; Bain, *Sitting in Darkness*, 79–80.

2. Hearings Before the Committee on the Philippines of the United States Senate 1902, vol. 2, 1428.

3. "Prisoners Not Murdered by American Troops," *San Francisco (CA) Call,* June 30, 1899, 1.

4. Linn, *Philippine War*, 64.

5. Bain, *Sitting in Darkness*, 9–10.

6. Bain, *Sitting in Darkness*, 24–35, 45–56.

7. Bain, *Sitting in Darkness*, 90.

8. Bain, *Sitting in Darkness*, 397, 52, 80–81.

9. Miller, *Benevolent Assimilation*, 70, 168–69, 180–81.

10. Bain, *Sitting in Darkness*, 15; "Deny Funston Swam the Bag Bag: Kansas Commissioners Say He Cannot Swim and Order Story Out of Textbooks," *New York Tribune* (NY), May 21, 1904, 1.

Chapter 10. Slander

1. "Record of Events," Regimental Returns, Twenty-Fourth Regiment, Co. I, March–April 1899.

2. Arnold, "Negro Soldiers in the U.S. Army," 120.

3. Theodore Roosevelt, "The Rough Riders," *Scribner's*, 435–36.

4. Steward, *Buffalo Soldiers*, 327; Roosevelt, "The Rough Riders," 436.

5. Letter from Sergeant Presley Holliday to *New York Age*, quoted in Gatewood, *"Smoked Yankees,"* 92–97.

6. Gatewood, *Black Americans*, 203.

7. Gatewood, *Black Americans*, 244.

8. "Colored Men Meet in Boston and Assert Their Rights," *New York Times*, August 17, 1900, 2.

9. Brundage, *Lynching in the New South*, 82–84.

10. *North Adams (MA) Transcript*, April 24, 1899, 1.

11. "Investigation into the True Story of Sam Hose Lynching," *Richmond (VA) Planet*, October 14, 1899, 1.

12. *Newnan (GA) Herald and Advertiser*, May 5, 1899.

13. "Negro Dies at the Stake," *New York Times*, April 24, 1899, 2.

14. "Investigation into the True Story," 1.

15. Sledd, "The Negro," 66, 70.

16. *Newnan (GA) Herald and Advertiser*, May 5, 1899; Sledd, "The Negro," 70.

Chapter 11 Stalemate

1. Gates, *Schoolbooks and Krags*, 104–5.

2. Roth, *Muddy Glory*, 55.

3. Wolff, *Little Brown Brother*, 178.

4. Linn, *Philippine War*, 100.

5. Marple, "The Philippine Scouts," 54; MacArthur quoted in Sexton, *Soldiers in the Sun*, 87–88.

6. Blount, *American Occupation*, 206, 196, 193; Miller, *Benevolent Assimilation*, 176; Vickers and Crandall quoted in "American Soldiers in the Philippines Write Home about the War," *History Matters*, http://historymatters.gmu.edu/d/58/.

7. Feuer, *Combat Diary*, 94.

8. Miller, *Benevolent Assimilation*, 74.

9. V. R. Jose, *Rise and Fall of Antonio Luna*, 283; Constantino, *A Past Revisited*, 228; Majul, *Mabini and the Philippine Revolution*, 215.

10. Agoncillo, *Malolos*, 520, 651–53.

11. Majul, *Mabini and the Philippine Revolution*, 217.

12. Mabini, *Philippine Revolution*, 2:271, 64.

13. Linn, *Philippine War*, 121.

14. Report of the Chief Bureaus, June 30, 1899, WDAR 1900, vol. 1, pt. 5, 467.

Chapter 12. Sequoia

1. Report of the Acting Superintendent of Sequoia and General Grant National Parks, in California, to the Secretary of the Interior, 1899 (U.S. Government Printing Office); *Salt Lake (UT) Tribune*, May 1, 1899; *San Francisco Chronicle*, April 29, 1899, 12.

2. *Boston Globe*, June 2, 1899.

3. Reports from James A. Moss to Secretary of the Interior, supplied by Ward Eldredge, curator for Sequoia and Kings Canyon National Parks.

4. Reports from James A. Moss to Secretary of the Interior.

5. "To forfeit to U.S. $5 per S.C. sentence June 7, '99," "Record of Events," Regimental Returns, Twenty-Fourth Infantry, Co. I, May–June 1899.

6. U.S. Army, Adjutant General's Office, *Correspondence Relating to the War with Spain*, 2:1018.

Chapter 13. The White Man's Burden

1. Kent, *America in 1900*, 116, quotes from *The Oregonian*, September 2, 1899: "In late 1899, fighting broke out between black and white soldiers on transport ships carrying them to the Philippines."

2. "To forfeit to U.S. $2 per S.C. sentence July 14, '99," "Record of Events," Regimental Returns, Twenty-Fourth Infantry, Co I, July–August 1899; *Manila Times*, September 18, 1901.

3. Stevens, *Yesterday in the Philippines*, 9, 10.

4. Gatewood, *"Smoked Yankees,"* 253.

5. Robinson, *Philippines*, 76.

6. Stevens, *Yesterday in the Philippines*, 201; McCallus, *Gentleman Soldier*, 76.

7. Stevens, *Yesterday in the Philippines*, 27; Robinson, *The Philippines, the War, the People*, 262.

8. John F. Bass, "In the Trenches—A Night on the Gunboat *Laguna de Bay*—With the 'Flying Column,'" in Wilcox, *Harper's History of the War in the Philippines*, 145; *Manila Times*, February 26, 1901, 1.

9. *Manila Times,* January 17, 1900; Gatewood, *"Smoked Yankees,"* 237.

10. J. D. Foner, *Blacks and the Military,* 92.

11. *Manila Times,* May 19, 1906, 1.

12. Moss, *Memories of the Campaign,* 37; James Alfred Moss, "Journal of a Trip through the Provinces of Pampanga, Nueva Ecija, and Pangasinan: Covering Nearly All the Territory Occupied by the 24th Infantry, from September 1899 to June 1902," Funston Papers, Kansas Historical Society, Topeka; Dentler, "In the Shadow of the White Man's Burden," 46; Goode, *Eighth Illinois,* 173.

13. Goode, *Eighth Illinois,* 172.

14. File on John Calloway, AGO 356799, RG 94, filed with AGO 17043.

15. McCallus, *Gentleman Soldier,* 75.

16. McCallus, *Gentleman Soldier,* 56.

17. "Colored Troops in the Philippines," *Richmond (VA) Planet,* September 30, 1899, 1.

18. "May Negroes Who Volunteer Get Ball-Stung," *Reporter* (Helena, AR), February 1, 1900.

19. "Blacks Should Not Enlist," *Broad Ax,* August 7, 1899 (this paper moved from Salt Lake City to Chicago in June 1899).

20. "To forfeit to U.S. $10 per S.C. sentence Sept. 11, '99," "Record of Events," Regimental Returns, Twenty-Fourth Infantry, Co. I, September–October 1899; *Salt Lake City (UT) Herald,* October 30, 1900, 8; "To forfeit to U.S. 5$ per S.C. sentence Sept. 22, '99," "Record of Events," Regimental Returns, Twenty-Fourth Infantry, Co. I, September–October 1899.

21. Linn, *Philippine War,* 139.

22. Linn, *Philippine War,* 137; WDAR 1901, vol. 1, pt. 5; McCallus, *Gentleman Soldier,* 108.

23. WDAR 1901, vol. 1, pt. 5.

24. Robinson, *Philippines,* 304; Muller, *Twenty Fourth Infantry, Past and Present;* McCallus, *Gentleman Soldier,* 98.

25. Gatewood, *"Smoked Yankees,"* 248.

26. *Richmond (VA) Planet,* November 11, 1899. In Louisiana, the year before, charges against Edward Gray had been dropped, and the young man, seriously ill, had struggled to make his way home. A mob of young white men caught up with him in the night and hanged him, creating outrage among not only African Americans but also much of the white community.

27. Gatewood, *"Smoked Yankees,"* 285.

28. McCallus, *Gentleman Soldier,* 108.

29. "Record of Events," Regimental Returns, Twenty-Fourth Infantry, Co. I, September–October 1899.

30. "Record of Events," Regimental Returns, Twenty-Fourth Infantry, Co. I, September–October 1899.

31. "Hay Appointed Second Lieutenant," *Daily Iowa Capitol,* March 15, 1899; Regimental Returns, Twenty-Fourth Infantry, Co. I, May–October 1899.

32. "Record of Events," Regimental Returns, Twenty-Fourth Infantry, Co. I, September–October 1899; *New York Times,* September 2, 1900.

33. *Collier's Weekly,* February 11, 1905, 13.

34. R. Thomas, *Little Gods,* 14.

35. R. Thomas, *Little Gods,* 17–18.

36. R. Thomas, *Little Gods,* 20.

37. R. Thomas, *Little Gods*, 19.

38. "The Degradation of Fagan," *New York Age*, April 30, 1905.

Chapter 14. Aguinaldo Adrift

1. May, "Why the United States Won the Philippine-American War, 1899–1902," 369: "[Aguinaldo] viewed guerrilla warfare as last resort of a beaten army."

2. J. R. M. Taylor, *Philippine Insurrection against the United States*, 2:221.

3. Constantino, *A Past Revisited*, 228–30.

4. Agoncillo, *Malolos*, 540.

5. Agoncillo and Guerrero, *History of the Filipino People*, 125.

6. Mabini, *Philippine Revolution*, 2:64.

7. Schumacher, "Socioeconomic Classes in the Revolution," 205; Bass, "The Situation in Luzon," 242; "Annual Report of Maj. Gen. MacArthur," Oct. 1, 1900, WDAR 1901, vol. 1, pt. 5, 61.

8. Guerrero, *Luzon at War*, 141.

9. Mabini, *Philippine Revolution*, 2:64; Vicente L. Rafael, "Introduction: Revolutionary Contradictions," in Guerrero, *Luzon at War*, 5; May, "Why the United States Won the Philippine-American War, 1899–1902," 365. May further stated, "Aguinaldo and other elite Filipinos were fighting the Americans because they wanted to rule, and not because they wanted to bring about a social revolution" (361).

10. Guerrero, "The Provincial Elites of Luzon during the Revolution, 1898–1902," in McCoy and C. de Jesus, *Philippine Social History*, 155.

11. Palmer, "White Man and Brown Man," 78; Guerrero, "Provincial Elites," 174; Majul, *Mabini and the Philippine*, 200.

12. May, "Why the United States Won the Philippine-American War, 1899–1902," 363; Kramer, *Blood of Government*, 122.

13. Kramer, *Blood of Government*, 122.

14. Blount, *American Occupation*, 529. On pages 187–88, Blount refers to "Mr. Root's nonsense . . . about 'the patient and unconsenting millions' dominated by 'the Tagalo tribe.'"

Chapter 15. Over the Hill

1. *Gazette* (Cleveland), September 19, 1900, quoted in Gatewood, *"Smoked Yankees,"* 257; "Record of Events," Regimental Returns, Twenty-Fourth Infantry, Co. I. January–February 1900.

2. Gatewood, *Smoked Yankees*, 217.

3. "Record of Events," Regimental Returns, Twenty-Fourth Infantry, Co. I, September–October 1899; AGO 403885, RG 94; *Leavenworth (KS) Times*, January 19, 1902, 6; "Record of Events," Regimental Returns, Twenty-Fourth Infantry, Co. I, November 1901.

4. Calloway letter to the *Richmond Planet* quoted in Gatewood, *"Smoked Yankees,"* 252.

5. Gatewood, *"Smoked Yankees,"* 253.

6. File on Calloway, AGO 356799, RG 94, filed with AGO 17043.

7. J. D. Foner, *Blacks and the Military*, 91.

8. According to Woolard, "The Philippine Scouts," 71: "Macabebe companies were really products of Pampangan tradition, distinctive solely because all came from one barrio of that province." See also Orosa, "The Macabebes"; Mallari, "The Warrior and Mercenary Culture of the Macabebes"; Tarnowski, "Macabebes and Moros." Others, like John Morgan Gates (*Schoolbooks and Krags*), speculate that the Macabebes were descendants of Mexican Indians sent by Spain as mercenaries during the years of the galleon trades.

9. Miller, *Benevolent Assimilation*, 81–82.

10. Linn, *Philippine War*, 161.

11. McCallus, *Gentleman Soldier*, 113, 118.

12. "Record of Events," Regimental Returns, Twenty-Fourth Infantry, Co. I. September–October 1899; *New York Herald*, March 17, 1912.

13. Linn, *Philippine War*, 145.

14. "Report of an Expedition to the provinces North of Manila, P.I., During the Months of September, October, November, and December 1899, Maj. Gen. H. W. Lawton, U.S.V., Commanding," WDAR 1900, vol. 1, pts. 5–7. This is a day-by-day telegraphic account of the campaign, including detailed reports of actions by officers of involved units, and captured dispatches of Aguinaldo's officers (125, 160).

15. WDAR 1900, vol. 1, pts. 5–7, 113 ("Intoxicating liquor is supplied by some party or parties in the town," leading Colonel Kennon to order the purveyor arrested and liquor and any related facilities destroyed); *St. Louis Post-Dispatch*, April 16, 1902.

16. Maj. Jno. T. Knight, November 6, 1899, WDAR 1900, vol. 1, pts. 5–7; Col. Lyman Kennon to Maj. Gen. Henry Lawton, WDAR 1900, vol. 1, pts. 5–7, 98, 142.

17. Sexton, *Soldiers in the Sun*, 183; A. G. Robinson, *Philippines*, 105.

18. Maj. Gen. Henry Lawton to Lt. Gen. E. S. Otis, WDAR 1900, vol. 1, pts. 5–7, 161.

19. Information slip on David Fagan, deserter, AGO 431081, RG 94; AAG Smith to AG Manila, February 19, 1901, RG 395/2133, Box 3, LS 593.

Chapter 16. Another Kind of War

1. Gen. Theodore Schwan to Maj. Gen. Henry Lawton, WDAR 1900–1901, vol. 1, pt. 6, 161.

2. Robinson and Schubert, "David Fagen," 75; Linn, *U.S. Army and Counterinsurgency*, 67–68, 78.

3. "Gave Their Parole," *Manila Freedom*, August 18, 1900, 1.

4. Report of November 29, 1899, WDAR 1900–1901 vol. 1, pt. 5, 389. Robinson and Schubert maintain that Fagen "headed toward the Arayat sanctuary" ("David Fagen," 74), but their notes do not support that contention. I found no other reference to Fagen joining Aquino's men on Mount Arayat, but rather the *St. Louis Post-Dispatch* (February 16, 1902) claim that he went east to join Garcia and Padilla at Papaya. This makes more sense as the next reference to Fagen, March 1900, places him with Padilla and Garcia at Papaya.

5. Sexton, *Soldiers in the Sun*, 185; Linn, *Philippine War*, 148–49; Lt. Castner to Maj. Gen. Lawton, November 29, 1899, WDAR 1900, vol. 1, pts. 5–7, 193.

6. Linn, *Philippine War*, 150–51.

7. Constantino, *A Past Revisited*, 232–33.

8. Constantino, *A Past Revisited*, 233; J. R. M. Taylor, *Philippine Insurrection*, 1:5, commentary on "telegraphic correspondence of E. Aguinaldo": "in the event of success in this attack [Manila Uprising] the so-called insurgent government would not have continued to call itself a republic. A republic does not award titles of nobility."

9. Mabini, *Philippine Revolution*, 26; "Chasing Aguinaldo through the Clouds," *New York Times*, December 14, 1899, 1.

10. Gen. Young to Lt. Gen. Otis, November 17, 1899, WDAR 1900–1901, vol. 1, pt. 3, 261; Otis to *Leslie's Weekly*, June 16, 1900, 462; Otis to Adjutant General, November 24, 1899; U.S. Army, Adjutant General's Office, *Correspondence Relating to the War with Spain*, 2:1107; Constantino, *A Past Revisited*, 231; Sturtevant, *Popular Uprisings*, 115–16.

11. Constantino, *A Past Revisited*, 231; Sturtevant, *Popular Uprisings*, 115–16.

12. Sturtevant, *Popular Uprisings*, 96–97.

13. Kerkvliet, *Huk Rebellion*, 5; Ochosa, *Tinio Brigade*, 15–18; Constantino, *A Past Revisited*, 217.

14. Linn, *U.S. Army and Counterinsurgency*, 67–68.

15. Wolff, *Little Brown Brother*, 290.

16. William Dinwiddie, "General Lawton's Last Fight," in Wilcox, *Harper's History*, 328–29.

17. Miller, *Benevolent Assimilation*, 205.

18. Dinwiddie, "General Lawton's Last Fight," 326.

19. Report of Maj. Gen. Otis, U.S. Army, Commanding Division of the Philippines, September 1, 1899, to May 5, 1900, WDAR 1900, vol. 1, pt. 5, December 3, 1899, 193.

20. Bass, "The Situation in Luzon," in Wilcox, *Harper's History*, 218–22.

21. Alejandrino, *Price of Freedom*, 174–75.

22. Report of Maj. Gen. Otis on Military Operations and Civil Affairs, September 1, 1899–May 5, 1900, January 5–6, 1900, 148–49; LeRoy, *The Americans in the Philippines*, 1:212n.

23. Report of Maj. Gen. Otis on Military Operations and Civil Affairs, September 1, 1899–May 5, 1900, Kobbé to Schwan, December 3, 1899, Kobbé to Schwan, December 4, 1900, WDAR 1901, vol. 1, pt. 5, 103.

24. Telegram from Funston in San Isidro to MacArthur in Manila, WDAR 1900, vol. 1, pt. 6, 498; "Pablo Padilla Must Be Tried," *Manila American*, January 3, 1902, 1; "Did Lacuna Build a Trap for Pablo Padilla?," *Leavenworth (KS) Times*, April 2, 1902, 2.

25. Report of Maj. Gen. Otis, Sept. 1, 1899–May 5, 1900, WDAR 1901, vol. 1, pt. 5, 198. Taylor writes that not more than 150 Americans were captured or missing—the "majority of them were recaptured or released." J. R. M. Taylor, *Philippine Insurrection*, 2:267.

Chapter 17. Billets-doux

1. Funston, *Memories*, 312.

2. "The Charmed Class Ring," *Washington Post*, March 12, 1912, 3 (from *New York Herald*).

3. WDAR 1900/1901, vol. 1, pt. 5, 133: "December 28, 1899. Near Talavera, 5 men Co. G (1 Sgt. Signal Corps) commanded by Private Thomas Clay, Co. G. Strength of enemy—50, Private Jesse Jones killed; Privates John Quarles and Edward Sanders, missing."

4. Report of Maj. Joseph E. Wheeler Jr. of Operations in Provinces of Nueva Ecija and Bulacan, March 20, 1900, WDAR 1900–1901, vol. 1, pt. 7, 505. Wheeler was ambushed on March 6.

5. General Grant to AG Manila, July 13, 1900, RG 395/2282, Box 1, TS Fifth District: "Capt. Roberts reports that there are in Pablo Tecson's camp near Tubigan two American prisoners, Privates Sanders and Quarles Co. G 24th Infantry who were captured December 28, 1899 near Talavera and have been held in various places since. They were in good health and spirits."

6. Report of Lt. Col. Markley, Twenty-Fourth Infantry, WDAR for year ending June 30, 1901, vol. 1, pt. 3, 134.

7. Kerkvliet, *The Huk Rebellion*, 8; for a description of Nueva Ecija and consequences of deforestation and rice-growing monoculture, see McClennan, "Peasant and Hacendero in Nueva Ecija," 236–47.

8. Funston, *Memories*, 314, 315.

9. *Chicago Tribune*, November 3, 1899; *San Francisco Call*, vol. 86, no. 155, November 2, 1899; *Chicago Tribune*, November 3, 1899; *Sacramento Daily Union*, vol. 98, no. 73, November 2, 1899.

10. *Chicago Tribune*, November 3, 1899.

11. Funston, *Memories*, 314, 315.

12. *Manila Times*, March 14, 1900; *English Crawford County Democrat*, March 22, 1900.

13. "Rebel Atrocities in Nueva Ecija," *Manila Times*, March 17, 1900, 2.

14. Guerrero, *Luzon at War*, 90 ("The ground rules established by Aguinaldo for political reorganization . . . carefully preserved the colonial elite"); 154 ("The lack of a firm land policy, in turn, suited the expectations of many members of the rural elite throughout Luzon, who proceeded to consolidate control over vast tracts of land"); Linn, *U.S. Army and Counterinsurgency*, 66.

15. Linn, *Philippine War*, 196.

16. "Kennon's Ilocanos," *Daily Northwestern* (Oshkosh, WI), September 13, 1900, 1; Blount, *American Occupation*, 119n, 246.

17. Ganzhorn, *I've Killed Men*.

18. Funston, *Memories*, 319–20.

19. "Talks of the Water Cure," *Messenger and Intelligencer* (Wadesboro, NC), April 24, 1902, 2.

20. "Talks of the Water Cure," 2.

21. Report of Maj. Joseph E. Wheeler Jr., March 16, 1900, WDAR 1901, vol. 1, pt. 7, 365; D. H. Smith, "American Atrocities in the Philippines," 282; Edward E. Brown, Philippine Diary Notebook, Department of Special Collections, Morris Library, Univ. of Delaware; Captain Chas. W. Wadsworth to Adj. 41st Inf. U.S.V., January 30, 1901, RG 395/2288, LR; Funston, *Memories*, 325: "In the meantime the captured man was put through a long examination, and finally agreed to lead us to the main insurgent camp." The reader is left to wonder what Funston's idea of "a long examination" entailed.

22. Funston, *Memories*, 314.

23. Funston, *Memories*, 377.

24. Report of Maj. Joseph F. Wheeler Jr., March 16, 1900—Engagement of 100 Americans against Padilla's 700 men, March 16, WDAR 1901, vol. 1, pt. 7, 365: "40 reported killed, many wounded, dragging themselves into the brush," "Lt. Jorge David captured," "supplies seemed woefully deficient"; Linn, *Counterinsurgency*, 71.

25. Taylor, *Philippine Insurrection*, 2:331: "The central committee has resolved the following: . . . the arrests of Pio del Pilar and Pantaleon Garcia will be made; they will be taken and summarily tried by court-martial and shot to death, as punishment for their treason."

Chapter 18. The Death of Captain Godfrey

1. "San Miguel Fight: Five Boys Killed, Seven Wounded," *Manila Freedom*, June 1, 1900, 1; "Filipinos Beat Them Back," *Baltimore (MD) Sun*, July 27, 1900, 10.
2. Report of Captain Charles D. Roberts to C.O. 35th Inf., U.S.V., July 15, 1900, AGO 459488, RG 94.
3. Report of Captain Charles D. Roberts to C.O. 35th Inf.
4. Report of Captain Charles D. Roberts to C.O. 35th Inf., 5: "I afterward learned that at least half of those engaged against us belonged to Col. Pablo Tecson's guerrillas."
5. *Davenport Weekly Leader*, July 24, 1900; letter from Lt. Hanson E. Ely.
6. *New York Times*, June 5, 1900; *Free Press* (Ozark, AL), June 14, 1900, 7.
7. Funston, *Memories*, 351.
8. Funston, *Memories*, 352.
9. Funston, *Memories*, 353.
10. Funston, *Memories*, 352; "Record of Events," Regimental Returns, 22nd Infantry, Co. A, June 1900, frame 182.
11. "Filipinos Killed Deserter Fagin," *St. Louis Post-Dispatch*, April 16, 1902, 12.
12. *St. Louis Republic*, February 5, 1902. After surgery in Kansas City, Funston returned for a "short sojourn in Iola" approximately February 7–20, 1902.
13. Funston to AG Manila, June 4, 1900, RG 395/2282, Box 1, TS.
14. "Filipinos Killed Deserter Fagin"; "Funston's Enemy," *Iola (KS) Daily Register*, April 23, 1902.

Chapter 19. "The Afro-American Traitor Called David"

1. Report of Captain Charles D. Roberts to C.O. 35th Inf., U.S.V., July 15, 1900, AGO 459488, NA, RG 94.
2. Report of Captain Charles D. Roberts to C.O. 35th Inf., 6.
3. Report of Captain Charles D. Roberts to C.O. 35th Inf., 6, 11.
4. "Report of Engagement on Mt. Balubad, Province of Bulacan, P.I., June 11, 1900, by Brig. Gen. Frederick D. Grant," WDAR 1901, vol. 1, pt. 7, 115–20; Linn, *Philippine War*, 271; account of engagement by Private Wheeley in "Filipinos Beat Them Back," *Baltimore Sun*, July 27, 1900, 10: "They seemed to be officered by Englishmen or Americans. . . . It was suicide to continue the fight with infantry, as artillery was needed. We returned to camp a sore and disappointed gang of lobsters."
5. Funston, *Memories*, 358.
6. "Record of Events," Regimental Returns, 22nd Infantry, June 1900, frame 182.
7. Ganzhorn, *I've Killed Men*, 177.
8. Lacuna to Lorenzo Tamayo, May 19, 1900, WDAR 1900, vol. 1, pt. 5, 120.
9. Report of Maj. Joseph E. Wheeler Jr., June 19, 1900, WDAR 1901, vol. 1, pt. 7, 370.

10. Funston, *Memories*, 370.

11. Report of Maj. Joseph E. Wheeler Jr., June 19, 1900, 372.

12. Funston, *Memories*, 361–62; Ganzhorn, *I've Killed Men*, 167.

13. Ganzhorn, *I've Killed Men*, 167.

14. Report of Maj. Joseph E. Wheeler Jr., June 19, 1900, 372.

15. Report of Maj. Joseph E. Wheeler Jr., June 19, 1900, 372, 373.

Chapter 20. Urbano Lacuna

1. Annual Report of Maj. Gen. MacArthur, Appendix 1: Guerrilla Tactics, Madrid, July 15, 1900, WDAR 1900/1901, vol. 1, pt. 5, 72.

2. Ochosa, *Pio del Pilar*, 61, 69, 85, 95; Linn, *Counterinsurgency*, 72.

3. Funston, *Memories*, 429; Linn, *Counterinsurgency*, 71, 72; Ochosa, *Pio del Pilar*, 61.

4. Funston, *Memories*, 357; Linn, *Counterinsurgency*, 73.

5. Funston, "Guerilla Warfare in the Philippines," 5.

6. *San Francisco Chronicle*, April 3, 1902. Funston left this anecdote out of his autobiography and does not appear to have brought up the matter elsewhere.

7. *New York Sun*, March 10, 1902, 1; *San Francisco Chronicle*, March 9, 1902, 1; "Funston Talked of War in the Philippines," *Weekly Gazette* (Colorado Springs, CO), March 13, 1902, 2.

8. Funston, *Memories*, 365; "Record of Events," Regimental Returns, Twenty-Fourth Infantry, reports Mitchell and his forty men to Manicling on June 24. Possibly the detachment was assigned to that post on the twenty-fourth but didn't actually move from San Isidro to Manicling until July 4.

9. Funston, *Memories*, 365.

10. "Record of Events," Regimental Returns, Twenty-Fourth Infantry, Company C, July 1900.

11. Funston, *Memories*, 365; Ganzhorn, *I've Killed Men*, 173.

12. "Record of Events," Regimental Returns, Twenty-Fourth Infantry, Company C, June–July 1900.

13. U.S. Army, Register of Enlistments, 1798–1914: 1895, 1898; Clark, "A History of the Twenty-Fourth," 56.

14. Funston to AG DNL, July 9, 1900, RG 395/2263, Box 2, TSR.

15. Funston to AG DNL, July 9, 1900, RG 395/2263, Box 2, TSR (separate telegram from the one mentioned in n14).

16. "Hamilton Japanese Receive Word That Aguinaldo Is Dead," *Journal News* (Hamilton, OH), 1, quoting description of Pilar from *American Review of Books*, February 1899.

17. Guerrero, "The Provincial and Municipal Elites," 174.

18. Funston to AG DNL, June 28, 1900, RG 395/2133, Box 2, L&TS.

19. J. R. M. Taylor, *Philippine Insurrection*, 2:331; Ochosa, *Pio del Pilar*, 113.

20. Funston to AG DNL, July 9, 1900, RG 395/2263, Box 2, TSR.

21. Funston to AG DNL, July 12, 1900, RG 395/2263, Box 2, TSR

22. Linn, *Counterinsurgency*, 71.

23. Report of Captain Charles D. Roberts to C.O. 35th Inf., U.S.V., July 15, 1900, 13; *Manila Times*, October 31, 1899.

24. Funston to AG DNL, July 12, 1900, RG 395/2263, Box 2, TSR.

25. "Pio Arrested," *Arizona Republic*, September 17, 1900, 1.

26. Tecson, *Remembering My Lolo*, 137.

Chapter 21. Mount Corona

1. Funston, *Memories*, 365–66.

2. Roosevelt, *Rough Riders*: "Day, who proved himself one of our most efficient officers, continued to handle the men to the best possible advantage. . . . L Troop was from Indian Territory. The whites, Indians, and half-breeds in it all fought with equal courage" (95); "Lieutenant Day, after handling his troop with equal gallantry and efficiency, was shot, on the summit of Kettle Hill" (149); *Manila Times*, October 12, 1900 ("revolver firing from the hip is practiced by Funston's mounted scouts under the direction of Lieut. R.C. Day, who holds the record for that style of shooting up to date. Competitive matches are soon to be held").

3. Funston, *Memories*, 367.

4. Funston, *Memories*, 367; Maj. Joseph E. Wheeler Jr., "Report of Operations in the Mountains of Nueva Ecija and Bulacan from July 16th to July 24th, 1900," WDAR 1901, vol. 1, pt. 7, 375.

5. Funston to AG, DNL, July 19, 1900, RG 395/2263 Box 2, TSR.

6. Linn, *Counterinsurgency*, 73.

7. Funston, *Memories*, 368.

8. *Harrisburg (PA) Daily Independent*, July 3, 1902, 4.

9. Lieutenant David R. Stone, 22nd Infantry, Company F, August 6, 1900, NA, RG 395, LTR 1358. (First two pages too dark to read, presumably addressed to regimental commanding officer.)

10. Lt. Stone, August 6, 1900; Ganzhorn, *I've Killed Men*, 175.

11. Funston, *Memories*, 372; "Tecson's Camp Destroyed," *Manila Freedom*, July 26, 1900, 1.

12. Ganzhorn, *I've Killed Men*, 175–77.

13. Funston, *Memories*, 372.

14. Report by 1st Sgt. H. D. Williams, Co. G, 34th Inf. U.S.V., July 25, 1900, RG 395, LTR 1358; Report of Maj. Joseph E. Wheeler Jr., July 24, 1900, WDAR 1901, vol. 1, pt. 7, 380.

15. Lt. Stone commends 1st Sgt. Ole Waloe, Company F, 22nd Inf., RG 395, LTR 1358.

16. Report of Maj. Joseph E. Wheeler Jr., July 24, 1900, 380.

17. Report of Maj. Joseph E. Wheeler Jr., July 24, 1900, 380.

18. Report, Lt. David Stone, RG 395, LTR 1358.

19. Report, Lt. David Stone, RG 395, LTR 1358; Report of Maj. Joseph E. Wheeler Jr., July 24, 1900, 382.

20. Report of Maj. Joseph E. Wheeler Jr., July 24, 1900, 382.

21. Ganzhorn, *I've Killed Men*, 177.

22. *Manila Freedom*, July 26, 1900; Report of Maj. Joseph E. Wheeler Jr., July 24, 1900, 380; Acting Adjutant Captain E. V. Smith to Funston, August 2, 1900, RG 395/2263, Box 2, TSR.

23. Report, Lt. David Stone, RG 395, LTR 1358.

Chapter 22. Alstaetter

1. Funston to AG DNL, August 6, 1900, NA RG 395/2263, Box 2, TSR.
2. "He Was Fagin's Prisoner," *Piqua (OH) Daily Call*, December 31, 1901.
3. AG Manila to Plummer, Baliaug, July 25, 1900, RG 395/2282, Box 1, TS.
4. AA Smith to Funston in San Miguel, August 2, 1900, RG 395/2263, Box 2, TSR.
5. Agoncillo and Guerrero, *History of the Filipino People*, 262; Strong, "Frederick W. Alstaetter 1897."
6. "Record of Events," Regimental Returns, Fourth Cavalry, Troop H, August 1900, frame 151.
7. Strong, "Frederick W. Alstaetter 1897"; *Manila Times*, August 3, 1900.
8. "He Was Fagin's Prisoner," *Piqua (OH) Daily Call*, December 31, 1901, 1.
9. "Lieut. Alstaetter's Ring," *Daily Herald* (Delphos, OH), December, 11, 1901, 3.
10. "Lieut. Alstaetter Talks of David Fagin," *New York Times*, December 10, 1901, 2.
11. "Promoted for the Capture," *Leavenworth (KS) Times*, December 10, 1901, 4.
12. Acting Adj. Smith to Funston, August 2, 1900, RG 395/2263, Box 2, TSR.
13. "Lieut. Alstaetter Talks of David Fagin," *New York Times*, December 10, 1901, 2.
14. "Lieut. Alstaetter Talks of David Fagin," 2.
15. "Americans' Serious Check," *New York Times*, August 5, 1900, 8.

Chapter 23. Funston's Great Roundup

1. Funston to AG DNL, August 12, 1900, RG 395/2263, Box 2, TSR.
2. Funston to AG DNL, August 18, 1900, RG 395/2263, Box 2, TSR.
3. AAG Alvord to Funston, August 10, 1900, RG 395/2263, Box 2, TSR.
4. J. R. M. Taylor, *Philippine Insurrection*, 2:276.
5. "Burt Mitchell Writes," *Iola (KS) Daily Register*, August 3, 1900, 1.
6. "Talks of the Water Cure," *Messenger and Intelligencer* (Wadesboro, NC), April 24, 1902, 2.
7. Funston to DNL, September 24, 1900, RG 395/2263, Box 3, TS; Funston to DNL January 8, 1901, RG 395/2263, Box 4, TSR; Funston to DNL, August 29, 1900, RG 395/2263, Box 4, TSR.
8. PIR 658-54.
9. "Filipino Ingenuity," *Saint Paul (MN) Globe*, September 29, 1900, 1.
10. May, "Why the United States Won," 365; Mojares, "The Hills Are Still There," in Shaw and Francia, *Vestiges of War*, n86; Rizal quoted in Ileto, "Bernardo Carpio," 10.
11. Ileto, "Bernardo Carpio," 26.
12. Guerrero, *Luzon at War*, 161, 234; "The revolution was being used as an excuse to swindle the people" (134) and "landgrabbing in Nueva Ecija" (158).
13. Ileto, *Pasyon and Revolution*, 80.
14. Lt. Col. Keller to Funston, August 16, 1900, RG 395/2263, Box 2, TSR, Maj. Wheeler to AA Smith, August 17, 1900, RG 395/2263, Box 2, TSR.
15. Lt. Col. Keller to Funston, August 16, 1900, RG 395/2263, Box 2, TSR; Maj. Wheeler to AA Smith, August 17, 1900, RG 395/2263, Box 2, TSR.
16. Gen. Funston to Maj. Wheeler, August 28, 1900, RG 395/2263, Box 2, TSR.

17. Gen. Funston to AG DNL, August 31, 1900, RG 395/2263, Box 3, TSR. Funston also reported "skirmish with small detachment commanded by David Fagin, the 24th Infty. deserter."

Chapter 24. Sergeant Washington and Captain Fagen

1. Wheeler to AAG 4th District, September 11, 1900, RG 395/1251, Box 3, LTR.
2. *Philadelphia Inquirer*, September 11, 1900; "Filipinos Look to Bryan," *Pittsburgh Daily Post*, September 10, 1900, 5.
3. AAG Smith to Commanding officer, Cabanatuan, September 3, 1900, RG 395/2263, Box 3, TS.
4. Fagen's commission, AGO 431081, NA, RG 94.
5. Funston to Mitchell, August 10, 1900, RG 395/2263, Box 2, TSR.
6. *Manila Times*, September 3, 1900, 1; Regimental Returns, Twenty-Second Infantry, September 1900.
7. Lt. Mitchell to AAG 4th Dist., September 19, 1900, RG 395/2261, Box 3, LR.
8. Lt. Mitchell to AAG 4th Dist., September 19, 1900.
9. Lt. Mitchell to AAG 4th Dist., September 19, 1900.
10. Funston to AG DNL, September 14, 1900, RG 395/2261, Box 3, LR.
11. Lt. Mitchell to AAG 4th District, September 19, 1900.
12. Ganzhorn, *I've Killed Men*, 172–73.
13. Ganzhorn, *I've Killed Men*; Lt. Mitchell to AAG 4th District, September 19, 1900.
14. "The Renegade Fagan," *Manila Times*, May 14, 1901.
15. Pvt. Patrick Shea to 1st Res. Hospital, Manila, January 11, 1901, RG 395/2263, Box 4, TR.
16. Kennon to AA Fourth District, September 24, 1900, RG 395/2263, Box 3, TR: "A negro with insurgents wounded in upper arm"; Jernigan to AA 4th District, December 4, 1900, RG 395/2263, Box 4, TR: "Among the dead was lieutenant Aguilar and one renegade American negro."

Chapter 25. Fall Offensive

1. Miller, *Benevolent Assimilation*, 145–46.
2. Wolff, *Little Brown Brother*, 318; Linn, *Philippine War*, 210–11; Miller, *Benevolent Assimilation*, 143.
3. Linn, *Counterinsurgency*, 52.
4. *San Francisco Call*, September 29, 1900, 1; "War All Over," *Mobile (AL) Weekly Monitor*, October 11, 1900, 1.
5. WDAR 1901, vol. 1, pt. 5, 63.
6. Schirmer, *Republic or Empire*, 211; Wolff, *Little Brown Brother*, 327; Miller, *Benevolent Assimilation*, 136.
7. Miller, *Benevolent Assimilation*, 144; Wolff, *Little Brown Brother*, 322; Jones, *Honor in the Dust*, 195.
8. Welch, *Response to Imperialism*, 65.
9. Scott, *Ilocano Responses*, 27; speech by McKinley in Racine, WI, October 17, 1899, *Public Opinion*, vol. 27, no. 17, October 26, 1899.
10. Karp, *Politics of War*, 107.

11. AA Smith to Morrison, September 23, 1900, RG 395/2263, Box 3, TR; *Manila Times*, September 24, 1900.

12. Linn, *Counterinsurgency*, 81–82; "Kennon's Ilocanos," *Daily Northwestern* (Oshkosh, WI), September 13, 1900, 1.

13. *Manila Times*, September 27, 1900, 1; *Kansas City Gazette*, October 1, 1900, 1; Bordua, "Col. Cushman Albert Rice."

14. AA 4th District to Kennon, Cabanatuan, September 24, 1900, RG 395/2263, Box 3 TR.

15. Wheeler to AA 4th Dist., October 2, 1900, RG 395/2263, Box 3 TR.

16. Wheeler to AA 4th Dist., October 2, 1900; Wheeler; "News from San Isidro," *Manila Times*, October 6, 1900.

17. WDAR 1900–1901, vol. 1, pt. 3, 216.

18. "Record of Events," Regimental Returns, 22nd Infantry, Co. A, October 1900, frames 168, 169.

19. "Record of Events," Regimental Returns, 22nd Infantry, Co. A, October 1900, frames 168, 169.

20. "Record of Events," Regimental Returns, 22nd Infantry, Co. A, October 1900, frames 168, 169.

Chapter 26. Old Scores

1. C. O. Cabanatuan to AA 4th District, October 19, 1900, RG 395/2261, Box 3, LS; Summary Court deposition of Pvt. Henry Clay taken by Capt. & Adj. J. B. Batchelor, Twenty-Fourth Infantry, December 17, 1900, AGO 403885, RG 94; Lt. Charles Hay Jr. to Adj. 24th Infantry, October 11, 1900, RG 395/2131 LS. The account of the attack is drawn from these two documents.

2. Letter from General Urbano Lacuna to Captains Dionisio and Lovero Santos, October 11, 1900, PIR 658, "Guerrilla desertions."

3. Kennon to AAAG Smith 4th District, October 12, 1900, RG 395/2263, Box 4, 2263: "one body of colored soldier, body horribly mutilated, privates cut off, great pieces of flesh cut out of legs, left arm and both legs presented appearance of having been flayed while man was alive, face beaten to a pulp and unrecognizable."

4. Hay to AAAG Smith, 4th District, October 11, 1900, RG 395/2388 LS.

5. Kennon to AAAG Smith, 4th District, October 13, 1900, RG 395/2263, Box 4, TS.

6. "Deserter Captured Leading Insurgents," *Leavenworth (KS) Times*, November 3, 1900, 1.

7. Funston to AG DNL, October 15, 1900, RG 395/2263, Box 4, TS.

8. "The Renegade Fagan," *Manila Times*, May 12, 1901, 1.

9. October 11, 1900, Funston to DNL, RG 395/2263, Box 4, TS.

10. Alejandrino, *Price of Freedom*, 176.

11. "Fagan Is Slippery," *Manila Freedom*, October 13, 1900, 1.

12. Alejandrino, *Price of Freedom*, 176.

13. "Fagan Is Slippery," 1.

14. Funston, *Memories*, 376.

15. Linn, *Counterinsurgency*, "The Nasty Little War," 63–86: no mention of Fagen.

16. Letter from Gen. Urbano Lacuna to Captains Dionisio and Lovero Santos, October 11, 1900, PIR 658.

17. *Wilkes-Barre (PA) Record*, November 2, 1900, 4.

18. "Who Fagan Was," *Wilkes-Barre (PA) Record*, March 21, 1901, 5.

19. Kennon to AAAG Smith, 4th District, October 13, 1900; *Wilkes-Barre (PA) News*, November 8, 1900, 4.

Chapter 27. "General Fagan"

1. Report by Capt. and Adj. J. B. Batchelor of investigation into ambush of Co. I, October 10, 1900, AGO 403885, RG 94, December 17, 1900.

2. Report by Capt. and Adj. J. B. Batchelor of investigation into ambush of Co. I, October 10, 1900.

3. Lt. Charles Hay Jr. to Adj. 24th Infantry, October 11, 1900, RG 395/2131, LS 1620.

4. Funston to AG DNL, October 11, 1900, RG 395/2263, Box 4, TR; Funston to Freeman, October 12, 1900, RG 395/2263, Box 3, TS.

5. Report by Capt. and Adj. J. B. Batchelor of investigation into ambush of Co. I, October 10, 1900.

6. Funston to AG 24th Infantry, December 17, 1900, AGO 483885, RG 94.

7. Report of Maj. Edwin B. Bolton, 24th Infantry, on engagement of October 10, 1900, forwarded by Col. H. B. Freeman, C.O. Twenty-Fourth Infantry, to AG DNL, RG 395/2131 LS 320.

8. Funston to AG DNL, October 15, 1900, RG 395/2263, Box 4, TR.

9. "Recaptured from Insurgents," *Manila Times*, October 16, 1900, 1.

10. "American Deserter a Filipino General," *New York Times*, October 29, 1900, 1.

11. *Manila Times*, October 25, 1900, October 26, 1900.

12. Lt. Quinlan, Phil. Cav. to AG San Isidro, October 26, 1900, RG 395/2263, Box 4, TR; account of attack drawn from *Manila Times* and primarily from the report of Lt. Whitfield, a five-page summary of pursuit of Fagen after raid on "Stonie": Lt. Whitfield, 22nd Inf. to Adj. 22nd Infantry, Arayat, October 29, 1900, RG 395, LTR 1706, Fourth District.

13. *Manila Times*, October 27, 1900, 1.

14. "On Deserter Fagan's Track," *Manila Times*, October 29, 1900, 3.

15. Lt. Quinlan, Phil. Cav. to AG San Isidro, October 26, 1900, RG 395/2263, Box 4, TR.

16. Lt. Whitfield, 22nd Inf. to Adj. 22nd Infantry, Arayat, October 29, 1900.

17. Lt. Whitfield, 22nd Inf. to Adj. 22nd Infantry, Arayat, October 29, 1900.

18. Lt. Col. Keller to AAG Smith, San Isidro, October 25, 1900, RG 395/2263, Box 4, TR; Lt. Col. Keller to AAG Smith, San Isidro, October 26, 1900, RG 395/2263, Box 4, TR: "After firing about ten minutes they boarded took the citizens money and jewelry and destroyed as much of the Stonie as they could took the capt. and his asst. prisoners and departed."

19. "Deserter Fagin's Record," *Salt Lake (UT) Tribune*, October 30, 1900, 3.

Chapter 28. "Negritos Soldados"

1. Bain, *Sitting in Darkness*, 87–88.

2. "Operator and Soldier Tells Rookie Story," *Lincoln (NE) Daily News*, June 8, 1914, 10.

3. "He Was Fagin's Prisoner," *Piqua (OH) Daily Call*, December 31, 1901.

4. "The Degradation of Fagan," *New York Age*, April 30, 1905.

5. Gatewood, *"Smoked Yankees,"* 280, quoting anonymous letter to *New York Age*, May 17, 1900.

6. Gatewood, *"Smoked Yankees,"* 245; letter from Private William R. Fulbright to *Freeman* (Indianapolis), in Gatewood, *"Smoked Yankees,"* 304–6.

7. Letter from Sgt. Preston Moore to *Freeman* (Indianapolis), October 22, 1900, in Gatewood, *"Smoked Yankees,"* 288–89; letter from S. T. Evans to friend Temple, March 30, 1900, in Gatewood, *"Smoked Yankees,"* 273–74.

8. Dentler, "In the Shadow of the White Man's Burden," 49.

9. Dentler, "In the Shadow of the White Man's Burden," 49, 45; Alejandrino, *Price of Freedom*, 176; Gatewood, *Black Americans*, 283.

10. Dentler, "In the Shadow of the White Man's Burden," 46.

11. Johnson, *History of Negro Soldiers*, 133.

12. Boehringer, "Imperialist Paranoia and Military Injustice," 323–58.

13. File on Calloway, AGO 356799, RG 94, filed with 17043.

14. File on Calloway, AGO 356799.

15. Funston, *Memories*, 343; "Record of Events," Regimental Returns, Twenty-Second Infantry, Troop A, Oct. 1900, frame 169.

16. Funston, *Memories*, 343; Dentler, "In the Shadow of the White Man's Burden," 49.

17. *Salt Lake (UT) Herald*, February 3, 1899.

18. File on Calloway, AGO 356799.

19. Dentler, "In the Shadow of the White Man's Burden," 50.

20. Letter Capt. A. Williams, Provost Marshall, San Fernando, to Adj. San Fernando, October 29, 1900, AGO 356799, RG 94, filed with 17043.

21. Col. Freeman to Gen. Wheaton, AGO 356799, RG 94.

22. *Manila Times*, June 7, 1907, 1; *Sunday Washington Globe* (Washington, DC), April 13, 1902, 7.

23. Gen. Wheaton to Gen. MacArthur, AGO 356799, RG 94.

24. Statement of John Calloway, Bilibid prison, December 11, 1900, AGO 356799, RG 94.

25. Major Inspector General Wills to AG of the Philippines, December 12, 1900, AGO 356799, RG 94.

26. Wills to AG Manila, December 12, 1900.

27. 3rd Endorsement, Headquarters Division of the Philippines, Major General Arthur MacArthur, Commanding, AGO 356799, RG 94.

28. John Calloway to AG U.S. Army, January 12, 1901, AGO 356799, RG 94.

Chapter 29. "The Courage of His Convictions"

1. *Manila Freedom*, October 13, 1900, 1; U.S. Army, Adjutant General's Office, *Correspondence Relating to the War with Spain*, 2:1001, August 31, 1900.

2. U.S. Army, Adjutant General's Office, *Correspondence Relating to the War with Spain*, 2:1237, December 25, 1900.

3. Linn, *Philippine War*, 214.

4. *New York World*, July 26, 1900.

5. Welch, *Response to Imperialism*, 65.

6. *New York Evening Post*, January 11, 1901.

7. "A Bryan Campaigner among the Insurgents," *Democrat and Chronicle* (Rochester, NY), October 30, 1900, 6.

8. Roth, *Muddy Glory*, 88; Schirmer, *Republic or Empire*, 258.

9. May, "Why the United States Won," 372.

Chapter 30. Alstaetter Revisited

1. "A Letter from Lieut. Frederick Alstaetter—His Gilded Cage," *Sandusky (OH) Daily Star*, November 23, 1900.

2. "Lieutenant Alstaetter Home," *Brooklyn (NY) Daily Eagle*, September 12, 1901, 9.

3. "He Was Fagin's Prisoner," *Piqua (OH) Daily Call*, December 31, 1901. This lengthy interview with Alstaetter is the source of the description of his captivity that follows and the quotations in this chapter except as noted.

4. "Renegade Fagan in Town," *Manila Times*, February 26, 1901, 1; "Funston's Enemy," *Iola (KS) Daily Register*, April 23, 1902.

5. Alejandrino, *Price of Freedom*, 176.

6. Strong, "Frederick W. Alstaetter 1897."

7. "He Was Fagin's Prisoner," *Piqua Daily Call*, December 31, 1901.

8. "Released Captive Joins His Corps," *Manila Times*, November 17, 1900, 1.

Chapter 31. A Christmas Souvenir

1. Linn, *Counterinsurgency*, 74; Funston to Kennon, October 13, 1900, RG 395/2133, Box 3, LTS.

2. Funston to AG DNL, October 14, 1900, RG 395/2263, Box 4, TR.

3. WDAR 1901, vol. 1, pt. 4, 132; Alejandrino, *Price of Freedom*, 175.

4. Lt. Col. Keller to AG San Isidro, December 2, 1900, RG 395/2263, Box 5, TR.

5. "Record of Events," Regimental Returns, Twenty-Second Infantry, November–December 1900, frame 177, Dec. 3: "Lieut. Sheldon with mounted detachment and Lieut. Day 34th Inf. with 4th District Mounted Scouts scouted through country east of Cabiao in search of Fagan's band. No results."

6. "Record of Events," Regimental Returns, Twenty-Second Infantry, November–December 1900, frame 177, Dec. 3: "Detachment of 42 men of Co. I under Lieut. Leonard with 2nd Lieut. Neely cooperating with party from Jaen, Nueva Ecija, went to San Francisco, N.E. on information that the band under Fagan was in vicinity. No result."

7. Funston, *Memories*, 180.

8. Ganzhorn, *I've Killed Men*, 185.

9. Ganzhorn, *I've Killed Men*, 185.

10. *Manila Times*, December 14, 1900, 1.

11. *Manila Times*, December 14, 1900, 1.

12. Funston, *Memories*, 180.

13. *Moulton (IA) Tribune*, December 14, 1900; *Daily Gazette* (Janesville, WI), December 7, 1900.

14. Jones, *Honor in the Dust*, 205.

15. *Leavenworth (KS) Times*, December 29, 1900, 1; Linn, *Philippine War*, 211.

16. Witt, *Lincoln's Code*, 357.

17. WDAR 1901, vol. 1, pt. 2, 93.

18. Jones, *Honor in the Dust*, 206.

19. "Army Wife's Xmas," *Iola (KS) Daily Register*, December 24, 1906, 6.

20. Magdalene Blankart to "My Angel Mother," December 26, 1900, Funston Papers, Kansas State Historical Society, Topeka.

21. AAG Smith to DNL Manila, WDAR 1901, vol. 1, pt. 5, 18.

22. "Sergt. Bailey," *Evening News* (Jeffersonville, IN), April 10, 1901.

23. Linn, *Counterinsurgency*, 74; WDAR 1901, vol. 1, pt. 3, 21: "Near San Isidro, Nueva Ecija, one mile wire carried away."

24. Funston to AG DNL, January 5, 1901, RG 395/2263, Box 5.

25. Funston to AG DNL, January 5, 1901, RG 395/2263, Box 5.

26. AAAG Smith to Lieut. Bridges, Cabiao, January 4, 1901, RG 395/2263, Box 5, TSR.

27. AAAG Smith to C.O. 22nd Inf. [Yeatman] at Arayat, January 5, 1901, RG 395/2263, Box 5, TSR.

28. Funston to AG DNL, January 6, 1901, RG 395/2262, Box 5, TSR.

29. Magdalene Blankart to "My Angel Mother," January 6, 1901, Funston Papers.

30. Funston to AG DNL, January 25, 1901, RG 395/2262, Box 5, TSR.

Chapter 32. The Revolution Falters

1. Wolff, *Little Brown Brother*, 334–35.

2. Brig. Gen. Thomas H. Barry, U.S.V., Chief of Staff, by Command of Maj. Gen. MacArthur, WDAR 1901, vol. 1, pt. 2, 95; U.S. Army, Adjutant General's Office, *Correspondence Relating to the War with Spain*, 2:1248.

3. Funston, "Guerilla Warfare in the Philippines," 5.

4. Ganzhorn, *I've Killed Men*, 187.

5. Funston to AG DNL, February 12, 1901, RG 395/2263, Box 5, TSR.

6. "The Situation at Manila," *Scranton (PA) Republican*, January 1, 1901, 1.

7. Report of Brig. Gen. F. D. Grant, Commanding Fifth District, DNL, WDAR 1901, vol. 1, pt. 3, 155–56.

8. "Renegade Fagan in Town," *Manila Times*, February 26, 1901, 1.

9. Principal Events in the Philippines Islands, WDAR 1902, 137; U.S., Buffalo Soldiers, Returns from Regular Army Cavalry Regiments, 1866–1916, Ninth Infantry, Company E, July 1901, Regimental Returns; "Deviltry of U.S. Deserters," *Honolulu Advertiser*, November 13, 1901, 11; San Juan, "An African American Soldier in the Philippine Revolution," 19.

10. San Juan, "An African American Soldier in the Philippine Revolution," 6–7; Gatewood, *Black Americans*, 290; Bonsal, "The Negro Soldier in War and Peace," 325–26.

11. Smith to AG DNL, February 19, 1901, RG 395/2133, Box 3, LS 593.

12. Smith to AG DNL, February 19, 1901.

13. Alejandrino, *Price of Freedom*, 175; Funston, "Guerilla Warfare in the Philippines," 5.

14. Ganzhorn, *I've Killed Men*, 197.

15. Investigation of Snyder letter, September 30, 1900, AGO 335956, RG 94.

16. Alejandrino, *Price of Freedom*, 110.

17. Linn, *Counterinsurgency*, 80; "Did Lacuna Build a Trap for Padilla?," *Manila Times*, April 2, 1902, 2.

18. AAAG Smith to AG DNL, March 9, 1901, RG 395/2263, Box 5, TSR.

19. Funston to Capt. Crittenden, Arayat, January 1, 1901, RG 395/2263, Box 5, TSR.

20. Linn, *Philippine War*, 266.

21. Alejandrino, *Price of Freedom*, 194.

22. RG 395/2263, Box 5, TSR.

23. Funston to AG DNL, March 1, 1901, RG 395/2263, Box 5, TSR.

24. AAAG Smith to AG DNL, March 15, 1901, RG 395/2263, Box 5, TSR.

25. "Lacuna Is Surrounded," *Manila Times*, March 22, 1901, 1.

26. "Macabebe Was a Fighter," *St. Louis (MO) Post-Dispatch*, January 19, 1902, 16.

27. AAAG Smith to AG DNL, March 15, 1901, RG 395/2263, Box 5, TSR.

28. "Lacuna Is Surrounded," *Manila Times*, March 22, 1901, 1.

Chapter 33. The Road to Palanan

1. The account of Aguinaldo's capture is drawn from these sources: Exhibit D, LS 2270, WDAR 1901, vol. 1, pt. 5; *Manila Times*, March 28, 1901, 1; Funston, *Memories*, 384–427; Segovia, *The Full Story of Aguinaldo's Capture*, 5–10; Bain, *Sitting in Darkness*, 96. Funston's full account of the capture of Aguinaldo is in his report to AG DNL, 122–30.

2. Miller, *Benevolent Assimilation*, 169: "Corbin had plenty of company in the War Department, where one reporter recorded that the general reaction to the news was, 'anybody but Funston.'"

3. Alejandrino, *Price of Freedom*, 177; Funston, *Memories*, 333–34; Funston to AG Manila, December 31, 1900, RG 395/2261, V. 4, LR 2115.

4. Witt, *Lincoln's Code*, 355.

5. Witt, *Lincoln's Code*, 358.

6. "A Graphic Description," *Manila Times*, March 28, 1901, 1.

Chapter 34. Surrender

1. Funston to AG DNL, May 19, 1901, RG 395/2263, Box 4, TSR.

2. Funston to AG DNL, March 21, 1901, RG 395/2263, Box 4, TSR.

3. "Unknown to Spain," *Harrisburg (PA) Daily Independent*, July 3, 1902, 4.

4. Alejandrino, *Price of Freedom*, 172.

5. Alejandrino, *Price of Freedom*, 174.

6. Alejandrino, *Price of Freedom*, 176.

7. Alejandrino, *Price of Freedom*, 172.

8. AAAG Smith to AG DNL, April 10, 1901, RG 395/2263, Box 4, TSR.

9. Lt. Mitchell, ADC to AG DNL, April 7, 1901, RG 395/2263, Box 4, TSR.

10. Alejandrino, *Price of Freedom*, 173.

11. Funston to AG DNL, April 10, 1901, RG 395/2263, Box 4, TSR.

12. AAAG Smith to AG DNL, April 26, 1901, RG 395/2263, Box 4, TSR.

13. Alejandrino, *Price of Freedom*, 173; Funston to AG DNL, April 29, 1901, RG 395/2263, Box 4, TSR.

14. AAAG Smith to Maj. Yeatman, Arayat, April 28, 1901, RG 395/2263, Box 4, TSR.

15. Alejandrino, *Price of Freedom*, 173.

16. Alejandrino, *Price of Freedom*.

17. Alejandrino, *Price of Freedom*, 174.

18. Funston, *Memories*, 429–31.

19. "Young Hero Visitor in City," *Evening Journal* (Wilmington, DE), November 20, 1901, 8.

20. *Hazel Green (KY) Herald*, July 4, 1901, 1.

21. Linn, *Counterinsurgency*, 86.

22. Alejandrino, *Price of Freedom*, 176.

23. Alejandrino, *Price of Freedom*, 177.

24. Funston, *Memories*, 356.

25. Funston, *Memories*, 434.

Chapter 35. Outcast

1. *Manila Freedom*, October 18, 1901, 1; Alejandrino, *Price of Freedom*, 196.

2. *Manila Times*, May 12, 1901, 1, and May 14, 1901, 1; *Army and Navy Journal*, June 15, 1901.

3. "Renegade Fagan Crops Up Again," *Manila Times*, September 18, 1901, 1.

4. Funston, *Memories*, 434.

5. Funston, *Memories*, 434; Funston, "Guerrilla Warfare in the Philippines," 5.

6. Lt. Corliss report to AG Second Separate Brigade, San Fernando, P.I., December 6, 1901, AGO 431081, RG 94, in Fagen file 56504.

7. "The Notorious Renegade Fagan's Career Is Ended," *Manila Times*, December 7, 1901, 1; "Notorious Fagan Killed," *Manila Freedom*, December 7, 1901, 1.

8. "The Notorious Renegade Fagan's Career Is Ended," 1.

9. Exchange of telegrams between Moss and Webster, AGO 431081, RG 94, in Fagen file 56504.

10. Exchange of telegrams between Moss and Webster; information slip on David Fagen, deserter, AGO 431081, NA, RG 94.

11. Exchange of telegrams between Moss and Webster; information slip on David Fagen; Proceedings of the Board of Officers convened at Headquarters Department of North Philippines, January 15, 1902.

12. Exchange of telegrams between Moss and Webster; information slip on David Fagen; LS 1160, 6th Endorsement, Captain E.B. Gose (also listed as LS 36).

13. "Fagan Reported Dead Just Once More," *Manila American*, December 7, 1901, 1.

14. "Fagan Reported Dead Just Once More," 1.

15. "Fagan Reported Dead Just Once More," 1; "Record of Events," Regimental Returns, Twenty-Fourth Infantry, Co. I, November–December 1901.

16. "Filipinos Killed Deserter Fagin," *St. Louis Post-Dispatch*, April 16, 1902, 1.

17. *San Francisco Call Sunday Magazine*, January 26, 1902.

18. *New York Sun*, March 10, 1903; "Funston Denounces Filipino Sympathizers," *San Francisco Chronicle*, April 3, 1902, 1, 9.

19. *Colorado Springs Weekly*, March 13, 1902.

20. *Winnipeg (MB) Free Press*, April 6, 1902.

21. "Teddy and Freddy," *New York World*, April 24, 1902.

22. "Funston's Enemy," *Iola (KS) Daily Register*, April 23, 1902, 1.

Chapter 36. The Renegade Comes to Town

1. "War, Pestilence, and Flood," *Inter Ocean* (Chicago), February 17, 1902, 12; Sturtevant, *Popular Uprisings*, 118; Fegan, "Social History of a Luzon Barrio," 99.

2. Kramer, *Blood of Government*, 155.

3. Jones, *Honor in the Dust*, 232–35.

4. Linn, *Philippine War*, 306.

5. *Bedford (PA) Gazette*, May 2, 1902.

6. Linn, *Philippine War*, 219; Ramsey, *A Masterpiece of Counterguerrilla Warfare*; Van Els, "Assuming the White Man's Burden," 619 ("American race hatred brought American forces in the Philippines to the brink of genocide. While no official policy of race extermination existed, many Americans expressed an almost unbelievable nonchalance about the deaths of thousands of Filipinos"); Ileto, *Pasyon and Revolution*, 170 ("When Malvar surrendered on 16 April 1902, he did so in order to save his region and its people from total destruction. . . . Faced with the prospect of genocide, Malvar had no choice").

7. May, *Battle for Batangas*, 254.

8. May, *Battle for Batangas*, 252.

9. Blount, *American Occupation*, 391 ("the American soldier in officially sanctioned wrath is a thing so ugly and dangerous that it would take a Kipling to describe him"); May, *Battle for Batangas*, 256.

10. *Boston Journal*, May 5, 1902.

11. Frederick W. Eddy, "Unrest Among the Filipinos," *Pittsburgh Daily Post*, July 19, 1903, 35; RPC, 1902, 185.

12. "Grant's Views," *Sandusky (OH) Daily Star*, May 20, 1901; RPC, 1902, 66; Constantino, *A Past Revisited*, 256.

13. Eddy, "Unrest among the Filipinos," 35.

14. Sturtevant, *Popular Uprisings*, 118; Constantino, *A Past Revisited*, 260; *Kansas City Daily Gazette*, September 29, 1902, 1; RPC, 1902, pt. 1, 185–86.

15. "Looks Like War in the Philippines," *Hawaiian Gazette* (Honolulu, HI), March 3, 1903, 5; RPC, 1902, pt. 1, 185–86.

16. Eddy, "Unrest among the Filipinos," 35; RPC, 1903, pt. 3, 29, Bandolerismo Statute, 34.

17. Hurley, *Jungle Patrol*, 88–89; Coats, "Philippine Constabulary," 112.

18. Coats, "Philippine Constabulary," 112–13.

19. Coats, "Philippine Constabulary," 114.

20. Hurley, *Jungle Patrol*, 76.

21. Hurley, *Red Epaulets*, 10–16.

22. Hurley, *Jungle Patrol*, 383–85.

23. Hurley, *Jungle Patrol*, 14.

24. Hurley, *Red Epaulets*, 5.

25. "American Negros in League," *Manila American*, November 14, 1902, 3.

26. "Negroes Lead Ladrone Bands," *Brooklyn Daily Eagle*, December 21, 1902, 6; "Led by Negroes," *Tennessean* (Nashville, TN), December 21, 1902, 5; "Ladrones Are

Led by Ex-Soldiers," *Inter Ocean* (Chicago, IL), December 21, 1902, 15; "Negroes Lead Ladrone Bands," *Chicago Tribune*, December 21, 1902, 30; "Negroes Lead Ladrone Bands," *Los Angeles Times*, December 21, 1902, 4.

27. "To Exterminate Ladrones," *Reading (PA) Times*, November 10, 1902, 1.

28. "Constabulary Encounters Large Force near Manila," *Manila Freedom*, February 5, 1903, 1; *Manila Times*, February 3, 1903, 1; *Manila Times*, February 10, 1903.

29. *Manila Times*, February 9, 1903, 1; *Manila Times*, February 11, 1903, 2.

30. "Renegade Fagans Last Seen in Manila," *Leavenworth (KS) Times*, March 17, 1903, 3.

Chapter 37. A People's War

1. Bass, "The Situation in Luzon," 218–22; Blount, *American Occupation*, 531.

2. Sturtevant, *Popular Uprisings*, 44.

3. Bain, *Sitting in Darkness*, 12; Miller, *Benevolent Assimilation*, 152; Welch, *Response to Imperialism*, 104; Kramer, *Blood of Government*, 201.

4. "Ladrones Punish Constabulary," *Manila Freedom*, February 21, 1903, 1; "Constabulary Put to Rout," *Manila Times*, February 3, 1903. 1.

5. "Luciano San Miguel Dies," *Manila Times*, March 28, 1903, 1.

6. Sturtevant, *Popular Uprisings*, 119.

7. RPC, 1902, 66; Constantino, *A Past Revisited*, 256; McCoy, *Policing America's Empire*, 133.

8. RPC, 1903, pt. 1, Reconcentration, 34.

9. Coats, "Philippine Constabulary," 205.

10. Coats, "Philippine Constabulary," 206.

11. RPC, 1905, V. XII, pt. 3, 55; "Alarming Disaffection Spreading in Northern Luzon," *Manila American*, May 19, 1906, 1.

12. Sturtevant, *Popular Uprisings*, 137; "Fuzzy-Wuzzies on Warpath," *Manila Times*, May 9, 1906, 1.

Chapter 38. "The Old Arch-Renegade Fagan"

1. "A Black Peril," *Manila Times*, May 5, 1906, 1.

2. "Negroes Living Quietly There," *Manila Times*, May 18, 1906, 1.

3. Sturtevant, *Popular Uprisings*, 119–21.

4. Coats, "Philippine Constabulary," 196, 198.

5. RPC, pt. 1, 1906, 420.

6. "Fagan Comes to Life," *Manila Times*, May 19, 1906, 1.

7. "Fagan Comes to Life," 1 (the photo had appeared previously in a Spanish-language paper in Manila, date unknown, under the heading "La Leyenda de Pagan"—The Legend of Fagan); Moore, "Browne, Thomas Alexander (1826–1915)." (*Robbery under Arms* is still highly readable.)

8. "Fagan Comes to Life," 1.

9. "Fagan Comes to Life," 1.

10. "Fagan Comes to Life," 1.

11. "Felizardo Did Not Leap to Death," *Manila Times*, March 3, 1906, 1.

12. "Fagan Again on Warpath," *Washington Post*, June 28, 1906, 1; "Big Fagan at Large?," *Press and Sun Bulletin* (Binghamton, NY), July 27, 1906, 6; *Appeal* (St. Paul, MN), July 2, 1906, 2, and others.

13. "Fagan Comes to Life," 1; *Washington Post*, June 28, 1906, 1.

14. RPC, pt. 1, 1906, 420.

15. RPC, pt. 2, July 1907, 402, 287; RPC, 1908, 331–32, 647, 652.

16. "Oust Island Bandit," *Rossville (KS) Reporter*, April 2, 1909, 3. (And other newspapers, mostly in Kansas, Harbord's home state.)

Afterword

1. Gatewood, *Black Americans*, 292; Rene G. Ontal, "Fagen and Other Ghosts: African-Americans and the Philippine-American War," in Shaw and Francia, *Vestiges of War*, 129–30; James Alfred Moss, "A Journal of a Trip Through the Provinces of Pampanga, Nueva Ecija, and Pangasinan; Covering Nearly All the Territory Occupied by the 24th Infantry, from Sept., 1899, to June, 1902," Funston Papers, Kansas State Historical Society, Topeka.

2. Linn, *Guardians of Empire*, 60; *Manila Times*, October 26, 1905.

3. "Worthless Renegades," *Manila American*, December 23, 1902, 1.

4. "Worthless Renegades," 1.

5. Report of the Philippine Commission, Bureau of Insular Affairs, 1903, pt. 1, 39.

6. "Renegades There," *Evening Herald* (Ottawa, KS), January 26, 1905, 1.

7. AGO 356799, RG 94, filed with AGO 17043; Boehringer, "Imperialist Paranoia and Military Injustice."

8. NA National Personnel Records Center, Record of Enlistment, John W. Calloway, No. 1261, 1899: "Reenl. Denied Jan. 17, 18. Noted on roll, Stafford Jan. 19, 1918. L.A.B."

9. Gatewood, *Black Americans*, 323.

10. "The Degradation of Fagan," *New York Age*, April 30, 1905.

11. Dean, *Rainier of the Last Frontier*.

12. Dean, *Rainier of the Last Frontier*, 265, 273, 337, 347.

A Note on Sources

1. Gatewood, *Black Americans*, 288–89.

2. Miller, "Compadre Colonialism," 205–6.

Bibliography

U.S. Government Documents, National Archives, Washington, DC

RG 94. Records of the Adjutant General's Office, 1780–1917.
RG 350. Records of the Bureau of Insular Affairs.
RG 395. Records of the U.S. Army Overseas Operations and Commands, 1898–1942.
Regimental Returns. 22nd Infantry, 24th Infantry, 4th Cavalry.
Microscopy 254. Philippine Insurgent Records, 1896–1901.

Government Publications and Documents

U.S. Army. Adjutant General's Office. *Correspondence Relating to the War with Spain, from Apr. 15, 1898 to July 30, 1902.* 2 vols. Washington, DC, 1902.
Annual Reports of the War Department, 1899–1908 (WDAR)
Annual Reports of the Philippine Commission, 1900–1908 (in WDAR)
Report of the Acting Superintendent of Sequoia and General Grant National Parks, in California, to the Secretary of the Interior, 1899. U.S. Government Printing Office.
U.S. Congress. Senate. Affairs in the Philippine Islands, *Hearings before the Committee on the Philippines of the United States Senate.* S. Doc. 331, 57th Cong., 1st Sess., 1902.

Newspapers

Appeal (St. Paul, MN)
Arizona Republic (Phoenix, AZ)
Atlanta Constitution
Baltimore Sun
Bedford (PA) Gazette
Boston Daily Globe
Boston Journal
Broad Ax (Salt Lake City, UT; Chicago)
Brooklyn Daily Eagle
Cedar Falls (IA) Semi-Weekly Gazette
Chicago Tribune

Daily Gazette (Janesville, WI)
Daily Herald (Delphos, OH)
Daily Iowa Capitol
Davenport (IA) Weekly Leader
Democrat and Chronicle (Rochester, NY)
Evening Herald (Ottawa, KS)
Evening Herald (Syracuse, NY)
Evening News (Jeffersonville, IN)
Free Press (Ozark, AL)
Harrisburg (PA) Daily Independent
Hazel Green (KY) Herald
Hawaiian Gazette (Honolulu)
Honolulu Advertiser
Inter Ocean (Chicago)
Iola (KS) Daily Register
Journal News (Hamilton, OH)
Kansas City Gazette
Leavenworth (KS) Times
Lincoln (NE) Daily News
Manila American
Manila Freedom
Manila Times
Messenger and Intelligencer (Wadesboro, NC)
Mobile (AL) Weekly Monitor
Moulton (IA) Tribune
New Times (Broward-Palm Beach, FL)
New York Age
New York Evening Post
New York Herald
New York Sun
New York Times
New York Tribune
New York World
Newnan (GA) Herald and Advertiser
North Adams (MA) Transcript
Oakland Tribune
Oshkosh (WI) Daily Northwestern
Philadelphia Inquirer
Piqua (OH) Daily Call
Pittsburgh (PA) Daily Post
Press and Sun Bulletin (Binghamton, NY)
Reading (PA) Times
Reporter (Helena, AR)
Richmond (VA) Planet
Roseville (KS) Reporter
Sacramento Daily Union
Salt Lake (UT) Herald

Salt Lake (UT) Tribune
Sandusky (OH) Daily Star
Scranton (PA) Republican
St. Louis Post-Dispatch
St. Louis Republic
St. Paul Globe
San Francisco Call
San Francisco Chronicle
Sunday Washington Globe (Washington, DC)
Tampa Weekly Tribune
Tennessean (Nashville, TN)
Washington (DC) Post
Weekly Gazette (Colorado Springs, CO)
Wilkes-Barre (PA) News
Wilkes-Barre (PA) Record
Winnipeg (MB) Free Press

Books

Agoncillo, Teodoro A. *Malolos: The Crisis of the Republic.* Manila: University of the Philip-
    pines Press, 1997.
Agoncillo, Teodoro A., and Milagros C. Guerrero. *History of the Filipino People.* 5th ed.
    Quezon City: R. P. Garcia, 1977.
Alejandrino, Jose M. *The Price of Freedom: Episodes and Anecdotes of Our Struggles for Freedom.*
    Manila: M. Colcol, 1949.
Aptheker, Herbert, *American Negro Slave Revolts.* New York: International Publishers, 1943.
Ayers, Edward L. *The Promise of the New South: Life after Reconstruction.* New York: Oxford
    University Press, 1992.
Bain, David Haward. *Sitting in Darkness: Americans in the Philippines.* New York: Penguin
    Books, 1984.
Bailey, Amy K., and Stewart E. Tolnay. *Lynched: The Victims of Southern Mob Violence.* Chapel
    Hill: University of North Carolina Press, 2015.
Barnett, Louise. *Atrocity and American Military Justice in Southeast Asia: Trial by Army.*
    Routledge Studies in the Modern History of Asia. New York: Routledge, 2010.
Beisner, Robert L. *Twelve against Empire: The Anti-Imperialist 1898–1900.* 1968. Repr.,
    Chicago: University of Chicago Press, 1985.
Birtle, Andrew J. *U.S. Army Counterinsurgency and Contingency Operations Doctrine, 1860–1941.*
    Washington, DC: Center of Military History, United States Army, 1998.
Blackmon, Douglas A. *Slavery by Another Name: The Re-Enslavement of Black Americans from
    the Civil War to World War II.* New York: Anchor Books, 2008.
Blount, James H. *The American Occupation of the Philippines, 1898–1912.* New York: G. P.
    Putnam's Sons, 1913.
Bonsal, Stephen. *The Fight for Santiago.* New York: Doubleday & McClure, 1899.
Brown, John Clifford. *Gentleman Soldier: John Clifford Brown and the Philippine-American War.*
    Edited by Joseph P. McCallus. College Station: Texas A&M University Press, 2004.
Brundage, W. Fitzhugh. *Lynching in the New South: Georgia and Virginia, 1880–1930.* Urbana:
    University of Illinois Press, 1993.

Carroll, John M., ed. *The Black Military Experience in the American West*. New York: Liveright, 1971.

Cashin, Herschell V. *Under Fire: With the Tenth U.S. Cavalry*. Niwot: University Press of Colorado, 1993.

Cirillo, Vincent J. *Bullets and Bacilli: The Spanish-American War and Military Medicine*. New Brunswick, NJ: Rutgers University Press, 1999.

Constantino, Renato. *The Philippines: A Past Revisited*. Vol. 1. Manila: Constantino, 1998.

Cosmas, Graham A. *An Army for Empire: The United States Army in the Spanish-American War*. College Station: Texas A&M University Press, 1994.

Dean, John M. *Rainier of the Last Frontier*. New York: *Thomas Y.* Crowell, 1911.

Du Bois, W. E. B. *The Souls of Black Folk*. 3rd ed. Chicago: A. C. McClure, 1903.

Dupuy, Col. Ernest R. *The Compact History of the United States Army*. New York: Hawthorne, 1961.

Elarth, Harold Hanne. *Story of the Philippine Constabulary*. Los Angeles: Globe, 1949.

Farwell, George. *Mask of Asia: The Philippines Today*. New York: Praeger, 1966.

Faust, Carl Irving. *Campaigning in the Philippines*. New York: Arno Press, 1970.

Feuer, A. B., ed. *America at War: The Philippines, 1898–1913*. Westport, CT: Praeger, 2002.

———. *Combat Diary: Episodes from the History of the Twenty-Second Regiment, 1866–1905*. New York: Praeger, 1991.

———. *The Santiago Campaign of 1898: A Soldier's View of the Spanish-American War*. Westport, CT: Praeger, 1993.

Fiske, Bradley, Rear-Admiral, U.S.N. *War Time in Manila*. Boston: Richard C. Badger, 1913.

Fletcher, Marvin Edward. *The Black Soldier and Officer in the United States Army, 1891–1917*. Columbia: University of Missouri Press, 1974.

Foner, Eric. *Nothing but Freedom: Emancipation and Its Legacy*. Baton Rouge: Louisiana State University Press, 1983.

Foner, Jack D. *Blacks and the Military in American History*. New York: Praeger, 1974.

———. *The United States Soldier between Two Wars: Army Life and Reforms, 1865–1898*. New York: Humanities Press, 1970.

Frederickson, George M. *White Supremacy: A Comparative Study in American and South African History*. New York: Oxford University Press, 1981.

Funston, Frederick. *Memories of Two Wars: Cuban and Philippine Experiences*. New York: Scribner's Sons, 1911.

Ganzhorn, John W. *I've Killed Men: An Epic Battle of Early Arizona*. New York: Devin-Adair, 1959.

Gates, John M. *Schoolbooks and Krags: The United States Army in the Philippines, 1899–1902*. Westport, CT: Greenwood, 1973.

Gatewood, Willard, *Black Americans and the White Man's Burden, 1898–1903*. Urbana: University of Illinois Press, 1975.

———. *"Smoked Yankees" and the Struggle for Empire: Letters from Negro Soldiers, 1898–1902*. Chapel Hill: University of North Carolina Press, 1989.

Gleeck, Lewis E. *Nueva Ecija in American Times: Homesteaders, Hacenderos, and Politicos*. Manila: Historical Conservation Society, 1981.

Goode, Corporal W. T. *The Eighth Illinois*. Chicago: Blakely, 1899.

Gosset, Thomas F. *Race: The History of an Idea in America*. New York: Schocken Books, 1965.

Guerrero, Milagros Camayon. *Luzon at War: Contradictions in Philippine Society, 1898–1902.* Madaluyong City, Philippines: Anvil, 2015.

Hair, William Ivy. *Carnival of Fury: Robert Charles and the New Orleans Race Riot of 1900.* 1976. Repr., Baton Rouge: Louisiana State University Press, 2008.

Hoganson, Kristin L. *Fighting for American Manhood: How Gender Politics Provoked The Spanish-American and Philippine-American Wars.* New Haven, CT: Yale University Press, 1998.

Hunt, Geoffrey. *Colorado Volunteer Infantry in the Philippine War, 1898–1899.* Albuquerque: University of New Mexico Press, 2004.

Hurley, Victor. *Jungle Patrol: The Story of the Philippine Constabulary.* New York: Dutton, 1938.

———. *Red Epaulets.* Edited by Suzanne J. Hurley-Kersh. Salem, OR: Cerberus Books, 2012.

Hurston, Zora Neale. *Mules and Men.* New York: Harper Perennial, 1990.

Ileto, Reynaldo C. "Bernardo Carpio: Awit and Revolution." In *Filipinos and Their Revolution: Events, Discourse, and Historiography,* 1–29. Quezon City: Ateneo de Manila University Press, 2003.

———. *Pasyon and Revolution: Popular Movements in the Philippines, 1840–1910.* Quezon City: Ateneo de Manila University Press, 1998.

Jahoda, Gloria. *Florida: A History.* 1976. Repr., New York: W. W. Norton, 1984.

Johnson, Edward A. *History of Negro Soldiers in the Spanish-American War.* Raleigh: Capital, 1899.

Jones, Gregg. *Honor in the Dust: Theodore Roosevelt, War in the Philippines, and the Rise and Fall of America's Imperial Dream.* New York: New American Library, 2012.

Jose, F. Sionel. *Dusk.* New York: Modern Library, 1992.

Jose, Vivencio R. *The Rise and Fall of Antonio Luna.* 1972. Repr., Manila: Solar, 1991.

Karnow, Stanley. *In Our Image: America's Empire in the Philippines.* New York: Random House, 1989.

Karp, Walter. *The Politics of War: The Story of Two Wars Which Altered Forever the Political Life of the American Republic (1890–1920).* New York: Franklin Square, 2003.

Kennedy, Stetson. *Palmetto Country.* 1942. Repr., Cocoa: Florida Historical Society Press, 2009.

Kent, Jacob Noel. *America in 1900.* Armonk, NY: M. E. Sharpe, 2000.

Kerkvliet, Benedict J. *The Huk Rebellion: A Study of Peasant Revolt in the Philippines.* New York: Rowman and Littlefield, 2002.

Kramer, Paul A. *The Blood of Government: Race, Empire, the United States, and the Philippines.* Chapel Hill: University of North Carolina Press, 2006.

Larkin, John A. *The Pampangans: Colonial Society in a Philippine Province.* Berkeley: University of California Press, 1972.

Leroy, James. *The Americans in the Philippines.* 2 vols. 1914. Repr., New York: AMS, 1970.

Levine, Lawrence W. *Black Culture and Black Consciousness: Afro-American Folk Thought from Slavery to Freedom.* New York: Oxford University Press, 2007.

Linn, Brian McAllister. *Guardians of Empire: The U.S. Army and the Pacific, 1902–1940.* Chapel Hill: University of North Carolina Press, 1997.

———. *The Philippine War, 1899–1902.* Lawrence: University Press of Kansas, 2000.

———. *The U.S. Army and Counterinsurgency in the Philippine War, 1899–1902.* Chapel Hill: University of North Carolina Press, 1989.

Litwack, Leon F. *Trouble in Mind: Black Southerners in the Age of Jim Crow.* New York: Vintage, 1999.

Mabini, Apolinario. *The Philippine Revolution*. Vol. 2. Ermita, Manila: National Historical Commission of the Philippines, 2011.

Majul, Cesar Adib. *Mabini and the Philippine Revolution*. 1960. Repr., Quezon City: University of the Philippines Press, 1996.

Marks, George P., ed. *The Black Press Views American Imperialism (1898–1900)*. New York: Arno Press, 1971.

May, Glen Anthony. *Battle for Batangas: A Philippine Province at War*. New Haven, CT: Yale University Press, 1991.

———. *A Past Recovered*. Manila: New Day Publishers, 1987.

McCallus, Joseph P., ed. *Gentleman Soldier: John Clifford Brown and the Philippine-American War*. College Station: Texas A&M University Press, 2003.

McCoy, Alfred W., ed. *An Anarchy of Families: State and Family in the Philippines*. Madison: University of Wisconsin Press, 2009.

———. *Policing America's Empire: The United States, The Philippines, and the Rise of the Surveillance State*. Madison: University of Wisconsin Press, 2009.

McCoy, Alfred W., and Edward C. de Jesus, eds. *Philippine Social History: Global Trade and Social Transformations*. Quezon City: Ateneo de Manila University Press, 1982.

McCoy, Alfred W., and Francisco Scarano, eds. *Colonial Crucible: Empire in the Making of the Modern American State*. Madison: University of Wisconsin Press, 2009.

McDonough, Gary W. *The Florida Negro: A Federal Writers' Project Legacy*. Jackson: University Press of Mississippi, 1993.

Meltzer, Milton, ed. *In Their Own Words: A History of the American Negro, 1865–1916*. New York: Thomas Y. Crowell, 1965.

Miller, Stuart Creighton. *Benevolent Assimilation: The American Conquest of the Philippines, 1899–1903*. New Haven, CT: Yale University Press, 1982.

Millis, Walter. *The Martial Spirit*. Chicago: Elephant Paperbacks, Ivan R. Dee, Publisher, 1989.

Mojares, Resil B. *Waiting for Mariang Makiling: Essays in Philippine Cultural History*. Quezon City: Ateneo de Manila University Press, 2002.

Morris, Edmund. *The Rise of Theodore Roosevelt*. New York: Modern Library, 2001.

Moss, James Alfred. *Memories of the Campaign at Santiago, June 6, 1898–Aug. 18, 1898*. San Francisco: Mysell-Rollins, 1899.

Muller, William G. *Twenty Fourth Infantry, Past and Present*. Ft. Collins, CO: Old Army Press, 1923.

Musicant, Ivan. *Empire by Default: The Spanish-American War and the Dawn of the American Century*. New York: Henry Holt, 1998.

Ochosa, Orlino A. *Bandoleros, Outlaws, Guerrillas of the Philippine-American War, 1903–1907*. Manila: New Day, 1995.

———. *Pio del Pilar and Other Heroes*. Manila: New Day, 1997.

———. *The Tinio Brigade: Anti-American Resistance in the Ilocos Provinces, 1899–1901*. Manila: New Day, 1989.

O'Connor, Richard. *Pacific Destiny: An Informal History of the U.S. in the Far East*. Boston: Little, Brown, 1969.

Olivares, José de. *Our Islands and Their People as Seen with Camera and Pencil*. Edited by William S. Bryan. St. Louis: N. D. Thompson, 1899.

Parker, John H. *The Gatlings at Santiago: The History of the Gatling Gun Detachment, U. S. Fifth Army Corps, During the Spanish-American War, Cuba, 1898*. Kansas City: Hudson-Kimberly, 1898. Facsimile edition reprinted by Denny Pizzini, 1996.

Paterson, Thomas G., and Stephen G. Rabe, eds. *Imperial Surge: The United States Abroad: 1890s–Early 1900s.* Lexington, MA: D.C. Heath, 1992.

Perez, Louis A., Jr. *The War of 1898: The United States and Cuba and Historiography.* Chapel Hill: University of North Carolina Press, 1998.

Peterson, Jean T. *The Ecology of Social Boundaries: Agta Foragers of the Philippines.* Urbana: University of Illinois Press, 1978.

Post, Charles Johnson. *The Little War of Private Post.* Boston: Little, Brown, 1960.

Ramsey, Robert D., III. *A Masterpiece of Counterguerrilla Warfare: Brigadier General J. Franklin Bell in the Philippines, 1901–1902.* Fort Leavenworth, KS: Combat Studies Institute Press, 2007.

Roberts, John W. *From Trickster to Badman: The Black Folk Hero in Slavery and Freedom.* Philadelphia: University of Pennsylvania Press, 1989.

Robinson, Albert Gardner. *The Philippines, the War, the People: A Record of Personal Observations and Experiences.* 1901. Repr., London: Forgotten Books, 2012.

Roosevelt, Theodore. *The Rough Riders: An Autobiography.* New York: Library of America, 1984.

Roth, Russell. *Muddy Glory: America's "Indian Wars" in the Philippines, 1899–1935.* W. Hanover, MA: Christopher, 1981.

Schirmer, Daniel B. *Republic or Empire: American Resistance to the Philippine War.* Rochester, VT: Schenkman Books, 1972.

Schubert, Frank N. *Voices of the Buffalo Soldier: Records, Reports, and Recollections of Military Life and Service in the West.* Albuquerque: University of New Mexico Press, 2008.

Scott, William Henry. *Ilocano Responses to American Aggression, 1900–1901.* Quezon City: New Day, 1986.

Segovia, Lázaro. *The Full Story of Aguinaldo's Capture.* Translated by Frank de Thoma. Manila, 1902.

Sexton, William Thaddeus. *Soldiers in the Sun: An Adventure in Imperialism.* 1939. Repr., New York: Books for Libraries. 1971.

Shaw, Angel Velasco, and Luis H. Francia. *Vestiges of War: The Philippine-American War and the Aftermath of an Imperial Dream, 1899–1999.* New York: New York University Press, 2002.

Sonnichsen, Albert. *Ten Months Captive among Filipinos.* New York: Charles Scribner's and Sons, 1901.

Sorensen, George Niels. *Iron Riders: Story of the 1890s Fort Missoula Buffalo Soldiers Bicycle Corps.* Missoula, MT: Pictorial Histories, 2000.

Stanley, P. W. *Reappraising an Empire: New Perspective on Philippine-American History.* Cambridge, MA: Harvard University Press, 1984.

Stevens, Joseph Earle. *Yesterdays in the Philippines.* New York: Charles Scribner's and Sons, 1899.

Steward, T. G. *Buffalo Soldiers: The Colored Regulars in the United States Army.* 1904. Repr., Amherst, NY: Humanity Books, 2003.

Sturtevant, David R. *Popular Uprisings in the Philippines 1840–1940.* Ithaca, NY: Cornell University Press, 1976.

Taylor, Arnold H. *Travail and Triumph: Black Life and Culture in the South since the Civil War.* Westport, CT: Greenwood Press, 1976.

Taylor, John R. M. *The Philippine Insurrection against the United States, 1898–1903: A Compilation of Documents and Introduction.* 5 vols. 1906. Repr., Pasay City, PI: Eugenio Lopez Foundation, 1971.

Tebeau, Charlton W. *A History of Florida*. Coral Gables, FL: University of Miami Press, 1980.

Tecson, Luis Zamora. *Remembering My Lolo, Simon Ocampo Tecson: Leader in the Siege of Baler*. Manila: National Commission for Culture and the Arts, 2011.

Thomas, Evan. *The War Lovers: Roosevelt, Lodge, Hearst, and the Rush to Empire, 1898*. New York: Little, Brown, 2010.

Thomas, Rowland. *The Little Gods: A Masque of the Far East*. 1909. Repr., London: Forgotten Books, 2012.

Tolnay, Stewart E., and E. M. Beck. *A Festival of Violence: An Analysis of Southern Lynchings, 1882–1930*. Urbana: University of Illinois Press, 1992.

Trask, David F. *The War with Spain in 1898*. Lincoln: University of Nebraska Press, 1996.

Welch, Richard E., Jr. *Response to Imperialism: The United States and the Philippine- American War, 1899–1902*. Chapel Hill: University of North Carolina Press, 1979.

Wells-Barnett, Ida B., *Mob Rule in New Orleans—Robert Charles and His Fight to the Death, the Story of His Life, Burning— Human Beings Alive, Other Lynching Statistics*. New York City: Arno Press and the *New York Times*, 1969.

Wernstedt, Frederick L., and Joseph E. Spencer. *The Philippine Island World: A Physical, Cultural and Regional Geography*. Berkeley: University of California Press, 1967.

White, Walter. *Rope and Fagot: A Biography of Judge Lynch*. New York: Knopf, 1929.

Wilcox, Marrion, ed. *Harper's History of the War in the Philippines*. New York: Harper and Brothers, 1900.

Wildman, Edwin. *Aguinaldo: A Narrative of Filipino Ambitions*. Boston: Lothrop, 1901.

Witt, John Fabian. *Lincoln's Code: The Laws of War in American History*. New York: Free Press, 2012.

Wolff, Leon. *Little Brown Brother: America's Forgotten Bid for Empire Which Cost 250,000 Lives*. 1960. Repr., Makati: Erewhon Press, 1971.

Woodward, C. Vann. *The Strange Career of Jim Crow*. Rev. ed. New York: Oxford University Press, 1996.

Worcester, Dean C. *The Philippines: Past and Present*. New York: Macmillan, 1930.

Articles

Aguilar, Mila D. "Fighting the Panopticon: Filipino Trickster Tales as Active Agency against Oppressive Structures." www.mda.ph/essays/academic-work/1168.pdf.

Arnold, Paul T. "Negro Soldiers in the U.S. Army." *Magazine of History with Notes and Queries* 11 (Jan.–June 1910): 119–25.

Bass, John. "Battle Scenes Described," "Manila's Night of Terror," "In the Trenches," "The Situation in Luzon," etc. In *Harper's History of the War in the Philippines*, edited by Marrion Wilcox. New York: Harper and Brothers, 1900.

Boehringer, Gil H. "Imperialist Paranoia and Military Injustice: Persecution and Redemption of Sergeant Calloway." In *Mixed Blessing: The Impact of the American Colonial Experience on Politics and Society in the Philippines*, 2nd ed., edited by Hazel M. McFerson, 323–58. Quezon City: University of the Philippines Press, 2011.

Bonsal, Stephen. "The Negro Soldier in War and Peace." *North American Review* 185, no. 616 (June 1907): 321–27.

Bordua, Rae. "Col. Cushman Albert Rice: Find a Grave Memorial." https://www.findagrave.com/memorial/98223927/cushman-albert-rice.

Chandler, Billy James. "Harmon Murray: Black Desperado in Late Nineteenth-Century Florida." *Florida Historical Quarterly* 73, no. 2 (October 1994): 184–99.

Clark, Michael J. "Improbable Ambassadors: Black Soldiers at Fort Douglas 1896–99." In *Buffalo Soldiers in the West: A Black Soldier's Anthology*, edited by Bruce U. Glasrud and Michael N. Searles, 221–41. College Station: Texas A&M University Press, 2007.

Clymer, Kenton J. "Humanitarian Imperialism: David Prescott Barrows and the White Man's Burden in the Philippines." *Pacific Historical Review* 44 (November 1976): 495–517.

Coffman, Edward M. "Batson of the Philippine Scouts." *Parameters* 7 (1977): 68–72.

Fegan, Brian. "The Social History of a Central Luzon Barrio." In *Philippine Social History*, edited by Alfred W. McCoy and Edward C. de Jesus, 91–133. Quezon City: Ateneo de Manila University Press, 1982.

Funston, Frederick. "Guerrilla Warfare in the Philippines." *Collier's Weekly*, March 22, 1902, 5.

Gates, John M. "The Philippines and Vietnam: Another False Analogy." *Asian Studies* 10 (1972): 64–76.

———. "The U.S. Army and Irregular Warfare." College of Wooster, Wooster, OH. http://discover.wooster.edu/jgates/files/2011/11/fullbook.pdf.

Gatewood, Willard B. "Negro Troops in Florida, 1898." *Florida Historical Quarterly* 49 (July 1970): 1–15.

Gillett, Mary C. "Medical Care and Evacuation during the Philippine Insurrection, 1899–1901." *Journal of the History of Medicine* 42 (April 1987): 169–85.

Guerrero, Milagros C. "The Provincial and Municipal Elites of Luzon during the Revolution, 1898–1902." In *Philippine Social History*, edited by Alfred W. McCoy and Edward C. de Jesus, 155–90. Quezon City: Ateneo de Manila University Press, 1982.

Hofstadter, Richard. "The Depression of the 1890s and Psychic Crisis." In *Imperial Surge: The United States Abroad, the 1890s–Early 1900s*, Problems in American Civilization, edited by Thomas G. Paterson and Stephen G. Rabe. Lexington, MA: D. C. Heath, 1992.

Kramer, Paul A. "Decolonizing the History of the Philippine-American War." Introduction to Leon Wolff, *Little Brown Brother: America's Forgotten Bid for Empire Which Cost 250,000 Lives*. New York: History Book Club, 2006.

Larkin, John A. "Philippine History Reconsidered." *American History Review* 87, no. 3 (June 1982): 595–628.

LeRoy, James A. "Apolinario Mabini on the Failure of the Filipino Revolution." *American Historical Review* 11, no. 4 (July 1906).

———. "Race Prejudice in the Philippines." *Atlantic Monthly* 90 (July 1900): 100–112.

Linn, Brian McAllister. "Guerrilla Fighter: Frederick Funston in the Philippines, 1900–1901." *Kansas History* 10 (Spring 1987): 2–16.

Mallari, Perry Gil S. "The Warrior and Mercenary Culture of the Macabebes." June 16, 2009. www.fmapulse.com/content/fma-corner-warrior-and-mercenary-culture-macabebes.

May, Glenn A. "Filipino Resistance to American Occupation: Batangas, 1899–1902." *Pacific Historical Review* 48 (November 1979): 531–56.

———. "Why the United States Won the Philippine-American War, 1898–1902." *Pacific Historical Review* 52, no. 4 (November 1983): 353–77.

McLennan, Marshall. "Changing Human Ecology on the Central Luzon Plain: Nueva Ecija, 1705–1939." In *Philippine Social History*, edited by Alfred W. McCoy and Edward C. de Jesus, 57–91. Quezon City: Ateneo de Manila University Press, 1982.

Miller, Stuart Creighton. "Compadre Colonialism." *Wilson Quarterly* 10, no. 3 (Summer 1986): 92–105.

Moore, T. Inglis. "Browne, Thomas Alexander (1826–1915)." *Australian Dictionary of Biography*, vol. 3. Melbourne: Melbourne University Press, 1969. adb.anu.edu.au/biography /browne-thomas-alexander-3085.

Orosa, Mario E. "The Macabebes." September 10, 2013. www.orosa.org/themacabebes .pdf.

Palmer, Frederick. "White Man and the Brown Man in the Philippines." *Scribner's Magazine*, no. 27 (January 1900): 76–86.

Powell, Anthony L. "An Overview: Black Participation in the Spanish-American War." Spanish-American War Centennial Website. www.spanamwar.com/AfroAmericans .htm.

Ramsey, Robert D. "Savage Wars of Peace: Case Studies of Pacification in the Philippines, 1900–1902." Long War Series Occasional Paper 24. Fort Leavenworth, KS: Combat Studies Institute Press, 2007.

Robinson, Michael C., and Frank N. Schubert. "David Fagen: An Afro-American Rebel in the Philippines, 1899–1901." *Pacific Historical Review* 44 (1975) 68–83.

San Juan, E., Jr. "An African American Soldier in the Philippine Revolution: An Homage to David Fagen." 2009. www.academia.edu/242727/A-Homage-to-David-Fagen.

Schubert, Frank. "Seeking David Fagen: The Search for a Black Rebel's Florida Roots." *Tampa Bay History* 22 (2008): 19–34.

Schumacher, John N. "Recent Perspectives on the Revolution." *Philippine Studies* 30, no. 4 (1982): 455–92.

———. "Socioeconomic Classes in the Revolution." *Budhi: A Journal of Ideas and Culture* 2, no. 2 (1998): 189–208.

Sledd, Andrew. "The Negro: Another View." *Atlantic Monthly*, July 1902.

Smith, D. H. "American Atrocities in the Philippines: Some New Evidence." *Pacific Historical Review* 55, no. 2 (May 1986): 281–83.

Strong, Paschal N. "Frederick W. Alstaetter 1897, Cullum no. 3747." https://www .westpointaog.org/memorial-article?id=25e62c32-917f-4069-a2b6-9da7900c4464.

Tarnowski, Amber. "Macabebes and Moros." June 4, 2010. https://www.army.mil /article/40345/macabebes-and-moros.

Van Els, Mark D. "Assuming the White Man's Burden: The Seizure of the Philippines, 1898–1902." *Philippine Studies* 43, no. 4 (1995): 607–22.

Welch, Richard E. "American Atrocities in the Philippines: The Indictment and the Response." *Pacific Historical Review* 43 (May 1974): 233–53.

Dissertations and Theses

Clark, Michael J. "A History of the Twenty-Fourth United States Infantry in Utah, 1896–1900." PhD diss., University of Utah, 1979.

Coats, George Yarrington. "The Philippine Constabulary: 1901–1917." PhD diss., Ohio State University, 1968.

Dentler, Jonathan. "In the Shadow of the White Man's Burden: Black Americans in and of the Philippines." Senior thesis, Columbia College, 2011.

Fletcher, Marvin Edward. "The Black Soldier and the United States Army, 1891–1917." PhD diss., University of Wisconsin, 1968.

Marple, A. D. "The Philippine Scouts: A Case Study in the Use of Indigenous Soldiers, Northern Luzon, the Philippine Islands, 1899." Master's thesis, U.S. Army Command and Staff College, Fort Leavenworth, KS, 1983.

McLennan, Marshall Seaton. "Peasant and Hacendero in Nueva Ecija: The Socio-Economic Origins of a Philippine Rice-Growing Region." PhD diss., University of California, Berkeley, 1973.

Scalice, Joseph. "'Pasyon, Awit, Legend': Reynaldo Ileto's *Pasyon and Revolution Revisited: A Critique.*" Master's thesis, University of California, Berkeley, 2010.

Woolard, James Richard. "The Philippine Scouts: The Development of America's Colonial Army." PhD diss., Ohio State University, 1975.

U.S. Army Military History Institute, Carlisle Barracks, Carlisle, PA

Batson, Matthew A. Cuban and Philippine Campaigns, 1898–1901. Letters.

Johnson, Richard. "My Life in the U.S. Army, 1899–1922." Unpub. autobiography.

Index

Page references in italics indicate an illustration. DF refers to David Fagen.